DELEGATION AND INTERNATIONAL OR(

Why do states delegate certain tasks and responsibilities to international organizations rather than acting unilaterally or cooperating directly? Furthermore, to what extent do states continue to control IOs once authority has been delegated? Examining a variety of different institutions, including the World Trade Organization, the United Nations, and the European Commission, this book explores the different methods that states employ to ensure their interests are being served and identifies the problems involved with monitoring and managing IOs. The contributors suggest that it is not inherently more difficult to design effective delegation mechanisms at the international level than at the domestic level. Drawing on principal-agent theory, they explain the variations that exist in the extent to which states are willing to delegate to IOs. They argue that IOs are neither all evil nor all virtuous, but are better understood as bureaucracies that can be controlled to varying degrees by their political masters.

DARREN G. HAWKINS is Associate Professor of Political Science at Brigham Young University.

DAVID A. LAKE is Professor of Political Science at the University of California, San Diego.

DANIEL L. NIELSON is Associate Professor of Political Science at Brigham Young University.

MICHAEL J. TIERNEY is Assistant Professor of Government at The College of William & Mary.

POLITICAL ECONOMY OF INSTITUTIONS AND DECISIONS

Series editors

Randall Calvert, Washington University, St. Louis
Thrainn Eggertsson, Max Planck Institute, Germany, and University of Iceland

Founding editors

James E. Alt, Harvard University
Douglass C. North, Washington University, St. Louis

Other books in the series

Alberto Alesina and Howard Rosenthal, *Partisan Politics, Divided Government, and the Economy*
Lee J. Alston, Thrainn Eggertsson and Douglass C. North, eds., *Empirical Studies in Institutional Change*
Lee J. Alston and Joseph P. Ferrie, *Southern Paternalism and the American Welfare State: Economics, Politics, and Institutions in the South, 1865–1965*
James E. Alt and Kenneth A. Shepsle, eds., *Perspectives on Positive Political Economy*
Josephine T. Andrews, *When Majorities Fail: The Russian Parliament, 1990–1993*
Jeffrey S. Banks and Eric Allen Hanushek, eds., *Modern Political Economy: Old Topics, New Directions*
Yoram Barzel, *Economic Analysis of Property Rights, 2nd Edition*
Yoram Barzel, *A Theory of the State: Economic Rights, Legal Rights, and the Scope of the State*
Robert H. Bates, *Beyond the Miracle of the Market: The Political Economy of Agrarian Development in Kenya, 2nd Edition*
Charles M. Cameron, *Veto Bargaining: Presidents and the Politics of Negative Power*
Kelly H. Chang, *Appointing Central Bankers: The Politics of Monetary Policy in the United States and the European Monetary Union*
Peter F. Cowhey and Mathew McCubbins, eds., *Structure and Policy in Japan and the United States: An Institutionalist Approach*
Gary W. Cox, *The Efficient Secret: The Cabinet and the Development of Political Parties in Victorian England*
Gary W. Cox, *Making Votes Count: Strategic Coordination in the World's Electoral Systems*
Gary W. Cox and Jonathan N. Katz, *Elbridge Gerry's Salamander: The Electoral Consequences of the Reapportionment Revolution*

Continued on page following index

DELEGATION AND AGENCY IN INTERNATIONAL ORGANIZATIONS

Edited by

DARREN G. HAWKINS
DAVID A. LAKE
DANIEL L. NIELSON
AND MICHAEL J. TIERNEY

CAMBRIDGE UNIVERSITY PRESS
Cambridge, New York, Melbourne, Madrid, Cape Town, Singapore, São Paulo, Delhi

Cambridge University Press
The Edinburgh Building, Cambridge CB2 8RU, UK

Published in the United States of America by Cambridge University Press, New York

www.cambridge.org
Information on this title: www.cambridge.org/9780521680462

© Cambridge University Press 2006

This publication is in copyright. Subject to statutory exception
and to the provisions of relevant collective licensing agreements,
no reproduction of any part may take place without
the written permission of Cambridge University Press.

First published 2006
Reprinted 2008

Printed in the United Kingdom at the University Press, Cambridge

A catalogue record for this publication is available from the British Library

ISBN 978-0-521-86209-7 hardback
ISBN 978-0-521-68046-2 paperback

Cambridge University Press has no responsibility for
the persistence or accuracy of URLs for external or
third-party internet websites referred to in this book,
and does not guarantee that any content on such
websites is, or will remain, accurate or appropriate.

Contents

List of figures	*page* vii
List of tables	viii
Notes on contributors	x
Preface	xv

Part I: Introduction   1

1. Delegation under anarchy: states, international organizations, and principal-agent theory
   DARREN G. HAWKINS, DAVID A. LAKE, DANIEL L. NIELSON, AND MICHAEL J. TIERNEY   3

Part II: Variation in principal preferences, structure, decision rules, and private benefits   39

2. Who delegates? Alternative models of principals in development aid
   MONA M. LYNE, DANIEL L. NIELSON, AND MICHAEL J. TIERNEY   41

3. US domestic politics and International Monetary Fund policy
   J. LAWRENCE BROZ AND MICHAEL BREWSTER HAWES   77

4. Why multilateralism? Foreign aid and domestic principal-agent problems
   HELEN V. MILNER   107

5. Distribution, information, and delegation to international organizations: the case of IMF conditionality
   LISA L. MARTIN   140

Contents

6 Delegation and discretion in the European Union
MARK A. POLLACK — 165

Part III: Variation in agent preferences, legitimacy, tasks, and permeability — 197

7 How agents matter
DARREN G. HAWKINS AND WADE JACOBY — 199

8 Screening power: international organizations as informative agents
ALEXANDER THOMPSON — 229

9 Dutiful agents, rogue actors, or both? Staffing, voting rules, and slack in the WHO and WTO
ANDREW P. CORTELL AND SUSAN PETERSON — 255

10 Delegating IMF conditionality: understanding variations in control and conformity
ERICA R. GOULD — 281

11 Delegation to international courts and the limits of re-contracting political power
KAREN J. ALTER — 312

Part IV: Directions for future research — 339

12 The logic of delegation to international organizations
DAVID A. LAKE AND MATHEW D. MCCUBBINS — 341

References — 369
Index — 394

Figures

1.1	International delegation decision tree	*page* 11
2.1	Types of agency relationships	45
2.2	Social percent of MDB projects, 1980–1999 (three-year rolling average)	55
2.3	Social preferences for the International Bank for Reconstruction and Development (World Bank), 1980–1999 with alternative models of the principal	64
3.1	Chain of delegation	79
4.1	Percentage of multilateral aid committed relative to total ODA committed	113
4.2	Public opinion in the EU net percentage with greater confidence in multilateral than bilateral organizations	121
5.1	State and staff preferences over stringency of conditionality	143
8.1	Implications of variation in institutional neutrality	248
8.2	Preference distributions regarding military intervention	251
9.1	Institutional design and IO slack	263
10.1	Change in the number and type of binding conditions, 3-year moving average	299
12.1	Delegation with communication	351
12.2	The knowledge condition	357
12.3	The conditions for successful delegation	359
12.4	Delegation with multiple principals	362

Tables

2.1	Hypothetical pivotal players	page 62
2.2	Hypothetical multiple principal	63
2.3	Logistic regression results with social loan as dependent variable using the Social Policy Index to generate principal preferences	67
2.4	Logistic regression results with social loan as dependent variable using the bilateral social foreign aid to generate principal preferences	70
3.1	IMF quota votes in the US Congress	88
3.2	Probit analyses of IMF quota votes in the 98th Congress	90
3.3	Probit analyses of IMF quota votes in the 98th Congress (robustness)	91
3.4	Probit analyses of IMF quota votes in the 105th Congress	92
3.5	Substantive effects of campaign contributions from money-center banks, district skill levels, and House member "ideology"	93
3.6	Random effects logit of IMF decisions to lend	99
3.7	OLS panel estimates of the size of IMF loans	101
4.1	Summary statistics for variables	127
4.2A	Multilateral commitments as % total ODA committed and OPINION1	128
4.2B	Multilateral commitments as % total aid committed and OPINION1	130
4.3A	Multilateral commitments as % total ODA committed and OPINION3	134

Tables

4.3B	Multilateral commitments as % total ODA committed and OPINION3	136
6.1	Delegation and discretion of executive powers, Consolidated Treaties	182
6.2	Executive powers delegated to Commission, Consolidated Treaties	184
6.3	Types of constraint in executive delegation, EC and EU treaties	185
7.1	Scope conditions: when agents matter	203
7.2	Court and Commission permeability and autonomy, 1955–2004	217
10.1	Conformity with First Conditionality Guidelines: Phasing, number of binding conditions and uniformity	295
10.2	Conformity with 1979 Second Conditionality Guidelines	298

Notes on contributors

KAREN J. ALTER is Associate Professor of Political Science at Northwestern University, specializing in international relations, international law, and in European Union politics. She is the author of: *Establishing the Supremacy of European Law: The Making of an International Rule of Law in Europe* (2001) and is working on a new book, titled *International Courts in International Politics: Four Judicial Roles and Their Implications for State–IC Relations*.

J. LAWRENCE BROZ is Associate Professor of Political Science at the University of California, San Diego. He is a specialist on international monetary and financial policies. His books are *International Origins of the Federal Reserve System* (1997) and *The Political Economy of Monetary Institutions* (2003), co-edited with William Bernhard and William Roberts Clark.

ANDREW P. CORTELL is Associate Professor of International Affairs at Lewis & Clark College. His publications include *Mediating Globalization: Domestic Institutions and Industrial Policies in the United States and Britain* (2005) and *Altered States: International Relations, Domestic Politics, and Institutional Change* (2002), co-edited with Susan Peterson.

ERICA R. GOULD is Assistant Professor of Politics at the University of Virginia. Her research focuses on international organizations and financial institutions. She is the author of *Money Talks: The International Monetary Fund, Conditionality and Supplementary Financiers* (forthcoming).

Notes on contributors

MICHAEL BREWSTER HAWES is a visiting instructor in the Department of Government at Georgetown University and a Ph.D. candidate in the Department of Political Science at the University of California, San Diego. He is completing a dissertation on Manipulative Multilateralism: Power and Informal Influence in International Organizations.

DARREN G. HAWKINS is Associate Professor of Political Science at Brigham Young University and director of the international relations program. He has published on human rights and democracy issues in *the Journal of Politics, International Studies Quarterly, Global Governance, Comparative Politics*, and the *European Journal of International Relations*, among other journals. He has also published *International Human Rights and Authoritarian Rule in Chile* (2002).

WADE JACOBY is Associate Professor of Political Science at Brigham Young University where he also directs the Center for the Study of Europe. He has published on institutional theory, political economy, international security, and European politics. He is the author of *Imitation and Politics: Redesigning Modern Germany* (2001) and *The Enlargement of the European Union and NATO: Ordering from the Menu in Central Europe* (2004).

DAVID A. LAKE is Professor of Political Science at the University of California, San Diego. He has published widely in international relations theory, international political economy, and international conflict studies. His latest books are *Entangling Relations: American Foreign Policy in its Century* (1999) and *Governance in a Global Economy: Political Authority in Transition* (2003), co-edited with Miles Kahler. He is a Fellow of the American Academy of Arts and Sciences.

MONA LYNE is Assistant Professor of Political Science at the University of South Carolina. Her research investigates the conditions under which collective actors are able to effectively delegate to their agents. Her major project examines this problem in the context of democratic elections, and is developed in her recently completed book manuscript, *The Voter's Dilemma and Democratic Accountability: A Transaction Cost Theory of Electoral Sanctioning*.

LISA L. MARTIN is Clarence Dillon Professor of International Affairs at Harvard University. She works in the areas of international political economy and international institutions. Her most recent publications include *International Institutions in the New Global Economy* (2005) and "The President and International Agreements: Treaties as Signaling Devices," *Presidential Studies Quarterly* (September 2005).

MATHEW D. MCCUBBINS is Chancellor's Associates and Distinguished Professor of Political Science at the University of California, San Diego, and Professor of Law at the University of San Diego School of Law. He is a Fellow of the American Academy of Arts and Sciences. The author of numerous articles and books on American politics, his most recent books are *Stealing the Initiative: How State Government Responds to Direct Democracy* (2001), with Elisabeth Gerber, Arthur Lupia, and D. Roderick Kiewiet; and *Setting the Agenda: Responsible Party Government in the U.S. House of Representatives* (2005), with Gary W. Cox. He was co-editor of the *Journal of Law, Economics, and Organization*.

HELEN V. MILNER is B.C. Forbes Professor of Politics and International Affairs and Director of the Center for Globalization and Governance at Princeton University. She has written broadly in international political economy, with a specific interest in the role of domestic institutions and politics, and is currently working on foreign aid, the global diffusion of the internet, and the relationship between globalization and environmental policy. She is the author of numerous books and articles, including *Interests, Institutions and Information: Domestic Politics and International Relations* (1997), and editor of *Political Science: The State of the Discipline III* (2002), with Ira Katznelson.

DANIEL L. NIELSON is Associate Professor of Political Science at Brigham Young University. His research focuses on international and comparative political economy, international relations theory, and comparative political institutions. He has published in *International Organization*, the *American Journal of Political Science*, and *Comparative Political Studies*.

SUSAN PETERSON is Professor of Government and Dean for Educational Policy in Arts and Sciences at The College of William and Mary. Her current research focuses on global health issues. She is the author of *Crisis Bargaining and the State: The Domestic Politics of International Conflict* (1996) and the co-editor, with Andrew Cortell, of *Altered States: Domestic Politics, International Relations, and Institutional Change* (2002). She is the editor-in-chief of *Security Studies*.

Notes on contributors

MARK A. POLLACK is Associate Professor of Political Science at Temple University. His research examines the role of international organizations in global and regional governance, with an emphasis on the European Union and on transatlantic relations. He is the author of *The Engines of European Integration: Delegation, Agency and Agenda Setting in the EU* (2003), and co-editor (with Helen Wallace and William Wallace) of *Policy-Making in the European Union* (2005).

ALEXANDER THOMPSON is Assistant Professor of Political Science at Ohio State University with research interests in international relations theory, international organization, and political economy. His current book manuscript, *Channeling Power: Coercion through International Organizations*, asks why states often conduct coercive policies through IOs rather than operate alone. His most recent articles appeared in *International Organization* and in the *Journal of Conflict Resolution*.

MICHAEL J. TIERNEY is Assistant Professor of Government and Director of the International Relations Program at The College of William and Mary. He has published articles on international relations theory and international organization. He is currently writing two books: *Greening Aid? Understanding Environmental Assistance to Developing Countries* (forthcoming, 2007); and *The Politics of International Organizations: Bridging the Rationalist-Constructivist Divide*, co-edited with Catherine Weaver.

Preface

This volume began with a set of questions asked at Park City, Utah, in May of 2002. The conference was titled "Delegation to International Organizations" and was organized by Scott Cooper, Darren Hawkins, Wade Jacoby, and Daniel Nielson, all of Brigham Young University. The conference asked why governments delegate authority to IOs, how they structure delegation relationships, and what problems result from such delegation. In many respects, this volume reflects the basic architecture of that early conference on the topic. We are thus grateful to the David M. Kennedy Center for International Studies; the College of Family, Home, and Social Sciences; and the Department of Political Science at Brigham Young University for making possible that initial exploration of ideas about international delegation.

While the broad themes of the volume were laid out in the spring of 2002, the scope of the project was narrowed and refined considerably during two conferences organized by Lisa Martin and held at Harvard University in December 2002 and April 2003. These meetings focused participants specifically on agency theory as a tool for understanding delegation to IOs. For funding and sponsoring these conferences, we are grateful to Harvard's Radcliffe Institute for Advanced Study and its Weatherhead Center for International Affairs.

To sharpen contributions to the volume, David Lake organized a final conference in Del Mar, California, in September of 2003. This meeting helped make clear the unifying themes of the volume. We are grateful to the Department of Political Science and the Institute for International, Comparative, and Area Studies at the University of California, San Diego; the University of California's Institute on Global Conflict and Cooperation and BYU's Kennedy Center for enabling that conference. We gathered a final round of commentaries and critiques during two

Preface

linked panels at the International Studies Association meeting in March 2004. We also thank the Reves Center for International Studies and the program on the Theory and Practice of International Relations at The College of William and Mary for financial support and maintenance of the project website.

We are grateful to many scholars who served as discussants at the various meetings. For their help in improving the ideas in this volume, we thank Ken Abbott, Michael Barnett, Jee Baum, Bill Bernhard, Tim Büthe, J. R. DeShazo, Peter Dombrowski, Daniel Drezner, John Ferejohn, Marty Finnemore, Jeff Frieden, Judy Goldstein, Peter Gourevitch, Lloyd Gruber, Miles Kahler, Robert Keohane, Barbara Koremenos, Beth Simmons, Kenneth Schultz, Ken Stiles, and Mike Thies. Anonymous reviewers for Cambridge University Press and *International Organization* (for the individual chapters submitted there) also provided useful feedback. While these scholars certainly do not agree with all the arguments we advance in this volume, the arguments and supporting evidence are much stronger because of their critiques.

With remarkably good cheer, all of the volume's contributors wrote multiple drafts of their papers in response to the comments received at the several conferences and lengthy comments from the editors. In addition, they served multiple times as discussants and commentators on one another's chapters. More than most academic projects, this volume represents the very best type of collaboration, where the joint efforts greatly outweigh the sum of the individual contributions. We are grateful to all of the authors for going that second (and third) mile on behalf of their co-contributors. This process has greatly strengthened our faith in the value of such collaborative scholarly endeavors.

We are also indebted to Randy Calvert, the series editor, and John Haslam at Cambridge University Press for their support and commitment to this project. Lynne Bush at the Institute on Global Conflict and Cooperation did an outstanding job in preparing the manuscript for review and publication.

PART I

Introduction

1

Delegation under anarchy: states, international organizations, and principal-agent theory

DARREN G. HAWKINS, DAVID A. LAKE, DANIEL L. NIELSON, AND MICHAEL J. TIERNEY

In December 1999, police fired tear gas and rubber bullets into a mob protesting the World Trade Organization meeting in Seattle. A central theme of this and similar anti-globalization protests is that the WTO, IMF, World Bank, and other global institutions are "runaway" international bureaucracies implementing a "Washington consensus" formulated by professional economists and other neo-liberals who have made their careers within these agencies (Stiglitz 2002; Rich 1994). Other critics charge that these international organizations (IOs) are imperialist tools of the powerful, exploiting poor and disadvantaged countries for the benefit of the West. Although they have not yet taken to the streets, American conservatives, at the other end of the spectrum, argue that these IOs fail to promote the interests of the United States (Meltzer Commission Report 1999; Krauthammer 2001).

Meanwhile, Europeans complain about the "democratic deficit" within the European Union (see Pollack 2003a: 407–14). As the EU expands its competencies and grows to twenty-five members, critics charge that the simultaneous deepening and broadening of the union is driven by unaccountable bureaucrats in the European Commission and the highly insulated judges of the European Court of Justice. Divorced from electoral pressures, these increasingly powerful EU institutions have allegedly escaped popular control. French and Dutch voters retaliated against the Brussels-led integration project by rejecting the proposed EU Constitution in June 2005.

Similarly, a variety of critics have excoriated the United Nations and its various agencies for their inability to take strong action on the one

---

We would like to thank Tim Büthe, David Dessler, Dan Drezner, Judy Goldstein, Mona Lyne, Mike Thies, Alex Thompson, and the participants in various workshops and panels for their feedback on earlier versions of this chapter.

Introduction

hand and for gross inefficiencies on the other. For victims in Bosnia, Rwanda, Congo, and elsewhere, states have preferred to fiddle while the world burns rather than give peacekeepers the authority and capacity to act (Gourevitch 1998; Power 2002; Barnett 2002). To many taxpayers in donor states, UN bureaucrats are seen as profligate globalists who spend first, budget second, and simply pass along the costs to member states. Corruption in the "oil-for-food" program in Iraq administered by the UN simply confirms pre-existing views of a skeptical American public.

In short, for some observers, IOs appear to be institutional Frankensteins terrorizing the global countryside. Created by their masters, they have slipped their restraints and now run amok. But for others, IOs seem to obey their masters all too well. Like the man behind the curtain in the *Wizard of Oz*, powerful Western countries use IOs to impose their will on the world while hiding behind the facade of legitimizing multilateral processes. Finally, other analysts claim that many IOs once served the purposes of their creators but were subsequently hijacked by other political actors to pursue undesirable ends. IOs become double agents, betraying their original purposes in serving new masters. While these debates rage among pundits, policy-makers and activists, students of international relations find themselves with few appropriate tools to assess these claims.

Contributors to this volume address these debates by drawing upon principal-agent (PA) theory – developed in other areas of the social sciences, especially economics and the study of American and comparative politics – and by examining IOs in their roles as agents variously responsible to member states. The seemingly incompatible perceptions of IOs persist in part because international organizations themselves vary widely in their range of activities and autonomy. Member states have tasked some IOs to act independently, even empowering them to sanction member states in order to facilitate dispute resolution or bolster treaty commitments. Yet other IOs are tightly constrained to follow the dictates of their member states.

To address such variation, this volume takes up two linked issues. First, why do states delegate certain tasks and responsibilities to IOs, rather than acting unilaterally or cooperating directly? Second, how do states control IOs once authority has been delegated? Specifically, what mechanisms do states employ to ensure that their interests are served by IOs? Overall, we find the causes and consequences of delegation to IOs to be remarkably similar to delegation in domestic politics. Despite assertions that international anarchy transforms the logic of politics and renders international institutions less consequential, we find considerable overlap between the reasons why principals delegate to domestic agents and why states delegate to IOs. We also find considerable similarity in the mechanisms domestic principals use to control their agents and those used by states to control IOs. There are, of course, important differences between the two arenas that we note below, but the similarities are striking.

This finding does not suggest that critics are incorrect to point to the problems of monitoring and controlling IOs. Underneath the charges leveled by anti-globalization protestors, for instance, are real concerns about opportunistic international bureaucracies. But the research presented in this volume suggests that it is not inherently more difficult to design effective delegation mechanisms at the international level than at the domestic level. There are variations in the ease of monitoring and controlling different IOs and in the extent to which states are willing to delegate to international agents. Nonetheless, these are questions of degree rather than kind. IOs are neither all evil nor all virtuous as their partisans too often suggest. Rather, they are better understood as bureaucracies that, like those within states, can be more or less controlled by their political masters. This volume helps to explain such variation.

Analytically, we treat IOs as actors in their own right. This furthers the development of an actor-oriented and strategic approach to international institutions. Much of the literature in international relations asks "do institutions matter?" Neo-realists, of course, are skeptical, whereas neo-liberal institutionalists claim that international institutions can and do facilitate interstate cooperation. More recently, scholars have moved beyond this debate to specify and test propositions about when and why states create international institutions and how they operate. Important new research has begun to advance a political approach in which strategic, forward-looking states intentionally adopt and design international institutions in pursuit of their goals (Goldstein et al. 2000; Koremenos, Lipson, and Snidal 2001).

We build on this work by reintroducing and emphasizing the importance of IOs as *actors* that implement policy decisions and pursue their own interests strategically. Most of the existing literature treats international institutions primarily as sets of rules (Simmons and Martin 2002: 192–94). We highlight the strategic behavior of IOs without ignoring the impact of rules on member states or IO staff. But we are primarily interested in a set of related questions: When and why do states delegate to an IO and what sets of rules govern that interaction? How do IOs behave once established; do they follow orders issued by their member states? To what extent do states foresee the problems that might occur by creating IOs as independent actors and how does that anticipation structure the relationship? In short, we seek to understand when, why, and how states create not only rules but also political actors who, in pursuing their own interests, might thwart the goals of states – or, at least, how these concerns might force states to expend valued resources to bring IOs to heel. By reinserting agency into institutionalist theory, we shed new light on the sources and difficulties of international cooperation.

This volume also seeks to contribute to the growing literature on PA theory in political science. First, the authors test a number of standard principal-agent hypotheses in new empirical settings (see chapters by Broz and Hawes, Gould, Martin, Milner, and Pollack, this volume). As results accumulate across sub-disciplines, scholars can be more (or less) confident in the general predictions that follow from specific variants of PA theory. Second, a number of chapters draw novel implications from PA theory that have not been deduced or tested before (see chapters by Thompson, Lyne, Nielson, and Tierney, and Hawkins and Jacoby, this volume). Third, in the international settings studied here some of the conditions that drive predicted outcomes in PA models – such as stability of decision rules, the heterogeneity of preferences, and the reflection of social power in formal decision rules – take on extreme values seldom witnessed in domestic politics. By testing models under these conditions, we help to establish scope conditions for the PA approach. Although the authors in this volume take principal-agent theory seriously, the project was not conceived as, nor is the final product, an uncritical celebration of this approach. Rather, in pushing the approach to a new area – the anarchic international system – we hope to identify the approach's weaknesses as well as its strengths.

In this introductory essay, we define the key terms employed in the volume and derive propositions regarding the nature and extent of delegation to IOs. Our arguments center on the interaction between the benefits to governments from delegating tasks to an IO, and the complications introduced by preference heterogeneity and power differentials among states. As the benefits increase, the probability of international delegation grows, all else equal. However, given a set of potential benefits, the probability of delegation to an IO decreases when preferences become more heterogeneous or voting rules fail to accord with the distribution of power among states. Following our discussion of the "why delegate" question, we then turn to the mechanisms of control used both domestically and internationally by principals to control their agents.

States, international organizations, and principal-agent theory

DEFINING DELEGATION

Delegation is a conditional grant of authority from a *principal* to an *agent* that empowers the latter to act on behalf of the former. This grant of authority is limited in time or scope and must be revocable by the principal. Principals and agents are mutually constitutive. That is, like "master" and "slave," an actor cannot be a principal without an agent, and vice versa. The actors are defined only by their relationship to each other.

The preferences of principals and agents are important determinants of outcomes in PA models. Nonetheless, the PA approach does not imply any particular assumptions about the preferences of actors. Rather, the preferences of both principals and agents are "filled in" as necessary by the specific assumptions of particular theories. The PA framework is employed to model the strategic interaction between these actors and to help make sense of the outcomes we observe. Further, the PA approach does not require that the actors be fully informed or motivated by material interests. Thus, the approach is equally consistent with theories that posit rational, egoistic, wealth-maximizing actors and those that assume boundedly-rational altruistic actors. What unites specific theories under the umbrella of "principal-agent theory" is a focus on the substantive acts of principals in granting conditional authority and designing institutions to control possible opportunism by agents.

The relations between a principal and an agent are always governed by a *contract*,[1] even if this agreement is implicit (never formally acknowledged) or informal (based on an unwritten agreement). To be a principal, an actor must be able to both grant authority and rescind it. The mere ability to terminate a contract does not make an actor a principal. Congress can impeach a president, and thereby remove him from office, but this power does not make Congress the principal of the President as we define it. Alternatively, Congress can authorize the President to decide policy on its behalf in a specific issue area – for example, to design environmental regulations – and then later revoke that authority if it disapproves of the President's policies. In this case, the Congress is indeed the principal of the President. To be principals, actors must both grant and have the power to revoke authority.

---

[1] Contracts are "self-enforcing agreements that define the terms of the relationship between two parties" (Lake 1996: 7). A principal delegating to an agent in a vertically integrated setting is an extreme form of a relational contract (Williamson 1985; Milgrom and Roberts 1992).

Introduction

Agents receive conditional grants of authority from a principal, but this defining characteristic does not imply that agents always do what principals want. *Agency slack* is independent action by an agent that is undesired by the principal. Slack occurs in two primary forms: *shirking*, when an agent minimizes the effort it exerts on its principal's behalf, and *slippage*, when an agent shifts policy away from its principal's preferred outcome and toward its own preferences. *Autonomy* is the range of potential independent action available to an agent after the principal has established mechanisms of control (see below). That is, autonomy is the range of maneuver available to agents after the principal has selected screening, monitoring, and sanctioning mechanisms intended to constrain their behavior. Autonomy and slack differ in subtle ways: autonomy is the range of independent action that is available to an agent and can be used to benefit or undermine the principal, while slack is actual behavior that is undesired.

Finally, as discussed in greater detail below, *discretion* is a dimension of the contract between a principal and an agent. Since it is often the most prominent feature of the contract, and often used as a synonym for autonomy, a brief digression is warranted. Discretion entails a grant of authority that specifies the principal's goals but not the specific actions the agent must take to accomplish those objectives.[2] As we explain later, discretion is an alternative to rule-based delegation. Where discretion gives the agent leeway the principal deems necessary to accomplish the delegated task, autonomy is the range of independent action available to the agent. Greater discretion often gives agents greater autonomy, but not always. To anticipate propositions we develop at greater length below, if a principal combines large discretion with mechanisms of control, the agent may have less autonomy than under rule-based delegation with less restrictive instruments of control. For example, UN weapons inspectors in Iraq enjoyed substantial discretion regarding which sites to inspect and how to gather evidence, but ultimately enjoyed little autonomy due to constant pressure from the United States and other members of the Security Council to produce specific results. Discretion is something the principal intentionally designs into its contract with the agent; autonomy is an unavoidable by-product of imperfect control over agents.

---

[2] A military commander may order her lieutenant to "take that hill," while leaving him considerable discretion regarding specific tactics. Alternatively, a commander may order her lieutenant to take the hill by a frontal assault at noon, leaving him with less discretion.

States, international organizations, and principal-agent theory

Principals incur *agency losses* or costs when agents engage in undesired independent action or when they themselves expend resources to contract with or monitor and control those agents. Since principals always incur some costs in contracting with or supervising agents – even with the most "sincere" types that are unlikely to slack – there are always agency losses associated with delegation. In choosing whether to delegate (or re-delegate), principals must weigh the benefits of delegation, discussed in the next section, against expected agency losses.

This conception of principals and agents hews closely to the classic definition of delegation in the PA literature (see Alchian and Demsetz 1972; Fama 1980; and Williamson 1985). It eschews definitions that broaden the scope of delegation to encompass any situation where the "principal" can affect the "agent's" incentives (see Bernheim and Whinston 1986). For example, Dixit, Grossman, and Helpman (1997) extend a principal-agent relationship to embrace all situations of influence. In this view, legislators are simultaneously agents of party officials, campaign contributors, and voters. Similarly, bureaucrats are agents of courts, the media, interest groups, and lawmakers.[3] But under our narrower definition of delegation, the legislators' principals are strictly voters, who are the only actors who grant authority to act on their behalf and are empowered to terminate the legislators' employment. Similarly, legislators or executives, or perhaps both, are the only actors that can write and terminate a contract with bureaucrats. This is not to say that the political influence of campaign donors, party leaders, interest groups, the media, and courts is trivial. Quite the opposite. We expect third parties will vigorously pursue their interests and may attempt to influence the principals, who then instruct their agents to act in certain ways. Alternatively, third parties may bypass the principals and try to influence agents directly, who may then act independently of their principals. However, third parties necessarily have a different relationship with principals and agents than those two actors have with each other.

These definitions of principals, agents and related terms are *relatively* theory-neutral. Many specific theories – employing particular assumptions regarding actor preferences or deriving preferences through

---

[3] If delegation is simply a situation where actor A can affect the payoffs that actor B receives, then nearly any strategic interaction would qualify A as the principal of B (and usually vice versa). Accepting such a broad definition would rob the approach of its analytic clarity and would make it much more difficult for analysts to deduce falsifiable hypotheses.

Introduction

inference or observation – can gainfully employ the principal-agent framework. Thus far, our use of the principal-agent approach has served as an analytic tool to identify important categories and dimensions of relationships that may be unfamiliar to international relations scholars. Such analytic tools are useful to the extent that they highlight understudied real-world phenomena or help us to understand more fully the phenomena that we already study without PA tools.

In the following sections we develop propositions about why states delegate and how they control agents. These arguments build on existing theories, which tend to be strongly rationalist. Yet the theoretical variation among those who study PA relationships is large, as reflected in this volume, and it would be a mistake to discuss "the" theory of delegation. We chart a middle course by forging a common language and identifying some generalizable answers to key questions that demonstrate the utility of a PA research program.

Delegation to IOs

Any theory of delegation must specify not only what delegation is, but also the alternatives to delegation. If we are to explain delegation, we must also be clear on what is "non-delegation." One possible construction of the dependent variable for this study is depicted in Figure 1.1. We distinguish first between whether states cooperate with one another – where, following Keohane (1984: 51–54), cooperation is defined as mutual policy adjustment – and then whether states choose to delegate authority or not to an IO. Conceptualized in this way, delegation to an IO is a particular form of international cooperation, broadly defined, and one of three possible outcomes.

Node 1. Unilateralism. In unilateral actions, there is no adjustment of policy and IOs are not the implementing agency for any policy. A recent example of unilateral action was the US war on Afghanistan, where the United States pursued its own preferences and implemented its policy choices without its traditional allies.[4] Other cases of unilateralism include Japan's war on the United States in 1941, the Smoot-Hawley Tariff of 1930, repeal of the British Corn Laws in 1846, and arguably the American policy on global warming today.

---

[4] After the fall of the Taliban regime other states cooperated by providing troops, aid, and other assistance.

States, international organizations, and principal-agent theory

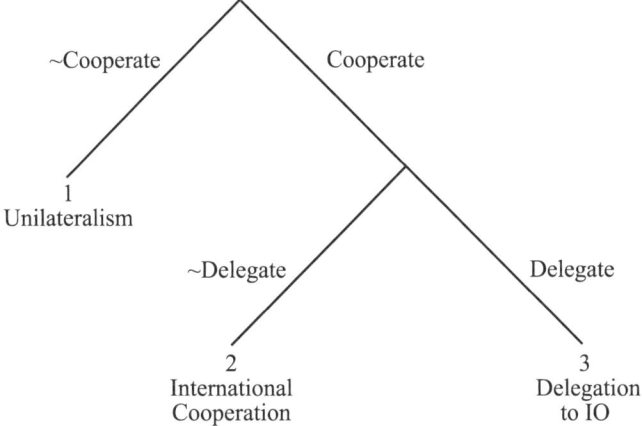

Figure 1.1. International delegation decision tree

Node 2. International cooperation. In "standard" international cooperation, the parties adjust policy but implementation is through strictly national laws or regulations. Cooperation can be achieved through a variety of mechanisms, all the way from unpublicized, informal agreements to legally binding multilateral treaties. Nonetheless, states themselves implement the policy rather than delegate authority to a third party. Examples include lowering tariffs under the GATT, arms reduction under START, bilateral foreign aid contracts, and restricting the production of specific chemicals under the Montreal Protocol on Ozone Depletion.

Node 3. Delegation to IOs. In a second form of cooperation, the paradigmatic case for this book, principals agree (or not) on a common policy and then delegate the implementation of that policy to an IO. Of course, even if states have jointly decided to delegate to an IO, questions remain over what tasks to delegate and how to control the IO. The chapters below provide many examples of such delegation.[5]

---

[5] Of course, states might also delegate authority to private firms, NGOs, or a third state rather than a formal international organization. For work that employs a similar PA framework to these phenomena see Martens et al. 2002; Cooley and Ron 2002. In this volume Lyne, Neilson, and Tierney examine a case where the US government shifts authority from an IO agent to a newly formed domestic agent in an attempt to minimize agency slack.

Introduction

Any satisfactory explanation of the decision to delegate to an IO also explains why not cooperation without delegation, and why not unilateralism. Delegation to an IO must be compared to the "next best alternative." In this volume, the "null policy" for delegation will be either unilateralism or international cooperation.

Delegation and recontracting

Several of the contributions to this volume address the initial act of delegation, while others pursue problems that result once delegation has taken place. While there are some clear differences between these endeavors, many of the hypotheses suggested for explaining why states delegate should also have observable implications for why states restructure – or fail to restructure – their relationship with an IO given the agency problems that result. This restructuring may include increased monitoring, new administrative checks, or enhanced screening and selection of agents (see below). It could also include choosing to withdraw authority from the IO (or "de-delegating"), re-delegating more precisely designated tasks, or authorizing new pursuits for the IO. While principals can never fully anticipate problems with IOs, they likely foresee some potential difficulties and thus design mitigation mechanisms in advance. We thus see the initial delegation and subsequent "re-delegation" endeavors as focusing on slightly different aspects of the same question: How and under what conditions do states conditionally grant authority to an IO?

WHY DELEGATE?

The literature on domestic delegation typically assumes that delegation occurs and then focuses on how principals design institutions to control their agents (McNollgast 1987, 1989). Congress can pass welfare legislation, for instance, but it is poorly suited to determine whether particular individuals pass a means-test to qualify for public aid. Thus, it appears unproblematic that Congress will delegate the implementation of its policy to some agent. However, not all domestic delegation stems from a principal's inability to do something itself. Congress can delegate to the President the authority to decide whether a particular country meets a human rights standard or if a policy is in the "national interest," but these are choices that Congress can (and often does) make itself (Epstein and O'Halloran 1999a).

States, international organizations, and principal-agent theory

In the international arena, the question "why delegate?" is central. States, especially powerful states, can accomplish unilaterally at least some of the tasks they delegate to IOs. Neo-liberal institutionalists have persuasively argued that cooperation can serve state interests (Keohane 1984; Martin 1992b). Delegation is not necessary for international cooperation. Why then do states delegate authority to an IO?

The benefits of delegation

All delegation is premised upon the division of labor and gains from specialization. These gains interact with all other benefits from delegation. We identify five additional benefits that may induce states to delegate to an IO: managing policy externalities, facilitating collective decision-making, resolving disputes, enhancing credibility, and creating policy bias. As the benefits from delegation increase, all else constant, we predict that states will be more likely to delegate authority to IOs.

Not surprisingly, given that delegation is a form of cooperation, many of the benefits we identify here overlap with incentives to cooperate more generally. Yet, our analysis goes beyond the sources of cooperation identified in the extant literature by showing how delegating to an IO can actually enhance the prospects for cooperation. As actors look "down" the decision tree described above and work backwards from possible outcomes to actual choices, the availability of attractive options at the terminal nodes increases the probability that actors will choose cooperation at the upper branch. In this way, understanding the benefits of delegation can also help augment explanations about when and why states cooperate.

Benefits do not always translate smoothly into international delegation; the mere fact that countries can gain does not mean that they will choose to grant authority to an IO. Two mitigating factors – preference heterogeneity and power balances – interact with benefits to affect the probability of delegation. We develop each of these arguments below.

Specialization. Inherent in all delegation is a division of labor. Rather than performing an act itself, the principal delegates authority to a *specialized agent* with the expertise, time, political ability, or resources to perform a task. Without some gains from specialization, there is little reason to delegate anything to anybody. In turn, the greater the gains from specialization, the greater the incentives to delegate (and the greater the agency losses the principal is willing to tolerate, if necessary, to capture these gains).

Introduction

Gains from specialization are likely to be greatest when the task to be performed is frequent, repetitive, and requires specific expertise or knowledge. One-time tasks capable of being performed by "anyone" are not likely to engender delegation; although the principal incurs opportunity costs in implementing the policy itself, this is offset by the inevitable costs in creating or finding and controlling an agent. Common tasks that require great expertise produce greater gains from specialization. The International Criminal Court, for example, centralizes the expertise needed for prosecuting war crimes and crimes against humanity, a task that states undertook with increasing frequency and intensity in the 1990s.[6] In this volume, Martin and Thompson both highlight the gains from specialized agents who can collect information that is useful to agents, including financial conditions in the developing countries (IMF) and the intentions of actors seeking to use force (Security Council).

Delegation to an IO is most likely when the costs of establishing the specialized agent are more than the benefits to any single state but less than the benefits to a collection of states. Peacekeeping provides a clear example. In most cases, no single state benefits enough from peacekeeping to pay those costs itself. Yet the benefits from peacekeeping are larger than any state's costs if burdens are distributed in politically viable ways (e.g. Bangladeshi and Nigerian soldiers with Western money). Resulting outcomes are not necessarily more effective than unilateral action (US peacekeepers acting alone might do a better job than Nigerians under UN command), but they do provide collective gains to states as a group.

Specialization allows others to provide services that states are unable or unwilling to provide unilaterally. States sometimes lack technical expertise, credibility, legitimacy, or other resources to make policy on their own. The greater the needs of states, the larger the gains from specialization and the more likely states are to delegate to IO agents, even though large agent capabilities also increase the possibility of shirking by those agents. States may delegate routine loan decisions to the World Bank and the IMF, for instance, but are likely to engage in coordinated action when those decisions become more important to state security, as with the Mexican peso crisis or the Russian financial crisis. Likewise, states may delegate some monitoring of weapons of mass destruction to

---

[6] The US representative to the Rome Conference argued explicitly that the transactions costs of setting up numerous regional courts, like those in the former Yugoslavia and Rwanda, were too great and that these tasks ought to be consolidated by creating the ICC. See Scheffer 1997.

an IO for reasons of credibility, but powerful states are unlikely to give up such monitoring capabilities themselves and are unlikely to delegate monitoring of other powerful states to an IO.[7]

Policy externalities. Principals benefit from cooperation and may delegate to an IO when there are large policy externalities (see Milner 1997: 44; Lake 1999: 44–52). The greater the externalities, the more likely states are to engage in mutually coordinated action. The gains from cooperation, however, can also be enhanced by delegating to an agent.

Policy externalities arise under two conditions, characterized as dilemmas of coordination and collaboration, respectively (Stein 1990; Martin 1992b). In coordination dilemmas, states seek to avoid mutually distasteful outcomes (exemplified by the Chicken game, where the actors desire to avoid the DD outcome) or enhance the certainty of their choosing mutually desired outcomes (exemplified by the "battle of the sexes" game, where the actors prefer to choose either CC or DD, but run some risk of choosing CD or DC "by accident"). Compared to other strategic problems, coordination dilemmas are relatively easy to solve – but no less important to world welfare. The risk that cooperation may fail in such situations arises from mistaken signals of resolve or other misperceptions.

Delegating authority to a *coordinating agent* can help resolve such dilemmas. Since the fact of agreement is typically more important than which policy is selected, states can reduce transactions costs by granting authority to some neutral, third party that can evaluate alternatives on more technical or social welfare criteria. In such cases, states are likely to grant significant discretion to their agents. Since cooperation may fail due to informational problems, states can also gain by delegating to agents to monitor their behavior, provide information about the various policy alternatives, or otherwise "endorse" various cooperative solutions (see Milner 1997; Lake and McCubbins, this volume). Such agents are likely to be granted significant discretion. International standards agencies, such as the International Postal Union or agencies to allocate the radio spectrum, are examples of IOs with broad discretion to coordinate national policies.

---

[7] For example, the United States and the Soviet Union insisted on monitoring each other in the SALT, INF, and START agreements, but they were willing to delegate significant authority to the IAEA to monitor the nuclear programs of developing countries.

Introduction

In collaboration dilemmas, the equilibrium outcome (or in cases of multiple equilibria, some range of outcomes) is sub-optimal. To realize cooperation in such strategic settings, states must bind themselves to act against their "natural" tendencies. Even so, states will typically retain incentives, at least in the short run, to "defect" from cooperation (the exemplary game is Prisoner's Dilemma). Nonetheless, states often try to develop some mechanism to restrain defection and facilitate cooperation.

Public goods constitute a major class of collaboration dilemmas. When states can benefit from a good (such as a clean environment) whether or not they contribute to its provision, the classic free rider problem arises and, in the absence of centralized provision, the outcome is likely to be sub-optimal. In such cases, states may benefit by delegating to an IO that they empower and finance to provide the public good. In the area of public health, the World Health Organization (WHO) provides an example, especially in the monitoring and control of infectious diseases (see Cortell and Peterson, this volume). In theory, states might also use multilateral development organizations to avoid policy externalities in the form of giving some countries too much aid and others too little, though Milner (this volume) finds no evidence for that hypothesis.

Alternatively, states may elect to contribute individually to public goods, but create agents to collect and reveal information about their efforts – often a necessary condition for successfully overcoming the free rider problem (see Keohane 1984; Abbott and Snidal 1998). Examples here include the Council of Europe, which monitors human rights practices; the International Atomic Energy Agency (IAEA), which monitors non-proliferation policies; and the Organization for Economic Cooperation and Development (OECD), which monitors macroeconomic policies of member states. Since states still have incentives to free ride, they might individually desire to control their agents but nonetheless collectively grant the IO a small amount of discretion so that it can more effectively provide public goods or, alternatively, police their individual contributions. Nonetheless, such *collaboration agents* are likely to possess far less leeway than their coordinating counterparts.

Collective decision-making. States may also delegate to IOs when they possess socially intransitive preferences or other problems of collective decision-making. That is, when states as a group are unlikely to reach a stable agreement on policy (i.e. will cycle through alternatives), they can delegate power to an *agenda-setting agent* to induce an equilibrium when one might not otherwise exist. This is a standard solution to the collective choice problem in domestic politics and may be reflected in the considerable agenda power given to the European Commission within the European Union (see Pollack 2003a: 84–85, and this volume).

Although the choice of institution or the leader of that institution may also be subject to collective choice dilemmas, presumably the IO and its leadership stand someplace near the median of the managing coalition of member states. On any particular policy choice, therefore, the leadership will try to move the group closer to its own ideal point and, therefore, closer to the managing coalition's collective preference.[8] Yet, we can anticipate a policy struggle over agenda control between states closer to the median of the group, who prefer to delegate agenda power to an IO they control, and powerful states with more extreme preferences who prefer to act unilaterally. We saw this in the wrangling between the United States and Britain, on the one hand, and the other members of the UNSC, on the other, over the disarmament of Iraq before the 2003 War in the Persian Gulf. The closer the membership's preferences and the politically weaker the preference outliers in socially intransitive settings, the more likely states will be to delegate to an agenda-setting IO or restructure an IO contract to provide agenda-setting authority.

Dispute resolution. States may also delegate authority to IO agents to resolve disputes between themselves. As international interactions have grown more rule-governed (Goldstein et al. 2000), there has been a corresponding increase in the use of third-party agents to resolve disputes. Such *arbitrating agents* can be important in securing the social benefits of cooperation – and it is this cooperation that helps to explain why states delegate to these agents in the first place.

The key problem in most interstate disputes is the incomplete nature of the contract among the principals. Although it is possible in theory to consider all possible future states-of-the-world and to negotiate ex ante the responsibilities and appropriate actions by all parties to an agreement in each of those states, in practice a large number of future conditions are left unconsidered in negotiations (see Williamson 1985). The anticipation of future conflicts over the terms of the contract, in turn, inhibits cooperation.

---

[8] In the context of American politics, this argument is pursued by Kiewiet and McCubbins 1991; and Cox and McCubbins 1993. They show, persuasively, that delegation can work in favor of the collective interests of the principals.

Introduction

When contracts are incomplete, the principals can lower their future transactions costs and secure cooperation by delegating authority to an agent who is empowered to decide disputes between the parties. In agreeing in advance to refer disputes to an arbitrating agent, the principals select (or create) agents who are known to be impartial and, more importantly, to possess a high degree of autonomy, as Alter's analysis in this volume illustrates. Agents that are expected to be biased or constrained to decide disputes on anything other than application of the relevant rules are unlikely to be acceptable to one or both parties to the agreement. Since the principals themselves disagree on what the contract implies, they cannot instruct the agent on exactly how to decide on the issue(s) under dispute. Principals, therefore, go to considerable lengths to select (or create) impartial agents with relatively high autonomy. In some cases, especially at the level of constitutional courts, the principals create not an agent, to whom they can both grant and revoke authority, but a *trustee*, to whom authority is permanently transferred, as Alter points out in this volume (see also Grant and Keohane 2005). For both agents and trustees, however, the purpose of the grant of authority is the same. The autonomy of the agent increases the likelihood that over some unknown number of future disputes regarding unforeseen issues, an individual principal is likely to "win" as many times as it "loses." This permits the agreement to go forward on a "risk neutral" basis.

Nonetheless, the principals still seek to constrain their arbitrating agents in a variety of ways, including specifying clearly the intent of their agreement – and therefore stipulating the principles to be upheld in dispute resolution – and agreeing on procedures, the types of evidence permitted, and the forms of argument to be followed should a dispute arise. Despite considerable discretion, principals do not grant agents the autonomy to decide disputes any way they want. If principals have designed the process well, the agent's decision will reflect what the architects of the agreement would have wanted on average even if they disagree on the particulars in a specific instance.

Credibility. States may delegate authority to an IO or revise an existing IO contract to enhance the credibility of their policy commitments (Martin 1992a; Stone 2002). Problems of credible commitment often arise under what economists call the time-inconsistency problem – actions that are in a political actor's long-term interest may not be in its interest at any particular moment. Although there are advantages in the long run to a balanced budget, for instance, at each moment politicians have incentives to satisfy the demands of their constituents for more services and less taxes through deficit spending. Credibility problems can also arise, as Pollack argues in this volume, when issues impose concentrated costs and diffuse benefits. Competition policies in the EU, for example, hurt producers but benefit all EU citizens and thus raise credibility problems for states with major producers adversely affected by the rules.

Principals can mitigate these problems by delegating policy to *enforcing agents* with high discretion and, typically, more extreme preferences so that, left to their own devices, the agents will move policy in the desired direction. To succeed in establishing policy credibility, it must also be costly for principals to revoke authority from their agents or to overturn their specific decisions, otherwise there is nothing to prevent the principals from promising to act in the long-term interest but then giving in to short-term temptation. Costs may arise from issue linkages, so that withdrawing on one dimension of policy threatens losses on other dimensions as well. Costs may also be imposed by others (say, international investors) who interpret the withdrawal itself as a signal of impending policy change (possibly a return to a more inflationary monetary policy) and react negatively (increasing the cost of borrowing to the state). The European Central Bank, designed to reflect Germany's comparatively conservative financial preferences, is an example of delegation to an enforcing IO to solve the time inconsistency problem. Currency areas in Francophone West Africa and Anglophone East Africa have been adopted for similar reasons (see Cooper 2004).

"Lock-in" (creating policy bias). Political decisions always create winners and losers, but political uncertainty is endemic; today's winners could be tomorrow's losers. Policy winners who want to continue to win in the future can bias policy in their favor through delegation. In domestic politics, political parties may alternate in power and, representing different coalitions of interests, enact different policies. In international politics, states may rise (or decline) in power, forcing a renegotiation of a more (or less) favorable agreement than was possible before (Powell 1999). Of course, these two arenas interact; domestic coalitions can seek to lock in their domestic benefits through international agreements (Moravcsik 2000).

In American politics, this is the widely discussed bureaucratic "lock-in" effect. As Moe (1990: 213, 222) put it, most political institutions "arise out of a politics of structural choice in which the winners use their

Introduction

temporary hold on public authority to design new structures and impose them on the polity as a whole." McNollgast (1987) demonstrates that administrative procedures acts have been used to structure the incentives of bureaucracies and insulate current policy beneficiaries from future change. Similarly, in some ethnically divided societies, consociational institutions have been constructed that lock-in the balance of ethnic power that exists at a particular moment and, in turn, delegate authority to elites (Lijphart 1977). The United Nations Security Council, empowered by the international community to defend international peace and security, has a permanent membership drawn entirely from the major victors of World War Two. This has served to lock-in the international balance of power as it existed in 1945.

Unlike arbitrating or credibility-seeking agents, such *policy-biased agents* do not necessarily need much discretion (though they may have it). Rather, principals ensure their utility by crafting careful mandates that are difficult to undo or by structuring voting rules in ways that ensure the continued dominance of those who hold power at the moment of the rule-drafting. For example, Moravcsik has argued that elites in unstable democracies created the European Court of Human Rights (ECHR) in order to secure democracy and bias future policy against autocratic elites who might try to seize power. The Court enjoys discretion, certainly, but more important to principals is its mandate protecting certain kinds of rights and decision rules that help ensure the Court is staffed by those sincerely committed to individual rights (Moravscik 2000). While this logic is sound, Hawkins and Jacoby (this volume) emphasize that the costs of adverse agent decisions can be quite high, and so in practice states have delegated very cautiously to the Court despite their strong incentives to lock-in policy.

Preference heterogeneity

While the gains from delegation may motivate states to grant conditional authority to IOs, they do not determine the outcome. Instead, benefits interact with the preferences and power of states to affect the probability and extent of delegation.

It is unlikely that all states share the same goals and policy preferences. Except in coordination dilemmas where states are largely indifferent between alternative equilibria or collective decision dilemmas plagued by social intransitivities, where delegation is a means of overcoming policy differences, delegation typically requires states to resolve their

States, international organizations, and principal-agent theory

policy conflicts before they can decide to grant conditional authority to an agent and, then, usefully instruct that agent on the action they want implemented. The greater the preference heterogeneity of any group of states, therefore, the less likely they will be to delegate to an IO. Similarly, the less similar their preferences, the less likely states will be to revise an existing delegation relationship (Nielson and Tierney 2003a; Lyne, Nielson, and Tierney, this volume). Since revising the relationship will likely produce a policy change, the greater the preference heterogeneity of states the more likely one or more members will prefer the status quo to the proposed outcome. Depending on the rules for institutional decision-making, this may allow states to veto any proposed revision of the delegation relationship and, thus, give the agent more autonomy (in this volume see Cortell and Peterson, Thompson, and Martin).

Institutional rules, power, and delegation

In addition to their preferences over policy, states also care about how institutional rules at the international level aggregate national preferences into policy and control over possible IO agents. Institutions aggregate preferences in different ways (Rogowski 1999). In the case of American politics, for instance, voters elect representatives at the local level, senators at the state level, and presidents at the national level. Not surprisingly, the House of Representatives, the Senate, and the executive all have different medians or "ideal points" on many policy issues despite their electoral connections to the same voters. Similarly, in the European Union, the Council of Ministers, representing voters as aggregated through national-level political institutions, differs in its positions from the European Parliament, elected directly by voters. Rules not only identify voting constituencies, they also govern how decisions are made in collective principals and they may tell agents (or not) how to resolve potentially conflicting instructions from different member states in the case of multiple principals.[9] Generally, the greater the number of states required to approve an action, the greater the autonomy of the agent. As with preference heterogeneity, decision-making rules requiring widespread support are likely to discourage delegation and to increase agent autonomy. Cortell and Peterson and Lyne, Nielson, and Tierney (this

---

[9] On the distinction between collective and multiple principals see Lyne, Nielson, and Tierney in this volume.

Introduction

volume) elaborate this logic and show how different rules for aggregating preferences result in different predictions for agent behavior.

Because institutional rules matter, they also interact with the power of different states to influence delegation outcomes. As depicted in the decision tree above, states weigh their ability to realize their aims by acting alone versus acting through an IO. Powerful states are able to obtain their goals through their own influence and capabilities. As a result, they have a more attractive "outside option" and, if they choose to do so, can more effectively realize their preferences (see Gruber 2000). When institutional rules fail to reflect accurately the distribution of power, powerful states will more readily choose to act alone outside the institution, in a "minilateral" group with like-minded states, or in concert with weaker states they can control. President George W. Bush's "Coalition of the Willing" in the 2003 Iraq War is a striking example.

When institutional rules reflect the power distribution, powerful states will more likely choose to act within the institution and delegate to the IO to reap the benefits of delegation discussed above. As Broz and Hawes suggest (this volume), the United States may be willing to work through the IMF because its weighted decision rules make it responsive to US concerns. Since powerful states are also likely to be large in absolute terms, the absolute benefits of delegation may be quite important.[10] The greater the benefits of delegation, of course, the greater the gap between rules and power the powerful states are likely to tolerate and still delegate to an IO. States that lack international influence will typically favor delegation because, first, they cannot affect international outcomes unilaterally and, second; they share in the benefits of delegation discussed above. To the extent that institutional rules do not reflect accurately the power distribution among states, moreover, the rules are likely to enhance their influence on world affairs, as in the United Nations General Assembly, for instance, where both large and small states all have one vote.[11] With weaker states normally disposed toward greater delegation,

---

[10] Large states may constitute a "privileged group" in providing public goods. See Olson 1965; Snidal 1985.

[11] Parks and Tierney 2004 demonstrate that multilateral granting agencies with rules closer to one country one vote, like the UNDP and the Montreal Protocol Fund, enable weaker states to realize their aid allocation preferences more fully than the weighted voting systems of multilateral development banks. On measuring power within IOs see Strand and Rapkin 2005.

States, international organizations, and principal-agent theory

the impetus for or against delegation to IOs typically originates from the more powerful members of the system.

Thus, in choosing to delegate to an IO, the existing institutional rules are important. Cortell and Peterson develop this point in their chapter. As important, the greater the divergence between power and institutional rules, the less likely the powerful states will be to delegate to IOs. As power is constantly in flux, and institutions are sticky and evolve slowly, this may well be an important impediment to international cooperation and delegation.

Summary

There are important benefits from delegation to IOs. By delegating, states reap gains from specialization, as well as capture policy externalities, facilitate collective decision-making, resolve disputes, enhance credibility, and lock-in policy biases. The larger these benefits, the greater the likelihood that states will choose to delegate to an IO. Similarly, the larger the gains, the greater the agency losses states will tolerate before revoking authority from an agent or renegotiating the agency contract. Delegating to an IO, in turn, is likely to enhance international cooperation as well.

Yet, despite the potential gains, states face at least two impediments to delegation. The more diverse the preferences of states, the less likely they are to agree to a common policy and delegate to an IO (see Martin and Lyne, Nielson, and Tierney, this volume). Similarly, as the distribution of power and institutional rules diverge, the less likely states will be to delegate to that IO. The most powerful states are critical to decisions about delegation and will be most likely to support delegation to international institutions that accurately reflect their global influence. By a similar logic, the greater the preference heterogeneity of states and the greater the divergence between institutional rules and the power of states, the fewer agency losses states will accept before abandoning the current contract or agent.

STRUCTURES OF DELEGATION

In any instance of delegation, there is a tradeoff between the gains from delegation and the agency losses that arise from the opportunistic behavior of the agent. The structure of the agency relationship – the form of delegation – is designed to manage this tradeoff and, specifically, to

Introduction

maximize the interests of the principals in a manner that is compatible with the incentives of the agents. In this section, we examine the incentives of agents and how principals design institutions to align these incentives with their own interests.

Agency problems

Central to PA theory is the assumption that agents pursue their own interests, subject to the constraints imposed upon them by their principals (Kiewiet and McCubbins 1991: 5). In other words, agents are opportunistic, which Williamson (1985: 30) famously defines as "self-interest seeking with guile." Since the preferences of the principals and agents are seldom aligned perfectly (see below), there is a natural and perhaps inevitable conflict of interest between the parties (Kiewiet and McCubbins 1991: 24). Principals try to control the behavior of their agents, but can do so only imperfectly and at some cost to themselves, inevitably suffering agency losses. Agency losses are partly endogenous to the agency relationship and vary in magnitude. The larger the agency losses relative to the available alternatives, the less likely states are to delegate authority to IOs or to maintain ongoing relationships with IOs.

Two features of the agency problem are critical. First, for agency slack to arise there must be some environmental uncertainty that renders it difficult for the principal to assess the agent's effort.[12] If no uncertainty exists, the principal can simply observe the outcome and infer the agent's actions in bringing about that result. In a world of perfect certainty, however much agents might try to obfuscate, their actions will eventually become known. But if there is uncertainty, the principal can discern only with difficulty whether an outcome arose because of the efforts of the agent or from some exogenous "shock." If the principal observes an unsatisfactory outcome, it cannot tell for sure whether this was the result of slack by the agent, in which case the latter should be sanctioned, or some unfortunate event that disrupted the best efforts of a sincere agent, who should not be punished. Conversely, if the principal receives a satisfactory or even better than expected outcome, it cannot tell if this is the product of the extraordinary efforts of a diligent agent or a "lucky break" for an otherwise slacking agent. It is this inability to distinguish

---

[12] On the important role of uncertainty, see Furubotn and Richter 2000: ch. 6. See also Koremenos, Lipson, and Snidal 2001.

the causes of policy success and failure that prohibits, in part, the principal from writing an optimal contract to control the agent (see below).

Second, agent specialization exacerbates the twin problems for the principal of hidden action and hidden information (Kiewiet and McCubbins 1991: 25). If the principal must learn everything that the agent knows and observe everything the agent does, the gains from specialization diminish accordingly. At the extreme, with perfect knowledge and monitoring, it is almost as if the principal has performed the task herself. Thus, to the extent that specialization is part of the motivation for delegating to an agent, the agent can act opportunistically by failing to disclose actions or information that might be beneficial to the principal. Specialization also typically inhibits the principal's ability to threaten contracting with other agents as a disciplining device to control the first agent. The greater the specialization, therefore, the greater the opportunity for agency slack.

The nature of the agent

In "hiring" an agent, a principal can create one of its own, thereby constructing from "scratch" an organization of her own design, or choose from among a pool of existing entities willing to serve as the agent. Creating a new agent is, of course, costly, but likely to produce one closer to the preferences and purposes of the principal. Choosing an existing agent avoids the start-up costs, but since no pool is infinitely large and diverse, the principal may be unable to find an ideal agent that perfectly mirrors her preferences and is optimally designed to perform the appointed task. This problem is compounded when principals must decide whether to re-delegate to an existing agent. Breaking relations with an existing agent imposes costs, but so does renewing a contract with a problematic agent.

Agent characteristics have not received much attention in the IO literature analysts typically assume that agents are designed by principals and therefore have no independent influence, or that adverse agent characteristics are controlled through selection and monitoring mechanisms (discussed below). Given a finite pool of possible agents and positive costs of creating new agents, however, the "exogenous" traits of agents are likely to matter, as Hawkins and Jacoby argue in their chapter (see also Moe 1990). This is not just a problem of delegating to IOs, but a problem inherent to all delegation. Nonetheless, despite their recent and accelerating growth (Shanks, Jacobson, and Kaplan 1996), the relatively

Introduction

limited number of existing IOs brings this constraint into sharp relief. The greater the costs of creating new agents and the larger the divergence between the "ideal" preferences and design of an agent and the traits of existing agents, the more difficult it will be to control the agent, the more costly mechanisms of control will be, and the greater will be the agent's autonomy. Several chapters below illustrate this argument while highlighting a range of agent characteristics. Cortell and Peterson argue that agents composed of international civil servants are likely to be more autonomous than those with staff seconded from national bureaucracies. Alter argues that courts as agents are likely to exhibit greater autonomy. For Gould, variation in agent tasks provides the main source of agent autonomy. Hawkins and Jacoby argue that agents have a variety of strategies available to make themselves more autonomous.

Principals anticipate many of these problems, which raise the costs of delegation. Hence, principals should carefully examine agent characteristics and not delegate where they cannot find a suitable agent. In support of this argument, Hawkins and Jacoby argue that principals often delayed delegation to the ECHR while they tried to ascertain the Court's preferences. Thompson argues that states delegated to the Security Council due to its heterogeneous preferences and the Council, in turn, failed to delegate enforcement to the United States due to concerns about US intentions. Martin finds evidence that states delegated more to the IMF when the staff's preferences reflected those of the principals. Lyne, Nielson, and Tierney find that despite such screening efforts, states sometimes make mistakes when selecting their agents and thus attempt to reform their agents (as in the case of the Inter-American Foundation) or to rescind delegated authority (as in the case of the Inter-American Development Bank). Such *ex post* measures by state principals focus attention on the mechanisms of control in any delegation relationship.

Mechanisms of control

Principals have five major mechanisms for controlling their agents. Broadly, principals attempt to structure the incentives of agents ex ante so that it is in the interests of those agents to carry out their principals' desires faithfully ex post. The form of delegated authority, then, is not given or fixed, but rather is endogenous to the agency relationship and largely designed by the principal to minimize the opportunistic behavior of the agent. However, principals cannot anticipate every contingency – particularly where agents are granted broad discretion or when the interests of the principals themselves shift over time. The mechanisms that principals use to control agents have been the subject of extensive research in the domestic politics literature. As we do not find significant differences between domestic and international mechanisms of control, this survey is brief.

Rules versus discretion. The contract between the principal and the agent specifies the scope of the authority delegated to the latter, the instruments by which the agent is permitted to carry out its task, and the procedures that the agent should follow in employing those instruments (McCubbins and Page 1987: 412). The precise nature of the contract will reflect many considerations, but contracts are often described as varying along a single dimension of rules versus discretion.

On the one hand, the principal can write detailed rules to the agent for carrying out its responsibilities. Under rule-based delegation, the principal instructs the agent on exactly how the agent is supposed to do its job. The use of rules may be partly a function of the purposes of delegation (discussed above) but it is, more often, a mechanism for constraining the agent. Rule-based delegation generally reduces the gains from specialization – as the principal must spend time and effort learning about the task and writing the rules – and reduces flexibility, as the tightly bound agent cannot respond as effectively to unpredictable changes in the environment. For this reason, rule-based delegation is relatively inefficient and will be used only when agents are difficult to control through other means. The World Bank provides an example. Member states allowed the Bank broad discretion until the mid-1980s when a fundamental change occurred in the preferences of a winning coalition on the Bank's executive board in favor of greater environmental protection. For several years, the coalition, led by the United States, tried ad hoc threats and *ex post* sanctions on the Bank but failed to establish a new equilibrium for their agent. Finally, the executive board designed new rules and institutions that now more tightly constrain the agent. These changes to the IO contract, entailing rule-based delegation, proved very expensive (Nielson and Tierney 2003a).

On the other hand, the principal can articulate its goals and leave the agent to figure out how best to fulfill its assigned mission. Under discretion-based delegation, the policy-making role of the agent is greatly enhanced. Discretion is most useful where uncertainty is high, and thus flexibility is necessary and valued (Cooter 2000: 94), or when the task requires highly specialized knowledge possessed only by the agent.

Discretion may also be useful when principals have heterogeneous preferences but not so extreme as to vitiate the gains from delegation. Rather than negotiating to a final policy, and incurring potentially large transactions costs in doing so, diverse principals may let the agent figure out where to set policy so that it cannot be overturned by a group of unhappy principals (McCubbins and Page 1987: 418). But for all these same reasons, discretion creates greater opportunities for opportunistic behavior by the agent. In this volume, Alter and Hawkins and Jacoby find that judicial agents capitalize on their high discretion to gain autonomy and exercise slack.

Monitoring and reporting requirements. Principals use *ex post* monitoring and reporting requirements, typically specified in the delegation contract, to reveal information about the agent's actions. The most important distinction is between "police patrols," which refer to direct monitoring of agents by principals to identify malfeasance, and "fire alarms," which rely upon affected parties outside the agency relationship to bring evidence of slack to the attention of the principals (McCubbins and Schwartz 1984). Fire alarms are typically more efficient, as the principal does not need to expend resources searching for slack where it may not exist, and potentially more effective, as parties harmed by the agent typically have strong incentives to publicize shirking and slippage. We see examples of both police patrol and fire alarm mechanisms at work in the European Union. Police patrols feature prominently in the EU's "comitology," where the Single European Act specifies various advisory, management and regulatory committees that oversee actions in all realms where the European Commission operates. As an effective fire alarm, aggrieved individuals can bring complaints before the European Court of Justice against any Commission action that affects them directly (Pollack 1997; see also Tallberg 2002b).

Screening and selection procedures. Principals also seek to reduce slack by selecting agents with preferences similar to their own. In doing so, principals seek agents who are likely to do what they themselves would do if they carried out the task directly. Screening and selection occur at both the leadership and agency levels. In domestic political systems, majorities typically select cabinet ministers and agency heads that reflect their views. In IOs a similar process of leadership selection unfolds (see Kahler 2001; Wade 2002). Principals can select between institutional agents with known biases or, at some cost, create a new agent with a defined policy preference. Either way, the principal attempts to select an agent naturally inclined to act as the principal would if implementing policy itself. By selecting a sympathetic agent, the principal can grant the agent greater discretion and employ less costly monitoring mechanisms while still minimizing agency slack.

However, agents have incentives to misrepresent their true preferences. Hence, principals face the problem of adverse selection when choosing an agent and, in international relations, screening and selection mechanisms may be rather weak. As noted above, the number of IOs, although growing rapidly, is still relatively small compared to the domestic arena. States can be expected to delegate authority to the most favorable IO, a practice sometimes known as "forum shopping," but the range of possible agents is still limited. At the same time, creating IOs with sympathetic preferences *de novo* is often costly. As Hawkins and Jacoby argue in this volume, this problem of a limited agent pool can create disincentives for delegation and greater scope for agent autonomy.

In addition, leaders of international organizations tend to be selected in less than fully competitive ways and are often difficult to remove, limiting the choice available to principals at any moment in time. By implicit agreement of the founding parties, for instance, the director of the IMF is always a European and the President of the World Bank is always an American. The Secretary General of the United Nations is selected from a list of regional candidates on a rotating basis. Such rules limit competition for office, deprive principals of a full range of candidates from which to choose, and may produce agents who do not represent the median member of the organization. The recent selection of Paul Wolfowitz as president of the World Bank is an obvious example, but is not atypical. The inability of member states to agree on the appointment of a prosecutor for the Yugoslav war crimes tribunal delayed the operation of that institution for more than a year and resulted in a weak choice that further delayed the institution's operation.

Institutional checks and balances. Principals can also structure agency relationships so that they contain institutional checks and balances that limit opportunistic behavior by agents. Within single organizations, checks are created by empowering bureaus with at least partially opposing mandates (e.g. in firms, production managers charged with maximizing output and controllers charged with minimizing production costs). In response to fears of a runaway international court, states carefully designed a series of safeguards in the International Criminal Court. The prosecutor can be checked by judges, initial court rulings can be checked by a more complete set of judges, the Security Council can check both prosecutors and judges, and individual states can check the court by seriously investigating cases themselves.

Checks are also created by empowering more than one agent or hiring agents with overlapping mandates. Competition between the agents will help reveal to principals the true costs of performing the task, the preferences of the agents, and so on. Although redundancy reduces the benefits of specialization, it may also reveal more and better information to the principal. The purview of the regional development banks overlaps with the World Bank's, and the banks often compete over projects and country portfolios. And in adjustment lending, the World Bank and the IMF are increasingly competitors.

Sanctions. Finally, principals can punish agents for undesired actions and reward agents for desired actions. This carrot and stick approach by principals can be applied to both individuals and bureaus to induce desired behavior.

Principals typically sanction agents through budgetary expansions and contractions. Agents that succeed in their missions are rewarded with larger budgets, allowing individuals to perform their jobs more easily or supervise larger staffs with compensatory benefits. Agents that fail are punished with smaller budgets, and may even be eliminated entirely. Broz and Hawes in this volume argue that the size of US funding creates incentives for the IMF to protect US money center banks in their loans to developing countries. In this case, the IMF appears responsive to the need for expanded budgets from the most important member of its collective principal.

Principals employ these mechanisms of control in varying combinations to achieve their aims. In some cases, the mix is determined by the availability of agents. In cases where agent preferences are especially hard to discern, principals are likely to write more extensive rules, employ tighter monitoring arrangements, create multiple agents, or use higher-powered sanctions. The mix is also likely to be affected by the purpose of delegation. When delegation is used to enhance the credibility of a principal's policy, for instance, considerable discretion must be given to the agent and visible sanctions will be counter-productive. Since it is the very independence of the agent and the agent's more extreme preferences that yields credibility, any overt control of the agent by the principal will actually diminish credibility. Similarly, dispute resolution

States, international organizations, and principal-agent theory

requires controlling the agent with a "light hand." Too much control, in these instances, undermines the purpose of the delegation. But in all cases, theory suggests mechanisms of control are intentionally designed and used to minimize agency slack.

Control mechanisms are costly and imperfect. Since resources are scarce (in the economic sense), principals never devote sufficient time or effort to control agents completely. Agents always possess some autonomy. As Gould shows in her chapter, principals find it more difficult to design control mechanisms for some IMF tasks than for others and, not surprisingly, the IMF has more autonomy in the areas that are more difficult to monitor. Alter argues that many of the control mechanisms designed by principals are inapplicable to international courts and that states have to find other ways to check courts. Despite the best efforts of principals, agents can turn autonomy into slack, depending on agent preferences and strategies.

Traditionally, PA approaches have focused on agent slack as the outcome of imperfect control, yet the presence of slack does not mean that delegation has failed or that it is not the best course of action available to states (Gould 2003). Slack is only meaningful relative to the gains from delegation and relative to the next best alternative available to states. Indeed, the greater the gains from delegation, the greater the agency slack states will tolerate. As a result, if slack is observed, one possibility is that the principal is reaping offsetting benefits. The principals can always reduce slack by tightening oversight, but this requires time, attention, and expertise. States choose the degree of delegation and control mechanisms to maximize their overall return, not just to minimize agency slack.

Agents as actors

While slack is one possible outcome of agent autonomy, we wish to draw attention to the possibility that agents may use their autonomy to influence future decisions by principals, an outcome that the term "slack" does not fully capture. When the agent pool is small or agents possess significant expertise, agents can lobby principals for more authority and resources, negotiate with principals the terms of their contracts, and even utilize their resources and knowledge to influence principals' preferences or strategies. In this volume, Thompson argues that the Security Council, acting as an agent of states, helped those states by providing valuable information about US intentions in the recent Iraq War. Hawkins and

Introduction

Jacoby argue that the ECHR has influenced state human rights policies and preferences. Moreover, when agents face complex principals they may play one member state against another, thus increasing their range of possible action or decreasing their principals' choice set (see Lyne, Nielson, and Tierney, this volume). This is often the case with administrative agencies in the United States, and we find international analogs in the European Union and the International Monetary Fund (see McNollgast 1987; Pollack 1997; and Martin, this volume, respectively).

Agents may also seek to increase the degree of autonomy that they possess, convincing states to delegate more authority to them or exercise less control. Agents can demonstrate to states through past successes – or use their resources to lobby member government officials – that they can be trusted with new tasks that obviate the need for a new IO. In this way agents can convince states to delegate new authority and resources to them rather than act unilaterally, cooperate without delegating, or delegate to a new IO. The unit cost of delegating thus may decrease as the number of tasks delegated to an apparently competent IO increases. In this volume, Thompson and Hawkins and Jacoby both examine agents who sought delegation and autonomy from principals, with contrasting outcomes. In Thompson's chapter, the United States was unsuccessful at trying to persuade the Security Council to delegate to it, while the ECHR was quite successful over time at encouraging further delegation and at gaining much greater autonomy.

This process of IO agents using their autonomy to influence principals is the central insight of neo-functionalism. In this literature, agents use autonomy to expand their influence through functional spillover, political spillover, and upgrading common interests (Burley and Mattli 1993). As Pierson (1996) and others recognize, however, much more than agent discretion is typically necessary for agents to influence principals. In particular, agents can gain more autonomy in a gradual process driven by member-state preoccupation with short-term concerns, the ubiquity of unintended consequences, and the instability of member-state policy preferences. Once agents have gained enough autonomy, principals may find it difficult to rescind authority due to institutional obstacles, such as the need for unanimous or supermajority votes to change the status quo. If we examine the prior link in the delegation chain, the logic for this institutional stasis becomes clearer. Societal groups may possess interests that coincide with the delegation of greater authority to the agent and may lobby political leaders to preserve or cede more clout to the agent. The European Union, for example, helps serve the interests of powerful

States, international organizations, and principal-agent theory

industrialists and investors, while the World Health Organization serves few social group interests in developed democracies. Hence, we should not be surprised to find that the European Commission has been more successful at turning autonomy into greater delegation than the WHO (see Cortell and Peterson, this volume).

In all, this dynamic of agent autonomy, slack, and influence has a substantial impact on the willingness of states to delegate in the first place, on the mechanisms and form of delegation, and on the restructuring that occurs to existing delegation contracts. Analysts should pay greater attention to these dynamic effects on delegation outcomes.

PLAN OF THE BOOK

To summarize, we provide a narrow definition of principal-agent relationships that distinguishes delegation from lateral strategic interactions. This narrower definition facilitates the development of falsifiable hypotheses in the short run and a viable research program in the long run. In addition, we distinguish delegation to IOs from unilateralism and cooperation alone. It is vital to keep these alternatives in mind when formulating hypotheses about when delegation will occur and what form it will take.

We also derive initial conjectures that have observable implications both for original decisions to delegate and for the restructuring of existing delegation contracts and provide an array of examples that illustrate the arguments. These initial propositions examine delegation from the viewpoints of principals contemplating or renegotiating contingent grants of authority and agents accepting delegation contracts. The remaining contributions to this volume follow up on these insights, challenging and extending them theoretically, as well as grounding them empirically.

Variation in principal characteristics

Each chapter in this volume assesses PA theories through one of two conceptual experiments – though some also interact the two. The first conceptual experiment examines exogenous variation (across cases or time) in some characteristic of the principal that is predicted to lead to some observable variation in the agent's behavior, authority or task, or in the mechanisms of control employed to guide the agent. Authors in this volume explore four important characteristics of principals (key

Introduction

independent variables) that are hypothesized to have an impact on agent behavior, authority, or the mechanisms of control.

Preferences of the principals. A number of chapters argue that the preferences of the principal determine the design of the contract, its mechanisms of control, and the subsequent behavior of the agent. At the same time, important disagreements exist among them about which principals and which preferences matter. Lyne, Nielson, and Tierney argue that alterations in the principal's preferences ought to induce change in agent behavior even if the principal does not re-contract or ratchet up control mechanisms. Given efficacious control mechanisms, a responsive agent should anticipate the principal's interests and adjust behavior accordingly. They find that as the preferences of member states evolved toward a greater emphasis on social protection during the 1980s and 1990s, multilateral development bank agents responded by making more social loans – but only when a large coalition favoring that preference emerged within the collective principal. When individual states delegate authority through trust funds, they often lack the control mechanisms necessary to control MDB behavior. Hence, as in the case of US delegation to the IADB in the 1960s, their only option may be to exit or dramatically restrict the delegation when faced with excessive agency slack. Broz and Hawes agree that principal preferences influence agent actions. Yet while Lyne, Nielson, and Tierney insist that scholars should avoid the temptation to focus on just one member state or even a small sub-group of member states, Broz and Hawes provide powerful evidence that the preferences of a single member of a collective principal can indeed influence agent actions. They find that the IMF responds to the influence of the US Congress by providing more loans for countries where US banks are exposed. For Broz and Hawes, the preferences of the US Congress as a principal of the IMF are fundamentally shaped by money center banks, outside actors in the PA relationship.

Milner agrees that principal preferences strongly influence agent actions, even in the unlikely case of US voters and the question of whether Congress allocates development aid bilaterally or multilaterally. Like Lyne, Nielson, and Tierney, Milner focuses on the substantive preferences of principals, in this case voter preferences for relatively altruistic development aid. She finds that as voter skepticism of foreign aid increases, Congress responds by distributing comparatively more multilateral aid.

States, international organizations, and principal-agent theory

The need for information. Martin, Pollack, and Thompson all argue that states' demands for more and better information influence their relations with IOs. For Martin, crisis situations produce a stronger need for information and states react by allowing IOs greater autonomy. She finds that IMF staff autonomy varies over time in response to the information needs of states. Pollack argues that states delegate to agents to gain better information but also to create more credible commitments. Like Martin, he hypothesizes that the greater the principals' need for information and credibility, the larger the agent's autonomy. Unlike Martin, he finds that in the European Commission, autonomy has little to do with the need for information and much more to do with the need for credibility and for speedy, efficient policy-making. Thompson argues that the needs of member states for information about the desirability of intervention have led them to delegate that authority to the Security Council.

Structure of the principal. Lyne, Nielson, and Tierney also argue that the nature of the contract between the principal(s) and agent ought to influence agent actions. When multiple principals hold independent contracts with the same agent, the outcome is likely to be less determinate than when agents face a collective principal composed of numerous member states acting in concert under a single contract. Of course, this implies that the collective principal possesses institutions that can effectively aggregate preferences and induce stable coalition formation among the members of the collective.

Decision-making rules within a collective principal. Relatedly, Cortell and Peterson, and Alter, maintain that unanimous decision rules within a collective principal provide greater room for agency slack than majoritarian rules (or rules that grant authority to a sub-set of great powers). Unanimous decision rules – allowing each state an effective veto – should increase the number of options that agents confront and should allow agents to select a policy closer to the agent's own ideal point. On the other hand, majoritarian decision rules should constrain the agent more closely because such rules more effectively aggregate member preferences and concentrate authority.

Variation in agent characteristics

The second conceptual experiment looks at exogenous variation in some characteristic of the agent, predicting observable variation in the principal's behavior or in the mechanisms of control adopted by the principal. As noted above, in many areas in which PA theory is applied, there are a large number of potential agents or it is not too costly to create a new agent. As a result, it often appears that principals select or design an "ideal" agent that corresponds to their preferences and is well suited to carry out its assigned tasks. In such cases, the attributes of the agents themselves appear to be relatively unimportant. As a consequence, this second conceptual experiment does not feature prominently in the existing PA literature. In international relations, however, neither the large-number nor low-cost conditions are consistently satisfied; hence, we have some reason to expect that varying characteristics of the agents may play an important role in delegation and its consequences. In this conceptual experiment, then, agent characteristics constitute the independent variables that should produce observable outcomes in the principal-agent relationship. The substantive chapters identify four important sets of variables.

Agent preferences. As with principal preferences, a variety of authors argue that agent preferences affect PA relationships. Hawkins and Jacoby, and Martin, both argue that states are more likely to delegate when they identify agents with preferences similar to their own. This argument suggests that state decisions to delegate can be influenced by the nature of the available IOs. Where IOs with similar preferences are in short supply, states are more likely to undertake tasks on their own rather than to delegate to an IO.

Drawing on the literature on delegation to committees in domestic legislatures, Thompson models the UN Security Council as an agent, hired by the membership or international community more generally, to screen proposals by others agents (the United States in his case) to use force for collective purposes. As in domestic legislative committees, it is the median and the distribution of preferences in the UNSC that determines whether it can provide a useful signal about the proposal of other agents. The fact that the Security Council has heterogeneous preferences makes it an attractive agent for all states seeking information. Milner also varies agent preferences, arguing that aid is delegated to a multilateral organization with more altruistic preferences when principals become suspicious of Congress, with its preferences for politicized aid.

Agent tasks or functions. The function or task assigned to the agent may alter the terms of the contract and the ability of the principal to monitor

States, international organizations, and principal-agent theory

and sanction that agent. Alter argues that international courts often undertake judicial review tasks that require substantial discretion and make the agent extraordinarily difficult for the principal to control. Gould argues that certain tasks within the IMF, especially negotiating agreements with borrowers, are simply harder for state principals to monitor effectively, and therefore the staff will have greater autonomy in these areas than in areas where tasks are more easily monitored. Cortell and Peterson argue that staffing arrangements influence agent autonomy. In an interesting twist, Thompson suggests that powerful states like the United States can sometimes be agents, as when the United States sought the blessing of the Security Council for invading Iraq. The United States sought this approval to demonstrate its benign intent in a case of preventive war.

Agent strategies and permeability. Hawkins and Jacoby argue that the permeability of agents to third parties can also increase agency autonomy and induce counter-reactions on the part of principals. When outside actors have broad or privileged access to agents, as Gould (this volume) suggests, they can pull the agents' actions toward their particular policy bias. Often principals design contracts for the purpose of giving this privileged access to specific outside actors. However, the influence of outside actors can also damage the interests of principals, and in such cases should induce principals to attempt to restrict third-party access or otherwise alter contract terms to bring outcomes back into line with their interests. However, agents have a variety of strategies available to them – a counterpart to principal control mechanisms – through which they can pursue autonomy. Hawkins and Jacoby argue the most important of these are interpretation (identifying new meanings for rules) and buffering (creating barriers between principals and agents).

The following chapters, of course, represent the beginning rather than the end of a research program on delegation to international organizations. The individual chapters develop one or more of the above conceptual experiments and arguments but do not individually or collectively provide a conclusive test of PA theory in international relations.

The final essay in this volume looks toward the future research agenda on delegation to IOs. Lake and McCubbins analyze how principals can learn about the behavior of their agents. Drawing upon recent work in domestic politics, they highlight the important role of third-party informants, or "external" sources of information. Pointing to the growth

Introduction

and importance of NGOs in world affairs, they suggest that these organizations may play a central role in facilitating monitoring and promoting delegation to IOs. Hence, their contribution may serve as an analytic bridge between the chapters in this volume, which focus on formal intergovernmental organizations and their member states, and the burgeoning literature on the role of NGOs and transnational politics in international relations.

PART II

Variation in principal preferences, structure, decision rules, and private benefits

2

Who delegates? Alternative models of principals in development aid

MONA M. LYNE, DANIEL L. NIELSON,
AND MICHAEL J. TIERNEY

INTRODUCTION

Principal-agent theory has proven a powerful tool for analyzing delegation relationships in a wide variety of settings, yet it remains underdeveloped in the study of international relations. Conventional wisdom holds that state principals face special, and often insurmountable, difficulties in realizing their interests when they delegate to international organizations (IOs). In this chapter we examine delegation to multilateral development banks (MDBs) and ask whether they are faithful agents. We demonstrate that analytic shortcuts commonly employed in the study of IOs can lead researchers to misleading conclusions about the faithfulness of IO agents.

In order to accurately assess whether delegation to IOs routinely leads to inordinate agency losses, analysts must first identify the actual principal(s) who has authority to delegate.[1] This requires careful attention to

---

For helpful suggestions and criticisms we are grateful to Jee Baum, Bill Bernhard, Lawrence Broz, Scott Cooper, John Ferejohn, Jeff Frieden, Erica Gould, Jay Goodliffe, Peter Gourevitch, Darren Hawkins, Wade Jacoby, Robert Keohane, David Lake, James Long, Lisa Martin, Eric Neumayer, Brad Parks, Mark Pollack, Phil Roeder, and Sven Wilson. For research assistance we thank Jessie Di Gregory, Steve Kapfer, Josh Loud, Dan Magleby, Chris Miller, Rich Nielsen, Chris O'Keefe, Phil Scarborough, and Jess Sloan. We are particularly grateful to Brendan Williams for his fantastic job doing archival research on the SPTF case study.

[1] In a seminal article on IO accountability Keohane and Grant (2005: 33) explain, "There is a clear tension between the concept of a World Bank that is accountable to poor people and one that is accountable to the U.S. Secretary of the Treasury." This is certainly correct, but either assumption would lead to a false negative (or positive) test. The formal principal of the World Bank is typically an authorized majority on the executive board, and assessments of Bank faithfulness within an agency framework should start with this assumption.

formal institutional rules, the structure of the principal, and the preferences of the principal(s). In this chapter we introduce the idea of complex principals – principals with more than one actor individually or collectively delegating to the same agent – and argue that these common conditions must be considered when assessing IO behavior. When we employ models that more accurately reflect the structure of the principal in a specific empirical setting, we find that delegation to IOs closely resembles delegation to domestic agents. Both domestic and international agents shirk under similar conditions, and principals employ familiar tactics in an attempt to rein in errant agents.

Our main point is simple: analysts should select the agency model that best reflects the real-world delegation relationship under study, since failure to do so will likely result in faulty interpretations of empirical results. We illustrate this central point with a qualitative analysis of the United States government's decisions to unilaterally delegate the administration of foreign aid for social policy through a trust fund at the Inter-American Development Bank (IADB) and later through the same trust's subsequent domestic administrator, the Inter-American Foundation (IAF). Although the deliberate shift from an international to a domestic agent suggests that the United States was unhappy with the results of its initial delegation to an IO, subsequent IAF performance reveals that it was not a demonstrably more faithful agent.

We suggest that the particular structure of the US principal may explain the apparent fecklessness of both agents. In presidential systems such as the United States, both the President and Congress have authority to delegate in the name of the US government. If these two independent principals are in conflict over the terms of the delegation, as they were in these cases, then the agent may exhibit behavior that is inconsistent with the preferences of either (or both) of these principals considered in isolation. We conclude that even when a single state is delegating to an IO, it may not be appropriate to adopt a single-principal model. If the government is composed of two independent principals that can unilaterally re-contract, then analysts must consider the impact of this multiple-principal structure in assessing the faithfulness of IO agents. These qualitative cases underscore that, in order to make sense of the empirical puzzles we observe or to make judgments about delegation success or failure, analysts must take care to employ an appropriate model of the principal.

Moving beyond unilateral delegation, we also examine the more common setting of multilateral delegation from a large number of member states to an IO. Here, many analysts suggest that international

Alternative models of principals in development aid

organizations are only nominally accountable to all their member states. Scholars interested in explaining IO behavior argue that IOs do not reflect the interests of most of their members (especially small states), or develop an internal culture that drives IO behavior, or echo the personal views of an autonomous leader (see Moravcsik 1998; Gilpin 2002; Barnett and Finnemore 2004; Sandholtz and Zysman 1989). We do not doubt that large member states often have more influence over IO behavior than small ones. We also agree that bureaucracies develop their own cultures and that charismatic leaders can engender change and shape the behavior of IOs in particular instances.

Nevertheless, analysts should exercise caution when generalizing about the irrelevance of particular member states, or when attributing primary causal weight for IO behavior to organizational culture or charismatic leaders. We argue for taking the formal decision-making rules seriously as mechanisms that serve to constrain delegation outcomes in predictable ways. Moreover, if rules are efficacious, then even small states can sometimes influence IO behavior. Too often scholars assume that formal decision rules are epiphenomenal and assert that a hegemonic state or small group of powerful states writes the rules and determines behavioral outcomes within an IO. With these analytic priors, IO behavior that does not conform to the preferences of a few powerful states in a relatively straightforward fashion will be (we believe, incorrectly) interpreted as unfaithful.

In order to address these problematic analytic and empirical shortcuts, we provide a series of systematic quantitative tests to determine whether MDBs follow the preferences of their principals. As in the prior case studies, we show that the model of the principal chosen by the analyst significantly alters the interpretation of empirical results. Modeling the principal properly allows for more accurate assessments of delegation success and agent faithfulness.

There are at least two requisites for a fair test of how well IO agents carry out the authoritative instructions of their principals. First, analysts must accurately model the structure of the principal and the rules governing decisions about agent contracts (Cortell and Peterson, this volume). We argue that our collective-principal model of delegation to MDBs, more accurately reflects the actual strategic interaction over multilateral lending that occurs among member states within MDBs than the more common conception of states as single principals or multiple principals. Second, a fair test requires systematic and reproducible measures of principal preferences and a large sample of cases that is drawn using established scientific methods. Hence, in the case of MDBs, an accurate test of agent compliance with principal preferences requires that we include all member states that are represented on the executive boards, provide systematic measures of each member's preferences, and explicitly model the formal decision rules that transform individual state preferences into collective preferences. Before we put our arguments about complex principals in empirical context, it makes sense to elaborate their conceptual underpinnings.

COMPLEX PRINCIPALS

The simplest PA relationships involve a single principal and a single agent. However, when more than one actor delegates to an agent, we are studying a complex principal. And in both domestic and international politics, principals are typically complex. A delegation relationship can have one or more principals, and a principal can either be an individual or a corporate entity containing more than one individual. Following Kiewiet and McCubbins (1991), when a single agent has more than one contract with organizationally distinct principals we label this a delegation relationship with multiple principals (Calvert, McCubbins, and Weingast 1989; Hammond and Knott 1996).

The second type of complex principal is designated as a collective principal. In the case of a collective principal, more than one actor designs and has authority over a common contract for a single agent. The most familiar delegation relationships in domestic politics and international relations involve a collective principal. Voters delegate to politicians, legislators delegate to party leaders, and nation-states delegate to international organizations. In all these situations a group of actors comes to a decision among themselves and then the group negotiates (or renegotiates) a contract with an agent. If the group cannot come to a decision a priori, then they cannot change the status quo. This goes for initial hiring decisions, for proposals to renegotiate the agent's employment contract, or for novel authoritative instructions. In all these collective-principal situations there is a single contract between the agent and his collective principal.

Collective principals are overwhelmingly the most common type of principal that we observe when analyzing IOs. Whether we are studying the World Bank, the IMF, the UN Security Council, or the WHO, all require a collective decision by a majority or super-majority of member states in order to alter the delegation contract between the member states

Alternative models of principals in development aid

Single principal — X → Agent

Multiple principals — X, Y, Z → Agent

Collective principal — XYZ → Agent

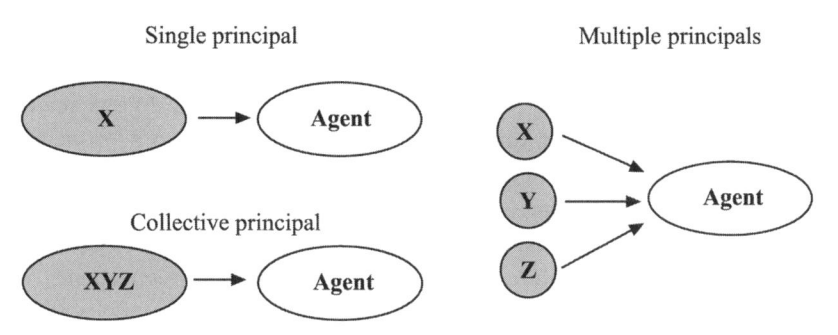

Figure 2.1. Types of agency relationships

and the IO secretariat. While the formal rules of some IOs allow individual states to veto a change to the status quo, few authorize an individual state to unilaterally re-contract with an IO agent. Since collective principals are most common in IR, we argue that a collective principal model should typically be used for analyzing delegation to IOs.

However, there are good reasons to consider both single-principal and multiple-principal models as alternatives. First, occasionally the decision-making rules within IOs do reflect a single – or multiple – principal setting.[2] Second, many scholars assume that the most powerful state within any IO will dictate outcomes there. Such a stance implies that the United States is often a single principal in many contemporary IOs. Third, since many PA models are imported from the American politics literature, where multiple-principal models are well developed, it makes sense to see how such models fare when explaining outcomes at the international level. Therefore, in the next two sections of this chapter we demonstrate the implications of adopting different models of principals – single, multiple, and collective – to explain the same empirical patterns.

Strikingly, getting the model right has significant implications for conclusions drawn from empirical results. In the next section we argue on a priori conceptual grounds that a multiple-principal model fits the politics of US social foreign aid delegation better than a single-principal

---

[2] In the next section of this chapter we explore the case of trust funds, where a single country is granted the authority (by the other IO members) to unilaterally contract with the IO secretariat. The clearest example of multiple principals in international relations is the European Union, where the Commission is responsible to both the Council of Ministers and the European Parliament. Both these principals can independently re-contract with the Commission (Nugent 2003). Also, Hix (2002) argues that both national and EU political parties are principals of the MPs in the European Parliament. For an alternative view see Pollack, this volume.

model because both the US President and Congress have the authority to unilaterally contract with the same agent. When agents are responsible for producing a single policy, theory suggests that a divergence of preferences among the multiple principals will create more room for agency slack (at least from the perspective of the principal whose preferences are not being enacted as policy).[3] Under these conditions the multiple-principal model predicts that the agent will shirk and aggrieved principals will attempt (often unsuccessfully) to redirect their agent. As important, when multiple-principal preferences converge, delegation becomes more attractive to all the principals and efforts to direct the agent will be more successful (Nielson and Tierney 2003a). A single-principal interpretation of the same cases would conclude (erroneously) that delegation had failed.

Further, in the third section of this chapter we argue that the correct conception for most IOs – and, hence, the MDBs lending multilaterally – is a collective-principal model. Indeed, modeling the MDBs appropriately as responsive to collective principals produces results that suggest that delegation often succeeds; modeling the banks inappropriately as responsive to single or multiple principals produces either false negatives or mixed results.

The different interpretations of results occur because these distinct principal structures have implications for how we model principal preferences and how contracts are designed. With multiple principals, modeling principal constraints on agent behavior requires that we capture the independent monitoring and sanctioning power of each of the principals. With collective principals, coalition politics – driven by the decision rules for aggregating members' preferences – will determine the shape of instructions to and contracts with agents. The significance of these conceptual points grows clearer as we apply them empirically, first qualitatively and then quantitatively.

US SOCIAL FOREIGN AID POLICY: SINGLE OR MULTIPLE PRINCIPAL?

In the 1960s the US government pursued similar foreign policy goals through delegation to an existing international agent, the Inter-American Development Bank (IADB), and later to a new domestic agent, the Inter-American Foundation (IAF). Hence, because the substantive issue and

---

[3] For theoretical underpinnings see Calvert et al. 1989; Hammond and Knott 1996; and Martin, this volume.

Alternative models of principals in development aid

the time period is similar, these cases serve as a useful comparison when assessing the faithfulness of IO agents compared to domestic alternatives (see Hawkins et al. and Milner, this volume). Normally, US influence over IADB-funded projects would be diluted, since the United States is only one member of the Bank and thus part of the Bank's collective principal. However, the establishment of a "trust fund" for a particular development purpose allows a donor to funnel money directly and unilaterally through a multilateral agent.[4] This novel delegation contract makes the two cases more comparable.

Conceiving the United States as a single principal

In 1960 the United States established the Social Progress Trust Fund (SPTF) at the IADB to fund small, grass-roots social projects and allocated $525 million to the Fund through early 1964. A May 1967 Report to the House Committee on Foreign Affairs reviewed projects funded through the SPTF. It documented numerous cases of extreme shirking on the part of IADB officials,[5] unwillingness to coordinate with USAID officials, and the lack of any results on the ground even though the vast majority of project funds had been released at least two years prior to the study. The report concluded that the IADB "is accountable to the U.S. Government for the [SPTF's] proper and effective use" and recommended a full review by the Government General Accounting Office (GAO) (US House Committee 1967a: 43).

Reacting to these lackluster results at the SPTF, the US government took three steps. First, it terminated new funding for the SPTF: after the initial appropriation in 1961, and one additional appropriation in February 1964, the United States announced in April 1964 that it would provide no fresh funds to the SPTF (US House 1964: 4). Any future SPTF money would be supplied only by repayments of prior loans from borrowing countries. Second, the United States acted to establish its own explicit oversight rights over the SPTF and all other trust funds. In November 1967, Congress amended the Foreign Assistance Act to provide for US auditing of the SPTF to assess "*how well* the funds have been

---

[4] The single donor does need the authorization of the MDB board, which represents all the other member governments. But once the collective principal that is the board has given its assent, the donor and the MDB agent contract directly with each other. This form of unilateral delegation to IOs has grown rapidly over the past decade and cuts against the archetypical form of collective delegation to IOs (World Bank 2004).
[5] For example, there was no permanent IADB representative in Brazil despite the fact that the country received the largest proportion of Bank funds.

Principal preferences, structure, decision rules, and private benefits

administered" (US House Committee 1967b: 32, emphasis added). Third, the United States created a domestic agent, the IAF, which was granted the lead role managing small US-financed development projects in Latin America and increasingly was authorized to administer the trust fund money that came back to the SPTF in repaid loans.

The IAF was created in 1969 as "the end-product of extensive congressional review of U.S. foreign assistance" in order to "help rectify identified shortcomings of previous U.S. programs for Latin America." The founding legislation gave the IAF a mandate remarkably similar to that of the original SPTF: to pursue small, grass-roots social development projects (US GAO 1982: 1–4). Roughly half of the IAF budget was funded through redirected SPTF loan repayments, and half from new congressional appropriations (US GAO 1979: 7), suggesting that the United States sought to realize the same development foreign policy goals by delegating to a more faithful domestic agent.

However, after the IAF's creation the US government repeatedly failed to monitor the IAF, to assert greater control over IAF's selection of grantees, or to encourage the desired coordination between the IAF and other US agencies. The criteria governing funding decisions became particularly controversial in the early 1980s. Following a 1981 Heritage Foundation report stating that the IAF funded many left-wing and nationalist organizations hostile to the United States, the Reagan Administration sought to redirect the agency. The Administration and its supporters argued that these funding choices were a direct consequence of an internal culture hostile to private enterprise and more concerned with maintaining a favorable image in Latin America than with serving US taxpayers. Members of the Board were successively replaced until it was dominated by a majority of Reagan appointees, who were all outspoken critics of previous IAF practices. In December 1983, this Reagan-backed majority ousted the Foundation's president and replaced him with one widely viewed as more business-oriented and loyal to the President (Omang 1985).

Despite these direct and forceful efforts at better vetting of grantees to ensure they were broadly in tune with US policies and practices, events in the mid-1990s revealed continued shirking by the IAF. Despite a prior warning from the US embassy in Ecuador, the IAF funded groups that, in 1997, publicly threatened an American businessman. Later that year an IAF-funded group supported a group responsible for the kidnapping of two American citizens. In 1998, an IAF grantee occupied a cathedral in Argentina in order to protest the local government (US GAO 2000;

Ryan 2000). According to a Congressional staffer, the Foundation's staff in Ecuador avoided all contact with the embassy and sought to act as an independent NGO rather than an agent of the US government (Lippman 1999; US GAO 2000). Finally, US government officials expressed outrage that even under these extreme circumstances, the grantees' contract was not immediately terminated, but was allowed to expire based on the original agreement (Lippman 1999). US officials concluded that the IAF had inadequate pre-screening procedures and displayed a general disdain for authoritative directives from the US government.

In addition to this inability to tighten control on vetting procedures, GAO reports in 1982 and 2000 document remarkably similar lapses at the IAF – a failure to coordinate with other US agencies, failure to follow established procedures for on-site monitoring, failure to document and report agency monitoring activity, and failure to ensure grantee compliance with reporting requirements. The 1982 GAO report reviewed 66 projects (which constituted 41 percent of all projects approved at the time of audit) and found that 29 had met, 25 had partially met, and 12 were not meeting their objectives, and that 38 were not self-sustaining (US GAO 1982: 1, 10).[6] The report found that grant funds were "not adequately accounted for or controlled, resulting in misuse and other improprieties," that monitoring visits "follow no discernable pattern to ensure full timely coverage of projects," and that "reports required were often delinquent" (US GAO 1982: ii, 7). Its final recommendations are to "carefully plan monitoring activities to provide coverage of all active grants" and "regularly check on grantees who are overdue in . . . reporting" as well as "establish explicit operating procedures" to ensure "active regular coordination with other governmental . . . development organizations" (US GAO 1982: 17, 26).

The 2000 GAO report reviewed program and financial documents for 50 of the 86 grants that were completed in 1999 and found that the requirement for documented annual monitoring visits was met in only 10 percent of projects, the requirement for embassy visits and documentation was met in only 63 percent of cases, Foundation contractors had submitted required reports in only 50 percent of projects, and financial audits were on time for only 25 percent of IAF grants (US GAO 2000). Despite calls for more coordination, better monitoring, and more

---

[6] Unfortunately, the 1982 GAO report does not define its criteria for concluding a project is fully, partially, or not meeting its goals. The general tenor of the report, however, demonstrates a willingness to give the IAF the benefit of the doubt.

Principal preferences, structure, decision rules, and private benefits

stringent reporting controls in the 1982 report, the 2000 report also recommended that the President "develop a management control mechanism to provide oversight of compliance with monitoring and auditing procedures" (US GAO 2000: 4–5).

This history suggests that the IAF is far from a perfect agent for the US government. Further, it is not obvious that the IAF is a more faithful agent than the IADB in administering the SPTF. In both cases the principal expresses displeasure with the utility of funded projects, agent failure to monitor projects, and agent failure to report and coordinate with other US officials. Moreover, the evidence suggests that the US government was not able to ensure proper vetting of grantees or better monitoring and coordination at the IAF than at the IADB. These very similar histories for two different agents with similar mandates at roughly the same time belie the notion that IO agents are necessarily less faithful than domestic counterparts. How can we better understand the apparent fecklessness of these two different agents?

Multiple principals within the US government

Our conclusions about the faithfulness of agents change considerably when we view those agents as responsive to two competing and independent principals. Since either US government branch can (re)contract with an agent regardless of the preferences of the other, predictably contradictory marching orders from distinct principals led to apparently feckless agents in both cases. At the very least, conflict among the principals allows the agents to pursue their independent preferences much more than if they had been accountable to a single principal or multiple principals that had similar preferences. In fact, the evidence suggests that when Congress and the Executive differ in their policy preferences, complaints about both the IO and the domestic agent arise and efforts at re-contracting subsequently occur. The poor performance by the IADB with the SPTF funds often followed from the conflicting goals the President and the Congress pursued with this agency. Similarly, the failure to alter the behavior of the IAF resulted from the fact that it became an important battleground in a larger war between the Reagan Administration and Congress over US foreign policy in Latin America.[7]

---

[7] Note that all three of the most critical GAO reports from 1973, 1982, and 2000 were published during times of divided government in the United States, where Congress was controlled by one party while the White House was controlled by the other.

Alternative models of principals in development aid

Presidential and congressional preferences over Latin American aid policy in the early 1960s cannot be understood without attention to the historical context. The President, who is generally held accountable for broad foreign policy successes or failures (Haggard 1988), had an overriding goal during this period: to counter the very real threat of communism in Latin America as exhibited and further exacerbated by Castro's rise to power in Cuba. Under these conditions, the President was more concerned with demonstrating effort and commitment in Latin America than in detailed compliance with the small-scale projects administered by the SPTF. Congress, in contrast, controls the purse-strings, and members of Congress face strong electoral pressures to act as good stewards of taxpayer dollars. Moreover, foreign aid is decidedly unpopular, and its scrutiny and management aligns with congressional incentives (Martens et al. 2002; Milner, this volume).

The available evidence from the period suggests an Executive relatively unconcerned with detailed compliance yet a Congress dismayed at the President's lackadaisical attitude. In the House Committee on Foreign Affairs report to amend the Foreign Assistance Act, it states that "The Executive has taken the position that the Social Progress Trust Fund . . . is not subject to audit by the General Accounting Office or other United States agencies, executive or legislative" (US House Committee 1967b: 32). In the same document, Congress amends the Act to explicitly assert congressional auditing rights over all projects for which the United States is the sole contributor as discussed above. It also states that "provision is made for the President to take such steps as are necessary to modify any existing agreements to conform to the auditing requirements newly prescribed" (US House Committee 1967b: 32). In short, the Congress acted to ensure, both retroactively and prospectively, that it would have auditing rights over any unilateral aid provided by the United States through trust funds at MDBs.

There is evidence for this same difference between the President and Congress in a mid-1964 report from the Treasury Department to Congress regarding proposed changes at the IADB. In a letter urging Congress to support and appropriate funds for an expansion of the Special Operations Fund at the IADB after SPTF was terminated, Treasury went to great lengths to assure Congress that internal changes at the IADB would guarantee greater compliance with US directives. The report emphasized the formation of a new review committee and a new high-level programming office staffed by a US national. This individual would rank among the senior management officials at the Bank and serve as

Principal preferences, structure, decision rules, and private benefits

principal staff advisor to the President for review of the Bank's objectives, policies, plans, and programs. The office would "prepare and recommend guidelines for the Bank's day-to-day operations . . . and assure that the Bank continues to make periodic appraisals of progress being made . . . in meeting planned social and economic objectives" (US House 1964: 9–10). In sum, this history of the SPTF suggests, first, that oversight was initially delegated to the IADB with few constraints, likely because the President had powerful overriding policy goals that gave him a strong incentive to favor a quick demonstration of commitment on the ground. Second, as soon as Congress gained information about the agent's poor performance, it acted both to terminate unilateral commitments to the problematic agent and to ensure that, in the future, both unilateral and multilateral aid programs would be subject to stringent oversight.

Turning to the IAF, the apparent failure to change agent behavior with regard to funding decisions, as well as coordination and oversight, also seems to stem from differences between the President and Congress. In this case, however, relations between the two branches degenerated into intense open conflict over Latin American policy. The IAF became a crucial battleground in this conflict, and in particular was an important symbol of a Democratic Congress's policy positions in opposition to the Reagan Administration. Congress's desire to constrain Reagan's Latin American policy, and the IAF's role in this larger conflict, meant that the Executive had difficulty ensuring compliance with the Administration's demands for improved vetting of grantees at the IAF. Conversely, it also meant that Congress had no interest in focusing attention on the IAF's failings that were cited in the 1982 GAO report.

In particular, Reagan's pro-right policies in El Salvador and, particularly, Nicaragua met with considerable resistance from Congress.[8] The IAF became a central battleground in this struggle over Latin American policy and with each attempt by the Reagan Administration to bend the IAF to its new vision, Congress pushed back. The Reagan Administration's initial strategy for gaining control of grantee vetting

---

[8] Already, in December of 1982, Congress expressed considerable misgivings about Reagan's Central American policy and passed the Boland Amendment prohibiting the use of US funds to overthrow the Nicaraguan government. In 1984, it passed the second Boland Amendment, prohibiting funding for the Contras, an expatriate force organized by the CIA to overthrow the Nicaraguan government.

Alternative models of principals in development aid

criteria was to replace the Foundation's top executives, but some members of Congress quickly noted that the IAF's president and his staff were directly answerable by law to the Foundation board, not to the White House (Clines 1983). Reagan responded by stacking the board with recess appointments and this Administration-backed board then dismissed Peter D. Bell, the IAF president. Congress's parry sent strong signals to the IAF that it had an ally in its battle with the Administration. Shortly after Bell's firing, Congress held hearings on his dismissal and indicated that it would not accept an IAF president who would remake the Foundation into a tool of Reagan's policies in Latin America. When Reagan appointed a businesswoman and Republican donor unknown in the development community, Congress used its ultimate sanction and cut the IAF's budget by 10 percent.

Finally, in the late 1990s we see detailed and coordinated intervention which leads to better performance at the IAF. After Senate Foreign Relations Committee Chair Jesse Helms publicized the problems at the Foundation in 1998, its budget was cut drastically, and Helms demanded a detailed response from the IAF president regarding new procedures to correct continuing problems (Lippman 1999).[9] In response to improvements in coordination with US embassies to ensure proper vetting of grantees and auditing reports that demonstrated better control of funds, the IAF's funding increased in the years 2001–05.[10] It is no surprise to agency theorists who study multiple principal settings that this period of budget expansion corresponded with unified Republican government and vastly refocused foreign policy goals in the wake of the September 11 terrorist attacks. The IAF's multiple principals now shared similar preferences, which enabled control from Washington and reduced agency slack. Conservative Republicans who were previously attempting to eliminate the agency now increased funding to its highest levels in two decades and authorized the IAF to draw down all the remaining funds from the SPTF that are on deposit at the IADB. When multiple principals agree on what policies to pursue, they are both more likely to delegate

---

[9] The IAF's budget was cut from $22 to $5 million from 1998 to 2000 and, according to one participant, was very nearly eliminated altogether. Interview with Senate Foreign Relations Committee staffer, July 2005, Washington, DC.

[10] On new procedures insuring coordination with embassies, see US House 2000. On improved financial control, see US House 2003.

Principal preferences, structure, decision rules, and private benefits

and more able to control their agents (see Nielson and Tierney 2003a; Hawkins et al. and Martin in this volume).

These results suggest that, if there are multiple principals involved in a delegation relationship, whether the two principals are in agreement about the terms of the delegation can create significant differences in patterns of agent behavior over time. As our discussion of both the SPTF and IAF cases suggest, it is misleading, but common, to conceive of "the US government" as the single principal of these agents. As conflict between Congress and successive US executive Administrations clearly illustrates, these agents receive distinct and sometimes contradictory instructions from their multiple principals that likely lead to inconsistent agent behavior. One of the two principals is thus often complaining about a feckless agent, while the other seeks to insulate the agent from "political meddling." Analysts employing a simple single-principal model might observe such behavior and conclude that delegation has "failed." In fact, we describe the first case of US delegation to the IADB in precisely these terms. But the observed pattern of agent behavior no longer appears aberrant with a model that considers all the multiple principals who actually have authority to delegate independently. A similar conceptual error may occur when analysts assume a multiple-principals model holds where a collective-principal model is more appropriate.

MODELING MDBS AS COLLECTIVE PRINCIPALS

In the year 1998, total dollars lent for social development at the World Bank – in education, health and safety nets – exceeded loans for the traditional sectors of energy, industry, mining, oil and gas, irrigation, transportation, and urban development combined. Since such "traditional" sectors had dominated the World Bank's portfolio since 1945, this change marked a major shift in lending behavior. Echoed among the regional MDBs, this trend toward social projects signals a wholesale change in the focus of multilateral development lending (Upton 2000; Nielson and Tierney 2003a). The trends in social lending at the three major development banks can be seen in Figure 2.2.

Conventional international relations (IR) theory suggests that this shift in MDB behavior should follow from the interests of the great powers, and particularly from the global hegemon. Yet the available data present an empirical puzzle. Preferences for social policy in the advanced industrial democracies – and in the United States especially – have not changed significantly over the last 20 years, and some measures even

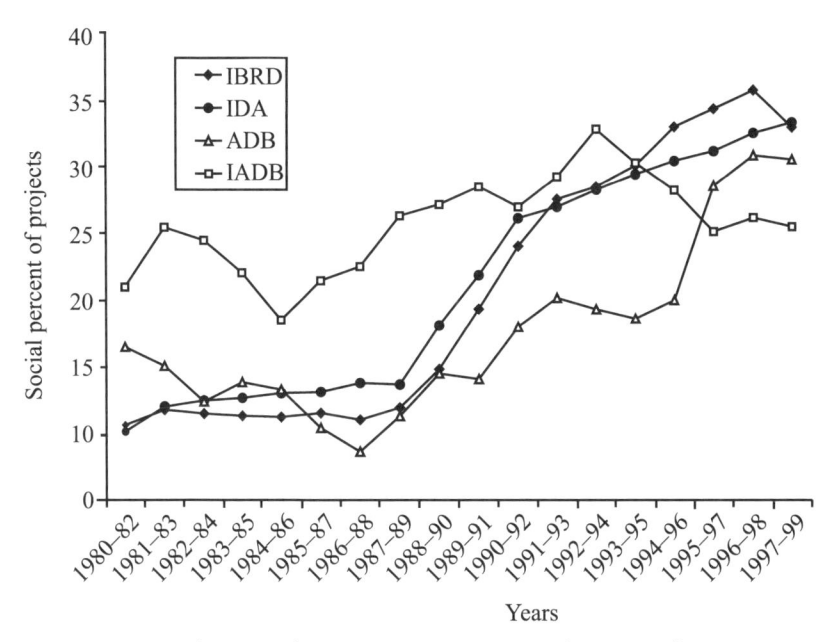

Alternative models of principals in development aid

Figure 2.2. Social percent of MDB projects, 1980–1999 (three-year rolling average)

suggest a decline since the mid-1990s. If we assume that MDBs are responsive to their most powerful members, then MDB social lending should not have increased over the past decade. But social lending moved dramatically upward. Common analytic shortcuts employed in the study of IOs would likely lead analysts to interpret this pattern as a case of MDBs defying their principals.

We argue that an accurate assessment of these trends requires reconsidering a number of analytic shortcuts commonly taken in the study of IOs. We improve on the existing literature evaluating the faithfulness of IO agents in four ways, and we test our new model with comprehensive data from the three major multilateral development banks. First, we develop two different measures of state preferences, and we systematically derive state preferences. Second, we introduce a new, collective-principal model of the decision-making process within MDBs and a systematic method for aggregating the preferences of member states for our model and the existing alternatives. Finally, we provide a systematic and comprehensive empirical analysis: we include all available observations of approved projects at the World Bank, the Inter-American Development Bank and the Asian Development Bank from 1980–99.

Principal preferences, structure, decision rules, and private benefits

Number of actors

In the study of IOs, the consensus view is that small states do not affect IO behavior in significant ways, and thus many empirical examinations explore the influence of great powers or the hegemon (Grieco 1990; Thacker 1999; Oatley and Yackee 2000, 2004; Yackee 2000; Nielson and Tierney 2003a). Small states, because they depend much more fully on the international system for their welfare, possess few attractive unilateral options for realizing the gains that IOs provide (Katzenstein 1985; Moravcsik 1998; Lake 1999). Moreover, because they are small, such states are susceptible to side-payments from the larger states (Moravcsik 1991, 25–26; Martin 1992a; Klepak 2003).

But this view discounts the fact that institutionalization of the international system varies from issue to issue and even from IO to IO within the same broad issue area (Keohane and Nye 1977; Stein 1990). In some IOs the formal rules that specify functional roles and the distribution of authority within an institution may actually reflect the "real" authority of various members – much as they do in institutionalized domestic polities.[11] If IO decision rules are efficacious, then we must include all member states in our derivation of the delegating principal's preferences. We believe this to be the case with multilateral development banks.

The voting power of member states and the project approval process within the MDBs are formally articulated in the Articles of Agreement and are similar to the decision process within a joint stock company. Member governments own shares in MDBs and thus have voting rights within the institutions. The number of shares owned by each state is roughly proportional to the amount of capital that each has paid in – an amount that is negotiated upon entry and adjusted depending upon a formula or periodic bargaining among member governments. The staff and management of the Bank typically develop projects in consultation with potential borrowing governments and then present individual projects to the executive board for approval.

If a majority of voting shares is cast in favor of a project, then Bank money is appropriated to cover agreed project costs. If a project fails to

---

[11] A crucial task for both IR and PA theorists is to specify the conditions under which these criteria will hold. Knowing this ex ante would help scholars to select cases amenable to institutional analysis. In this chapter we simply adopt the assumption that institutions are efficacious and test to see whether empirical patterns are consistent with our expectations.

Alternative models of principals in development aid

attract a majority of shares casting votes, then the loan request is rejected. Hence, the politics of loan approval at the MDBs requires the construction of voting majorities on the board. Observers and board members note that projects lacking majority support rarely reach the board. Further, formal roll-call votes are not often taken when a clear consensus in support of a project exists. While both these observations are accurate, all negotiations within the board take place in the shadow of the formal majority rule.[12]

Given these decision rules, we argue that the preferences of all member states within an MDB ought to be considered when attempting to explain or predict the behavior of IO agents and ultimately the substantive outcomes that result from this behavior – the type (and amount) of loans made by these MDBs. The selection of relevant member states is not the only analytic choice we believe deserves closer scrutiny. Scholars should systematically derive preferences for member states.

Derivation of individual member states' preferences

In the case of social lending at the MDBs, we derive two independent measures of member governments' preferences based on their behavior in two realms other than multilateral finance: domestic social policy and bilateral aid for social projects. For the first measure, we assume that countries with redistributive welfare states at home should be interested in seeing similar policies and institutions take hold in developing countries. This is a strong assumption. However, there is a growing body of literature demonstrating that domestic social policy preferences map very well onto foreign policy for social purposes.[13]

Our second measure uses the proportions of foreign aid targeted to social purposes for each donor and recipient, which arguably reflect the social foreign policy preferences of governments more directly. We assume that those governments interested in giving or receiving more bilateral social aid will lobby for similar policies on MDB executive boards. Of course, we recognize that even if bilateral aid is a reasonable proxy for donor country preferences, it may reflect the interests of recipient nations less well, since recipients may have less influence over

---

[12] As the former US Executive Director to the ADB explains, "Management is not going to bring a project to the Board unless it knows the project will be approved." Interview with Cinnamon Dornsife, June 2005. See also Piercy interview, June 2005.
[13] See, in particular, Noel and Therien 1995; also Imbeau 1988, 1989; Stokke 1989.

the type of bilateral grants they receive than they have over the loan contracts that they negotiate with MDBs. Objections might be raised about either measure of preferences, and thus we employ both here. If we find similar results using both measures, this lends greater confidence to our argument. Modeling country preferences is the first step in testing PA arguments; the next step requires systematic aggregation of those preferences.

Modeling multiple principals

The leading multiple-principals model suggests that the agent scans the range of principal demands and identifies a point that maximizes the compensation offered by the multiple principals. Principals with more power and resources thus have a greater impact on agent behavior. This is the general result of the original treatment of the common agency problem, by Bernheim and Winston (1986).[14] In the Bernheim–Winston equilibrium, the multiple principals all truthfully offer compensation schedules to the agent that accurately reflect their interests and expected gains from delegation. This allows the agent to select an action that maximizes the joint gains to both the principal and the agent.

This model is a good place to start for scholars who wish to model delegation with many independent principals and a single agent who must come to some discrete decision. We can operationalize this model in a relatively straightforward fashion. If analysts have a reasonable proxy for principal resources and a means of locating principals in a policy space according to their preferences, the ideal points for each principal can be imputed where the compensation offered is at its maximum, with the rest of the schedule reflecting the shape of the individual principal's indifference curve. Once all of these compensation schedules are specified, we can compute which of these offers maximizes the vector sum for the agent, and identify a unique equilibrium. We display an example of this model in table 2.2.

Modeling a collective principal

Since most PA relationships studied by scholars of IOs more closely reflect a collective-principal structure, we develop a generalizable

---

[14] For these authors, and most other economists, common agency is equivalent to a multiple-principals structure. They do not consider collective principals.

Alternative models of principals in development aid

collective-principal model that can be employed by empirically oriented researchers. The key problem here is how to model the decision rules that determine how the members of the collective principal will come to a joint decision. We draw on coalition theory in comparative politics, which suggests ways in which coalitions can be built given majority voting rules. The coalition model we employ highlights pivotal players in coalition formation. It allows us to construct an aggregate measure of the collective principal preference (Laver and Schofield 1990; Garrett and Tsebelis 1996).

The pivotal-players model emphasizes the role of veto players in the coalition-formation process. That is, of the many possible connected majority coalitions that might form in unidimensional issue space, some potential members might be "pivotal" in the sense that the combination of their centrist position and their size makes them very attractive coalition partners. Thus, pivotal players can veto a large set of the possible winning coalitions that might form and can extract policy benefits from their coalition partners that their size alone would not necessarily predict.

The simplest intuition distinguishing the multiple-principals model from the collective-principal model is that the collective-principal model better captures the constraints that collective decision-making places on those members with the most votes. The multiple principals vector-sum model implies that outcomes will be closest to the preferences of the most powerful player. In contrast, the collective-principal model explicitly models coalition dynamics which can inflate or diminish the influence of a player, relative to its size, depending on where they are located within the policy space.

EMPIRICAL APPLICATIONS: MDB SOCIAL LENDING

Data and dependent variables

We apply these alternative models to social lending at the MDBs. Our dataset consists of more than 6,600 loans issued by the World Bank, the Inter-American Development Bank and the Asian Development Bank from 1980 to 1999. The dependent variable is a dummy variable – it takes the value of 1 when the MDB project in question is intended for social development, otherwise the value is 0. We classify MDB projects as "social" when the primary intent is to address the following issues: education, health, general welfare, and social safety nets. We identified the universe of projects from the banks' annual reports and analyzed project descriptions to code every loan.

Independent variables

Using the two datasets described above, we derive the social policy preferences of member states year-by-year since 1980 and track member states' voting shares in the MDBs over time. In order to obtain a composite measure of social policy preferences of MDB member states, we constructed a social policy index (SPI).[15] We gathered data for 179 countries on 13 distinct measures of social policy-making and social outcomes in three areas: education, health, and social protection. Data on these variables were gathered from World Development Indicators (World Bank 2001b).

We standardized the measures, aggregated them into six overall indicators (education outcomes, education expenditures, health outcomes, health expenditures, fertility rate, and social security expenditures), and then averaged them to generate the social policy index (SPI). We used 1996 as a baseline year from which we calculated a pooled time series for all 179 countries. Our SPI is a comparative measure of social policy outcomes, not an absolute measure. The higher a country's score on our index, the more socially "progressive" are its social outcomes for a given year compared to the 179 countries in the index in 1996. This offers us a relative measure of social policy, which varies over time for a given country and varies across countries within a given year.[16]

Our second measure of social policy preferences uses statistics on bilateral foreign aid compiled from the Organization for Economic Co-operation and Development's (OECD) Creditor Reporting System database. Using the same coding system we used for MDB loans, we coded each bilateral grant into social and non-social categories. The percentage of social projects was then computed as a proportion of total projects committed by donor countries or obtained by recipients to derive an overall measure of social foreign policy preferences for each country by year from 1980 to 1999.

We operationalize the collective principal's preference in the following manner. For each bank year we arrayed all countries from highest to

---

[15] For our exemplar, see Esty 2001.
[16] For details on the index, see http://fhss.byu.edu/PolSci/Nielsond/PlaidWebsite/ResearchIndex.htm.

Alternative models of principals in development aid

lowest for our two measures of preferences (SPI and bilateral social aid percentages). We then summed all possible values of the voting shares of countries adjoining one another, creating a matrix of all potential coalitions. The matrix was 179 by 179 for the bank year with the greatest number of members.

For all of the coalitions where the sum of voting shares was greater than .50, we computed the consequence to the potential coalition of each extreme partner's defection. If the defection of a partner on one of the ends of the potential coalition would cause the coalition's collapse (vote shares fell below .50), we counted this as an instance where the defecting country would prove "pivotal." We summed all such instances and then gave each country a "pivotalness" score based on the proportion of all instances where the given country proved pivotal to a potential coalition. We then weighted all countries' SPI and SFA scores by the pivotalness share. Finally, we summed the products of all of the countries' SPI and SFA values multiplied by their pivotalness shares to produce the collective principal's social preferences for each bank year.

We provide a simple example of this technique in table 2.1. Along a ten-point scale in issue space, all possible contiguous coalitions are identified. In this example there are five such potential coalitions: (1) ABC, (2) ABCD, (3) ABCDE, (4) BCD, and (5) BCDE. For the first coalition, either actor A or actor C could prove pivotal by defecting. For coalitions 2 and 3 there are no critical defectors (defection does not collapse the coalition below 0.5). For coalition 4 either actor B or D could prove pivotal. And for coalition 5, only actor B could critically defect. The total number of potential critical defections is 5, with actors A, C, and D each proving pivotal in 20 percent of the critical defections, and actor B in 40 percent. Actor E is never pivotal. We then weight each actor's ideal point by the "pivotalness" share. Finally, we sum each of these products to produce an overall preference for the collective principal of 5.2.

A different outcome is predicted by the multiple-principals model, which predicts agent behavior based on the maximum weighted sum of the compensation schedules offered by the principals, with the weights reflecting the principals' resources. To create a proxy for this, we set ideal points for all members of the three MDBs equal to the countries' SPI score or bilateral aid percentage for a given bank year. We then compute compensation schedules weighted by the countries' actual contributions (capital subscriptions) to the banks. This produces a single equilibrium where the weighted sum of the compensation schedules can be maximized.

Principal preferences, structure, decision rules, and private benefits

Table 2.1. *Hypothetical pivotal players*

Actor	Vote Share	Ideal	Pivotal	Ideal* Pivotal
A	0.2	2	0.2	0.4
B	0.3	5	0.4	2.0
C	0.1	6	0.2	1.2
D	0.3	8	0.2	1.6
E	0.1	9	0.0	0.0
			Sum	5.2

Actors' ideal points:

A				B	C		D	E	
1	2	3	4	5	6	7	8	9	10

A hypothetical example is given in table 2.2. Here, we compute offered compensation schedules based on ideal points and voting shares. We set the maximum offer at the principal's ideal point and then reduce the offer uniformly over the other possible outcomes, setting a floor of zero, and weight the offer by capital subscriptions/voting share.[17] In this hypothetical, there are two policy outcomes where the compensation is maximized: 5 and 6, with an average of 5.5.

Operationalizing the hegemon's preferences at the MDBs is straightforward. We multiplied the United States' SPI and bilateral social aid scores by its voting share for each bank each year. We would expect that hegemonic influence would vary from bank to bank depending on the degree to which the hegemon dominated the other member states. Since voting share at each of the banks is scaled to country GDP, vote share might be reasonably used as a proxy for the weight of hegemonic influence from bank to bank.

Figure 2.3 displays the proxy measures of principal preferences for the IBRD from 1980 to 1999 produced by the three distinct models using the SPI measure. The SFA measure produced a qualitatively similar graph. As noted previously, it is the marked tendency in IR scholarship to focus solely on the most powerful players in an IO to the exclusion of all other actors. While this is often convenient analytically, it is equivalent to setting the weights for all of the neglected actors at zero. As the

---

[17] Allowing negative offers (sanctions) does not matter in predicting the outcome provided that they are uniformly scaled across the actors.

Table 2.2. *Hypothetical multiple principal*

Actor	Ideal	Vote share	Compensation schedules									
			1	2	3	4	5	6	7	8	9	10
A	2	0.2	0.16	0.20	0.16	0.12	0.08	0.04				
B	5	0.3	0.06	0.12	0.18	0.24	0.30	0.24	0.18	0.12	0.06	
C	6	0.1		0.02	0.04	0.06	0.08	0.10	0.08	0.06	0.04	0.02
D	8	0.3				0.06	0.12	0.18	0.24	0.30	0.24	0.18
E	9	0.1					0.02	0.04	0.06	0.08	0.10	0.08
Overall agent compensation			0.22	0.34	0.38	0.48	0.60	0.60	0.56	0.56	0.44	0.28

Principal preferences, structure, decision rules, and private benefits

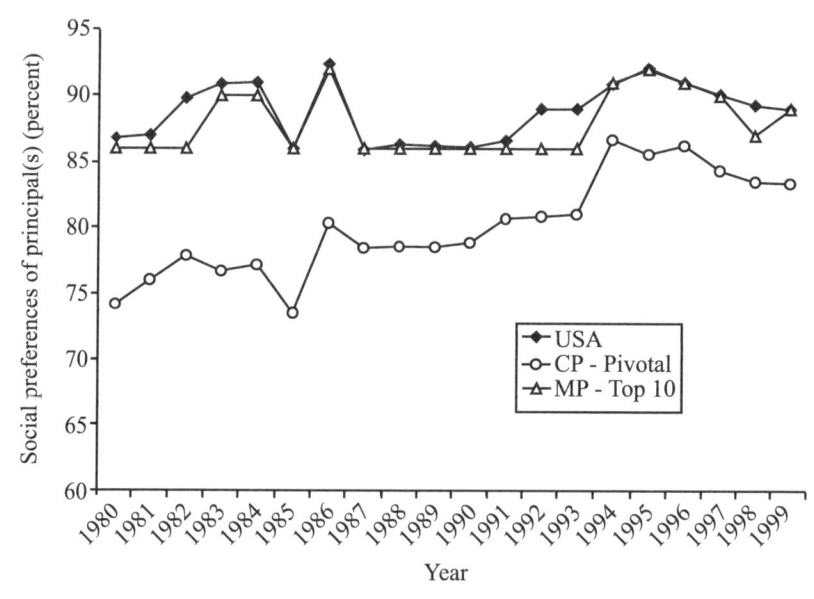

Figure 2.3. Social preferences for the International Bank for Reconstruction & Development (World Bank), 1980–1999 with alternative models of the principal

figure indicates, these distinct modeling choices produce significantly different principal preferences.

As illustrated in figure 2.3, the measure for social preferences for the United States and the multiple-principals proxy using the top ten member countries track one another quite closely. This is almost certainly because the United States and most of the other top ten World Bank members share closely aligned social preferences compared to the vast majority of member countries. As depicted, both measures produce high numbers for principals' social policy preferences with a relatively flat trend over the twenty years.[18] But the preferences of the United States and the top ten voting members of the Bank do not reflect the preference distribution of the other 169 member countries. Of course, the number of countries examined in a multiple-principals model is arbitrary. To address this problem we specified three different multiple-principals models, the first employing the preferences of the five leading donors to each bank, the second to the G-7 countries, and the third to the top ten donors.

---

[18] Ten multiple principals, while a small number, is actually much larger than the number usually considered in IR studies. See Moravscik 1998, Pollack 2003, Nielson and Tierney 2003a, and Martin in this volume.

Alternative models of principals in development aid

The top-five and top-ten models arbitrarily set a limit on the number of states considered and thus are vulnerable to criticisms of unreliability. The G-7 model is better grounded theoretically in that these seven states actually coordinate policy through regular meetings. However, for the two regional banks – the Inter-American and Asian Development Banks – several members of the G-7 have marginal voting shares that are significantly smaller than large regional players, such as Brazil, Argentina, India, and Indonesia. The theoretical foundation for the G-7 measure thus proves much shakier for the regional banks.

Controls

In addition to the independent variables that are central to our argument, we include a large number of control variables. We include dummy variables for each bank, expecting differences across the banks that our proxy variables for social preferences might not capture. Overall GDP and GDP per capita in 1995 dollars are standard comparative measures and control for the size of a given country's economy and its relative wealth, respectively (World Bank 2001b).

We also control for the objective need that given borrower countries might have for social loans, employing measures for Infant Mortality, Measles Immunizations, Physicians per Thousand, Public Health Expenditures, Paved Roads, Primary School Enrollment, Public Education Expenditures, Literacy Rate, Social Security Expenditures, and Fertility Rate. Domestic Savings Rate, Exports as Percent of GNP, GDP Growth, and Agriculture Value Added are all standard economic controls and might be expected to affect the overall probability that a loan – of any type – will be issued to a given country in a given country year (World Bank 2001b).[19]

Methods and results

We employed a set of basic logistic regression models, clustered by country (since loans within countries – but not across countries – should be related). These different models represent alternatives for the same independent variable. This means that the models are non-nested – they cannot encompass one another and thus should not be included in the

---

[19] Here, we tested for collinearity and removed all collinear controls that were duplicated or not theoretically justified.

Principal preferences, structure, decision rules, and private benefits

same regression. They are also highly collinear, particularly the hegemonic and the multiple-principals models. For these reasons we ran the variables separately rather than pooling them in the same model.

Because there is a two-year project cycle on average at the MDBs, we lagged all of our independent variables by two years. The loans approved for each year, which comprise our dataset, should reflect the interests of the executive board members from two years before a given annual portfolio is announced more than they reflect the current interests of the board. Thus, all results reported in tables 2.3 and 2.4 for each variable reflect the effects of independent variables lagged by two years.

We argue that the received wisdom that state principals do not control their IO agents deserves re-examination. Thus we vary the number of member states included in the principal as well as the model of the principal in order to evaluate whether analytic short-cuts commonly employed in the literature are likely to affect results. We expect that when we accurately model the relationships between member states and their IO agent and include all member states in the analysis, the results will show that principal preferences are significant predictors of agent behavior. We should model IOs as subject to collective principals.

As seen in tables 2.3 and 2.4, employing different models of the principal, and varying the number of states included, do lead to different results. In Models 1A and 1B, the social preferences of the United States (the hegemon) weighted by voting share in the MDBs proved significant at the .001 level, but in a negative direction. That is, the odds that a given loan would be social actually decreased significantly as the weighted social preferences of the United States increased. This suggests that hegemonic influence may not be determinant of social lending at the MDBs in the expected direction.[20] Employment of this model thus might lead researchers to conclude (we believe, erroneously) that delegation failed in this case.

In Models 2A and 2B, the proxy for multiple principals' social preferences for the top five donor countries did not prove significant at conventional levels. In Models 3A and 3B the social preferences proxy for the G-7 countries acting as multiple principals was significant for both our measures of preferences at the .05 level. While the coefficient for the G-7 variable in these latter two models is relatively large, the variable

---

[20] This result flies in the face of other quantitative evidence in other issue areas at other IFIs where the United States purportedly determines outcomes. See Oatley and Yackee 2000, 2004; Thacker 1999.

Table 2.3. *Logistic Regression Results with Social Loan as Dependent Variable Using the Social Policy Index to Generate Principal Preferences*

Independent Variable		Model 1A Hegemon	Model 2A Multiple Principals (Top 5)	Model 3A Multiple Principals (Group of 7)	Model 4A Multiple Principals (Top 10)	Model 5A Collective Principal (Pivotal)
USA Social Preferences	Coeff.	−0.142***				
	St. Err.	0.033				
Social Prefs. – Top 5 States	Coeff.		1.149			
	St. Err.		0.623			
Social Prefs. – Group of 7 States	Coeff.			3.599*		
	St. Err.			1.493		
Social Prefs. – Top 10 States	Coeff.				0.786	
	St. Err.				0.740	
Social Prefs. – Majority Coalition	Coeff.					3.143***
	St. Err.					0.744
Infant Mortality	Coeff.	−0.003	−0.003	−0.003	−0.003	−0.003
	St. Err.	0.002	0.002	0.002	0.002	0.002
Physicians per 1000	Coeff.	−0.151*	−0.153	−0.155	−0.150	−0.156*
	St. Err.	0.074	0.080	0.080	0.080	0.076
Measles Immunization	Coeff.	0.004*	0.007***	0.007***	0.007***	0.004**
	St. Err.	0.002	0.001	0.001	0.002	0.002
Health Expenditures	Coeff.	−0.048	−0.060	−0.062	−0.061	−0.053
	St. Err.	0.031	0.035	0.035	0.035	0.032

(continued)

Table 2.3 *(continued)*

Independent Variable		Model 1A Hegemon	Model 2A Multiple Principals (Top 5)	Model 3A Multiple Principals (Group of 7)	Model 4A Multiple Principals (Top 10)	Model 5A Collective Principal (Pivotal)
Fertility Rate	Coeff.	0.007	−0.011	−0.007	−0.012	0.003
	St. Err.	0.047	0.049	0.049	0.049	0.047
Primary School Enrollment	Coeff.	0.002	0.001	0.001	0.001	0.001
	St. Err.	0.003	0.003	0.003	0.003	0.003
Public Expenditures on Education	Coeff.	−0.041*	−0.044*	−0.047*	−0.045*	−0.043*
	St. Err.	0.018	0.018	0.019	0.018	0.017
Illiteracy	Coeff.	0.003	0.003	0.003	0.003	0.002
	St. Err.	0.004	0.004	0.004	0.004	0.004
Social Security Expenditures	Coeff.	0.000	0.001	0.000	0.001	0.000
	St. Err.	0.005	0.006	0.006	0.006	0.005
Paved Roads	Coeff.	0.003	0.003	0.003	0.003	0.003
	St. Err.	0.002	0.002	0.002	0.002	0.002
Agriculture Value Added	Coeff.	−0.010*	−0.009*	−0.009*	−0.009*	−0.010*
	St. Err.	0.004	0.004	0.004	0.004	0.004
GDP per capita (in thousands)	Coeff.	0.049*	0.040	0.041	0.039	0.046
	St. Err.	0.024	0.025	0.025	0.025	0.024
GDP in 1995 USD (in billions)	Coeff.	0.759***	0.726***	0.715***	0.729***	0.701***
	St. Err.	0.179	0.182	0.186	0.184	0.182

Independent Variable		Model 1A Hegemon	Model 2A Multiple Principals (Top 5)	Model 3A Multiple Principals (Group of 7)	Model 4A Multiple Principals (Top 10)	Model 5A Collective Principal (Pivotal)
GDP Growth	Coeff.	0.001	0.000	0.000	0.000	0.000
	St. Err	0.005	0.005	0.005	0.005	0.005
Exports as Percent of GNP	Coeff.	0.006*	0.007*	0.007*	0.007*	0.006
	St. Err.	0.003	0.003	0.003	0.003	0.003
Domestic Savings Rate	Coeff.	−0.006	−0.006	−0.006	−0.006	−0.005
	St. Err.	0.003	0.004	0.004	0.004	0.004
IBRD Dummy	Coeff.	−0.274	−0.462**	−0.462**	−0.465**	−0.434**
	St. Err.	0.167	0.153	0.154	0.153	0.153
ADB Dummy	Coeff.	−0.928***	−0.281	−0.413**	−0.336*	−0.098
	St. Err.	0.185	0.161	0.151	0.169	0.159
IADB Dummy	Coeff.	1.920***	−0.016	−0.242	−0.102	0.208
	St. Err.	0.527	0.167	0.133	0.179	0.155
Constant	Coeff.	1.416	−1.755*	−3.986**	−1.444	−3.218***
	St. Err.	0.678	0.718	1.396	0.778	0.738
Number of Observations		6636	6636	6636	6636	6636
Log Likelihood		−3804	−3825	−3823	−3826	−3814
Wald Chi-Square		192***	145.1***	187.2***	145.91***	164.26***

Notes: * $p < .05$
** $p < .01$
*** $p < .001$

Table 2.4. *Logistic Regression Results with Social Loan as Dependent Variable Using the Bilateral Social Foreign Aid to Generate Principal Preferences*

Independent Variable		Model 1B Hegemon	Model 2B Multiple Principals (Top 5)	Model 3B Multiple Principals (Group of 7)	Model 4B Multiple Principals (Top 10)	Model 5B Collective Principal (Pivotal)
USA Social Preferences	Coeff.	−0.162***				
	St. Err.	0.032				
Social Prefs. – Top 5 States	Coeff.		0.525			
	St. Err.		0.658			
Social Prefs. – Group of 7 States	Coeff.			2.014*		
	St. Err.			0.897		
Social Prefs. – Top 10 States	Coeff.				0.804**	
	St. Err.				0.245	
Social Prefs. – Majority Coalition	Coeff.					2.786***
	St. Err.					0.492
Infant Mortality	Coeff.	−0.003	−0.003	−0.003	−0.003	−0.004
	St. Err.	0.002	0.002	0.002	0.002	0.002
Physicians per 1000	Coeff.	−0.163*	−0.150	−0.152	−0.149	−0.152
	St. Err.	0.076	0.081	0.081	0.081	0.078
Measles Immunization	Coeff.	0.005**	0.007***	0.007***	0.008***	0.006***
	St. Err.	0.002	0.001	0.001	0.001	0.001
Health Expenditures	Coeff.	−0.052	−0.062	−0.062	−0.064	−0.059
	St. Err.	0.031	0.035	0.035	0.036	0.034

Independent Variable		Model 1B Hegemon	Model 2B Multiple Principals (Top 5)	Model 3B Multiple Principals (Group of 7)	Model 4B Multiple Principals (Top 10)	Model 5B Collective Principal (Pivotal)
Fertility Rate	Coeff.	0.004	−0.014	−0.015	−0.013	0.004
	St. Err.	0.047	0.049	0.049	0.049	0.048
Primary School Enrollment	Coeff.	0.001	0.001	0.001	0.001	0.002
	St. Err.	0.003	0.003	0.003	0.003	0.003
Public Expenditures on Education	Coeff.	−0.043*	−0.046*	−0.046*	−0.045*	−0.043
Illiteracy	St. Err.	0.018	0.019	0.019	0.019	0.018
	Coeff.	0.003	0.003	0.004	0.004	0.004
	St. Err.	0.004	0.004	0.004	0.004	0.004
Social Security Expenditures	Coeff.	0.001	0.001	0.001	0.001	0.001
	St. Err.	0.005	0.006	0.006	0.006	0.006
Paved Roads	Coeff.	0.003	0.003	0.003	0.003	0.003
	St. Err.	0.002	0.002	0.002	0.002	0.002
Agriculture Value Added	Coeff.	−0.009*	−0.009*	−0.009*	−0.009*	−0.009*
	St. Err.	0.004	0.004	0.004	0.004	0.004
GDP per capita (in thousands)	Coeff.	0.000	0.000	0.000	0.000	0.000
	St. Err.	0.000	0.000	0.000	0.000	0.000
GDP in 1995 USD (in billions)	Coeff.	0.691***	0.737***	0.722***	0.726***	0.729***
	St. Err.	0.186	0.183	0.185	0.185	0.190
GDP Growth	Coeff.	0.000	0.000	0.000	0.001	0.001
	St. Err.	0.005	0.005	0.005	0.005	0.005

(continued)

Table 2.4 *(continued)*

Independent Variable		Model 1B Hegemon	Model 2B Multiple Principals (Top 5)	Model 3B Multiple Principals (Group of 7)	Model 4B Multiple Principals (Top 10)	Model 5B Collective Principal (Pivotal)
Exports as Percent of GNP	Coeff.	0.006	0.007*	0.007*	0.007*	0.006
	St. Err.	0.003	0.003	0.003	0.003	0.003
Domestic Savings Rate	Coeff.	−0.005	−0.007	−0.007	−0.007	−0.006
	St. Err.	0.004	0.004	0.004	0.004	0.004
IBRD Dummy	Coeff.	−0.387*	−0.466**	−0.460**	−0.419**	−0.430**
	St. Err.	0.156	0.153	0.152	0.153	0.158
ADB Dummy	Coeff.	−0.636***	−0.464**	−0.408**	−0.502**	−0.322
	St. Err.	0.160	0.157	0.142	0.154	0.153
IADB Dummy	Coeff.	0.637*	−0.284*	−0.245	−0.330*	−0.408**
	St. Err.	0.211	0.144	0.133	0.141	0.141
Constant	Coeff.	0.175	−0.934*	−1.460**	−1.160*	−1.450**
	St. Err.	0.483	0.472	0.496	0.456	0.467
Number of Observations		6636	6636	6636	6636	6636
Log Likelihood		−3812	−3826	−3824	−3821	−3807
Wald Chi-Square		206***	149***	144***	185***	252***

Notes: $^*\ p < .05$
$^{**}\ p < .01$
$^{***}\ p < .001$

itself has a much smaller range (between .86 and .92), indicating that while statistically significant, its substantive impact is minor.

In Model 4A, the proxy for the top ten multiple principals' social preferences using our social policy index was not significant, though in Model 4B the proxy using bilateral aid dollars for social projects was significant at the .01 level. These results for the various multiple principals' models are decidedly mixed: in half of the instances they suggest that the multiple principals' preferences drive social lending outcomes at the MDBs and in half they do not. Thus, if analysts were to adopt the multiple principals model as the appropriate conceptualization of multilateral delegation to MDBs, they might once again, as in the case of the hegemonic model, conclude (we believe, erroneously) that principals exercise only limited control over their agents.

For the collective principal model the proxy for collective social preferences proved positive and significant at the .001 level in both Models 5A and 5B. The results for Model 5A, for example, suggest that an increase from the minimum pivotal-weighted preference of .50 (the IADB in 1981) to the maximum of .87 (the IBRD in 1994) was on average related to a .15 increase in the probability that a given loan would be social. Given that only 27 percent of all loans in the dataset were social loans, a .15 increase in the probability for social loans suggests substantive as well as statistical significance.

These results demonstrate that decisions about how to model the principal and the number of states included do have important implications for the results generated. We believe they also provide strong support for the view that, at least in the case of MDBs, member state principals do control their IO agents. Researchers commonly employ a model that approximates the multiple-principals model we employed here, and we have shown that in half of the instances, such a modeling choice would lead to conclusions of delegation failure. We have argued on a priori conceptual grounds that the collective-principal model is the more accurate model of actual PA relationships governing multilateral delegation to MDBs. And this model consistently demonstrated a substantively and statistically significant relationship between principal preferences and agent behavior.

Alternatively, scholars often examine only the hegemon or a few powerful states in studying IO behavior,[21] but we have shown that

---

[21] The most prominent example for researchers employing qualitative analysis is probably Moravcsik 1998. For examples of this practice with quantitative analysis see Thacker 1999; Nielson and Tierney 2003.

varying the number of states included alters the results.[22] We have argued once again on a priori conceptual grounds that if rules governing interaction between member states delegating to IOs are efficacious, then small states will also, at times, influence IO behavior. And indeed, both of the collective principal models which included all states showed that principals do exercise control over MDB behavior. In sum, we believe that on a priori conceptual grounds, we can have far more confidence in the statistical results that demonstrate that MDB agents do follow the preferences of their collective principal than in the alternatives.

CONCLUSION

The goal of this chapter was to demonstrate that choices about modeling the principal in delegation to IOs have important implications for empirical results and thus for conclusions about whether IO behavior is consistent with principal preferences. We introduced the idea of complex principals and argued that researchers must carefully consider whether the principal(s) delegating to IOs are best modeled as a single principal, multiple principals, or a collective principal. First we presented a qualitative case study of US delegation to an international (IADB) and then subsequently to a domestic (IAF) agent to pursue virtually identical goals. We argued that researchers should exercise caution in concluding that this replacement of a poorly performing international agent with a domestic alternative provides affirming evidence for the view that domestic agents are more faithful than international agents. Often policy differences between the President and Congress over the terms of the delegation contract drove agent behavior or enabled agent autonomy. We concluded that even when a single state delegates to an IO (or a domestic agent), researchers should first consider the impact of multiple principals before drawing conclusions about delegation failure.

[22] When *all* of the member countries are included, the proxy for the multiple principals' preferences does prove significant in the expected direction. This is an interesting result that is very likely driven by the fact that voting shares are exactly equivalent to compensation schedules at the MDBs. But this is a very special case for two reasons. First, we have employed a very simple model of the multiple principal as a first analytic cut. Changing any of our simplifying assumptions would likely mean the results of the collective and multiple principal models diverge. Second, in cases where voting shares in the collective principal are not equivalent to compensation schedules offered by each multiple principal, even this simplified model of the multiple principal would very likely give different results from the collective principal model, even when all states are included.

Alternative models of principals in development aid

In the second section we examined delegation from member states to MDBs and we argued that the appropriate model for understanding principal preferences in this case was a collective principal model.[23] We also argued that accurate tests of the faithfulness of IO agents required systematic derivation of individual member state preferences and inclusive quantitative tests. As our results show, the distinction between collective and multiple principals is demonstrably important for empirically oriented researchers. We argued on analytic grounds that the collective principal model is superior to a single or a multiple-principals model when studying MDBs (and most other IOs), because it more accurately reflects the strategic interaction taking place within the institution. This more accurate model consistently demonstrated a strong statistical and substantive relationship between principal preferences and loan patterns. We believe the greater accuracy of our model, combined with our systematic derivation of preferences and our analysis of comprehensive data, justifies the conclusion that our study provides strong evidence that member state principals do control their MDB agents. This is consistent with findings in other issue areas of MDB lending (Nielson and Tierney 2003, 2005).

We conclude that when testing principal-agent relationships, the number of principals considered and the model employed of the principal matter. It is quite possible that arbitrarily restricting the number of states analyzed, or failing to model the complex principal correctly, will generate false negative (or positive) findings. That is, analysts may conclude that agents are not responsive to principals when in fact agents may well be responsive, just not to a truncated set of member states that does not accurately reflect the operative principal. Similarly, analysts who do not explicitly consider procedures for aggregating preferences within a collective principal may often be evaluating agent behavior based on a conception of agent marching orders that does not correspond to the operative collective principal's mandate.

But the modeling issues involving principals, once properly identified, do not introduce challenges to the conceptual underpinnings of

---

[23] From 1980–2000 Congress and the President were more unified on multilateral aid than they were on bilateral aid. This follows in part from the fact that multilateral aid has more features of a collective good and that many reforms instituted in the 1960s and 1970s protected donor contributions at the MDBs. Hence, the simplifying assumption that presidential democracies (like the United States) can be treated as unified actors in a collective principal is more plausible for the period under study.

Principal preferences, structure, decision rules, and private benefits

principal-agent models. To be sure, they are complicating factors. And, particularly, we should not assume a single principal even in the case of delegation from a single state if it has a separation of powers system, and we should not conflate multiple principals with a collective principal nor truncate the set of principals considered. But if scholars model the structure of the principal and the dynamics of collective contract design accurately, our analysis suggests that the basic insights of PA theory hold, even "under anarchy."

3

US domestic politics and International Monetary Fund policy

J. LAWRENCE BROZ AND MICHAEL BREWSTER HAWES

INTRODUCTION

Emerging market crises of the 1990s stimulated new interest in the political motivations that shape International Monetary Fund (IMF or Fund) lending decisions.[1] We take up this topic, analyzing the interests and influence of the IMF's most powerful member, the United States. Instead of specifying an aggregate "national interest" for the United States, we ground our approach in domestic politics. One of our arguments is that American "money-center" banks comprise a key constituency for the IMF and lobby on its behalf.[2] US policy-makers, in turn, use their influence at the Fund to ensure that countries in which American banks are highly exposed fall under the IMF's insurance umbrella. In short, we provide microfoundations for IMF lending and identify a possible source of "moral hazard" in the lobbying activities of US banks.

We thank Mat McCubbins, J. R. DeShazo, Michael Hiscox, James Vreeland, David Lake, Lisa Martin, Jeffry Frieden, William R. Clark, Erica Gould, Joseph Joyce, Devesh Kapur, Louis Pauley, Shanker Satyanath, Beth Simmons, and Michael Tierney for comments and Mark Farrales and Molly James for research assistance. We also thank participants at the Annual International Society for New Institutional Economics Conference (ISNIE), Tucson, AZ, September 30–October 3, 2004; the Public Lectures Seminar at the UCLA Department of Political Science, June 2, 2003; and the 2003 Annual Meeting of the American Political Science Association, Philadelphia, August 28–31, 2003.

[1] See Thacker 1999; Vreeland 1999; Przeworski and Vreeland 2000; Oatley and Yackee 2004; Barro and Lee 2001; Bird and Rowlands 2001; Dreher and Vaubel 2001; Joyce 2002.
[2] Money-center banks specialize in wholesale and international banking and are located in financial centers like New York, Chicago, and San Francisco. Their clients include governments, corporations, and other banks. Citigroup, JPMorgan Chase & Co., and Bank of America fit the description.

Principal preferences, structure, decision rules, and private benefits

We are not the first to identify money-center banks as an important constituency for the IMF. A radical "dependencista" version of the argument has been around since the 1960s and a more orthodox variant is currently circulating (Barro 1998; Soros 1998; Stiglitz 2002). One claims the existence of a "Wall Street–Treasury complex" (Bhagwati 2002: 8–9). Other studies (Gould 2003; Oatley and Yackee 2004) examine the extent to which commercial banks exert a systematic influence on IMF lending.[3] Still, some fundamental questions remain: How do bankers and other private actors influence an international organization like the IMF? Why would IMF officials be responsive to the interests of private actors?

These are tough questions, not least because they involve incentives and actions of private and public actors at multiple levels of collective decision-making. Furthermore, the IMF is not a particularly transparent institution. Its members do not vote formally on country loan arrangements or on other aspects of their day-to-day business, and much of the IMF's "consensus-building" is done informally, outside of executive board meetings. In addition, the Fund imposes a 20-year gag rule on minutes of board meetings – yet another procedure that makes it difficult to ascertain the underlying motivations behind Fund decisions.

Like other chapters in this volume, we are motivated by the growing scholarly interest in international organizations, and by concern with the "principal-agent" problem that can confound the operation of these organizations (Hawkins et al., this volume). But unlike chapters that take a unitary actor approach to the formal principals of such organizations, we focus on the pecuniary interests of private individuals (voters and interest groups) within a key principal: the United States.[4] By establishing links between US private actors and domestic politicians, and then between domestic politics and international decision-making, we elucidate the micro-incentives that underpin the behavior of complex international organizations like the IMF. In short, we examine incentives and outcomes at both the domestic and the international levels of analysis.

Figure 3.1 illustrates our approach. The "chain of delegation" begins with private individuals in the United States and ends at the IMF, with the US delegate representing US interests, which are endogenously determined. To derive the interests of private actors with respect to IMF and its policies, we ask: Who benefits and who loses from IMF policies? To

---

[3] Gould (this volume) also discusses banks in her analysis of Fund conditionality.
[4] Milner (this volume) comes closest to the spirit of our analysis in that she also focuses on domestic politics.

US domestic politics and IMF policy

Influence, monitoring

Private actors (voters and groups) → Congress (legislators) → Executive (President, Secretary of the Treasury) → IMF (US Executive Director)

Distributional effects

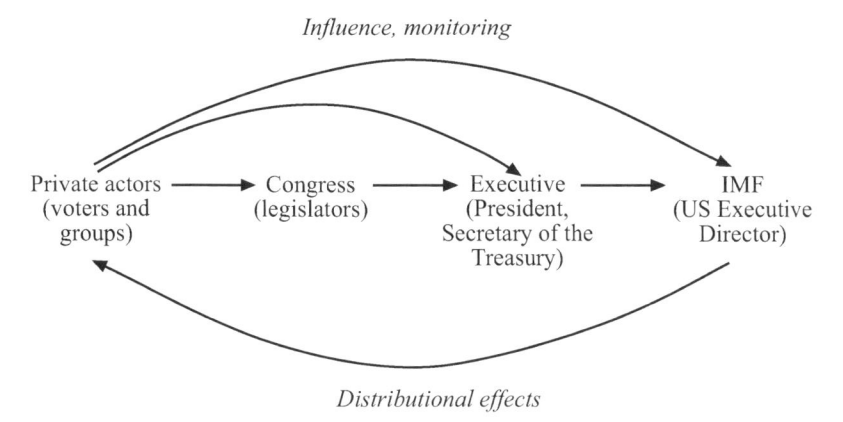

Figure 3.1. Chain of delegation

address this distributional issue, we look to the economics literature on international financial rescues and to the literature on economic globalization more generally. Next, we assume that private actors advance their international financial policy goals through one of three channels: either directly to the IMF (top arrow) as in Gould (2003); via the Executive Branch (second arrow); or by way of Congress. Although Congress rarely monitors the day-to-day operations of the Fund, it plays an active role in funding decisions, which require congressional authorization and appropriations. We analyze voting in the US House of Representatives on IMF funding increases as a means to establish the links between private actors and domestic politicians. Finally, we evaluate IMF behavior to see if it is consistent with our arguments about the domestic distributional effects of IMF policy. At this level, we employ a "revealed preferences" approach. Due to the absence of transparency at the IMF, we analyze IMF lending outcomes *as if* the institution was pursuing the interests of US private actors (e.g. money-center banks).

Our results are encouraging. At the congressional level, we find that campaign contributions from money-center banks have a large and significant impact on the propensity of members to vote in favor of increasing the US quota contribution to the IMF. We also find that members representing districts with greater proportions of net "winners" from economic globalization are more likely to favor increasing the IMF's resources. We anticipate the first result because IMF financial rescues provide insurance to private creditors, allowing banks to retain the gains from international lending while distributing losses, when they occur, to

Principal preferences, structure, decision rules, and private benefits

the public sector. We predict the second result because the IMF, in pursuing its mandate to protect the world economy from financial shocks, encourages globalization and its attendant distributional consequences.

At the IMF level, we find that the size of an IMF loan to a country is positively and significantly related to the degree of money-center bank exposure in that country, controlling for other factors. An important implication of this result is that moral hazard in international finance is at least partly a function of the interests of private actors seeking to externalize the risks of cross-border lending.

The chapter is organized as follows. In section two, we provide background on the organization of the IMF and illustrate shortcomings in the scholarly work on the IMF, particularly the lack of attention to individual incentives. In the next three sections, we address these flaws. Section three contains our arguments and evidentiary strategy. Section four is the empirical analysis of congressional roll call votes on IMF quota increases, and section five explores the determinants of IMF lending. The final section is the conclusion, which discusses the implications of these findings.

ORGANIZATION OF THE IMF

The IMF supports global trade and economic growth by providing assistance to countries facing balance-of-payments problems. The IMF obtains its financial resources from member country subscriptions, which are known as "quotas." Each country's quota is calculated by a formula reflecting the relative size of its economy, using various measures of output and trade. But quotas are also important because they determine members' voting power in the organization.

Each member country has 250 "basic" votes, plus one additional vote for each part of its quota equal to SDR 100,000. As basic votes comprise only a small fraction of total votes, control of the IMF is heavily weighted toward its larger members.[5] The United States is the largest member with a quota of SDR 37.1 billion (about $54.2 billion) and 371,743 votes (17.1 percent of the total). By contrast, Palau has but

---

[5] While we acknowledge Lyne, Nielson, and Tierney's (this volume) concern with small members and coalition-building in "collective principal" international organizations, we focus on the United States because it is unambiguously the IMF's most powerful member. Our approach, however, could be applied to any member or group of members.

281 votes (0.013 percent of the total). The United States has even greater clout over certain important decisions – like changing quotas – that are subject to special 85 percent majorities. With 17 percent of the votes, the United States is the pivotal actor on quota changes and many other IMF decisions.

Organizationally, the IMF has two representative bodies, the board of governors and the executive board, both with weighted voting.[6] While the board of governors has ultimate authority for running the IMF, it has delegated nearly all its powers to the executive board. The executive board is the main decision-making body on the day-to-day business of the Fund.

Formal votes are not taken by the executive board. The board's decision rule (Rule C-10 of the Fund's Rules and Regulations) dates to the origins of the IMF and came at the insistence of the United States and the United Kingdom. The rule prescribes that "the Chairman shall ordinarily ascertain the sense of the meeting, in lieu of a formal vote." A "sense of the meeting" means that the chairman of the executive board (i.e. the managing director of the IMF) surmises whether a position is supported by executive directors having sufficient votes to carry the question *if* a vote were taken (Van Houtven 2002: 23). We are interested in the political economy of these decisions, so we focus on the motivations and influence of large members.[7] The problem is that the "sense of meeting" voting procedure makes it difficult to discern influence by any member and shrouds motivations behind a veil of "consensus."

One solution is to infer motivations and influence from patterns of IMF lending ex post, filling in the black box of IMF decision-making by reading backwards from IMF outcomes to member government interests. Several papers follow this "revealed preferences" approach, hypothesizing a positive association between the size of a debtor country's loan from the IMF and that country's "political proximity" to the United States (Thacker 1999; Barro and Lee 2002; Dreher and Jensen 2003; Stone 2004). The standard proxy for "political proximity" is the fraction of times the United States and the country in question vote identically in the UN General Assembly. The results generally support the argument.

While this approach purports to elucidate IMF policy-making, it has shortcomings. One problem is that the micro-incentives of

---

[6] See Martin and Gould (both this volume) for details on the IMF's governance structure.
[7] For the influence of small members, see Lyne, Nielson, and Tierney (this volume).

decision-makers are not defined. IMF officials advance an aggregate goal – their home country's "national interest"– instead of being motivated by individual incentives conditioned on the institutional environment. While there may in fact be personal benefits (costs) that accrue to executive directors that take positions favoring (opposing) allies, these incentives are not identified ex ante, leaving a gap in the logic of the causal story. Another problem is the indirect relationship between the argument and the evidence. The argument predicts executive directors' individual positions within the IMF's main decision-making body. Evidence, on the other hand, is from aggregate IMF lending outcomes. While research in political economy is often forced by data constraints to resort to indirect evidence, we should be cautious of inferences drawn at one level but tested at another.

We acknowledge that IMF directors' positions are difficult to discern, and that simplifying behavioral assumptions can yield theoretical and empirical insights. However, we think it is problematic to infer motivations from IMF outcomes without more direct evidence that executive directors maximize the objectives claimed by analysts.

APPROACH AND ARGUMENT

To avoid this and other problems associated with the lack of transparency of IMF decision-making, we develop our argument from the bottom up. We start with private actors within large shareholding countries like the United States, treating them as potential constituencies of the IMF. We define the interests of private actors in narrow pecuniary terms: the IMF's policies have distributional effects that give private actors stakes in what the organization does. We then move east along the chain of delegation to an institutional level in which individual voting on Fund policy *is* formal and observable – the US Congress.[8] We assume that domestic legislators care about re-election and therefore take positions that reflect voter and interest group stakes in the policy. Our results suggest that legislators' positions are indeed shaped by the lobbying activity of banks and other constituency goals.

We then move to the IMF level, where we expect US representatives to advance the interests of American banks, among other things. Since we can't observe this influence directly, we analyze IMF lending *as if* the US

---

[8] Some decisions that the Fund makes must be ratified by Congress (e.g. quota increases), which opens a window into the otherwise opaque politics of the IMF.

delegate was the dominant decision-maker actively pursuing the interests of private US constituencies. We are agnostic on the mechanism by which private actor interests are communicated to the IMF (see figure 3.1), but our results suggest that such communication does take place. We find that the size of an IMF loan to a country is positively and significantly related to the degree of US money-center bank exposure in that country, controlling for other factors. Although such "third-party actors" are not direct principals of the IMF according to the conceptual framework of this volume (Hawkins et al., this volume), our findings suggest that bankers do influence agent behavior.

Private actors and the IMF

Among third-party private actors, the portion of the financial sector in the United States that invests in and lends to emerging market economies is a key beneficiary of IMF activities (Oatley and Yackee 2004). This is because IMF financial assistance, even if intended to help stabilize the international financial system, is a form of insurance for creditors and a source of moral hazard. A moral hazard is an action that encourages the very behavior that the action seeks to prevent. With respect to the IMF, moral hazard arises when IMF crisis assistance encourages private investors to assume risks that they might otherwise shun in an attempt to reap greater financial returns. The idea is that private investors and lenders to developing countries over-commit to emerging economies because of the expectation, based on previous experience, that the IMF will provide the foreign exchange liquidity that will allow them to exit the country in time of crisis without having to bear their full losses.[9] As creditors, they are aware that they will be bailed out in case of a balance-of-payments crisis. For example, at the time of the 1995 Mexican crisis, private investors suffered no crisis-related losses as a result of the bailout. This encouraged excessive risk-taking, and set the stage for the Asian crisis two years later. In this crisis, investors and foreign banks did suffer losses, although these losses were less than they would have been in the absence of the $100 billion IMF rescue.

[9] The IMF encourages moral hazard, both with creditors and debtor nations, but there is a vigorous ongoing debate on the extent of the problem (Jeanne and Zettelmeyer 2001; Dreher and Vaubel 2001). The International Financial Institutions Advisory Commission, or Meltzer Commission, which Congress chartered to evaluate and recommend US policy toward the IMF after the Asian crisis, viewed moral hazard to be the most important problem in international finance.

Principal preferences, structure, decision rules, and private benefits

IMF bailouts allow private creditors to retain the gains from international lending and distribute at least part of the losses to the public sector. When the IMF provides funds to a member government, that government often uses the IMF funds to repay private creditors (Bird 1996: 477–511). Financial market participants are aware of this risk transfer. Demirguc-Kunt and Huizinga (1993) found that unanticipated increases in US government financial commitments to the IMF caused the market capitalization of exposed US money-center banks to increase. They concluded that the "stock market expects virtually all additional resources provided to debtor countries [by the IMF] to be used for debt service to commercial banks"(Demirguc-Kunt and Huizinga 1993: 443). While moral hazard and the risk subsidy to private actors may be an inevitable consequence of stabilizing financial markets (Rogoff 1999), our argument is simply that creditors with assets in developing countries are among the most important beneficiaries and therefore are likely to be strong supporters of the IMF. We expect money-center banks to lobby (provide campaign contributions) in support of the IMF.

Other private actors are affected by IMF policies. Among unorganized constituencies (voters), the actors that gain and lose from having the IMF stabilize the world economy can be identified via international trade theory. Stolper and Samuelson (1941) identified the winners and losers from economic globalization in terms of factors of production, such as high-skilled and low-skilled labor, from which factor owners derive their incomes. Owners of locally abundant factors tend to gain more than average from globalization, while owners of scarce factors tend to lose. In the United States, the relatively scarce factor is low-skilled labor, and thus the group most likely to lose from globalization is low-skilled labor (Wood 1994). As trade has increased with nations where low-skilled labor is relatively abundant (and hence cheap), organized labor in the United States has mobilized against globalization, and received protection in less-skilled intensive industries in return (Haskel and Slaughter 2000; Baldwin and Magee 2000). By contrast, highly skilled labor is abundant in the United States relative to the rest of the world, and thereby benefits from globalization.

Existing individual-level data from public opinion surveys provide empirical support for the argument. Scheve and Slaughter (2001: 267–92) suggest that workers with college degrees or advanced skills support liberalization of international trade, while those with less education and fewer skills resist such initiatives. Our extension to the analysis of IMF policy recognizes that the Fund's mandate to protect global trade and economic integration from financial disorder is a benefit to private actors that gain from such integration. We thus would expect people with high (low) skills to support (oppose) the IMF. But we do not expect them to lobby. As discussed below, diffuse interests such as high- and low-skilled workers find representation via the electoral calculations of legislators.

Congress and the IMF

Although it has delegated some important functions to the executive branch – the President appoints the executive director to the IMF, and the executive director is ordered by law to clear his or her decisions with the secretary of the Treasury – Congress has the final authority to determine the terms of US involvement in the IMF, which originate with the Bretton Woods Act of 1944. While it does not carefully monitor most aspects of Fund behavior, Congress plays an active role on certain issues, especially funding increases.

On major IMF policy changes, such as an increase in the US quota contribution, Congress maintains direct authority. Under Section 5 of the Bretton Woods Act, US participation in a quota increase must be approved by the US Congress (Wertman 1998b). In fact, no general increase in IMF quotas has taken effect without Congress consenting to the US increase (Boughton 2001: 858).

On other issues, Congress is weakly to moderately active in monitoring IMF policy and shaping the agenda that US appointees to the IMF and the Secretary of the Treasury must advance. In 2001, the General Accounting Office reported that Congress had established 60 legislative mandates prescribing US policy goals at the Fund (US General Accounting Office 2001). These mandates cover a wide range of policies, including labor standards, international trade, human rights, and weapons proliferation. In every case, Congress directs the secretary of the Treasury to instruct the US executive director to use his "voice and vote" on the executive board of the Fund to pursue specific policies as part of his duties (Wertman 1998a: 1–22).[10]

We analyze congressional voting on quota increases because voting to increase quotas is a straightforward way to indicate support for the IMF (more resources allow the Fund to make more stabilization loans).

---

[10] As an international organization, the IMF is exempt from US law, so Congress must work through the secretary of the Treasury to influence IMF behavior.

Principal preferences, structure, decision rules, and private benefits

Legislators' positions on quota increases are likely to be shaped by many factors, including partisan identity, political ideology, and expectations about the future consequences of IMF rescues (the moral hazard problem). However, elections and the possibility of being voted out of office bind legislators to the interests of constituents. We make the standard assumption that legislator behavior is self-interested and derives, at least in part, from the desire to remain in office. This assumption implies that members of Congress make decisions on IMF policy based upon how these policies affect them personally (which is to say, electorally), without regard for the policies' national or international effects. The link to private actors involves both campaign contributions from organized groups such as money-center banks, and votes of citizens affected by the distributional impact of IMF policy such as high-skilled workers.

Campaign contributions provide legislators with resources for political advertising, which can be helpful in winning support from voters. Legislators thus respond to organized groups with clear stakes in a policy and money to invest in politics (Grossman and Helpman 1994). However, legislators also are sensitive to unorganized constituencies via the election processes. Legislators calculate the distributional effects of a policy on voting constituencies within their districts and take positions on the policy that reflect these districts' interests (Denzau and Munger 1986; Arnold 1992; Bailey 2001). These calculations occur even in the absence of direct influence and lobbying, meaning that constituents don't actually have to vote on the basis of the policy for this mechanism to be effective.

IMF policy-makers and IMF policy

IMF decision-making procedures give the US executive director extraordinary influence. The absence of roll call voting at the IMF, however, makes it difficult to directly observe US positions and motivations. We cannot resolve this problem. What we can do is determine if IMF decisions are consistent with the motivations we uncover at the level of domestic politics. Specifically, we predict that the IMF will tend to give more support to countries in which US money-center banks have greater exposure. This assumes that the US executive director and/or the secretary of the Treasury are agents of these private actors. Scholars who report a "Wall Street connection" would have little difficulty with this assumption (e.g. Stiglitz 2002). However, it may also be the case that members of Congress, as agents of banking interests, or bankers themselves, communicate these policy goals to the Treasury Department. These paths of influence are depicted in figure 3.1.

DATA AND ANALYSIS: CONGRESSIONAL ROLL CALL VOTING ON IMF QUOTA INCREASES

Under the IMF's Articles of Agreement, a general review of the adequacy of Fund quota resources must be conducted at least every five years. If a review results in the approval of a quota increase, Congress must ratify the US increase. Historically, these requests for increases in the quota have been the occasion for rigorous congressional examinations of the IMF, its operations, and its loan programs. During these debates, members of Congress are occasionally required to vote. These roll calls provide a window into the politics of the IMF, and an opportunity to determine if constituency pressures are involved.

We analyze congressional votes on the quota increases that followed the IMF's Eighth and Eleventh General Review of Quotas, which occurred in 1983 and 1998, respectively. These were the only quota increases for which "clean" role call votes could be found.[11] Table 3.1 provides summary information on the roll call votes we analyze. These four votes represent the universe of clean roll calls on IMF funding since 1973.

Three of the votes (V286, V287, and V313) occurred in 1983 following the IMF's Eighth General Review. The context was the Latin American debt crisis, which provoked worries in Congress that a quota increase would fund a bailout of the commercial banks (Bordo and James 2000: 32). Our three votes were on amendments that would strip the omnibus spending bill of the IMF quota increase.

The fourth and most recent roll call (V109) involved a motion in 1998 to return $18 billion in new funding for the IMF to a House emergency supplemental spending bill. The House had stripped the IMF increase from the bill and the motion instructed the conference committee to return it, thus providing the IMF with $18 billion in new

---

[11] Congress typically includes IMF funding in large omnibus spending bills, which makes it difficult to isolate legislators' positions on the IMF issue. However, we were able to identify amendments and motions to the 1983 and 1998 spending bills that dealt exclusively with IMF quota increases. These are "clean" votes in the sense that a vote for or against reflects a member's position on increasing US contributions to the IMF.

Table 3.1. *IMF quota votes in the US Congress*

Roll call number	V286 H.AMDT. 306 (HR 2957)	V287 H.AMDT. 307 (HR 2957)	V313 H.AMDT.341 (HR 2957)	V109 Motion to Instruct Conferees (HR 3579)
Congress	98th	98th	98th	105th
Date	7/29/1983	7/29/1983	8/3/1983	4/23/1998
Sponsor	McCollum (R-FL)	Patman (D-TX)	Corcoran (R-IL)	Obey (D-WI)
Summary	To amend HR 2957 to strike the language authorizing the Governor of the IMF to consent to an increase in the quota of the United States. [A "no" vote is a vote in favor of the IMF quota increase.]	To amend HR 2957 to eliminate provisions in the bill requiring continued US participation in the IMF. [A "no" vote is a vote in favor of the IMF quota increase.]	To amend HR 2957 to strike the language that increases US participation in the IMF General Arrangements to Borrow from $2 billion to $4.25 billion, and authorizes the Secretary to consent to an increase of the US quota in the IMF. [A "no" vote is a vote in favor of the IMF quota increase.]	To allow the House and Senate to pass identical spending bills, providing the IMF with $18 billion for quota increase and to establish the New Arrangements to Borrow (NAB). [A "yes" vote is a vote in favor of the IMF quota increase.]
Result	Y = 182 N = 227	Y = 178 N = 226	Y = 174 N = 249	Y = 186 N = 222
Partisan split	Dem: Y = 90, N = 158 Rep: Y = 92, N = 69	Dem: Y = 89, N = 155 Rep: Y = 89, N = 71	Dem: Y = 82, N = 177 Rep: Y = 92, N = 72	Dem: Y = 164, N = 28 Rep: Y = 22, N = 193

US commitments. On April 23, 1998, Congress defeated Obey's motion by a vote of 186 to 222, stalling the appropriation of funds for the IMF for another six months.

We have two hypotheses. First, we expect the probability a House member will vote in favor of the IMF quota call to increase with a member's affinity with money-center banks. Money-center banks are among the most direct beneficiaries of IMF rescues, and legislators with ties to these banks, as proxied by campaign contributions, will support their policy preferences. Second, we expect variation in skill levels of constituents across House districts to influence member voting. Specifically, we anticipate that the higher (lower) the skill level of constituents, the more likely a member will be to vote for (against) the IMF quota increase. This captures our argument that members relate to the IMF as an organization that promotes global economic integration, and take positions on IMF votes that reflect how diffuse constituencies fare distributionally from globalization.

To identify money-center banks, we use the regulatory classification in the Federal Financial Institutions Examination Council's (FFIEC) "Country Exposure Lending Survey." The FFIEC compiles data on the international exposure of US banks and aggregates these data into two categories, "money-center" banks and "other banks," for confidentiality reasons. Because the FFIEC survey identifies the specific banks that comprise the money-center group, we were able to obtain a list on which to base our collection of campaign contribution data. For campaign contributions, we use the Federal Election Commission's data on contributions from Political Action Committees (PACs). Each money-center bank identified by the FFIEC maintains a PAC to channel funds to members of Congress. Our constructed variable is BANK_PAC: the sum of campaign contributions from all money-center banks to a House member in the two electoral cycles preceding the IMF quota vote.

We measure constituent skill levels in two ways: by educational attainment and by occupational classification. COLLEGE is the share of district population with four years of college. SKILLS is the percentage of district workers in executive, administrative, managerial, professional, and professional specialty occupations (see the Appendix for variable descriptions and sources).

Table 3.2 presents results from Probit analyses of the three 1983 roll calls (robust Huber/White standard errors are in parentheses). In Models 1–3, we control only for member "ideology" as proxied by a member's first dimension DW-NOMINATE score (Poole and Rosenthal

Table 3.2. *Probit analyses of IMF quota votes in the 98th Congress*

	(1)	(2)	(3)	(4)
DV: 1 = Yes 0 = No (a no vote *favors* IMF quota)	V286	V287	V313	V313 (add'l controls)
Constant	0.804***	0.836***	0.640***	0.305
	(0.203)	(0.204)	(0.198)	(0.338)
DW-Nominate	1.885***	1.835***	1.788***	1.785***
	(0.201)	(0.204)	(0.192)	(0.195)
Bank_PAC	−0.212***	−0.237***	−0.180***	−0.186***
	(0.049)	(0.054)	(0.047)	(0.049)
College	−13.165***	−13.820***	−12.204***	−14.307***
	(3.3)	(3.332)	(3.225)	(4.044)
Income				0.025
				(0.024)
Mexican Origins				0.756
				(0.69)
Observations	409	404	423	423
Prob > chi^2	0.0000	0.0000	0.0000	0.0000
Log Likelihood	−218.035	−215.778	−227.955	−226.932

Robust standard errors in parentheses

Note: * significant at 10%; ** significant at 5%; *** significant at 1%

1997). The first dimension of the DW-Nominate score is usually interpreted as capturing a member's ideological position on government intervention in the economy. We include it to pick up some of the individual attributes that sway member voting. Since higher values denote a more "conservative" ideology, we expect a positive sign on the regression coefficients – more conservative members should oppose increasing the IMF resources because IMF bailouts create moral hazard, and have other ill effects on incentives. While we find evidence of this effect, our variables of interest, BANK_PAC and COLLEGE, are invariably correctly signed and highly significant. The more campaign contributions from banks and the higher the education level in a district, the more likely a member is to vote against the amendments stripping the IMF of its quota increase. In Model 4, we include controls for district INCOME (median household income) and MEXICAN ORIGINS (share of district population of Mexican ancestry). The later control is intended to capture any effect that proximity to Mexico – the first victim of the

US domestic politics and IMF policy

Table 3.3. *Probit analyses of IMF quota votes in the 98th Congress (robustness)*

	(1)	(2)	(3)	(4)
DV: 1 = Yes 0 = No (a no vote *favors* IMF quota)	V286	V287	V313	V313 (add'l controls)
Constant	1.334***	1.156***	1.247***	1.118***
Party	−0.670***	−0.621***	−0.756***	−0.759***
	(0.136)	(0.136)	(0.134)	(0.136)
Bank_PAC	−0.217***	−0.234***	−0.190***	−0.193***
	(0.052)	(0.057)	(0.049)	(0.049)
Skills	−2.645***	−2.227***	−2.522***	−2.517***
	(0.758)	(0.801)	(0.719)	(0.785)
Income				0.006
				(0.02)
Mexican Origins				0.722
				(0.713)
Observations	409	404	423	423
Prob > chi^2	0.0000	0.0000	0.0000	0.0000
Log likelihood	−252.851	−250.786	−256.952	−256.385

Robust standard errors in parentheses

Note: * significant at 10%; ** significant at 5%; *** significant at 1%

debt crisis – might have on member voting. Our core results are not affected by the inclusion of these controls.

As a robustness check, we ran Probits using alternative measures of district skill level and member ideology. Table 3.3 contains results substituting SKILLS (share of population working in high-skills industries) for college attainment and PARTY (1 = Dem, 0 = Rep) for DW-Nominate scores. Our findings are robust to these substitutions.

The vote on Obey's 1998 motion (V109, 105th Congress) would seem to be a difficult one for our argument since members voted very strongly along party lines – only 28 Democrats and 22 Republicans broke ranks with their parties. Nevertheless, our main variables are signed correctly (positive, since a "yes" vote on Obey's motion would fund the IMF) and significant in several alternative models, as shown in table 3.4. Model 1 controls for member ideology with DW-Nominate. We prefer Model 2, which controls for PARTY, since this model has better explanatory power, as indicated by the reduced log-likelihood ratio, and directly controls for

Principal preferences, structure, decision rules, and private benefits

Table 3.4. *Probit analyses of IMF quota votes in the 105th Congress*

	(1)	(2)	(3)
DV: 1 = Yes 0 = No (a yes vote *favors* IMF quota)	V109	V109	V109
Constant	−0.508**	−2.186***	−1.854***
	(0.236)	(0.288)	(0.359)
DW-Nominate	−2.678***		
	(0.215)		
Party		2.526***	2.519***
		(0.177)	(0.18)
Bank_PAC	0.015**	0.021***	0.020**
	(0.007)	(0.008)	(0.008)
College	2.120*	3.539***	2.908**
	(1.125)	(1.127)	(1.2)
Net Imports			−2.218**
			(1.121)
Net Exports			1.423
			(1.99)
Mexican+Korean+Thai			0.322
			(0.683)
Observations	408	407	407
Prob > chi^2	0.0000	0.0000	0.0000
Log likelihood	−151.497	−140.859	−138.867
Robust standard errors in parentheses			

Note: * significant at 10%; ** significant at 5%; *** significant at 1%

the partisan nature of the vote. Model 3 adds variables that reflect potentially relevant district characteristics. MEXICAN+KOREAN+THAI is the share of district population of ethnic groups originally from three countries that suffered major currency crises in the 1990s. Our estimates do not support a relationship. NET IMPORTS and NET EXPORTS capture the effect of district industrial characteristics. Members representing districts that face strong import competition are expected to oppose funding the IMF, since the Fund pursues an essentially pro-trade mandate. Members with export-oriented industries in their districts, on the other hand, should support IMF funding (see Appendix for construction of these variables). Our results provide partial support for this argument, as NET IMPORTS is both negative and significant.

In table 3.5, we provide a substantive interpretation of the results and a sense of the magnitude of the effects. Using models from tables 3.3

US domestic politics and IMF policy

Table 3.5. *Substantive effects of campaign contributions from money-center banks, district skill levels, and House member "ideology"*

	Bank_PAC	College	DW-Nominate	Party
V286 (98th Cong) Table 2, Model 1	0.179***	0.112***	−0.267***	
V287 (98th Cong) Table 2, Model 2	0.194***	0.117***	−0.262***	
V313 (98th Cong) Table 2, Model 3	0.146***	0.098***	−0.258***	
V109 (105th Cong) Table 4, Model 1	0.059**	0.07*	−0.344***	
V109 (105th Cong) Table 4, Model 2	0.079***	0.115***		−0.788***

Notes: Values represent the *change* in the predicted probability of voting in favor of an IMF quota increase ("no" on V286, V287, V313, and "yes" on V109) as each variable of interest is increased by one standard deviation over its mean, holding other variables at their means. "Party" indicates the change in predicted probability of moving from a Democrat to a Republican (from 1 to 0).
*$p < .10$, ** $p < .05$, *** $p < .01$

and 3.5, we simulated the predicted probability of observing a vote in favor of increasing the IMF quota, and then examined how the predicted probabilities *change* as our explanatory variables increase one standard deviation from their means, holding all other variables at their mean values.[12] The effects are substantively large. For example, a one-standard-deviation increase in BANK_PAC, the measure of campaign contribution from money-center banks, increases the likelihood that a member will support IMF funding by 17.9 percentage points in the case of V286 (table 3.2, Model 1). Note that the effect is smaller in the case of the 1998 vote (V109, Models 1 and 2), but still not trivial. The average effect (across all five models) of increasing campaign contributions by one standard deviation is to increase the probability of supporting the IMF by 13.1 percentage points.

We obtain similarly large substantive effects for COLLEGE, our measure of district skill levels. Increasing the share of district population with a college diploma by one standard deviation increases the probability a member will support IMF funding by 10.2 percentage points, on average (11.2 points on V286, 11.7 points on V287, 9.8 points on V313, 7 points

[12] The simulations were performed with Clarify, a statistical software program (Tomz et al. 1998; King et al. 2000).

Principal preferences, structure, decision rules, and private benefits

on V109, Model 1, and 11.5 points on V109, Model 2). Note that the effects are quite large even where PARTY has an overwhelming impact on voting (V109, Model 2).

Discussion

The positive relationship between campaign contributions from money-center banks and member support for the IMF clashes with research on contributions from special interests more generally: there is little evidence that campaign money influences member voting (Hall and Wayman 1990; Snyder 1992; Wright 1996). One possibility is that contributions from banks are different than money from other sources. For example, the banking industry is one of the largest contributors to member campaigns. Commercial banks rank in the top ten in terms of total giving (PAC, individual, soft money) to Congress among more than 80 industries (Makinson 2003). This may help explain why our study and others (e.g. Kroszner and Stratmann 1998) find an effect of bank money on congressional roll call voting. However, our estimates on bank campaign money may also be inflated due to some unmodeled constituency effect. Perhaps member voting is tied to the importance of international banking activity in a district. To control for this, we added a dummy variable for districts that are home to money-center banks (in downtown New York, Chicago, Boston, and San Francisco). We also created a variable to capture the importance of banking in employment terms, as the share of a district's population employed in large commercial banks. Neither of these variables was significant, and their inclusion did not affect the size or significant level of BANK_PAC.

A broader concern is whether special interests target members with similar positions or "buy votes" when they give contributions (Hall and Wayman 1990; Bronars and Lott 1997). We are agnostic on this issue. It makes little difference to our argument whether banks give money to reward members who share their policy preferences or give money to sway their votes; either way, the money is an observable indication of a relationship in which members are more likely to vote the way banks want. Nevertheless, the relatively small sums involved do not suggest that banks are directly buying votes. With members receiving $952 on average from banks in the 1981–84 electoral cycles (with a maximum of $20,200), they would be selling their votes very cheaply relative to the benefits. In light of these small numbers, campaign contributions might be understood as a form of political participation, like voting or attending a political rally (Ansolabehere, et al. 2003).

Our other finding, that higher district skill levels increase the probability a member will support the IMF, is also open to alternative explanations. Our interpretation is that member positions on rescues reflect the relative wage effects of globalization on district constituencies. However, the result also could suggest that more educated constituents are more "cosmopolitan," and therefore better able to understand the need for international financial rescues. But while a college education or a high skill occupation could give rise to an internationalist outlook, there is no compelling reason why these attributes imply support for rescues. Academic economists are divided on the issue, with a handful taking public stances against rescues on moral hazard grounds (Calomiris 1998; Meltzer 1998; Schwartz 1998). More education might make people more likely to support other foreign economic policies, like trade liberalization, where the overwhelming majority of academic opinion favors free trade. But on rescues, no such unanimity exists. Therefore it is difficult to attribute the results on skill endowments to the constituents' level of education.

Our argument also requires that constituents and members of Congress understand the connections between IMF rescues and economic globalization, and between globalization and relative income shares. Do people really connect the dots that run from the IMF bailouts preserving global economic integration to economic integration having distributional consequences? Evidence from peak organizations, industry groups, and congressional testimony suggests they do. For example, organized labor connected the dots when the executive council of the AFL-CIO adopted a resolution in 1998 urging Congress to reject US participation in the IMF unless borrowers adopted strict labor standards: "The IMF defines its mission narrowly, as protecting the interests of international capital". . . it should be reformed to ensure that bailout programs serve a broader set of social and economic goals, including "commitment to and vigorous enforcement of international labor and human rights." Corporate organizations and export interests connect the dots by taking pro-IMF stances, as when the US Chamber of Commerce included a Senate vote on IMF funding (S 1768) in its 1998 legislator ratings. The Chamber strongly supported IMF funding "as a way to aid financially troubled nations whose economic health impacts businesses in the United States" (US Chamber of Commerce 1998: 4). Socialist Congressman Bernie Sanders of Vermont also connected the dots:

What precedent is this [Asian] bailout setting, and what does it say about our role in the globalization of the international economy? If the U. S. Government cannot protect millions of workers, small business people, and family farmers in this country . . . should we really be responding to every bank and business failure throughout the world? America must rethink the nature of our relationship to the global economy – and our obligation to millions of needy Americans. (Sanders 1997)

IMF LENDING PATTERNS

We have shown evidence suggesting a relationship between campaign contributions by money-center banks and congressional voting on IMF issues. In this section, we check to see if money-center bank influence carries through to IMF policy decisions. Our findings suggest that IMF lending decisions are correlated with the size of US commercial banks' loans outstanding in IMF member countries. Our analysis focuses on the relationship between US banks and the IMF, but not exclusively. As decision-making in international organizations is often the product of collective bargaining between powerful members (Lyne, Nielson, and Tierney, this volume), we begin with US banks, and then extend the analysis to include the loan exposures of banks from other major IMF donors (England, France, Germany, and Japan).

Two questions about IMF behavior motivate the analysis. First, does the extent of commercial bank loan exposure make the IMF more likely to bail out a country facing a currency or debt crisis? Second, with all other factors being equal, does greater private bank loan exposure induce the IMF to provide larger loans to a country? In order to examine these questions, we adopt a two-stage approach. In the first stage, we look solely at the decision by the IMF to offer assistance; in the second we examine the amount of assistance approved by the IMF. We treat the decision to lend as separate from the actual amount of assistance because of the potential for endogeneity: the decision to support a country may serve as a "seal of approval," inducing further lending from the private sector.

Our data set spans twenty years, from 1983 to 2002. During this period, the IMF approved 369 loans under the Stand-By and Extended Fund Facilities (EFF) programs, with an average loan size of 636 million Special Drawing Rights (SDRs). In the first stage of our analysis, our dependent variable is a binary variable, representing whether or not a member country received an IMF loan in a given year. In the second stage, we analyze the size of IMF loans approved for member countries.

As our prior analysis focused on the ties between money-center banks and the US Congress, the chief explanatory variable for this part of the analysis is the country exposures of these same money-center banks abroad. For reasons of confidentiality, individual banks do not disclose the geographic profile of their foreign loans. However, the Federal Financial Institutions Examination Council (FFIEC) does collect, aggregate, and publish this information for the *group* of money-center banks, in order to track the overall lending behavior of these banks. Thus, our key independent variable is the amount owed to US money-center banks by each IMF member country (US_BANKS).[13] Furthermore, since the United States is not the only major international lender with a strong voice in IMF decision-making, we also include the foreign lending behavior of major banks from England, France, Germany, and Japan.

Our theory does not lead us to predict that increased private-sector bank lending will necessarily *cause* a country to require IMF assistance, but rather, that of those countries experiencing debt or currency crises in a given year, the IMF will be more likely to provide assistance to those members with larger debts to banks in the Fund's top-five donor countries. Consequently, in order to predict IMF lending behavior, we must include in our model the principal variables used to predict and identify sovereign debt and currency crises that might lead countries to need IMF assistance in the first place.

Economists at the IMF and elsewhere have developed models of currency and debt crises in order to establish an Early-Warning-System (EWS) that can be used by the Fund in its surveillance of the world's economies. EWS models use economic and political variables in order to predict economic crises before they occur. Kaminsky, Lizondo, and Reinhart (1997) critically review EWS models and identify the economic indicators that yield the best predictive power. Drawing on their conclusions, we include several economic indicators related to the countries' overall debt, debt profile, international reserves, and economy in our analysis to obtain a more accurate and realistic model of IMF lending behavior. We also include an indicator of financial crises, generated by Caprio and Klingebiel (2003). Since receipt of IMF assistance is an indication of economic instability, and since that instability may persist

---

[13] These figures represent the total amount of loans by US money-center banks outstanding in the IMF member country. As there is significant annual variation in total money-center bank lending, while lending patterns to individual countries remain relatively constant, we have elected *not* to scale this variable as a percentage of the total banks' annual lending portfolio, instead opting for the more stable actual dollar amounts.

beyond the duration of the Fund's assistance, we also include a dummy variable representing whether a member country has received any Stand-By or EFF loans over the prior decade.

International politics may also affect IMF decision-making. To control for these influences, we follow Barro and Lee (2002) and include UN voting affinity scores for Fund member countries vis-à-vis the major powers.[14] Similarly, we include loans from the World Bank, on the grounds that IMF might be more willing to lend to countries that are receiving development assistance from the World Bank. A set of additional controls round out the model: year dummies, a time trend, and dummy variables for regions and economic groupings (e.g. Latin America, Africa, developed countries, as well as countries belonging to the British Commonwealth and the French *Francophonie*).

Data and analysis: IMF outcomes

We expect greater commercial bank exposure to increase the likelihood of IMF assistance for countries in economic crises. To evaluate this claim, we ran a time-series cross-section Logit model of our binary dependent variable (if a member country received an IMF loan in a given year) on our independent variables and controls. The results, presented in table 3.6, provide modest support for our argument.[15] The baseline model includes all variables except UN affinity scores, our proxies for "international politics." Note that including UN affinity scores has little substantive effect on our results. In both models, the exposure of US money center banks (US_BANKS) is positively and significantly (at the 10 percent level) related to the likelihood that the IMF will provide a loan to a country, other factors considered. Substantively, the estimate suggests that a one standard deviation increase in US bank loan exposure (roughly $4 billion) increases the probability of receiving an IMF loan by approximately 3.4 percent.

When we consider the loan exposures of banks from Britain, France, Germany, and Japan, the results are less consistent. While the coefficient for German private bank loan exposure (GERMANY_BANKS) is

---

[14] Affinity scores for Germany are unavailable.
[15] Our substantive results are stable across methodological specifications. We obtained nearly identical results (in sign, magnitude, and level of significance) for our indicator of US bank lending using robust standard-errors, fixed-effect estimators, and controls for temporal auto-correlation.

Table 3.6. *Random effects logit of IMF decisions to lend*

DV: IMF decision to lend (1 = Yes, 0 = No)	(1) Baseline model	(2) Base with UN affinity scores
US_Banks	.155*	.172**
	(.080)	(.088)
UK_Banks	−.122	−.029
	(.090)	(.100)
France_Banks	−.053	.016
	(.121)	(.141)
Germany_Banks	.296***	.260**
	(.102)	(.110)
Japan_Banks	−.143	−.060
	(.096)	(.088)
Prior IMF loans	.790**	1.30***
	(.347)	(.380)
Financing	.103**	.056
	(.048)	(.052)
IBRD loans	.200	.084
	(.179)	(.127)
Short-Term Debt	−.029**	−.054***
	(.013)	(.017)
Reserves/Imports	.019	−.042
	(.051)	(.057)
Debt	−.379	−.393
	(.310)	(.300)
Money_Supply/Reserves	.014*	.010
	(.008)	(.007)
Trade	.011**	.010**
	(.005)	(.005)
Debt_Service	.385*	.182
	(.221)	(.219)
US_TBill	.183	.268
	(.123)	(.193)
Reserves (Change)	2.40e-11	9.22e-12
	(3.40e-11)	(5.29e-11)
Economic Crisis Dummy	.637	.275
	(.259)	(.291)
US_UN_Affinity		2.15
		(1.80)
UK_UN_Affinity		−2.52
		(5.47)
France_UN_Affinity		−.042
		(5.57)
Japan_UN_Affinity		4.33
		(3.45)

(continued)

Table 3.6 *(continued)*

DV: IMF decision to lend (1 = Yes, 0 = No)	(1) Baseline model	(2) Base with UN affinity scores
Observations	951	675
Groups	96	89
Log likelihood	−375.02	−252.2
Standard errors in parentheses		

Note: * significant at 10%; ** significant at 5%; *** significant at 1%

positive and significant, those for Britain, France, and Japan vary in sign, and are statistically insignificant. These results appear to suggest that the United States and Germany exert a dominant influence on Fund decision-making. However, these indicators exhibit a high degree of multicollinearity. Britain, France, Germany, and Japan are all home to major international banks with lending portfolios that strongly reflect US bank lending. Correlations between US lending and these other countries' bank lending range from $r = 0.45$ to $r = 0.60$. Despite this overlap, which may lead to underestimation of foreign influence in Fund decision-making, we include these other countries' lending exposures because it is unrealistic to assume that these countries do not affect IMF decisions. Combined, they constitute another 23 percent of voting rights on the IMF, endowing them with clout similar to that of the United States in Fund decision-making.[16]

Our second hypothesis relates to the *size* of IMF loans given to countries that receive Stand-By or EFF assistance. Using the same economic indicators and control variables, we expected to see a positive relationship between the amount of US (and other contributors') bank lending to a country and the size of the loan it receives from the IMF. As our cases are now limited to just those countries receiving IMF assistance, our sample size drops to 165.

The results, presented in table 3.7, suggest that the amount of IMF support a country receives is positively and significantly (at the .05 level) related to US commercial bank exposure.[17] According to this model, an increase in the size of US lending of one standard deviation yields an

---

[16] Pooling the lending portfolios of Britain, France, Germany, and Japan into a single "foreign lending" indicator does not substantially alter the results for our key explanatory variable (in sign, magnitude, or level of significance).

[17] As with our first-stage analysis, our statistical results are stable across alternate specifications.

Table 3.7. *OLS panel estimates of the size of IMF loans*

DV: Amount of IMF loan	(1) Baseline model	(2) Base with UN affinity scores
US_Banks	.119**	.124*
	(.053)	(.069)
UK_Banks	.026	.046
	(.061)	(.086)
France_Banks	−.142*	−.201
	(.076)	(.135)
Germany_Banks	.049	.031
	(.064)	(.088)
Japan_Banks	−.006	.057
	(.057)	(.074)
Prior IMF Loans	−.503**	−.392
	(.214)	(.252)
Financing	.092***	.086**
	(.035)	(.042)
IBRD	−.189	−.137
	(.129)	(.169)
Short-Term Debt	−.023***	.019
	(.008)	(.015)
Reserves/Imports	.007	−.016
	(.038)	(.046)
Debt	.402**	−.345
	(.195)	(.281)
Money_Supply/Reserves	−.004	−.003
	(.004)	(.005)
Trade	−.007**	−.007
	(.003)	(.005)
Debt_Service	.467***	.375*
	(.149)	(.210)
US_TBill	.108	.079
	(.098)	(.148)
Economic Crisis Dummy	.436***	.174
	(.155)	(.192)
US Bank Total Lending	−.712***	−.657*
	(.264)	(.395)
US_UN_Affinity		−1.91
		(1.22)
UK_UN_Affinity		2.44
		(3.68)
France_UN_Affinity		−1.44
		(4.36)
Japan_UN_Affinity		1.29
		(2.55)

(continued)

Principal preferences, structure, decision rules, and private benefits

Table 3.7 *(continued)*

DV: Amount of IMF loan	(1) Baseline model	(2) Base with UN affinity scores
Observations	165	116
Groups	58	50
Prob > Chi^2	0.00	0.00
Standard errors in parentheses		

Note: * significant at 10%; ** significant at 5%; *** significant at 1%

increase in the IMF loan of approximately 1.5 million SDRs. The results for other countries' lending portfolios were inconsistent across models, and statistically insignificant. This seems to suggest that the IMF policies do reflect the interests of major private actors within its powerful members, and that lending practices of US banks may have greater influence on Fund decision-making than that of their foreign counterparts.

CONCLUSION

Our foray into the political economy of the IMF helps resolve some issues, but raises others. We began by identifying the private actors within large member countries that have pecuniary stakes in IMF activities. This step is often ignored in the study of international organizations, even though such organizations are nearly always created and maintained through domestic legislation in powerful member states. We then established that the organized segment of this constituency, money-center banks, actively participates in domestic politics by supplying legislators with campaign funds. Judging from our empirical results, members of Congress appear, in turn, to be responsive to these appeals, as well as to the interests of unorganized groups benefited or harmed by the IMF's pro-globalization mandate. The final link in the causal chain was to analyze IMF outcomes. Although our results at this level provide some support for the argument that the IMF acts in ways that reflect the interests of money-center banks, our evidence is modest and indirect. We have no direct evidence showing that the US executive director at the Fund is a dutiful agent of Congress. We have no direct evidence that Congress compels the US delegate to advance the interests of private international banks. In fact, we have ignored a level of delegation that is probably crucial to IMF outcomes: the delegation from Congress to the executive branch that gives the US Treasury secretary and the US executive director the predominant authority for the day-to-day business of the Fund.

We justify our lack of attention to this agency relationship in the standard, unsatisfying way: one need not actually observe monitoring and punishment for principals to effectively control agents, because foresightful agents *anticipate* the boundaries of acceptable action and stay within them. Is this how the supposed "Wall Street connection" actually operates to promote the interests of the international investment community? We are certain only that more research is necessary.

Overall, our multilevel arguments and statistical tests provide some insight into the complex relationship between private actors and the IMF. This relationship begins with the distributional goals of private actors and moves to the domestic legislatures of powerful member governments via the electoral connection. However, on all but the most important IMF decisions (e.g. quota increases), national legislatures have no direct influence over policy. As an international organization, the IMF is not subject to domestic law. Therefore, legislatures like the US Congress must work through their agents at the IMF to influence Fund policy. In researching this chapter, we found dozens of US laws formally requiring the US executive director to use his "voice and vote" at the IMF to pursue congressional goals. Our sense of the anecdotal evidence is that the US executive director has a good deal of flexibility in deciding how to interpret and implement these mandates. In short, the US executive director is far from a perfect agent of Congress. Yet, even though the chain of delegation may be long and indirect, the evidence we found suggests that domestic politics may influence policy-making by international organizations.

Appendix: data and sources

Africa: Dummy variable indicating African countries.

ASEAN: Dummy variable indicating countries that are a member of the Association of South East Asian Nations.

Bank_PAC: Campaign contributions from money-center bank political action committees to candidates in the two electoral cycles preceding the roll call votes. Money-center banks are identified by the Federal Financial Institutions Examination Council (FFIEC), *Country Exposure Lending Survey*. PAC contributions are from the Federal Election Commission.

Principal preferences, structure, decision rules, and private benefits

College: Share of district population with four years of college (*Congressional Districts of the United States*, US Bureau of the Census).

Commonwealth: Dummy variable indicating countries that are members of the British Commonwealth (http://www.thecommonwealth.org/).

Debt: Total external debt owed to non-residents repayable in foreign currency, goods, or services. Includes publicly guaranteed and private non-guaranteed long-term debt, IMF credit, and short-term debt (debt with a maturity of one year or less and interest in arrears on long-term debt). In current US dollars (*World Development Indicators* (WDI)).

Debt_Service: Public and publicly guaranteed debt service. The sum of principal repayments and interest paid on long-term obligations of public debtors and long term private obligations guaranteed by a public entity. In current US dollars (WDI).

Developed Countries: Dummy variable for developed economies.

DW-Nominate: The first dimension of the DW-Nominate score, which is interpreted as capturing a member's ideological position on government intervention in the economy. Higher values denote a more conservative ideology (McCarty et al. 1997).

Economic Crisis Dummy: Dummy variable indicating whether or not the country experienced a systemic banking crisis during that year (Caprio and Klingebiel 2003).

Financing: Financing from abroad (obtained from non-residents). Includes all government liabilities (other than those for currency issues or demand, time, or savings deposits with government) or claims on others held by government and changes in government holdings of cash and deposits but excludes government guarantees of the debt of others. Central government only (WDI).

France_Banks: Total foreign claims of French banks on individual countries, in millions of US dollars (BIS).

France_UN_Affinity: Voting affinity score of countries relative to the French position in the United Nations General Assembly (Gartzke and Jo 2002).

Francophonie: Dummy variable indicating countries that are members of the French "Francophonie" (http://www.francophonie.org/membres/etats/).

Germany_Banks: Total foreign claims of German banks on individual countries, in millions of US dollars (BIS).

IBRD: The sum of International Bank for Reconstruction and Development (IBRD) and International Development Association (IDA) loans to a country, in current US dollars (WDI).

IMF Loans: Amount of IMF loans approved under the Stand-By and Extended Fund Facilities during the fiscal year, in millions of Special Drawing Rights (IMF Annual Reports 1983–2002).
Income: Median district household income (*Congressional Districts of the United States*).
Japan_Banks: Total foreign claims of Japanese banks on individual countries, in millions of US dollars (BIS).
Japan_UN_Affinity: Voting affinity score of countries relative to the Japanese position in the United Nations General Assembly (Gartzke and Jo 2002).
Latin America: Dummy variable indicating Latin American countries.
Mexican Origins: Share of district population of Mexican ancestry (*Congressional Districts of the United States*).
Mexican + Korean + Thai: Share of district population of Mexican, Korean, and Thai ancestry (*Congressional Districts of the United States*).
Money/Reserves: Money and quasi money (M2) to gross international reserves ratio (International Financial Statistics (IFS)). Gross international reserves include holdings of monetary gold, special drawing rights, reserves of IMF members held by the IMF, and holdings of foreign exchange under the control of monetary authorities (WDI).
Net Imports: Percent district population aged 16 years and over employed in net import industries. Net import industries are two-digit SIC manufacturing sectors where the ratio of imports to consumption is greater than the ratio of revenues from exports to total industry revenue (*County Business Patterns*, Bureau of the Census). County-level employment data was aggregated up to the congressional district level using the procedure in Baldwin and Magee (2000).
Net Exports: Percent district population aged 16 years and over employed in net export industries. Net export industries are two-digit SIC manufacturing sectors where the ratio of revenues from exports to total industry revenue is greater than the ratio of imports to consumption (*County Business Patterns*).
Party: 1 = Democrat; 0 = Republican.
Prior IMF Loans: Dummy variable indicating whether or not the country received IMF assistance during the prior ten years (IMF, various years).
Reserves: Change in net international reserves resulting from transactions on the current, capital, and financial accounts. Includes changes in monetary gold, SDRs, foreign exchange assets, reserve position in the IMF, and other claims on non-residents net of liabilities constituting

foreign authorities' reserves, and counterpart items for valuation changes and exceptional financing items. In current US dollars (WDI).

Short_Term_Debt: Short-term debt (percentage of total external debt). Short-term debt includes all debt having an original maturity of one year or less and interest in arrears on long-term debt (WDI).

Skills: Share of district population aged 16 years and over employed in executive, administrative, managerial, and professional specialty occupations (*Congressional Districts of the United States*).

Trade: Sum of exports and imports of goods and services, as a share of gross domestic product (WDI).

UK_Banks: Total foreign claims of UK banks on individual countries, in millions of US dollars (Bank for International Settlements, "Consolidated Foreign Claims on Reporting Country Banks on Individual Countries" (BIS)).

UK_UN_Affinity: Voting affinity score of countries relative to the British position in the United Nations General Assembly (Gartzke and Jo 2002).

US_Banks: Total amount owed US money-center banks by foreign borrowers (excluding revaluations gains on foreign exchange and derivative products) as of March 31 of the reporting year (FFIEC).

US Bank Total Lending: Total owed to US money-center banks by foreign borrowers (excluding revaluations gains on foreign exchange and derivative products) as of March 31 of the reporting year (FFIEC).

US_TBill: Nominal US Treasury Bill rate (IFS).

US_UN_Affinity: Voting affinity score of countries relative to the US position in the United Nations General Assembly. Voting affinity scores are measured on a −1 to 1 scale using Signorino and Ritter's "S" score, for three categories of voting behavior (with/abstain/against). A score of 1 indicates complete similarity of voting positions with the United States, while a score of −1 indicates complete dissimilarity of voting (Gartzke and Jo 2002).

Year Trend: Time trend variable, in years, from 1983 to 2002 with 1983 equal to 1.

4

Why multilateralism? Foreign aid and domestic principal-agent problems

HELEN V. MILNER

INTRODUCTION

Why do countries sometimes use multilateral strategies and institutions for pursuing their foreign policies? Since World War Two the advanced industrial countries – basically, the OECD countries – have chosen to distribute part of their foreign aid through multilateral organizations, such as the European Union (EU), World Bank, IMF, UN, and regional development banks (RDBs). In particular I want to understand why these countries have chosen to delegate varying amounts of aid to these international organizations over the past 40 years. The delegation of aid-giving to multilateral organizations is surprising; it reduces a country's control over its own foreign policy and has the potential to increase principal-agent problems associated with all spending programs. The other choice that these countries had was to use their own bilateral aid agencies to select projects and oversee aid expenditures, which was the traditional practice prior to the 1960s. So the question addressed is why delegate the provision of foreign aid to a multilateral organization instead of using traditional bilateral channels.[1]

I would like to especially thank Erica Gould, Ken Abbott, Robert Keohane, Mike Tierney, Lisa Martin, Alex Thompson, Dan Nielson, David Lake, Darren Hawkins, Barbara Koremenos, Ruth Ben-Artzi, and Peter Rosendorff for their comments, and all the participants at the conferences on Delegation to IOs, Radcliffe, Cambridge, MA, Dec. 13, 2002 and UCSD, La Jolla, CA, Sept. 19–20, 2003, also those at USC and at Duke University. Robert Trager, Megumi Naoi, Patrick Leblond, Qiang Zhou, and Thomas Kenyon have provided excellent research assistance. Research support for this project also came from the Center for Advanced Study in the Behavioral Sciences, Stanford, CA.

[1] In this volume Lyne, Nielson, and Tierney address a similar question by examining the US decision to delegate, and then rescind, such authority to the Inter-American

Principal preferences, structure, decision rules, and private benefits

The total amount of such multilateral aid is not inconsequential. For instance, the World Bank gives aid in two main forms. The International Bank for Reconstruction and Development (IBRD) uses its donor subscription base as collateral to borrow money on world capital markets, which it then lends at below market interest rates to developing countries. In 2001 the IBRD committed roughly $10.5 billion in low interest loans (World Bank 2001a). For the poorest who cannot afford even these rates, the bank makes interest-free credits available through its other arm. The International Development Association (IDA) of the World Bank, founded in 1960, gives out grants from moneys it collects from about 40 donor countries. In fiscal year 2001 it gave out roughly $6.8 billion in aid (World Bank 2001b). Donors must agree to replenish this money every three years. And it supplies only about 25 percent of total World Bank aid funds. In addition to these organizations, the EU, UN, and the RDBs provide substantial aid funds yearly.[2] For 1999, the EU's total commitments approached 8 billion euros (Holland 2002: 89).

The literature on foreign aid is large so I concentrate on that which discusses donor giving (not the impact on recipients) and multilateral (rather than bilateral) giving. The literature on donors focuses on a debate over the motivations of donors. Simplifying, this literature points to two main motivations: the satisfaction of recipient needs or of donor political goals. Does aid promote economic development and meet the needs of recipients, or does aid largely contribute to the foreign policy or economic interests of the donor? A large part of the literature finds that donor interests seem to better explain the nature and allocations of aid given (e.g. Alesina and Dollar 2000; Dudley and Montmarquette 1976; Maizels and Nissanke 1984; McKinlay and Little 1977, 1978;

Development Bank. As Ruggie (1993: 6–14) notes, multilateralism minimally involves the coordination of policies among three or more states. But substantively, it implies more: that behavior is coordinated on the basis of generalized organizing principles, which tend to entail both the indivisibility of the member's behavior for achieving their goals and some form of diffuse reciprocity, as opposed to specific forms.

[2] The RDBs are the African Solidarity Fund, African Development Bank, Asian Development, Central American Bank for Economic Integration, Andean Development Corporation, Caribbean Development Bank, East Caribbean Central Bank, Inter-American Development, Nordic Development Fund. The EBRD gives aid (as loans only) primarily to the ECE countries and Russia; this aid is classified as Official Aid (OA), not ODA; hence it is not counted here.

Burnside and Dollar 2000).[3] Much of this literature shows that the neediest countries do not receive the most aid and that much aid is tied to the donor's interests. As Alesina and Dollar (2000: 33) conclude, "the pattern of aid giving is dictated by political and strategic considerations. An inefficient, economically closed, mismanaged non-democratic former colony politically friendly to its former colonizer receives more foreign aid than another country with similar levels of poverty, a superior policy stance but without a past as a colony." More recent work, such as Lumsdaine (1993), has argued that humanitarian motivations are primary. A good deal of research suggests, however, that bilateral aid is more tied to donor interests than is multilateral aid, which is often more needs-based in its orientation. This debate remains important and vigorous, but it concerns us mainly in what it has to say about multilateral versus bilateral aid giving.

Why is aid given multilaterally? The existing literature, inspired largely by Rodrik (1996), suggests two principal reasons that make multilateral organizations superior to bilateral relationships. The first is an informational one. Since information about recipients is a collective good, it will tend to be underprovided by individual donors. Multilateral agencies are supposedly better at providing information, especially that necessary to monitor the recipient. The second argues that the interaction of multilateral organizations with recipient countries is less politicized than that between donor countries and recipients. If the multilateral organization has some autonomy from its member states, then it can better exercise aid in a conditional way, that is, by making aid conditional on policy changes, than can an individual donor. In addition, if a recipient can play numerous potential donors off one another, the donors may end up giving more aid and getting less influence. Under these conditions, a multilateral institution may be seen as an aid-giving cartel, designed to maximize the donors' influence by presenting a unified front to the recipients. As discussed in the introduction to this volume, multilateralism may be chosen to reduce policy externalities. But these reasons would seem to make multilateral aid preferable in most conditions, leading to the prediction that it should inexorably supplant

---

[3] Countries, of course, are often seen to differ in their motivations: the United States and France are usually characterized as pursuing their foreign policy goals, although of different types; Japan is often viewed as pursuing its economic interests, while Sweden is more attuned to recipient needs (Dudley and Montmarquette 1976; McKinlay 1979; McKinlay and Little 1977, 1978; Schraeder et al., 1998).

bilateral aid. This has not occurred; instead, most aid is still given bilaterally.[4] This fact suggests that only under certain conditions do acquiring better information, having less politicized relations, and forming an aid-giving cartel become important enough to justify multilateralism. Identifying these conditions is the next important step for advancing such claims. Moreover, since Rodrik's own data do not support these two claims strongly, we are left with an outstanding puzzle.

The argument here relies on domestic politics and principal-agent problems in the donor countries. It claims that the preferences of donor governments and their publics are likely to diverge. Donor governments desire to use foreign aid for political and economic purposes that are related to donor interests. Publics, however, are more interested in addressing the needs of the recipient countries, i.e. their economic development. Publics are reluctant to give their tax dollars for aid when it is controlled by their own government since they have a hard time monitoring the government and they know it has incentives to give aid politically. But since multilateral aid organizations are both reputed for giving more needs-based aid and cannot be as directly controlled by any government, publics will trust more in them to give higher quality aid. It is the fact that multilateral aid agencies have collective principals (Lyne, Nielson, and Tierney, this volume) that gives them their ability to help domestic leaders. When publics are more skeptical about aid, governments will find it in their interest to give more multilateral aid. By doing so, the public is more willing to allocate resources to foreign aid. All sides end up better off: the government can distribute a larger amount of aid than otherwise, and the public gets higher quality aid through multilateral allocation. As Darren Hawkins, David A. Lake, Daniel Nielson, and Michael J. Tierney claim in the introduction, multilateralism can serve a credibility enhancing function, but here a domestic one.

This chapter attempts to explain variations in the pattern of multilateral aid giving over time and across countries using this principal-agent theory of multilateral allocation. Data on multilateral aid exist for the 27 OECD donors, i.e. those in the OECD's Development Assistance Committee (DAC), for the period from 1960 to 1999; sixteen of these

---

[4] Only 12 percent of all of my country-year observations for the percentage of multilateral aid committed relative to total aid are greater than 50 percent. The median amount of multilateral aid committed relative to total aid is about 32 percent, meaning that bilateral aid-giving is the norm.

Foreign aid and domestic principal-agent problems

countries have continuous data over the 40-year period. The data show that public opinion toward aid is an important factor in the choice of allocation between multilateral and bilateral aid within donor countries. The more the public dislikes aid in the prior period, the more the government is induced to spend on multilateral aid in the next period. Multilateral aid thus helps solve a domestic principal-agent problem. Domestic politics may be a reason that governments choose to use multilateral international institutions.

THE PUZZLE? THE COSTS OF MULTILATERAL AID FOR DONOR COUNTRIES

A central purpose of the donation of foreign aid is to influence the recipient's policy choices or other behavior by providing the country with additional resources. These additional resources may be used to continue an existing policy which the donor approves. For instance, American lend-lease aid to Britain during World War Two was intended to increase British resources so that they would and could keep fighting the Nazis. More strongly, aid may be used to alter a recipient state's behavior or policies. The use of conditionality by the World Bank is an example. Aid is influential to the extent that its termination would affect (benefit or hurt) the recipient. It is, of course, a central form of positive sanctions and hence a primary tool of statecraft (Baldwin 1985).

The delegation of aid provision to an international institution is thus puzzling. Why would countries relinquish (some) control over their donations of aid if they are a useful instrument of statecraft? Multilateral aid has not supplanted bilateral aid. For the United States in the late 1990s, for instance, only 25 percent of its aid was multilateral; it is greater than that for many EU countries. It is just that since the 1960s the OECD countries have chosen to give both bilaterally and multilaterally. Historically, this is unusual.

There are at least two puzzles here. The decision by one country to channel its aid through an international institution, rather than donating it bilaterally, is puzzling since this is likely to increase the principal-agent problems facing donors. This choice adds another link in the chain of delegation involving foreign aid, and thus may exacerbate the principal-agent problems inherent in all government spending programs (Lake and McCubbins, this volume). Unless the country completely controls the international institution, it is unlikely that aid provision will be the same as if it were done bilaterally. There is bound to be some slippage between the desired goals of any one country and the actions of its agent, the international institution.

Second, in a multilateral setting the principal-agent problem becomes even more acute. As noted by other chapters in this volume (Martin; Lyne, Nielson, and Tierney), with many principals collectively trying to direct an international institution, the slippage between the goals of each country and the institution's final output will likely grow. For instance, the World Bank resembles a global cooperative, which is owned by member countries, and in which control is shared by these members. The size of a country's shareholding depends on the size of the country's economy relative to the world economy. Together, the largest industrial countries (the Group of Seven) have about 45 percent of the shares in the World Bank. Thus the rich countries have a good deal of influence over the Bank's policies and practices. The United States has the largest shareholding, at about 17 percent, which gives it the power to veto any changes in the Bank's capital base and Articles of Agreement (85 percent of the shares are needed to effect such changes). According to the Bank however, virtually all other matters, including the approval of loans, are decided by a majority of the votes cast by all members of the Bank. Hence even if the United States has an effective veto, it still cannot decide aid matters on its own; it must compromise with the other members of the Board – the Bank's collective principal, a fact which would seem to give the Bank greater latitude.

The OECD countries are a diverse set of principals with regard to foreign aid provision. They have distinct preferences regarding the amount, type, and distributive criteria for aid-giving. The Scandinavian countries donate much larger portions of their GDPs to aid and give this aid to a wide variety of countries with limited attention to their international political alliances; in contrast, the United States gives a much smaller portion of its wealth to aid and usually targets countries that are political allies. Sweden and Norway gave aid equivalent to 0.8 percent of the GDP in 2000; the United States gave only 0.1 percent of its GDP. The top three recipients of US aid are Russia, Egypt, and Israel; the top three for Sweden and Norway include Tanzania, Mozambique, and South Africa (OECD 2001).

Coordinating aid-giving among such countries is likely to be difficult, and costly. It is also likely to increase the range of outcomes that the agent can implement, and hence to decrease the control that each country exercises over the agent. As Hammond and Knott (1996) and Lyne, Nielson, and Tierney (this volume) show, if collective principals

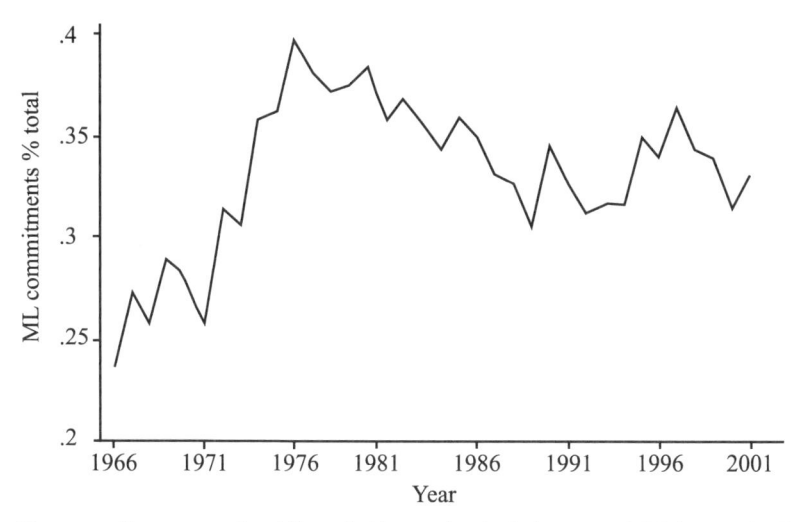

Foreign aid and domestic principal-agent problems

Figure 4.1. Percentage of multilateral aid committed relative to total ODA committed

have different preferences and coordination is costly, the best they can do often is to agree to limit the agency's discretion so that it cannot adopt a policy that is worse for any principal than the initial status quo. As these coordination costs rise or equivalently as the differences among the principals' preferences grow, the agency may gain autonomy. The point is that each OECD country is losing control over aid policy by delegating collectively to a multilateral international institution. As argued in the introduction, if member states are rational, it must be the case that the benefits of multilateral aid outweigh these costs.

As figure 4.1 shows, the average commitment of aid to multilateral organizations by OECD countries has varied over time.[5] As a percentage of total aid, it appears to have risen in the late 1960s and early 1970s, and then to have fallen from around 1976 to 1990. After 1990 it rose and fell, leaving the levels similar at the beginning and end of the decade.[6] It is also the case that countries change the amount that they

---

[5] The OECD defines multilateral aid as that made to an international institution whose members are governments and whose contributions are pooled with other amounts received so that they lose their identity and become an integral part of the institution's financial assets, and the pooled contributions are disbursed at the institution's discretion (OECD 1999: 81).

[6] All data on foreign aid are from the OECD (2001). See the data at http://www.oecd.org/dac/stats/. They are for annual multilateral commitments of aid by each country divided by total ODA commitments. Actual disbursements of aid follow a very

delegate to multilateral organizations over time. Interestingly, for example, Italy went from being in the bottom half of multilateral donors in the 1960s to being the biggest multilateral donor by the 1980s. This cross-national and longitudinal variation in multilateralism is the puzzle motivating this inquiry.

THE BENEFITS OF MULTILATERAL AID FOR DONOR COUNTRIES

Most authors seem to agree that multilateral giving will be different than bilateral aid. They suggest that multilateral aid will in itself be less attached to any country's foreign policy goals and more humanitarian in orientation. It is the collective principal relationship, as defined in the second chapter of this volume, that creates the possibility for multilateral aid agencies to be useful to donors. As Balogh noted almost 40 years ago, "bilateral aid was often based on irrelevant criteria aimed at political ends, subject to changes and interruptions from budget to budget, and thus unsatisfactory for [mitigating] inequality in the world . . . [There was also a] tendency for bilateral aid to be tied to grandiose projects when an equal or greater need was for general aid to overall programs of development" (1967: 328).

Since then, research has confirmed that multilateral and bilateral aid are quite different. For instance, multilateral aid tends to be given to poorer countries on average than does bilateral aid (Maizels and Nissanke 1984). As Lumsdaine (1993: 40) states, "Aid channeled through [multilateral] sources – almost a third of the total – could not even be identified as coming from a particular donor. Many donors consciously undertook to direct a large proportion of their aid to the neediest recipients, and multilateral institutions tended to favor large, poor recipients even more than bilateral aid programs." By and large, aid given through multilateral fora cannot be "tied" to purchases from a country's firms, hence undermining the pursuit of donor economic interests. As Martens et al. (2002: 47) note, "a multilateral agency may be able to [better] resist the pressure to make loans for purely political purposes than would the aid arm of a single country." Indeed, in the mid-1960s, Senator William Fulbright argued that all aid should be given multilaterally since this form was the only one that would truly promote

---

similar pattern, being correlated at about 0.85 with commitments. Later I discuss why I use commitments here.

Foreign aid and domestic principal-agent problems

economic development, but was never able to persuade any government of this (Balogh 1967: 328–29).[7]

In most of the debate on multilateral versus bilateral giving, states have been considered as unitary rational actors. But, as I have argued elsewhere, they may be better analyzed as collective entities composed of rational actors with different preferences (Milner 1997). This perspective allows us to see the strategic interaction within states as an important element of the aid delegation game.[8]

The redistribution of assets internationally is a policy that tends to have limited domestic support, especially when publics are asked to pay for it. Publics tend to have less sympathy for this goal than for similar ones at the domestic level. For instance, in 1998 the last Eurobarometer poll of 15 EU countries shows that on average for all countries over 31 percent think foreign aid should be decreased, and in countries like Belgium and Germany a majority preferred to decrease aid than to increase it even when they were not asked to pay for it. And in the United States a Gallup poll for 2000 showed that 47 percent desired to reduce foreign aid, while 49 percent wanted to keep it the same or increase it. Foreign aid then is not a policy where policy-makers can count on strong public support. However, most policy-makers realize that aid is an important element of foreign policy and desire to use this tool. In a democracy especially then foreign aid-giving may be subject to strong domestic pressures.

Foreign aid in general poses a principal-agent problem. Like all public spending, it involves long chains of delegation. Publics pay taxes to their governments who then spend this money on various programs including foreign aid. Hence publics first delegate to elected representatives decisions about the levels of taxation and allocations across different spending programs. Bureaucrats, who are the agents of the elected politicians, then implement these decisions. Multilateral delegation of aid adds a further link; aid moneys then pass through some multilateral organization which, as the donors' agent, makes decisions about the distribution

---

[7] A second point about multilateral aid is that it is often given for long periods of time. Moseley notes that "the very existence of multilateral aid agencies [means that] individual members' subscriptions to those multilateral bodies are contractually fixed several years in advance" (1985: 378). This process is contrasted with bilateral aid programs where yearly allocations are more common.

[8] See also Lyne, Nielson, and Tierney in this volume where domestic conflict between the President and Congress often affects the nature and the extent of delegation to both bilateral and multilateral aid agencies.

Principal preferences, structure, decision rules, and private benefits

of aid but then passes on to its agents the actual implementation of these decisions.

As Martens et al. (2002) claim, the main difference with foreign aid is that the final link in the feedback chain of delegation is broken. The foreign recipients cannot vote for more or less aid, nor can they usually express their opinion of whether the aid was useful or not and worth the tax monies. On the other side, the real donors – i.e. the publics who pay taxes – also cannot see for themselves how their aid monies were used.

> The most striking characteristic of foreign aid is that the same people for whose benefit aid agencies work are not the same as those from whom their revenues are obtained; they actually live in different countries and different political constituencies. This geographic and political separation between beneficiaries and taxpayers blocks the normal performance feedback process: beneficiaries may be able to observe performance but cannot modulate payments as a function of performance. (Martens et al. 2002: 14)

Therefore, foreign aid adds at least two elements to the delegation chain that are distinct from domestic spending programs. Longer chains of delegation and the fact that, unlike with domestic spending programs where voters can see for themselves the benefits of the spending, voters in donor countries cannot measure aid performance reliably mean additional principal-agent problems.

As the principal-agent literature points out, the two most prevalent problems arising from this relationship are moral hazard and adverse selection (e.g. Laffont and Martimort 2002; Martens et al. 2002). Moral hazard arises when agents take actions that are not fully observed by their principals and when these actions promote goals of the agents that differ from those of the principal. Adverse selection occurs when an agent has private information unknown to the principal that the agent manipulates to promote outcomes adverse to the principal's interests. All principal-agent relationships carry the potential for these sub-optimal outcomes, but in the foreign aid arena they are likely to be worse given the two problems noted above that make this area different.

In the foreign aid area, the information problems are extremely severe. Voters in the donor countries have an impossible time evaluating how aid is being used in the recipients. As noted above, the feedback loop is broken and the public paying taxes for aid has little knowledge to use to reward or punish their agents for foreign aid outcomes. Moreover, as Martens et al. (2002) show, moral hazard and adverse selection also arise in information provision about and evaluation of aid programs. Because of this, rational publics know that what their governments tell them about aid programs is going to be heavily biased. This information problem would not be as acute were it not for the fact that the agents' and principals' interests in aid are likely to diverge. But publics know that the slippage between their preferences for aid and those of their government may be substantial. And they know that their governments have private information about the benefits of aid. Because they know these problems exist, the public will be reluctant to support aid, i.e. to pay taxes for it.[9]

Consider a simple game between voters in a donor country and the agents of that voter, her government or executive branch. The public supports aid for needs-based reasons and is willing to pay taxes for that purpose, but prefers low levels of aid, if any, when it is used for political purposes. The executive likes aid for political purposes; it provides another foreign policy tool. And more tools are always better than fewer. The executive must also worry about the preferences of aid suppliers in the donor country. These interest groups are the direct beneficiaries of aid policies, and they are profit maximizers who give campaign contributions. These interest groups prefer aid for commercial reasons; that is, they want aid given in such a way that maximizes their profits. Agents' preferences vis-à-vis aid differ from those of their principals.

The quantity and quality of aid are linked in terms of actors' preferences. All actors worry about the quality of the aid given. Hoadley (1980) points out that the DAC has four quality targets for donor countries. First, grants are preferred to loans; roughly 84 percent of ODA is supposed to be grants, instead of loans. Second, DAC members should give at least 90 percent of this grant aid to the worst off countries. Third, donors should give less aid that is tied to donor purchases.[10] Last, aid should be given mostly to the very poorest countries to ensure that it is humanitarian aid. Each of these quality indicators implies aid that is less political, less commercial, and less tied to donor's self-interests, and more humanitarian and responsive to recipient needs. Multilateral

---

[9] In the concluding chapter of this volume, Lake and McCubbins specify the informational conditions for successful delegation.

[10] "The tying of aid is an act of self-interest designed to protect the donor's balance of payments, stimulate its private sector exports, and return a portion of aid to the treasury via taxation" (Hoadley 1980: 132).

organizations are far more likely to give aid according to these criteria than are bilateral aid programs, which are beset by special interest pressures and concerned with foreign policy problems.

In general, the public by a large majority in most countries prefers aid that is humanitarian to aid that is political. As Lumsdaine (1993: 43) points out, "Publics when asked consistently said aid should go to needy countries that would use it well rather than being used to promote narrow national interest. In one poll of ten European countries, 75 percent favored giving aid to the neediest LDCs rather than those of strategic, political, or economic importance to their own countries." And a recent study of public opinion toward aid (McDonnell, et al. 2003: 20) points out that "In most cases, the overwhelming [public] support for foreign aid is based upon the perception that it will be spent on remedying humanitarian crises."

For the executive, of course, the political nature of aid is what makes it a foreign policy tool; hence the executive is not likely to appreciate a purely humanitarian approach to aid. Moreover, as special interest groups grow in importance to donor executives, their desire for commercially oriented aid will also make executives use aid for reasons opposed by donor publics. As noted above, multilateral organizations, however, tend to give aid in more humanitarian ways, or at least in ways that are less tied to any single donor's self-interest and are surely less commercial. Multilateral aid is going to be closer to the public's preferences.

The government will often have preferences that differ from voters' and face pressures to take actions that diverge from the optimal aid policy preferred by voters. First, capture by interest groups can divert leaders from the policy most preferred by its principal, the voters. Second, governments may also desire to use aid to promote their general foreign policy goals, many of which may have no relation to the needs of the recipients. The government controls what information is given to the public about the results of foreign aid spending. The information about the performance of aid spending is private information held by the government; that is, publics have a hard time knowing how their governments allocated aid, and whether that aid served donor interests or those of the recipient. The principal-agent relationship makes it likely that the government will present only biased information to the public.

The public knows this and hence has little way to judge the performance of aid and thus the benefits that it derives from paying for it. As a recent study of foreign aid and public attitudes toward it claims, more than other policies, international development cooperation is characterized by a large gap between its opacity for the public, and its relevance for this very public's concerns about global "bads" (epidemics, threats to the environment, financial instability and crises, etc.) and "goods" (the call for greater justice at the global level). . . . Greater transparency of international development policies in donor countries, as well as a stepping up of efforts towards accountability of public authorities, are thus needed. (McDonnell et al. 2003: 30)

Because of these information problems, taxpayers will tend to believe that the benefits of aid are less than political leaders say and thus they will be unwilling to provide as much aid as may be optimal from their point of view. As Smillie et al. claim about public opinion toward aid,

Typically more aware of its failures than its successes, people were concerned that aid is being wasted. Not only do [voters feel that] global problems seem to be getting worse, but "bureaucratic bungling and mismanagement" have diverted assistance away from those who most need it, and have given way to a legacy of "horror stories about rusty tractors and railways to nowhere."

(Smillie et al. 1998: 23)

Political leaders know that this is how voters think. They desire to have a foreign aid budget and will thus try to find ways to publicly commit to an aid regime that provides higher benefits to voters. Multilateral aid programs provide exactly this commitment mechanism. As in Mansfield et al. (2002) where signing an international trade agreement that binds protectionist leaders to freer trade improves their welfare, here a similar process is at work. Giving (more) aid to a multilateral forum ties the leader's hands relative to that aid but also makes the voters more likely to approve of greater aid overall. Thus executives choose some portion of multilateral aid depending on how voters view the ex ante benefits of foreign aid.

For this mechanism to work, some members of the public must know that the government is committing more aid to multilateral organizations than previously. Publics in donor countries, however, are notorious for their lack of information about foreign aid. But two mechanisms at least exist by which voters may learn about a government's aid policy without much effort. First, the multilateral organizations themselves may broadcast widely the fact that governments are giving them more or less aid. Indeed, the OECD has a very public mechanism for alerting publics and other governments to the behavior of its members: the country-specific aid policy reviews that it conducts (OECD 1999). These reviews may signal to the attentive public what their own government is doing in this area. The OECD's DAC has targets for the amount and type of aid-giving

Principal preferences, structure, decision rules, and private benefits

it expects from members (they usually have agreed to these targets) and the reviews specifically ask about the percentage of multilateral giving.

Second, attentive publics and public organizations (NGOs) within a donor country with strong preferences about aid-giving may act as endorsers for other voters. Voters or organizations that care about foreign aid a lot may well invest in the resources to follow what their governments are doing, and they may publicize this information or use it to recommend for and against certain political candidates. For instance, since 1993 a group of NGOs has produced an evaluation of aid programs, called The Reality of Aid. A main goal of this group is to publicize the behavior of the OECD countries vis-à-vis their aid-giving (OECD 1999: 107). The use of "endorsers" such as these has been shown to be important in other areas of politics (e.g. Lupia 1992, 1994; Lupia and McCubbins 1994a; Milner and Rosendorff 1996; Milner 1997; Grossman and Helpman 2002; Thompson, this volume; and especially Lake and McCubbins, this volume). Information on the multilateral content of a donor government's aid is available directly or indirectly from these sources for voters, especially for those who care about the issue.

When the public is very hostile to aid, governments should have to commit larger sums to multilateral programs to reassure voters and induce them to vote for higher aid programs. When voters are more favorable to aid, governments will have to do less to reassure them and aid can be less multilateral. Since governments cannot provide unbiased information to voters about the benefits of aid and voters know this, they must use multilateral aid organizations as signaling devices about their intentions. When they commit to multilateral aid, leaders signal that they are going to use this for more humanitarian purposes and less political or commercial ones. This signal is credible because the donor government cannot control the multilateral organization (completely) and because the organization has a reputation for more needs-based aid-giving.

Do publics really believe that multilateral organizations are better aid providers than their own governments? In many OECD countries, publics often have more confidence in international organizations, such as the EU, than they do in their own governments. Italy, for instance, is a classic case of this; domestic corruption is perceived to be widespread, while the EU, among other international organizations, is perceived to be much "cleaner." Although many Americans express doubts about international organizations, in most of the OECD countries, especially the Scandinavian ones, international organizations are seen very

Foreign aid and domestic principal-agent problems

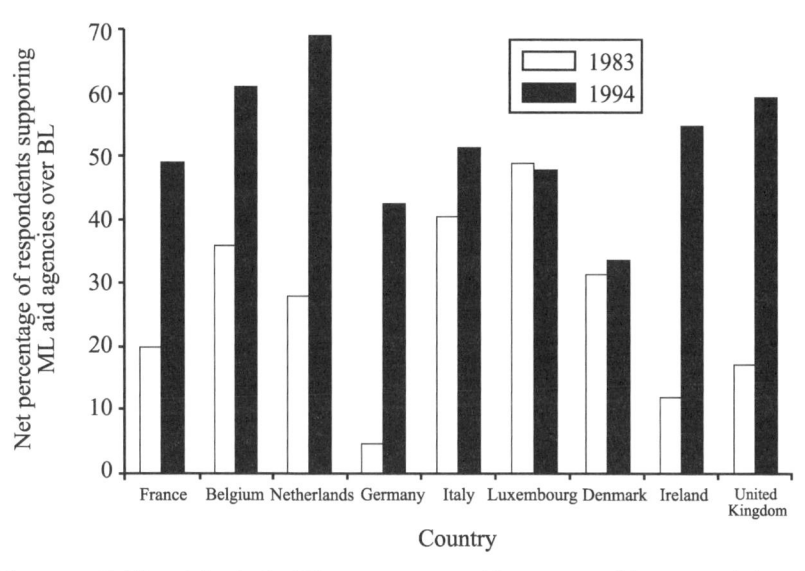

Figure 4.2. Public opinion in the EU: net percentage with greater confidence in multilateral than bilateral organizations

favorably and are often preferred as a means of foreign policy to purely domestic institutions. The Eurobarometer surveys of public opinion support this contention. In 1983 the Eurobarometer asked its members to identify which five groups provided the most useful help to the third world countries. The choices were the national government, the EU, international organizations like the UN, business and industry, and voluntary organizations. In the ten countries responding, the percentage believing it was international organizations like the UN always outnumbered the percentage saying it was the national government. In 1994 the Eurobarometer asked ten of its member countries again the following question: which one of the following do you think is the most effective way for EU countries to give humanitarian assistance; is it each EU country's own individual government, the EU, the UN, or NGOs? For every country, the EU far outpolled the national governments and so did the UN in all but two cases. Figure 4.2 shows the net percentage of positive responses for the EU and international organizations (i.e. the multilateral organizations) after subtracting from them the percentage in favor of the national government. As can be seen, the publics in these countries have far more confidence in multilateral organizations giving aid than in their own governments. Multilateral organizations for aid-giving are thus often seen as better aid providers than their own governments. Multilateralism thus may be an appealing strategy for governments who face credibility problems with their own voters.

The main hypothesis follows from this model. Multilateralism should be favored when governments most need to reassure their publics about their intentions in aid-giving; that is, when domestic principal-agent problems are the worst. The more skeptical the public is about the (ex ante) benefits of foreign aid, the more likely that governments will turn to multilateral aid organizations for aid-giving. This credible signal provided by multilateral giving will induce voters in donor countries to give more aid overall and thus will benefit executives, even though they lose control of the portion that is multilateral. All groups in the donor country gain from this since the government gets more aid and the public gets higher quality aid.

EMPIRICAL ANALYSIS

What factors account for the varying amount of aid that countries give to multilateral organizations relative to their total aid budgets? To address this question, I will examine the data on total multilateral commitments of ODA flows as a percentage of total ODA commitments per country-year (OECD 2001).[11] The data here are for commitments, not disbursements. Given our model, the commitments data – i.e. what countries have decided to provide each year – are preferable, since actual disbursements depend on conditions in both the donor and recipient. Data for 27 DAC countries, with 16 of them having data for all 40 years from 1960–2000, exist. Recent members, such as South Korea (10 years), Greece (4 years), Turkey (8 years), Poland (2 years), the Czech (2 years) and Slovak (1 year) Republics, only have data for a few years. Countries, such as Ireland, Luxembourg, New Zealand, Portugal, and Spain, also have data for about 20–30 years only. This gives a total of 643 observations for the main dependent variable.

The literature discussed above suggests a number of hypotheses that one must control in testing the claims made here. First, certain economic characteristics of countries might make them more or less interested in multilateralism. A country's size, as measured by its population (log of population, LN POP), could have some impact.[12] Smaller countries

---

[11] See http://www.oecd.org/dac/stats/.
[12] Population and GDP are highly correlated among this group (r = .93); the log of population is also highly correlated (r = .70). Both measures proxy for a country's size. I use the former since I also include GDP per capita.

might be more multilateral in their orientation since they may not have the economic or political weight to influence other countries bilaterally. A country's level of wealth, as measured by its real per capita GDP (GDP PC), could also affect the choice of multilateral over bilateral. Wealthier countries would be expected to rely on bilateral means more often. A country's extent of ties to the international economy is also important. More trade dependent countries, as measured by their ratios of exports and imports to GDP (TRADE), should be more likely to apply bilateral provision of aid so that they can more directly influence their trading partners, actual and potential. In addition, the amount a country's government spends indicates an interest in or positive attitude toward government aid for the poor, at home and abroad. Government spending as a percentage of GDP (GOV EXP) should be positively related to multilateralism then. All data for these variables comes from the World Bank's (2001b) *World Development Indicators*.

In addition, features of the international system may affect all countries similarly. Donor collusion may also be promoted by external pressures. American hegemony over the period might play a role in fostering multilateral commitments since the United States could be expected to enforce the multilateral rules and punish free riding. Declining US hegemony then would be expected to undermine multilateral giving. On the other hand, the loss of American hegemony might make the demand for effective multilateral coordination rise, and thus promote multilateral aid giving. Thus the extent of American hegemony may matter. Higher levels of US hegemonic power, as measured by America's total trade relative to world trade (US HEGEMONY), may induce greater cooperation among donors, thus increasing the amount of multilateral aid they give. An alternative measure is US GNP relative to the world's total GNP.

Second, strategic competition at the world system level may affect the donor game. The OECD countries were members of the Western security alliance and during the Cold War one would expect that they might desire and be better able to coordinate their policies. Indeed the more intense the competition between East and West during the Cold War, the more aid that might be given, but also the more multilateral aid that might be given. Heightened external competition should increase the will and capacity of the Western countries to coordinate their aid policies to overcome both free-riding and being exploited by recipients. The end of the Cold War in 1989 and the collapse of the USSR in 1991 brought about a precipitous decline in aid flows from the Soviet Union after 1990 (which coincided with a large decline in aid from the OPEC Arab

Principal preferences, structure, decision rules, and private benefits

countries). These changes should have had the effect of reducing OECD aid but also of decreasing the amount given multilaterally. As Arvin says, "Freed from the strategic constraints of the Cold War, donors may feel less tied to a common security agenda and thus more able to pursue their own independent ODA policies" (Arvin 2002: 28). The measure of Cold War competition that I use is an indicator that equals 2 before 1989, 1 from 1989 to 1991, and 0 from then on (COLD WAR).[13] The Cold War should intensify Western countries' cooperation in aid promoting multilateral aid. It should be positively related to the percentage of multilateral aid.

Other factors relating to each country's relations with the rest of the world may also be of significance. A country's relative power, as measured by the size of its GDP as a percentage of US GDP, may indicate how much influence a country can wield on its own. Countries with less relative power (GDP %US) may be more likely to use multilateralism for giving aid since this may increase their influence over recipient countries. In addition, whether a country is a member of the European Union may make a difference. One might expect that countries willing to join the EU and give up substantial control over their domestic and foreign policies to such a multilateral institution may be much more sympathetic to multilateralism in general.

In terms of domestic politics, the model suggests a number of important characteristics for determining a government's choice between multilateral and bilateral aid. Political parties may have different policy preferences regarding foreign aid. This may result from the fact that their core constituents have different preferences about the matter. If so, then giving aid in a multilateral forum may be a means of "locking in" larger amounts of aid than could be given otherwise. One might expect that parties on the left part of the political spectrum would be more interested in foreign aid. Lumsdaine makes this argument explicitly about the preferences of parties on the left; he claims that left parties' greater support for the domestic welfare state translates into more support for foreign aid. "In country after country, the politicians and political parties that strongly advocated aid were those on the left, and factions within political parties that advocated aid were those which

---

[13] I also looked at two alternative variables to measure the extent of Cold War competition: a dummy that equaled 1 in all years previous to 1990 and a dummy that equaled 1 in all years previous to 1992. These are the alternative dates one could assign to the ending of the Cold War.

Foreign aid and domestic principal-agent problems

were concerned with idealistic causes" (Lumsdaine 1993: 139). If this is true, governments dominated by left parties may be more likely to give aid multilaterally

The partisan orientation of a government may thus matter. I expect that left governments have a greater propensity to give aid multilaterally. I include a variable called PARTISAN, which uses the Comparative Manifesto Project dataset on party programs to code governments and should be negatively related. I use the Gabel and Huber method of calculating party partisanship (Gabel and Huber 2000).[14]

To test my argument, I include a variable measuring public opinion on foreign aid in each country over time (OPINION). Primarily, I use data from a question about aid that asks whether the respondent thinks that their government gives too much, the right amount, or too little foreign aid to poor countries. The percentage saying the right amount plus the percentage saying too little are added together and then from this I subtract the percentage saying too much aid is given. This variable then measures the net public opinion that is favorable to foreign aid in each country that year. I assume that this tells us about the benefits that taxpayers in donor countries believe foreign aid brings them. High levels of favorable opinion indicate a belief that the benefits of aid are high. When voters are optimistic about aid, then governments need to re-assure them less about these benefits, and hence prefer to use multilateral aid less. However, when voters are pessimistic about the value of aid, leaders desire to reassure them by providing more multilateral aid, which voters see as a signal that aid will be dedicated to humanitarian assistance. I expect a negative relationship between opinion and multilateral aid.

Collecting data on public opinion about foreign aid is not simple. I have 222 observations for the donor countries from 1963 to 2001. I have data for the 15 current EU countries from 1976 to 1998, and sporadic data for the United States, Canada, Japan, Australia, and Norway.[15] A composite measure of favorable attitudes toward aid was

---

[14] They take each party in government and create the government score by weighting them by their percentage of seats among the winning coalition. For presidential systems, the variable is constructed as a simple average of the score for parties in control of the legislature and the President's party score. The partisanship variable ranges in theory from 0 to 10, with higher numbers denoting more right-wing governments. The expected sign of PARTISAN then is negative.

[15] The EU data come from eleven Eurobarometer surveys over the past three decades: 1976, 1979, 1980, 1981, 1983, 1987, 1991, 1993, 1994, 1996, 1998. Two general

constructed from different public opinion polls. All those in favor of increased or the same levels of spending on foreign aid were counted as favorable toward aid, and all those favoring decreased spending were subtracted from this. These net percentages of respondents in favor of aid (OPINION1) were then used. If one worries about listwise deletion problems and believes that public opinion may be quite stable over time, then imputing values for the intervening years between public opinion surveys may make sense. For years in between where no survey was performed, data were added by using two different methods. First, the last value available was used for all intervening years (OPINION2). Second, a linear extrapolation was used to fill in values for intervening years (OPINION3). Using these two methods, observations for this variable (OPINION) rise to 418. Unfortunately, this number remains smaller than the data on foreign aid available (643 total observations). I expect that rising public opposition to aid will lead policy-makers to prefer multilateral over bilateral aid. Hence OPINION should be negatively related to the dependent variable.

Finally, I include a variable to capture the total amount of aid committed in the previous period. It may be that multilateral commitments as a percentage of total commitments are changing because total ODA is changing; that is, the denominator is changing and not the numerator. The measure of total ODA commitments as a percentage of GDP (TOTAL COMMIT) for each country in each year is examined as well.

The time series cross-section data used necessitate attention to problems of heteroskedasticity as well as panel and serial correlation. The data include less than 26 countries over 40 years, which means that T is fairly large and often bigger than N and therefore the use of panel-corrected standard errors is appropriate. I sometimes include a time counter variable to pick up linear trends over the period, but this is often dropped since it is never significant and is highly correlated with both the Cold War and the US hegemony variables. I use OLS regressions with panel-corrected standard errors, including country fixed effects and a lagged dependent variable for estimation. Table 4.1 presents the summary statistics for all the variables used.

Tables 4.2A and 4.2B present the results from these regressions for OPINION1, which contains only the original data on public opinion.

questions were used. One asked whether the respondent favored increased, decreased, or no change in foreign aid. The other asked whether the respondent was highly favorable, favorable, opposed, or highly opposed to increased foreign aid.

Foreign aid and domestic principal-agent problems

Table 4.1. *Summary statistics for variables*

Variable	Obs	Mean	Std. Dev.	Min.	Max
ML PC	668	0.33	0.15	0.02	0.92
OPINION1	222	45.59	30.35	−54	96.40
OPINION2	418	43.84	31.95	−54	96.40
OPINION3	418	44.29	29.81	−54	96.40
LN POP	772	16.61	1.37	12.81	19.44
GDP PC	756	20656.35	8838.63	2654.08	52675.27
GOV EXP	729	18.59	4.68	7.32	29.88
TRADE	735	63.13	38.26	9.33	238.70
PARTISAN	686	7.57	0.82	4.66	9.37
TOTAL COMMIT	624	2.72E-09	2.05E-09	7.75E-11	1.18E-08
US HEGEMONY	772	0.27	0.02	0.24	0.31
GDP % US	756	0.15	0.25	0.00	1
YEAR	853	1983	12.31	1960	2002

The lagged dependent variable (LAG ML PC) is positive and significant as expected. A multilateral orientation once acquired seems to stay in place. But note that this variable is nowhere near unity, suggesting that unit root problems might be unimportant. The economic variables match expectations generally, but often do not attain conventional levels of significance. A country's size (LN POP) seems to be negatively related to its multilateral giving, although never significantly. Its wealth (GDP PC) is negatively and often significantly related to multilateralism. Richer and bigger countries tend to give less multilateral aid. Overall government spending as a portion of GNP (GOV EXP) is unexpectedly negative, and usually quite significant. This result implies that as government expenditure rises, executives are less willing to give to multilateral aid organizations. Governments that are better able to tax and spend domestically have less need and desire to use multilateral institutions to distribute their foreign aid. It may be an indicator of government capacity rather than of preferences for spending on the poor, as speculated above.[16]

---

[16] This negative relationship does not disappear if one eliminates partisanship either. The correlation between them is surprisingly low and positive (r = .10).

Table 4.2A. Multilateral commitments as % total ODA committed and OPINION1

Dependent variable	(1)	(2)	ML PC (3)	(4)	(5)
OPINION1	−0.0005***	−0.0005***	−0.0005**	−0.0005***	−0.0005***
	(0.0002)	(0.0002)	(0.0002)	(0.0002)	(0.0002)
GDP PC	−0.0000*	−0.0000	−0.0000**	−0.0000*	−0.0000
	(0.0000)	(0.0000)	(0.0000)	(0.0000)	(0.0000)
LN POP	−0.0694	0.0113	0.0025	−0.0704	−0.0575
	(0.1368)	(0.1487)	(0.1366)	(0.1353)	(0.1390)
GOV EXP	−0.0068*	−0.0067*	−0.0079*	−0.0068*	−0.0068*
	(0.0040)	(0.0040)	(0.0044)	(0.0041)	(0.0041)
PARTISAN	0.0208***	0.0223***	0.0212***	0.0208***	0.0209***
	(0.0075)	(0.0075)	(0.0073)	(0.0076)	(0.0074)
LAG ML PC	0.4239***	0.4195***	0.4175***	0.4242***	0.4225***
	(0.0803)	(0.0802)	(0.0806)	(0.0802)	(0.0805)
YEAR		−0.0015			
		(0.0023)			
TRADE			−0.0013		
			(0.0009)		
COLD WAR					0.0023
					(0.0108)
US HEGEMONY				0.0289	
				(0.3744)	
Constant	1.3590	2.9674	0.2435	1.3706	1.1537
	(2.2213)	(3.8046)	(2.2135)	(2.2023)	(2.2672)

Dependent variable			ML PC		
Observations	176	176	176	176	176
# countries	21	21	21	21	21
R2	0.84	0.84	0.85	0.84	0.84
Wald chi²	523726	855	7015	322866	2257
Prob > chi²	0.00	0.00	0.00	0.00	0.00

Note: OLS with panel-corrected standard errors in parentheses, using STATA 8.2 (xtpcse). ALL IVs, except the year counter, are lagged one period. Country fixed effects included.
Two-tailed tests: * significant at 10%; ** significant at 5%; *** significant at 1%.

Table 4.2B. *Multilateral commitments as % total aid committed and OPINION1*

Dependent variable	ML PC			
	(1)	(2)	(3)	(4)
OPINION1	−0.0005***	−0.0005***	−0.0005***	−0.0005**
	(0.0002)	(0.0002)	(0.0002)	(0.0002)
GDP PC	−0.0000*	−0.0000	−0.0000	−0.0000
	(0.0000)	(0.0000)	(0.0000)	(0.0000)
LN POP	−0.0602	−0.0856	−0.0660	−0.0587
	(0.1288)	(0.1413)	(0.1379)	(0.1964)
GOV EXP	−0.0067*	−0.0063	−0.0074*	−0.0076*
	(0.0041)	(0.0040)	(0.0041)	(0.0044)
PARTISAN	0.0211***	0.0220***	0.0213***	0.0228***
	(0.0074)	(0.0078)	(0.0075)	(0.0077)
LAG ML PC	0.4240***	0.4158***	0.4204***	0.4044***
	(0.0803)	(0.0819)	(0.0798)	(0.0829)
GDP %US	0.1219			0.0160
	(0.3578)			(0.4638)
TOTAL COMMIT		−2.8717e+06		−4.8841e+06
		(4188308.5832)		(4377359.0430)
EU			−0.0381*	−0.0214
			(0.0207)	(0.0253)
COLD WAR				−0.0015
				(0.0144)
US HEGEMONY				0.0256
				(0.4378)

Dependent variable		ML PC	
YEAR			0.0006
			(0.0042)
TRADE			−0.0014
			(0.0011)
Constant	1.2013	1.6036	1.3117	0.0246
	(2.0845)	(2.2873)	(2.2383)	(6.5158)
Observations	176	176	176	176
Number of countries	21	21	21	21
R2	0.84	0.84	0.84	0.85
Wald chi²	10614	1994	3631	28442
Prob > chi²	0.00	0.00	0.00	0.00

Note: OLS with panel-corrected standard errors in parentheses, using STATA 8.2 (xtpcse). ALL IVs, except the year counter, are lagged one period. Country fixed effects included.
Two-tailed tests: * significant at 10%; ** significant at 5%; *** significant at 1%.

Principal preferences, structure, decision rules, and private benefits

The impact of the international system seems limited. American hegemony, measured either as a percentage of world trade or world GNP, is positive as expected but not significant. It seems to have no discernible effect on countries' choices about aid-giving. The dynamics of the Cold War also had no consistent impact on multilateral aid-giving; although always positive, it was never significant.[17] The structure of world politics seemed to play little role in conditioning aid-giving. On the other hand, being a member of the EU seemed to matter. But its impact was unexpected. Joining the EU seemed to lower a country's multilateral contributions.

Domestic politics, in contrast, plays an important role. But this impact was often contrary to expectations. Partisanship was almost always significant; a government's partisan orientation mattered. But this result was contrary to expectations: right governments consistently gave more multilateral aid than did left ones. Given the view of left governments as more sanguine about aid in general, it is hard to understand this result. It could be that right governments are more willing to give aid to multilateral organizations because such organizations are staffed with actors whose preferences are more similar to right parties than are their domestic aid-giving bureaucracies. Right governments may thus avoid bilateral aid and support multilateral giving as a means of controlling their home bureaucracies. Or the result may arise from the fact that right-wing governments like aid less than left ones and can cut bilateral aid more easily than multilateral, thus driving the multilateral percentage of aid higher. Overall, this result is robust and puzzling.

My hypothesis about public opinion is supported strongly by the data. The regressions using public opinion in table 4.2 show that it has the anticipated impact.[18] This result occurs with all three versions of the public opinion variable, as can be seen from tables 4.2A and 4.2B

---

[17] The Cold War variable is never significant, whether I use the version that marks a change both in 1989 and 1991 or a dummy for 1989 or 1991.
[18] An interesting issue not addressed here is what impact public opinion toward aid has on overall aid budgets. Some, such as McDonnell et al. (2003, 17) claim it has none: "Trying to link those levels of public support with ODA levels almost inevitably leads to the conclusion that the former does not have a direct influence on the latter. Indeed, on the whole, and in spite of some differences among OECD Member countries, foreign policy decisions, and more particularly those relating to aid and international development cooperation, are hardly influenced, at least directly, by the general public's preferences. Governments' strategic priorities, perceptions of political leaders and decision makers, the influence of domestic vested interests and specific pressure groups, or the role of other government

Foreign aid and domestic principal-agent problems

and 4.3A and 4.3B. As the public in donor countries grows more favorable toward aid in general, the government is less likely to choose multilateral aid-giving. This finding suggests that public opposition to foreign aid may enhance the probability that executives favor multilateral giving. When publics are skeptical about the benefits of aid, governments are more likely to turn aid over to multilateral organizations in order to reassure taxpayers that their money is being well spent (i.e., spent on aid that is more likely to have humanitarian motivations).

These results are quite robust as well. The results in tables 4.2A and 4.2B do not depend on the version of the public opinion variable used; tables 4.3A and 4.3B replicate these results using an interpolated version of the public opinion data, OPINION3, which linearly imputes data for public opinion. The results here are very similar to those in tables 4.2A and 4.2B. But note that the number of observations is much larger here, and hence worries about listwise deletion of cases should be alleviated. Using another interpolated version of the public opinion data, OPINION2, which simply uses the last value for all periods in between two surveys, the results obtained are virtually identical to those in tables 4.3A and 4.3B. The public opinion variable is always negative and statistically significant.

The results are also robust to a wide variety of changes in the model. As can be seen from tables 4.2A and 4.2B and 4.3A and 4.3B, adding variables does not seem to affect the coefficients on the public opinion variables much, if at all. When the public is skeptical about the benefits of aid, holding numerous other factors constant, leaders are more likely to choose multilateral aid-giving in the next period. Could it be that the amount of multilateral aid committed actually affects public support for aid? That is, does an exogeneity problem exist? Regressing public opinion about aid on the percentage of multilateral commitments shows no significant results. Multilateralism in previous periods has no significant relationship to current public opinion about aid. It is also apparent from tables 4.2B and 4.3B that the results are not driven just by changes in the denominator of the dependent variable. Including a measure of the total amount of aid commitments (TOTAL COMMIT) does not affect the results concerning public opinion, nor does it usually have a significant relationship to current multilateral commitments of aid.

---

departments and actors in the public domain appear to be much more influential factors." Preliminary data suggest this is not the case.

Table 4.3A. *Multilateral commitments as % total ODA committed and OPINION3*

Dependent variable	(1)	(2)	(3) ML PC	(4)	(5)
OPINION3	−0.0003**	−0.0003*	−0.0003**	−0.0004**	−0.0004**
	(0.0002)	(0.0002)	(0.0002)	(0.0002)	(0.0002)
GDP PC	−0.0000***	−0.0000	−0.0000***	−0.0000*	−0.0000***
	(0.0000)	(0.0000)	(0.0000)	(0.0000)	(0.0000)
LN POP	0.0155	0.0640	0.0264	0.0480	0.0144
	(0.1124)	(0.1371)	(0.1150)	(0.1130)	(0.1126)
GOV EXP	−0.0093***	−0.0092***	−0.0096***	−0.0094***	−0.0094***
	(0.0035)	(0.0036)	(0.0036)	(0.0036)	(0.0036)
PARTISAN	0.0156**	0.0164***	0.0156**	0.0159***	0.0154**
	(0.0062)	(0.0063)	(0.0061)	(0.0061)	(0.0063)
LAG ML PC	0.4159***	0.4156***	0.4155***	0.4108***	0.4162***
	(0.0755)	(0.0753)	(0.0759)	(0.0752)	(0.0754)
YEAR		−0.0010			
		(0.0021)			
TRADE			−0.0002		
			(0.0007)		
U.S. HEGEMONY					0.0668
					(0.2925)
COLD WAR				0.0090	
				(0.0088)	
Constant	0.0585	1.1560	−0.1095	−0.5208	0.0626
	(1.8394)	(3.3262)	(1.8741)	(1.8536)	(1.8413)
Obs	337	337	337	337	337

Dependent variable			ML PC		
# countries	21	21	21	21	21
R2	0.75	0.75	0.75	0.76	0.75
Wald chi²	125279	23928	142467	23148	134195
Prob > chi²	0.00	0.00	0.00	0.00	0.00

Note: OLS with panel-corrected standard errors in parentheses, using STATA 8.2 (xtpcse). ALL IVs, except the year counter, are lagged one period. Country fixed effects included.
Two-tailed tests: * significant at 10%; ** significant at 5%; *** significant at 1%.

Table 4.3B. *Multilateral commitments as % total ODA committed and OPINION3*

Dependent variable	ML PC			
	(1)	(2)	(3)	(4)
OPINION3	−0.0004**	−0.0004**	−0.0003*	−0.0004*
	(0.0002)	(0.0002)	(0.0002)	(0.0002)
GDP PC	−0.0000***	−0.0000	−0.0000***	−0.0000
	(0.0000)	(0.0000)	(0.0000)	(0.0000)
LN POP	0.0099	−0.0366	0.0155	−0.0348
	(0.1115)	(0.1175)	(0.1125)	(0.1747)
GOV EXP	−0.0094***	−0.0081**	−0.0093***	−0.0091**
	(0.0035)	(0.0035)	(0.0036)	(0.0037)
PARTISAN	0.0151**	0.0180***	0.0155**	0.0172***
	(0.0061)	(0.0062)	(0.0062)	(0.0065)
LAG ML PC	0.4150***	0.3933***	0.4159***	0.3784***
	(0.0756)	(0.0752)	(0.0755)	(0.0773)
GDP %US	−0.1690			−0.4355
	(0.3251)			(0.4191)
TOTAL COMMIT		−8.93e+06**		−1.11e+07**
		(4398367.41)		(4659486.84)
EU			0.0017	0.0110
			(0.0339)	(0.0306)
COLD WAR				0.0079
				(0.0105)
US HEGEMONY				−0.2080
				(0.3239)
YEAR				0.0010

Dependent variable		ML PC	
TRADE			(0.0033)
			−0.0009
			(0.0008)
Constant	0.1640	0.8602	0.0582	−0.9594
	(1.8215)	(1.9105)	(1.8399)	(4.8208)
Observations	337	337	337	337
Number of countries	21	21	21	21
R^2	0.75	0.76	0.75	0.76
Wald chi^2	21888	20220	134073	7543
Prob > chi^2	0.00	0.00	0.00	0.00

Notes: OLS with panel-corrected standard errors in parentheses, using STATA 8.2 (xtpcse). ALL IVs, except the year counter, are lagged one period. Country fixed effects included.

Two-tailed tests: * significant at 10%; ** significant at 5%; *** significant at 1%.

Principal preferences, structure, decision rules, and private benefits

These results and the robustness checks add strong empirical support to the model's main proposition. Multilateralism responds to domestic politics, and seems related to the overcoming of principal-agent problems internally. Public opposition to foreign aid prompts governments to search for mechanisms to shield aid from the public's skepticism, and the commitment of aid to multilateral institutions allows governments to protect their aid budgets while better satisfying the public which desires greater needs-based aid-giving.

CONCLUSIONS

This chapter has explored why countries choose to allocate their foreign aid through multilateral channels rather than through bilateral ones. Giving aid through multilateral institutions represents a fairly new procedure for most countries. Moreover, aid given through multilateral means looks different than other forms of aid. It is much harder for donors to exercise direct influence when using multilateral aid-giving. This aid is not tied; it tends to be given to the poorest countries – i.e., those most in need; and it is often given as grants, instead of loans. Thus this aid may be of higher quality than bilateral aid, but it is surely of less direct political utility to donor governments.

The puzzle concerning multilateral aid can thus be rephrased as one about why donor countries would be willing to exchange political influence for higher quality aid. Under what conditions does this exchange make sense for political leaders in donor countries? Some scholars, as noted above, have speculated that multilateral aid occurs because it is more effective or efficient. It can solve donor information problems, facilitate collusion among them, and/or make the conditionality of aid more effective and less political. If this is the case, then the puzzle is why isn't more aid given multilaterally; why just one-third of all aid? Why are rational leaders making inefficient choices two-thirds of the time? Clearly, leaders in donor countries perceive a loss from giving aid multilaterally, and hence optimize the allocation of it on the margin.

Under what conditions is giving aid through multilateral institutions an optimal choice for national governments? I argue that this choice is made to solve a domestic principal-agent problem. Like all government spending programs, foreign aid entails a delegation process from voters/taxpayers to elected governments to bureaucrats. In foreign aid the principal-agent problem is further exacerbated since the principals have very little information about the benefits they receive from their tax money spent on aid. Aid goes to recipients in foreign countries who cannot vote in the donor country, and taxpayers in donor countries have little knowledge of how their tax dollars are spent in these foreign countries. The feedback link between spending and its benefits is broken in foreign aid. Hence voters in donor countries have to rely upon limited and biased information provided by their governments, whose agencies all have incentives to misrepresent aid's benefits. Voters know that governments have private information about aid, and they know that their agents have goals that differ from their own. They formulate beliefs about the benefits of foreign aid and gauge their willingness to pay for it relative to these benefits. When they are pessimistic about the value of aid, voters will not want to allocate money to the aid budget. Their agents thus need to find a way to reassure some voters at least. One way to do this is to give some portion of aid through a multilateral agency, which some voters at least believe to be a higher quality dispenser of aid. Hence as public opinion about foreign aid becomes more negative, executives are increasingly likely to channel more aid through multilateral organizations to reassure voters. Multilateral aid institutions thus can solve a principal-agent problem for donor countries.

The data here support this proposition. As public opinion vis-à-vis foreign aid becomes more negative, more aid is channeled through multilateral organizations. This result holds even when controlling for a wide variety of other factors. In sum, governments may delegate aid delivery to international institutions when their publics lack information about the consequences of aid and fear that their governments will deviate from their wishes concerning its use. By using the international organization to send aid, the government issues a credible signal about the use of foreign aid; the collective principal relationship to the multilateral agency allows it to be useful to national leaders. In this way, the presence of international institutions can make domestic as well as international actors better off by helping to solve a principal-agent problem in domestic politics. Political leaders in democracies will have greater motivations to create and maintain multilateral international institutions in these types of situations. As the introduction to this volume notes, multilateralism will be chosen when the benefits for principals outweigh the costs, but it should be remembered that these benefits can be largely domestic.

5

Distribution, information, and delegation to international organizations: the case of IMF conditionality

LISA L. MARTIN

States delegate authority to international organizations (IOs) for many reasons. Incentives to delegate fall under the general heading of informational concerns, such as monitoring behavior or providing scientific expertise, and distributional concerns, making sure that policies reflect major state interests. This chapter elaborates the informational and distributional logics of delegation, draws observable implications from them, and uses these propositions to examine the development of policies regarding conditionality within the International Monetary Fund (IMF).

Some would argue that the IMF has achieved greater agency or autonomy than IOs in any other sphere of activity. I use the definition of autonomy presented in the introduction to this volume: the range of potential independent action available to the agent (I also sometimes use the term *agency* to refer to the same concept). Initially, the IMF was merely a set of rules regulating member state behavior rather than an organization with any autonomy. However, it quickly transformed into an active organization. Much of this transformation took place via debates about the use of Fund resources by members, leading to the practice of conditionality.

I begin by setting out two potential sources of variation in the autonomy of IOs: distributional conflict and the demand for information. I develop a number of expectations about how the delegation of authority should vary in response to the concerns. In the IMF, these concerns take the form of divergence of preferences among the executive directors

---

I thank Devesh Kapur, Jeff Frieden, James Boughton, Miles Kahler, and participants in the Cambridge workshop on the Political Economy of International Finance and the BYU conference on delegation to international organizations. My thanks for research assistance go to David Singer and Ethan Handelman.

The case of IMF conditionality

(EDs) and private information held by the staff. I then examine the historical development of rules and procedures governing the use of conditionality in the IMF to provide evidence relevant to these hypotheses.

I distinguish between formal agency, which is the amount of authority states have explicitly delegated to an IO, and informal agency, which is the autonomy an IO has in practice, holding the rules constant. Both formal and informal autonomy fit within the definition of autonomy adopted in this volume. Formal autonomy refers to state decisions about the explicit rules that delegate authority to IOs; informal autonomy refers to IOs' ability to maneuver within the existing rule structure. My conception of informal autonomy conforms closely to the puzzle studied by Erica Gould in this volume, and her chapter on the IMF provides further details on how the IMF staff uses the informal autonomy it gains through delegation.

Overall, the picture of agency and delegation is a complex one. Traditional IMF practices of not publicly airing many of the details of its internal proceedings make a definitive study of the agency issue difficult. Autonomy varies. The staff may simultaneously be tightly constrained in some aspects of its activity, while enjoying close to a free hand in other dimensions. The distributional and informational frameworks help us to analyze the causes of IMF structure and actions, thus providing greater insight into its functions as an international institution. For example, they help us to understand the substantial delegation of authority that took place in the 1950s, and challenges to that delegation in the 1970s. IOs gain autonomy as the result of intentional state decisions to delegate authority, not through a careless process driven by the staff (Barnett and Finnemore 2004: 56–58). In the case of the IMF, Fund staff and management have autonomy when it works to the interests of the executive board (EB), and the historical evidence clearly demonstrates that decisions about delegation are thoroughly debated and considered; the autonomy of staff does not emerge by accident.

DISTRIBUTIONAL CONFLICT AND PRIVATE INFORMATION AS SOURCES OF AUTONOMY

When states create an IO and endow it with some agency, they necessarily delegate a certain degree of authority to it. However, the level of delegation varies greatly across IOs, over time, and across issues. Some IOs have attained substantial autonomy, while others can do little without explicit consent from member states (Cortell and Peterson 2001;

Principal preferences, structure, decision rules, and private benefits

Nielson and Tierney 2003a; Pollack 1997). I argue that two sets of factors help us to understand variation in the level of delegation. One is distributional conflict, meaning conflicts of interest among member states. The other is informational concerns, especially private information that might be held by the IO staff. In developing these rationales for delegation, I draw explicitly on a principal-agent framework, where member states are understood as principals and the IO as an agent. In the case of the IMF, I simplify by assuming that the EB, which directly represents member states, is the principal, and that the management and staff (treated as a unitary actor) is the agent.

Distributional concerns

The introduction to this volume refers to preference heterogeneity as a potential source of IO autonomy. Preference heterogeneity can also be understood as distributional conflict, since it means that different principals prefer that different outcomes prevail. To illustrate and develop the argument, assume a simple, one-dimensional space over which member states make decisions. In the case of the IMF, this space ranges from loose conditions on drawings to rigorous conditions. States' ideal points will array themselves along this continuum. I assume that the IO staff also has a preference on this spectrum. The preferences of states and the IO will vary over time and across countries. For the IMF, states' preferences will be influenced by both economic and political factors. They will be concerned about the economic consequences of programs for the international financial system, but also about their political relationship with borrowers. For example, they may prefer looser conditions for states that are political allies, wishing to spare them the domestic upheaval that tight conditions often cause. In the IMF case, I assume that state interests are reflected by the EDs. As the IO staff is not directly responsible to any particular member state, being made up of international civil servants, I assume that its preferences are driven primarily by economic ("technocratic") considerations.

Figure 5.1 illustrates how state and staff preferences might appear for a particular program or policy choice. For tractability, I identify only five states, which could be thought of as groups of like-minded states. I assume that the staff makes a proposal for a program, and the members approve this proposal by majority vote. States' ideal points are represented by the numbers 1 through 5. The staff's ideal point is indicated by the letter S.

The case of IMF conditionality

```
    1           2           3    S      4           5
```

Loose   Tight
conditions   conditions

Figure 5.1. State and staff preferences over stringency of conditionality

The assumption of a staff proposal and majority votes by members is a strong one, and may not be appropriate for all IOs. However, it is accurate for the case of the IMF, and some version of a staff proposal and state approval is appropriate for most IOs. In the IMF case, the states are represented by EDs who make up the EB. EDs have different numbers of votes, depending on whom they represent. One important question is whether the EB can amend staff proposals, or whether they are presented with a "take it or leave it" offer. Technically speaking, in the IMF the board has the right to do whatever it wants, and so could amend proposals. But in practice, amendments would be controversial and cumbersome, subject to charges of political interference. Because conditions have been agreed in prior negotiations with the borrowing country, attempts to amend would mean sending the staff back for renegotiation. These considerations mean that, in practice, the board almost never considers amending staff proposals.[1] It therefore seems a reasonable simplification to assume that proposals to the board are essentially take-it-or-leave-it offers (Gold 1984: 392; Garritsen de Vries 1985: 987).

Given this decision-making framework, on any individual program the staff can have substantial influence over the content of the program or policy finally approved. The staff can propose the program closest to its own preference that is able to muster majority support. The EB will only veto a staff proposal if a majority finds the status quo – i.e. no program – more to its liking than the proposal.

This simple setup leads to a few preliminary propositions about staff autonomy, understood as the staff's ability to influence the content of programs. First, observe that staff influence is likely to grow when the status quo is strongly disliked by most states. In this case, nearly any proposal will be able to gain a majority, so the staff can present something close to its ideal point. This observation could lead us to suggest, for example, that in times of crisis that threaten the international financial

---

[1] Stone (2002) notes some extraordinary circumstances in which the staff is forced to amend its proposals because of EB disapproval.

system, IMF staff will have substantial influence, as EDs will be anxious to move away from the status quo. On the other hand, when dealing with relatively minor borrowing countries, or with chronic problems that do not pose any immediate threat to the international system, EDs are more willing to live with the status quo. In this case, the staff will have to be more attentive to ED preferences, effectively limiting its autonomy.

A second observation is that the distribution of preferences among states will have implications for staff influence. When state preferences diverge, stretching along the entire policy continuum, there is more likely to be a wide range of proposals that could gain majority approval. This gives the staff room for maneuver, as they can choose the proposal within this space that comes closest to their ideal point. In contrast, when state preferences converge, the staff will have less flexibility. Now a smaller set of proposals is likely to gain approval, constraining the staff to make a proposal within this smaller space. I therefore expect that staff autonomy will be greater when there is disagreement among states about the desired policy (the degree of conditionality in the IMF case). Such disagreement allows the staff to play states off against one another.[2]

The hypotheses developed so far focus on informal agency – the autonomy of staff given a stable set of rules. However, this setup also suggests likely changes in the rules governing staff activities as a result of the distribution of state preferences. Recognizing that the staff might have significant autonomy on any individual decision, states have searched for ways to put ex ante constraints on staff activities. They can specify guidelines for policies or provide more direct oversight of staff activities, for example. Under what conditions are states likely to put stringent constraints on the staff?

One straightforward expectation is that a state is more likely to delegate significant formal authority when it believes that staff preferences are in line with its own. If the staff is perceived as an outlier – preferring far looser or tighter conditions than the majority of states – states will recognize the potential use of agenda-setting power to force an outcome

---

[2] I should note that this proposition differs from that developed in the introduction to this volume, where the claim is made that greater preference heterogeneity will make states less likely to delegate authority. The difference arises because I am considering informal autonomy here: the autonomy the staff has, holding the rules constant. Given a priori delegation decision and constant rules, greater heterogeneity should increase the room for maneuver available to the staff. This proposition is actually anticipated by the introduction's argument that preference heterogeneity makes it difficult for states to restructure an existing delegation relationship.

The case of IMF conditionality

far from what they would prefer. Under these conditions, states are likely to reclaim authority, perhaps setting more explicit guidelines for policy or exercising more direct oversight. On the other hand, when the staff is perceived as "like-minded," states will be willing to allow it substantial flexibility. This proposition is consistent with that in the introduction to this volume, where the "nature of the agent" is proposed to influence patterns of autonomy.

Following this logic, it also follows that those states whose preferences are closest to those of the staff will be the strongest proponents of staff autonomy. Those who perceive their interests as at odds with the staff will argue for tighter constraints, clearer guidelines, and so on. Thus, the distribution of state and IO preferences provides us with some general hypotheses about delegation of formal authority to IOs, and IO autonomy given a stable pattern of rules. Four distributional hypotheses will structure the following empirical discussion:

(D1) When states are most dissatisfied with the status quo, as during crises, they will allow the staff the most autonomy.

(D2) Given a stable set of rules, as state preferences diverge, staff autonomy will increase.

(D3) States will delegate more authority to the IO staff when it believes that staff preferences are in line with its own.

(D4) Those states with preferences closest to the staff's will be the most willing to delegate authority to the IO.

Informational concerns

Another important source of variation in IO autonomy comes through consideration of informational concerns. In many circumstances, such as design of IMF programs, a great deal of information is required for drafting policies that are likely to be effective. This dynamic is anticipated by this volume's introduction, where "specialization" is seen as a source of delegation and autonomy. Even when states oversee activities closely, it is often impossible for state representatives to have the necessary expertise to craft complex, effective programs in a timely fashion. Thus states rely heavily on staff memos and proposals.

The IO thus has both an important responsibility and an additional source of flexibility. Staff members are responsible for collecting and being the repositories of necessary economic and political information to design policies that are likely to succeed. In the IMF case, they must collect information on a wide variety of economic variables. They also are expected to acquire knowledge that is more political in nature that will help provide a judgment about a program's likely success. For example, is a government likely to live up to the terms of a Letter of Intent? Or will it fail to meet these terms, either voluntarily or because of stiff domestic resistance? Without information like this, the IMF's lending programs cannot be effective, and may even be counter-productive.

States thus confront a dilemma. On the one hand, they face incentives to delegate authority to the staff to collect information and use it in designing high-quality programs. On the other, delegation can result in the staff acquiring private information that it may not share accurately or in a timely manner. This private information could become a source of substantial flexibility. For example, consider a situation where the IMF EB prefers loose conditions on a loan, perhaps because the borrowing country is a political ally of the major shareholders. The staff, in contrast, believes that far-reaching policy changes are necessary, so that tight conditions are appropriate. The staff may be able to use its private information to exaggerate the economic difficulties facing the borrower, or to minimize the political difficulties, thus convincing the board to approve tighter conditions than it otherwise would have preferred.[3]

Another complication arises for the IMF in that borrowing countries are often reluctant to reveal vital information. The EDs represent a diverse, worldwide constituency. Any borrowing country is likely to face political adversaries on the board. Countries will therefore be reluctant to reveal sensitive information. However, if borrowers will not reveal the information, programs will rest on a shaky foundation. The EDs thus have incentives to convince borrowers to reveal information fully to the staff, while assuring them that this information will not be leaked or used for political purposes. One way of providing such assurance is to allow the staff to treat some information as confidential. Similar considerations arise when a quick decision is necessary. When the EB believes that it is necessary to put together a program quickly, it will not have the time to carefully review all the relevant information, and will find itself relying more heavily on what the staff chooses to reveal. The board therefore faces a tradeoff between the perceived urgency of any program and the desire to reduce the staff's informational advantage.

---

[3] One could perhaps see such an outcome as an example of agents influencing principals, as outlined in the introduction to this volume. However, in the interests of keeping the argument as straightforward as possible, I prefer to interpret such a dynamic as a standard use of agent autonomy rather than changing principals' preferences.

The case of IMF conditionality

I thus expect that states constantly perform a juggling act with respect to IO ability to collect information and requirements to reveal this information to member states. In situations where designing a strong program is of vital importance – for example, in a financial crisis – I expect states to be willing to allow the IO greater leeway in keeping information private. The same is true when states believe that the staff has preferences close to their own, as argued above. Concerns about private information held by the staff will influence decisions about where staff members are stationed. Stationing staff overseas, rather than in the organization's headquarters, allows them to collect more information, but may also increase their leverage vis-à-vis states.

Two information hypotheses will be examined in the following empirical discussion:

(I1) Staff will gain the capacity to collect information, and keep it private, when the demand for high-quality information is intense, as in crisis situations.

(I2) The staff will become more constrained in their informational capacities when their preferences are believed to deviate from those of the major member states.

THE EVOLUTION OF IMF DECISIONS ON CONDITIONALITY AND GUIDELINES

A focus on principal-agent issues illuminates the structure of the IMF and the evolution of conditionality. The relationship between the EB and the management and staff is central to the overall agency issue, and the management and staff have agenda-setting power when it comes to proposing loan programs and the conditions attached to them. I ask how agenda-setting power translates into autonomy of the staff from the executive board by considering distributional and informational sources of autonomy. I find substantial support for the hypotheses outlined above, particularly those based on informational considerations.

IMF structure

The IMF organizational structure consists of a board of governors, the EB, a managing director (MD), deputy managing directors, and a staff of civil servants. The board of governors is made up of political representatives of the IMF's member states, primarily finance ministers. It has ultimate authority for running the IMF. However, the IMF's Articles of

Principal preferences, structure, decision rules, and private benefits

Agreement allow the governors to delegate nearly all their powers to the executive board, and they have done so (Gold 1984: 389). In the early years of the Fund, the governors sometimes attempted to take a more active role. For example, at one time they established committees to discuss the annual report. However, attendance was low, and the idea of such devices was quickly dropped (Southard 1979: 3).

The EB, now made up of 24 EDs, therefore operates as the IMF's permanent decision-making body and conducts day-to-day business. It is in permanent session in Washington. Five EDs are appointed by one large state each. The rest are elected by constituencies that have no fixed makeup and are quite diverse. Each ED has a number of votes that are linked to each member state's quota (contribution to IMF financial resources). These quotas are, in turn, loosely based on each member's financial weight in the world economy. Some IMF decisions require an 85 percent or 70 percent majority of votes on the EB. However, my focus here is on approving loans (called drawings in IMF parlance). Approval of loans requires a simple majority vote of EDs, although in practice the EB works by consensus, rarely taking explicit votes. The United States has about 18 percent of total votes.

The IMF staff has grown over time as the membership and activities of the Fund have grown, now numbering over 2,000. Each department head reports to the MD, who is appointed for a five-year term. By tradition, the MD is always a European, while an American is first deputy managing director. The MD's constitutional position, compared to that of the heads of many other IOs, is quite strong. Since the MD is the chair of EB meetings, he is "in a position to control the agenda, direct the discussion, and by this means influence the board's decisions" (Strange 1973: 286). Some MDs have taken more advantage of this agenda-setting power than have others.

The staff is crucial to the work of the EB. The board carries out its work largely on the basis of memos and papers prepared by the staff. Staff members carry out negotiations with countries that are interested in drawing on Fund resources, undertake regular surveillance activities, and prepare reports on all member states. Many staff members are regularly stationed outside Washington, in countries that have extensive dealings with the IMF.

Over time, the primary mechanism for releasing Fund resources to member states, and the primary conduit for conditionality, has become the stand-by arrangement. A country wishing to have access to Fund resources negotiates a stand-by arrangement with the management

The case of IMF conditionality

and staff. After approval by the EB, this arrangement allows the country to draw on Fund resources on a specified schedule, under certain conditions. Letters of Intent attached to stand-by arrangements specify the actions that the borrowing country pledges to undertake.

My concern is with the procedures that go into negotiation and approval of IMF programs, and how these procedures affect the relative influence of the EB and the staff and management. Because the EB cannot approve a program without a proposal from the staff, a useful starting point in understanding this complex principal-agent nexus is to recognize that the staff has agenda-setting power, while the EB has the power to accept or reject staff proposals. If the staff anticipates that the outcome of board decisions will not be to its liking, it could refuse to present a program in the first place, providing it with gatekeeping power. Once a program is in place, agenda-setting power takes the form of assessing whether the borrower has lived up to the conditions of the loan and recommendations about whether to release the next stage of the drawing.

The decision to attach conditions to IMF drawings in itself conferred some autonomy on staff and management. As the exact content of conditions would inevitably be subject to staff input, any use of conditionality provides it with authority. Therefore, understanding the Fund's early decisions to use conditionality and the procedures it developed to set conditions illuminates important aspects of the agency issue. These early decisions are also important because the procedures have changed surprisingly little over the last fifty years, in spite of massive change in the content of conditions, the scale of lending, and the variety of countries involved. More recently, the Fund has reviewed conditionality practices and explicitly promulgated guidelines. Although open discussions about issues of staff authority and autonomy are not frequently available in the public record, they do at times arise and suggest that the framework introduced above helps us understand the structure of EB-staff relations.

The first years

The Articles of Agreement negotiated by John Maynard Keynes and Harry Dexter White at Bretton Woods left the issue of conditionality intentionally vague. The positions of Keynes and White, and the politicians that they represented, were predictable as Britain was certain to have to draw on Fund resources, while the United States would be the major source of these resources. The debate between automaticity, favored by Keynes, and conditionality, favored by White, played out

Principal preferences, structure, decision rules, and private benefits

over the first few years of the Fund, and was settled in the United States' favor by 1952. The early signals indicated that automaticity would prevail (Robichek 1984: 67). Keynes was anxious to avoid giving the Fund "wide discretionary and policing powers" (Dell 1981: 1). He believed that the Bretton Woods agreement endorsed his view that the Fund's "initiative and discretion" should be limited. His preferences were shared by virtually the entire membership other than the United States. Internal Fund memos and congressional hearings affirm that the United States wanted the Fund to be able to limit access to its resources.[4] The United States settled for the requirement that governments make representations as to their intentions for using resources (Dam 1982: 117).

The United States opened the door to conditionality by assuring that the Articles of Agreement required that Fund resources could only be used for purposes consistent with the Fund's principles. If the EB could question members' representations, "then there was the possibility that it might be able to exercise some discretion under cover of an assessment of need" (Dam 1982: 117). Ambiguity in the Bretton Woods agreement allowed US negotiators to tell Congress that drawings would be subject to conditions, while other countries believed that unconditional drawings would be possible. Keynes, aware of congressional resistance to the agreement and anxious to assure its passage, did not publicly dispute the US interpretation. By 1947, the EB decided that it had the right to challenge a member's representation about the purposes to which it would put Fund resources. This wedge allowed the principle of conditionality to develop.

However, the first MD, Camille Gutt, expressed views consistent with automaticity (Dell 1981: 8), while the United States continued to insist on the board's right to scrutinize requests for drawings. Between 1949 and 1951, drawings from the Fund nearly came to a halt, due to a combination of Marshall Fund aid substituting for IMF resources and deadlock about mechanisms for using them. No drawings occurred during 1950, and the entire amount drawn from October 1949 until September 1951 was only $76.8 million, while repayments of earlier drawings to the Fund during this period were $67.7 million (Horsefield 1969, 1: 276).

During this period, the EB as well as the staff and management paid a great deal of attention to developing procedures that would allow an

---

[4] Broz and Hawes (this volume) illustrate the consistent connection between the preferences of the US Congress and IMF activities.

The case of IMF conditionality

increase in drawings. The concept of automaticity disappeared during these discussions. A number of staff proposals emerged. At first, the staff questioned whether the EB had the legal right to specify the terms of drawings, claiming that the board had either to approve a drawing with no conditions, or to reject it entirely (Horsefield 1969, 1: 279). The staff proposed continuous consultations after a drawing occurred, with the Fund then cutting off further use of resources if the policies adopted were not appropriate. Many EDs felt that this procedure was too severe. After this rejection, the staff changed its tune, and suggested that the Fund might be able to suggest to members appropriate policies, and to make following them a prerequisite for the right to draw. This proposal also aroused concern. While the United States supported the staff view, others "said that they doubted the Fund could go as far as the staff had suggested in interpreting the Fund's powers" (IMF Archives S1723, EB Minutes, Meeting 285, February 12, 1948).

The United States throughout this period insisted that conditions be attached to the use of resources, and that the Fund's Articles of Agreement allowed, in fact required, such conditions. A memo from the US ED in March 1948 argues that the Articles provide "ample powers to establish conditions on borrowing members . . . with respect to the economic policies of the borrowing members while they are in debt to the Fund" (IMF Archives S1720).

New MD Ivar Rooth presented a plan in November 1951, known as the "Rooth Plan," that finally broke the deadlock. This plan became the basis of stand-by arrangements. After extensive discussions and some modifications by a staff working party, the Rooth Plan was approved in February 1952. The basic idea of the plan was that drawings of greater resources would result in greater stringency of conditions. Members would agree with the Fund on a plan to assure policy changes and repayment of the drawing within a specified time before the EB would approve the stand-by arrangement.

This formal development of conditionality reflected actual board practice in the years 1948–52.[5] Over this period, requests for drawings were often challenged on the grounds of policy problems that would lead to an inability to repay. For example, an informal request from Colombia in May 1948 for a purchase of $12.5 million was put on hold because the current measures in place to improve Colombia's economic situation

---

[5] The archival evidence seems to contradict the claim by Williamson (1982: 11) that lending during the early years essentially reflected the principle of automaticity.

were "insufficient." The board specified that a "strong policy of monetary stabilization" was necessary, and said it would approve the request if Colombia "prepared to take the proper steps" (Archives S1720, Memo from Taylor to Brand, November 5, 1948). The EB adopted similar policies toward Peru and Chile (Archives S1720, Memo from van Campenhout to Brenner, March 16, 1948; Archives S1720, EB Minutes, Meeting 240, December 23, 1947).

The development of the principle of conditionality went hand-in-hand with a shift in responsibility from the EB to the staff. In the first two years of the Fund, EDs played an active role in negotiations, heading field missions. EB Minutes from 1947 establish the following early principles:

> Liaison between the Fund and each member should normally be carried out by the Executive Director concerned, the Managing Director, and staff members. In particular cases a mission might be sent out as had been done recently, but such special contacts should be carried out only after decision by the Executive Board. (Archives S1720, Meeting 170, May 20, 1947)

This statement illustrates the tight constraints on staff autonomy that the EB initially attempted to maintain. At times, EDs questioned staff judgments on particular policy issues, such as advice to Iran on its exchange rate, or to Colombia on fiscal issues. Such questions continually raised the issue of staff autonomy, and EDs attempted to delegate enough authority to the staff to allow them to do their jobs, but to maintain control. For example, US ED Southard was unhappy with a staff report on Iran, and "expressly reiterated his support for the independence of the staff, even while declaring that he could not agree that technical reports should be submitted by the Fund with which the board disagreed" (Horsefield 1969, 1: 471).

The practice of EDs participating in missions stopped in 1948, with a board decision clarifying the division of responsibility between the board and the staff. But from 1948 until the early 1950s, the EB continued to keep a tight rein on staff missions. The "composition of each staff mission was subject to Board approval, and the Board outlined detailed instructions for them" (Horsefield 1969, 2: 11). Furthermore, members routinely discussed their prospective requests for drawings directly with the US ED prior to submitting a formal request. This practice ended by 1956. Susan Strange sees this as an "important shift of responsibility from the United States to the Fund" (Strange 1973: 279). EB oversight of staff missions also became less stringent. As staff members conducted missions, they had to make a number of immediate decisions that were only subject to review

The case of IMF conditionality

afterwards, indicating their agenda-setting function. Overall, by the late 1950s and early 1960s, the complex process of policy-making meant that "the management and the staff ha[d] a large measure of responsibility" (Horsefield 1969, 2: 11). That "in later years the influence of the staff tended to grow is undeniable" (Horsefield 1969, 1: 471).

Miles Kahler (1990: 96) also notes that the staff gained autonomy in the early 1950s, and began to exercise it. The EB stopped attempting to revise individual country programs. He indicates reasons that are consistent with the informational framework for delegation: "The United States supported these expansions of staff autonomy. In part it had no choice; meticulous design of country programs required a degree of expertise and information that executive directors and their staffs could not provide" (Kahler 1990: 96). He also notes, however, that national governments retained control over the general outlines of policy.

Strange finds the same pattern of shift from a dominant EB to more staff authority. "At first ... the secretariat was very much overshadowed by the Executive Board, to whom it was subordinate, and operated mainly as the board's advisor" (Strange 1973: 267). However, once consultations with members became common, the staff acquired more authority. Strange identifies the pressure of business – the need to make decisions in a timely manner – as one factor contributing to greater staff autonomy. For many matters, the staff adopted the so-called "lapse-of-time procedure." "In effect, this meant that the board backed up staff decisions automatically, unless an executive director having an objection or query was reasonably prompt in raising it" (Strange 1973: 267).

The reasons that historian Margaret Garritsen de Vries indicates for this substantial shift of authority from the EB to the staff with the development of conditionality echo the informational and distributional rationales for delegation. She argues that frequent staff–ED contact meant that staff could convey information informally to EDs, so that explicit oversight was unnecessary; and that over time EDs came to have more confidence in the staff. Another reason that the staff gained authority over time was their accumulated expertise. Growth of membership and turnover on the board meant that it did not build up the kind of institutional memory that the staff gained over time.[6] Thus, the desire to draw on high-quality information led to greater delegation of authority to the staff.

---

[6] See also Finch (1994).

Principal preferences, structure, decision rules, and private benefits

Keith Horsefield argues that moving the venue of negotiations from Washington to members' capitals substantially enhanced staff influence. He points out the informational advantages this shift gave to the staff:

> It ... led to the staff acquiring a much more intimate knowledge of the problems of each member country than was possible for any Executive Director except the one who had been appointed or elected by that country. It was a small step from this to the evolution by the staff, in discussions with members, of programs for the reform of their economies; and an even smaller step to the inclusion of conditions in stand-by arrangements which reflected these programs and undertakings which members had given to observe them. Yet the result was that the Board came to be faced with draft stand-by arrangements and letters of intent that had been prepared by the staff in consultation only with the member country – or at most with the Executive Director immediately concerned – and which contained conditions drafted by the staff itself. (Horsefield 1969, 1: 472)

One controversial issue associated with the shift of venue was whether the ED concerned would be able to review draft country consultation reports before the staff presented them to the board. "The Management/staff successfully argued that the whole consultation process would be frustrated if, in effect, the staff had to negotiate the contents of the report ... This was another important step in establishing the operational independence of the staff" (Southard 1979: 10).

Horsefield calls this shift nothing short of a "revolution." Not surprisingly, some EDs protested. At the 1951 annual meeting, some governors expressed similar views. The governor representing Australia decried the "tendency of the Fund, which according to my information is constantly pressed on the Executive Board by a section of the staff, to interpret the law in such a way as to expand the functions of the Fund, and thus indirectly the influence of the staff" (Horsefield 1969, 1: 270). However, the informational demands of drafting effective programs eventually convinced the board that it had little option but to embrace this delegation of authority. The shift of authority to staff was not evidence of a runaway agency or lack of attention on the part of principals, but an intentional choice determined by the need to tradeoff direct control for high-quality information. This interpretation of staff autonomy stands in sharp contrast to that of Barnett and Finnemore (2004: ch. 3), for example, who see the staff as authoritative and influential because of their legitimacy and bureaucratic incentives, not because of rational decisions by their principals.

Horsefield also draws attention to the conflict of interest among EDs that the distributional framework highlights. He argues that "the principle reason for the strengthening of the staff's position was that it had

The case of IMF conditionality

opportunities for exercising initiative, and took them" (Horsefield 1969, 1: 472). For example, the staff sent an important report on international reserves and liquidity to Fund members without board review. Horsefield identifies "a clash of views amongst Executive Directors . . . which might have made it impossible to present an agreed Board report" as the permissive condition for this exercise of staff autonomy (Horsefield 1969, 1: 472).

US ED Frank Southard has published his own analysis of the evolution of board–staff relations during this early period, and concurs with the conclusions reached by the official historians: "[I]n the end, the result was a strong Management/staff and an Executive Board that acted largely on Management recommendations" (Southard 1979: 7). Southard also provides evidence that the model is realistic in assuming that EDs do not, in practice, have amendment power over individual country programs proposed by the staff. While the board does revise general policy papers and annual reports, reports "on country consultations, including those recommending the use of Fund resources, were not to be revised unless actual errors were found" (Southard 1979: 9). In addition, he shows the effective gatekeeping power exercised by the staff and management, as the EB decided, after much controversy, that it would not consider requests for the use of resources in the absence of a recommendation by the staff. Some countries have threatened to go directly to the board to evade this staff gatekeeping authority, but these threats have never been carried out, as the EB has made it clear that it would vote "no" in such a circumstance (Southard 1979: 10).

Evolution of mechanisms

Mechanisms for implementing stand-by arrangements evolved during the 1950s. Concerns about agency issues – in particular, mechanisms to assure that the EB had oversight power in spite of increasing staff activity – continually appeared during this period. One notable instance was MD Rooth's parting address in 1956. Here, he emphasized the "delicate" nature of relations between the EB and the staff and management. He was particularly unhappy with the tendency of EDs to discuss problems with other EDs, rather than with the management. As the Fund had not been as active in the mid-1950s as Rooth desired, he felt that its achievements fell short of its promise. He located the source of this "failure . . . in the difficult problem of the respective responsibilities of the Executive Directors and the management and staff . . . Mr. Rooth emphasized anew the desirability of entrusting to the management and staff of the Fund the

Principal preferences, structure, decision rules, and private benefits

application of its policies and the day-to-day Administration of its activities" (Horsefield 1969, 1: 424). Rooth's successor, Per Jacobsson, came into office with a similar view: that the EB "sat rather too heavily on the back of the Managing Director" (Southard 1979: 5).

The early years, in which the practice of conditionality was invented and institutionalized, thus set the framework that still exists for relations between the EB and the staff. This period saw a considerable delegation of authority. The EB retains control over general policy decisions, and its delegation of authority was intentional. The staff gained agenda-setting and gatekeeping power over specific programs. The reasons for this delegation lie in the informational and distributional criteria discussed above, with more emphasis on the informational rationales at this stage. Two later changes in the formal procedures deserve mention: the promulgation of guidelines on conditionality in 1968 and 1979.

A set of explicit guidelines for conditionality was first established in 1968. These guidelines emerged in response to concern on the part of some EDs about the content of conditionality and excessive staff influence on these conditions. Those EDs representing developing countries raised the concerns, especially in response to a program negotiated with the UK in 1967. A sterling crisis arose, and the MD was instrumental in negotiations with the UK. This situation contrasted starkly with the last major episode involving the UK, in 1956. Then, the decisive negotiations occurred between the UK's ED and the US secretary of the Treasury (Southard 1979: 20). In 1967, the MD demonstrated that he could specify the terms on which the Fund would provide assistance, and used this leverage to convince the UK to devalue the pound. Negotiations were confidential, and EDs not informed of their progress. This decision to allow the MD substantial autonomy showed evidence of deliberation, not lack of attention on the part of EDs. They considered, for example, whether the Group of Ten might be a better body for handling this sensitive situation. However, both the UK and the EB preferred that the IMF take a leading role (Strange 1976: 140).

However, the outcome of these negotiations led to an uproar among developing countries, as they perceived the conditions agreed in the negotiations as far more lenient than those attached to programs with developing countries. The program contained no provisions for phasing of drawings, no performance clauses, and few monetary or credit ceilings (Dell 1981: 12–13). This leniency was especially criticized because the loan was for a large amount, $1.4 billion, in the UK's highest credit tranche, and therefore should have included stringent performance criteria. Instead, provisions for reviews and consultations substituted for the usual quantitative performance requirements.

The MD, Pierre-Paul Schweitzer, anticipated that developing countries would review the terms of the UK program closely, and so spent considerable time explaining the reasoning behind the agreed plan. His major justification was that the devaluation of a major currency like the pound sterling potentially threatened the international monetary system. "In these circumstances, it seemed to him that all of the financial support which the Fund could make available to the member ought to be forthcoming *en masse* whenever needed" (Garritsen de Vries 1976: 341).

In spite of Schweitzer's justifications, developing country EDs complained that this episode revealed a lack of equality of treatment, and argued in favor of uniform standards. Their discontent led to a general review of use of the Fund's resources, resulting in the 1969 guidelines on conditionality. The review began with a staff paper arguing in favor of continuation of the existing policies, on the grounds that individual design of each program was necessary. One could also read this argument as favoring continuing staff discretion. The staff's position was supported by developed countries, but not by developing countries. They demanded some criteria that would guide the number and content of performance clauses.

The outcome of EB discussions was a set of guidelines approved in September 1968. These guidelines reflected the demands of developed countries, as they recognized that "no general rule as to the number and content of performance criteria can be adopted in view of the diversity of problems and institutional arrangements of members" (Decision No. 2603-(68-132), September 20, 1968). The board also decided, however, in line with the preferences of developing countries, that "the number of performance criteria . . . should be limited to those considered truly necessary for determining whether the objectives of a member's stabilization program were being achieved" (Dell 1981: 12). In addition, it developed standard texts for consultation and performance clauses in stand-by arrangements. Thus, while the guidelines left substantial staff discretion and primarily codified existing practice, they can be read as an attempt to limit this discretion.

Over the next few years, the EB devoted greater attention than had previously been the case to reviewing the details of staff negotiations. Any changes in existing performance criteria recommended by the staff had to be approved by the EB, and policies demanded by the board became more specific. The board also demanded, and received, reviews of the financial models used by the staff in their negotiations. It asked for more evidence on the results of previous programs, and greater quantification to allow them to oversee programs more easily.

This increased oversight by the EB continued in the 1970s. Members of the EB, "and those in developing countries in particular, were ever vigilant to constrain the fund's management and staff as to the scope of the conditionality they could pursue in negotiations with prospective borrowers" (Polak 1991: 53). Developing country views were, temporarily, reflected in the United States, as the Nixon Administration expressed deep dissatisfaction with the management of the Fund in 1971. MD Schweitzer was criticized by US officials for allowing Fund staff too much leeway (James 1996: 244).

The 1976 annual meeting saw the airing of extensive criticism of the staff (Garritsen de Vries 1985: 493). EDs from developing countries began explicitly to call for "a close involvement of the Executive Board in the application of the Fund's policies to particular countries by having the Executive Board set up specific guidelines and constraints" (Garritsen de Vries 1985: 502). The Syrian ED expressed a similar view: the EB "ought to have a larger role in the application of conditionality to individual members. As it was, conditions were not approved ex ante by the Executive Board, that is, before the program was finalized; they were determined by the management and staff and approved only ex post by the Executive Board" (Garritsen de Vries 1985: 503).

A review of the guidelines in 1979 reflected this intensified vigilance, with a further attempt to set standards for the number and content of conditions. The emphasis was on limiting the number of performance criteria and preconditions used. The guidelines gave the EDs "closer participation in the negotiating process" (Garritsen de Vries 1985: 505). Periodic reviews of the guidelines took place in the late 1980s and late 1990s, but did little to change their basic structure.

How to interpret these debates about guidelines for conditionality? They lend support to the distributional framework. During the 1960s and 1970s, conflicts of interest on the EB grew as developed countries ceased to have any realistic possibility of drawing on Fund resources. Their interests in conditionality thus moved closer to the long-held views of the United States, while developing countries preferred loose conditions. The divergence in views was increased as the industrial countries believed that the conditions of many post-oil shock programs were too lenient (Kahler 1990: 104).

The distributional framework predicted that such polarization of preferences on the EB, given a stable set of formal procedures, would in

The case of IMF conditionality

practice increase the flexibility of the staff, as they could play EDs off against one another. In fact, it was during the 1970s that EDs expressed concerns that the management and staff were essentially setting policies, not just implementing them (Kahler 1990: 104). In reaction to this increased practical autonomy, the EB attempted to change the rules so as to rein in the staff, as expected. In addition, these debates provide firm support for the expectation that EDs with preferences closest to those of the staff should be the most willing to grant the staff significant autonomy. Attempts to rein in the staff came primarily from the developing countries, which saw the staff as imposing conditions that met the demands of developed countries.

PRECONDITIONS AND TREATMENT OF CONFIDENTIAL INFORMATION

The previous section has examined the historical evidence relating to the development of procedures for conditionality. I now turn to two additional issues relevant to the agency problem: the use of preconditions in programs and provisions for the treatment of confidential information. The issue of preconditions has become important since the mid-1970s, when they became common, and the problem of confidential information has run throughout the life of the Fund. Both present the potential for the staff to gain substantial autonomy.

Preconditions are actions that the staff and management require a member to take before they will present any program to the EB for approval. Preconditions evolved to address problems of monitoring and credibility. The 1979 guidelines on conditionality recognized the use of preconditions as associated with the need to establish credibility. With conditions written into programs in the usual manner, questions continually arose about who would monitor these conditions, whether members would really live up to them, and whether release of further Fund resources would really be dependent on their achievement. Requiring a member to meet certain standards before any program is presented circumvents all of these difficulties.

However, as John Williamson points out, the use of preconditions creates a new problem, one that is central to the issue of staff autonomy. The problem is "the absence of *ex ante* control by the Executive Board over the actions of the staff" (Williamson 1982: 36). Since staff set these preconditions, determine when countries have met them, and can refuse to present programs to the board until the preconditions are met, they could become the source of an exceptionally high degree of autonomy. Williamson recognizes the problem, but also argues that the ex post power of the EB to ask about what preconditions the staff has demanded might serve as an adequate constraint on the staff and explain why the board has gone along with the use of preconditions.

The 1979 guidelines on conditionality attempted to put limits on the use of preconditions. The guidelines state that: "A member may be expected to adopt some corrective measures before a stand-by arrangement is approved by the Fund, but only if necessary to enable the member to adopt and carry out a program consistent with the Fund's provisions and policies" (Decision No. 6056-(79/39), March 2, 1979). EDs have continued to allow the use of preconditions, indicating their satisfaction with current procedures – or at least a calculation that the benefits of using them outweigh the possible losses from increased authority for the staff. A 1986 review indicates that while the management and staff establish preconditions, they do so "against the background of discussions in the Executive Board with respect to previous programs or Article IV consultations" (IMF 1986: 7). However, there is also evidence that staff have at times used preconditions to evade what they see as excessive political interference by the EB. For example, in the case of Russia in the early 1990s, persistent intervention against the recommendations of the staff led to the increased use of preconditions (Åslund 2000: 25). Randall Stone's (2004) careful study of IMF programs in Africa indicates that such political interference is a primary reason for the economic failure of programs, lending support to the idea that the staff would have incentives to attempt to limit it.

When preconditions and "prior actions" became relatively common, in the late 1970s, the EB spent some time discussing their use and implications. A report in August 1978 acknowledged concern:

Several Executive Directors suggested that the requirement of prior actions by members should be altogether eliminated. Normally, Executive Directors are not formally informed of these measures until the request for a stand-by arrangement is presented to the Executive Board for approval; these measures therefore do not receive the Board's endorsement at the time they are discussed between the member and the staff. (IMF 1978: 6)

Other EDs found the use of preconditions necessary in some circumstances. Not surprisingly, the staff agreed with the latter position, arguing that they established a groundwork that allowed for effective programs.

The report went on to an explicit discussion of agency issues. Beginning from the presumption that preconditions are sometimes essential,

The case of IMF conditionality

the question became one of associating the EB more closely with their determination. The difficulty is that the necessary measures could only be identified in the process of discussions between the staff and the country's financial authorities. The report recommended informal contacts between the MD and EDs to keep the EB informed, but against any formal EB discussion of evolving preconditions. A review a couple of years later showed continuing EB concern with the issue, but EDs agreed to continue using preconditions on a case-by-case basis (IMF 1983: 7).

A second source of staff autonomy that has frequently met with concern on the part of the EB is the treatment of confidential information. In the course of negotiations with members, the staff often acquires information that the member would prefer to keep confidential. Analysts of the Fund have noted the "delicacy" of discussions between the staff and members (Gold 1984: 392). If a member does not anticipate that such information will remain private, it may refuse to disclose it, undermining the potential for a successful program.

In the early years of the IMF, the EB assumed that it would be privy to all information shared with the staff. However, as staff negotiations gained in importance, EDs moved toward a willingness to allow the staff and management to keep some information private. The original Articles of Agreement and Rules and Regulations made no reference to the treatment of confidential information. However, questions about the access of EDs to such information arose quickly, coming on the EB's agenda as early as March 1947.

The EB's early decision established an equal right of all EDs to any information; the ED representing the member concerned could not have privileged access to information. The EB decision "specified that every member of the Executive Board was entitled to request and receive all the information in the possession of the Fund" (Garritsen de Vries 1985: 991). However, revealing some sympathy for the desire of members to protect sensitive information, the MD adopted the practice of requesting a member's consent before disclosing information to EDs. This practice at least allowed members to know what information was being disclosed, and what remained confidential.

The situation changed after the mid-1950s with increased intensity of staff activity. In what historian Garritsen de Vries (1985: 990) calls a "salient advance in the Fund's policymaking," the EDs became willing to allow the MD to keep confidential information from them. This development was perceived as going hand-in-hand with allowing the MD or staff to take the initiative in raising issues with members.

Principal preferences, structure, decision rules, and private benefits

Questions about how to treat confidential information arose again in the 1970s, reflecting the growing difference in perspectives between developed and developing countries, as well as new issues on the IMF's agenda. The MD, Johannes Witteveen, at times carried out lengthy private negotiations. As negotiations dragged on, the EB inevitably became worried that it was being excluded (Garritsen de Vries 1985, 1006). Concerns grew that the retention of confidential information by the staff unduly increased the power of staff technicians in negotiations (Buira 1983: 133). "There is striking testimony that the amount of information which has been available to Executive Board members as a basis for their decisionmaking has, in fact, been limited" (Eckaus 1986: 245).

When the question of confidential information arose again, the issue was whether the technical assistance provided by the staff should first be cleared with the ED concerned. This question provoked strong feelings on the part of the MD and staff, as they felt that it was of "prime importance" (Garritsen de Vries 1985: 994). They worried that this precedent would mean that any information provided by a member would be available to all governments. They also emphasized the importance of the existing delegation of authority to the success of the Fund: "If Executive Directors were to direct the Managing Director in conducting the ordinary business of the Fund, the Fund could become a minor institution, with no effective relations with member governments" (Garritsen de Vries 1985: 994).

The EDs discussed the issue extensively, and endorsed the existing practices. "In short, the Executive Board decided that the Managing Director and the staff would continue to have considerable freedom with respect to confidential information" (Garritsen de Vries 1985: 994). However, they also took some steps to shore up existing procedures, reining in the staff to a mild extent. Staff reports would be available to EDs unless a member specifically requested that they not be. The staff was directed to discuss the issue of confidentiality with members, encouraging them not to withhold information unless it was absolutely necessary to do so. The attempt to encourage members to release information became stronger in recent years, with the IMF under great pressure to increase the transparency of its operations. The MD was instructed to hold more frequent informal discussions with EDs to keep them apprised of the progress of negotiations. The EB also took the step of establishing a committee to deal with any conflicts over access to information that the MD could not resolve. However, this committee does not appear to have been used.

The case of IMF conditionality

Thus, the pattern is of a substantial delegation to the staff in the mid-1950s, with modest attempts to put more limits on their access to private information in the late 1970s and today. Garritsen de Vries (1985: 992) summarizes the logic behind these explicit decisions to allow the management and staff access to private information:

> The major theme running through these Executive Board decisions was that such treatment of confidential information would enable the Fund to promote its purposes and exercise its powers more effectively. A minor theme was that the information, or conclusions based upon it, would often be provided to the Executive Board in some circumspect form.

The EB thus kept tight control over decisions about confidential information, while the content of these decisions amounted to a substantial delegation to the staff. As the informational framework suggests, when high-quality information is in demand, greater delegation is likely to occur.

CONCLUSION

Delegation of authority to an IO leads to a certain degree of autonomy on the part of the staff working for the IO, and can be analyzed using the concepts of principal-agent relationships. The case of the IMF illustrates these relationships. Two analytical frameworks provide insight into variation in staff autonomy and influence. One, a distributional framework, focuses on the preferences of states and staff members. The other considers informational demands as a motivation for delegating authority. These perspectives provide a mechanism for understanding the evolution of staff authority on IMF conditionality. They suggest six propositions about how staff agency, formal and informal, will vary. By way of conclusion, I summarize how the IMF's historical evidence stacks up against these six expectations.

First, the distributional perspective suggested that states will delegate more authority when they are most dissatisfied with the status quo (D1). During crises states have been more willing to allow the staff substantial autonomy, consistent with this hypothesis. Second, as state preferences diverge, staff autonomy should increase (D2). As the positions of developed and developing countries became polarized in the 1960s and later, the IMF staff found itself with more flexibility and influence. In response, the EB attempted to put more formal constraints on staff activities. In contrast, when the preferences of the EB converge – as during a crisis, for example – the staff finds itself having to respond more directly to EB demands.

Principal preferences, structure, decision rules, and private benefits

Third, states should be more willing to delegate authority to the staff when staff preferences are close to those of member states (D3). The strongest evidence in favor of this proposition comes from the early years of the IMF. As EDs learned that they could "trust" the staff, they delegated significant authority to staff members. A closely related expectation is that those states with preferences close to those of the staff will be the most willing to delegate authority (D4). Strong support for this proposition arises in the debates over conditionality of the 1960s and 1970s, when EDs representing developing countries consistently complained about staff autonomy and searched for ways to put tighter constraints on staff actions.

Other expectations concentrate on informational issues. IO staff will gain autonomy as the demand for high-quality information increases (I1). This is probably the most compelling explanation for staff agency that appears throughout IMF history. Demand for the necessary information to design programs with some probability of success led to the stationing of staff overseas, the withdrawal of EDs from negotiations, and other steps that substantially increased staff authority. On the other hand, states will constrain the staff's ability to collect private information as states' preferences diverge (I2). Evidence of this effect is apparent in decisions about the treatment of private information and the use of preconditions during the 1970s, when polarized ED preferences led to attempts to force the staff to reveal more information to the EB.

Overall, the process by which the IMF makes decisions on conditionality and the historical evolution of this process show that the staff does, in fact, have substantial autonomy and influence.[7] However, this finding is not evidence of a runaway agency. Instead, decisions about how much authority the staff should acquire have been deliberated and argued thoroughly by the EB. The EB has chosen to delegate authority to the staff in order to resolve distributional and informational problems associated with the use of Fund resources. At the same time, the board retains the power to retract and restrict staff autonomy, and at times exercises this power. The IMF's practices regarding conditionality thus suggest that the distributional and informational frameworks presented here provide a valuable tool for understanding the general problem of delegation of authority to IOs.

---

[7] One ED from the Netherlands, who had previously served on the staff, complained that he had more influence when he was a senior staff member ("The 'Yes' Men Atop the IMF," *Wall Street Journal*, May 12, 1983).

6

Delegation and discretion in the European Union

MARK A. POLLACK

The European Union (EU), like other international organizations (IOs), is composed of its member states. The governments of those member states have signed and ratified successive treaties outlining the objectives and institutions of the Union, starting with the European Coal and Steel Community of 1951 and continuing through the creation and institutional elaboration of today's European Union. As in any international organization, the member governments of the EU have assigned to themselves the central role in the governance of the Union. At the same time, however, the EU's member governments have created and allocated increasing powers and discretion to a number of supranational organizations, including the executive Commission, the European Court of Justice (ECJ), the European Central Bank (ECB), the European Parliament (EP), and a growing number of independent agencies which are delegated regulatory and/or informational functions in specific issue-areas. Although clearly the creation, or agents, of the member governments, these supranational organizations possess powers and preferences distinct from those of their member-state principals, and they have frequently been posited by both practitioners and academic observers as the embodiment of the project of European integration, and indeed as the "engines" or "motors" of the integration process.

The delegation of such powers to supranational organizations, the editors of this project point out, raises two fundamental and linked issues. First, why do states choose to delegate certain tasks and responsibilities

---

I would like to thank the editors as well as Bill Bernhard, Andrew Cortell, Mona Lyne, Helen Milner, Alex Thompson, and the participants in the Harvard and UCSD workshops on Delegation to International Organizations for comments on earlier drafts of this chapter.

Principal preferences, structure, decision rules, and private benefits

to IOs, rather than merely acting unilaterally or cooperating directly? In the case of the European Union, why have member states chosen to create an executive Commission and other supranational agents, and delegate an ever-growing array of functions to them? Second, how do states control IOs? Having delegated authority to IOs, what mechanisms do states employ to ensure that their interests are served? (Hawkins, Lake, Nielson, and Tierney, this volume). As applied to the EU, this question focuses our attention on what Thatcher and Stone Sweet (2002) call the "how" of delegation, namely the institutional design of international agents and the control mechanisms created to limit their discretion.[1]

The leading approach to such questions, the editors point out, has been and remains a principal-agent approach derived from rational choice theory. The principal-agent approach to delegation adopts a functional logic, explaining delegation decisions in terms of the functions performed by agents, with the most commonplace claim being that political principals delegate powers to agents in order to lower the transaction costs of policy-making. The institutional form of delegation, in this view, reflects the complex, issue-specific calculations of principals, who design various control mechanisms in order to tailor the discretion of their agents so as to maximize the gains, and minimize the losses, of delegation. In the principal-agent approach, therefore, a desire by political principals to reduce the transaction costs of policymaking explains both the "why" and the "how" of delegation.

In this chapter, I formulate and test a variety of principal-agent hypotheses about the conditions under which EU member governments delegate powers and discretion to the EU's primary executive agent, the European Commission.[2] The chapter is organized in four sections. In the first section, I set out a simple principal-agent model of delegation, and derive from it several testable hypotheses about the functions likely to be delegated to supranational agents and the institutional design of

---

[1] Thatcher and Stone Sweet's third question, "With What Consequences?", focuses on the nature of the principal-agent relationship after the moment of delegation, and more specifically on the autonomy of the agent and its ability to influence policy outcomes in ways unintended or undesired by the principals. For the sake of tractability, I bracket this important but complex question in the current chapter.

[2] The discussions of PA analysis and of delegation to the Commission in this chapter draw extensively from Pollack 2003a. For contrasting discussions of EU delegation to the European Court of Justice, and the extraordinary discretion that it enjoys vis-à-vis its political principals, see Pollack (2003a: ch. 3) and Karen Alter's contribution to this volume.

the control mechanisms created to limit Commission discretion. The second section examines the empirical record of the Commission's delegated functions, including an historical analysis of the EU's original design as well as a functional and cross-sectoral analysis of Commission discretion, which I argue fit closely with the predictions of PA models. The third section focuses in particular on the role of the European Parliament (EP) nomination and censure of the Commission. This central and growing role of the EP, I argue, demonstrates the limits of purely functional explanations of delegation, and suggests the importance – at least at the margins – of normative concerns about democratic legitimacy in the design of the EU's institutions; it also raises the intriguing question whether the Parliament has emerged as a collective or multiple principal of the Commission alongside the EU's member states. In the fourth and final section, I conclude that principal-agent analysis has proven to be a fruitful approach to the study of international delegation, explaining variation in member-state decisions to delegate powers to IOs, as well as variation in the subsequent influence of those IOs over policy outcomes. The primary challenge for future research, I argue, consists of moving beyond the "parallel demonstration of theory" – namely, that the principal-agent approach allows us to explain delegation decisions and agents' influence *within* a number of IOs – and begin explaining international delegation and agency *across* international organizations.

PRINCIPAL-AGENT ANALYSIS: DELEGATING FUNCTIONS, LIMITING DISCRETION

Generally speaking, the delegation of powers by a group of *principals* (such as domestic legislators or member governments) to an *agent* (such as a regulatory agency or a supranational organization) is a special case of the more general problem of institutional choice or institutional design: Why do a group of actors collectively decide upon one specific set of institutions rather than another to govern their subsequent interactions? The basic approach of rational choice theory to this problem of institutional choice is *functional*: that is to say, institutional choices are explained in terms of the functions that a given institution is expected to perform, and the effects on policy outcomes it is expected to produce, subject to the uncertainty inherent in any institutional design (Keohane 1984; Koremenos et al. 2001).

Within American politics, a growing literature on the institutional design of delegation examines the *transaction costs* involved in the

Principal preferences, structure, decision rules, and private benefits

making of public policy, which make it difficult for re-election-minded members of Congress to produce efficient policies and satisfy their constituents. Off-the-shelf models from American politics emphasize two specific transaction costs of policy-making that might be reduced through delegation (see e.g. Epstein and O'Halloran 1999a; Huber and Shipan 2000). (1) *Informational* transaction costs arise when legislative principals are confronted with a complex policy environment, and often require technical information and expert advice in order to craft effective public policies. In order to produce the necessary information, legislators design political institutions that employ policy experts, and create incentives for those experts to provide policy-relevant information for legislators. (2) In addition to these informational concerns, legislative principals may encounter a second transaction cost, namely the problem of *credible commitment*; that is to say, a group of legislators may find that it "pays" electorally to commit themselves to certain kinds of policies, but that they cannot credibly bind themselves or their successors to maintain those policies in the future. For this reason, legislators may often delegate powers to bureaucratic agents (such as Congressional committees, regulatory agencies, or independent central banks) who, because of their independence and their insulation from day-to-day electoral pressures, are more able to commit themselves to maintaining a given policy in the future. These two transaction costs, and the prospect of reducing them, also play a central role in Keohane's (1984) functional theory of international regimes, in which international institutions facilitate cooperation among states both by reducing the transactions costs of international negotiations ex ante, and by monitoring compliance and identifying transgressors ex post.

In formulating and testing such PA models, it is vital to specify and operationalize ex ante the types of functions that principals might be expected to delegate in order to reduce transaction costs. Indeed, without such specification, transaction-cost models can become tautological: principals delegate powers to agents in order to reduce transaction costs, and we know that those powers reduce transaction costs because principals are willing to delegate them. For this reason, I derive from the PA literature in American politics the hypothesis H1 that principals should delegate four key functions to their agents, namely: (1) monitoring compliance with agreements among the principals; (2) solving problems of "incomplete contracting," most notably by adjudicating disputes among the principals about the meaning of previous agreements; (3) adopting credible, expert regulation of economic activities in areas where

Delegation and discretion in the European Union

the principals would be either ill-informed or biased; and (4) setting the parliamentary agenda so as to avoid the endless "cycling" of policy alternatives that might otherwise result from the possession of agenda-setting power by the principals themselves.

In the case of the European Union, then, we should find EU member governments delegating these four types of functions to agents such as the Commission. Such a pattern of delegation would support the hypothesis that member-state principals are indeed motivated primarily by a desire to minimize the political transaction costs of international cooperation. A random pattern of delegation, by contrast, or a pattern in which authority is systematically delegated for functions other than those specified above, would suggest that member states are motivated by concerns other than the minimizing of transaction costs.

Studying the delegation of powers in isolation, however, is of limited utility without a further examination of the institutional form of delegation, which can limit the discretion of agents in the conduct of their delegated functions.[3] Specifically, when delegating authority to an agent, principals can also adopt various control mechanisms to limit the discretion of that agent, and hence the prospect of agency losses. These control mechanisms can be divided into two broad categories: ex ante administrative procedures and ex post oversight procedures. Administrative procedures define more or less narrowly the scope of agency activity, the legal instruments available to the agency, and the procedures to be followed by it. By contrast, oversight procedures consist of the various institutional mechanisms that principals can use to (1) monitor agency behavior, thereby correcting the informational asymmetry in favor of the agent, and (2) influence agency behavior through the application of positive and negative sanctions. Among the formidable array of sanctions at the disposal of legislative principals are control over appointments, control over budgets, and the possibility of overriding agency behavior through new legislation (Hawkins et al., this volume).

If these control mechanisms were costless, one would be expect principals to adopt the full range of administrative and oversight procedures in all cases in order to minimize or eliminate agency losses. These mechanisms, however, are not costless. Strict administrative controls, for

---

[3] The term "discretion" as employed in this chapter follows the definition and operationalization in Epstein and O'Halloran 1999a, and can be roughly equated with the use of "autonomy" in the editors' introduction to this volume.

Principal preferences, structure, decision rules, and private benefits

example, tend to produce rigid and inefficient policies, while oversight procedures and sanctions may impose significant costs for principals as well as agents. In addition, both types of oversight, by limiting the autonomy of agents from their principals, also limit their credibility as independent regulators.

Given these costs, principal-agent models predict that principals will select control mechanisms carefully, tailoring the mix of control mechanisms to the nature of the functions delegated and the characteristics of specific issue-areas. In delegating to agents, that is, principals attempt to choose the "right" institutions to minimize agency losses at an acceptable cost to themselves. However, as Huber and Shipan (2000: 9) point out, the "right" institutions may vary considerably depending upon the nature of the political environment: "One size does not fit all." Rather, they argue, the institutional design of control mechanisms can be considered as a dependent variable, which in turn reflects other factors of the political environment, which are the independent variables for the purpose of explaining institutional choice.

Over the past half-decade, rational choice scholars have put forward a wide range of hypotheses about the specific aspects of the political environment that might be expected to influence the decision by principals to allocate discretion to regulatory agents; but two factors already mentioned – the demand for policy-relevant expertise and the demand for credible commitments – have been singled out by various authors as the most important motivations for delegation and the most important determinants of agent discretion.

First, the existence of imperfect information – or more specifically, legislators' need for policy-relevant information – is often cited by rational choice scholars as justification for the delegation of powers from legislators such as the US Congress to regulatory agencies such as the Environmental Protection Agency or the Food and Drug Administration. The argument here is straightforward: the empirical world is inherently uncertain, and legislators face constant demands for policy-relevant information about the state of the world. Under such circumstances, legislators may find it useful to delegate power to a regulatory agency, which is assumed to provide policy-relevant expertise and thereby improve the quality of regulation while reducing the workload of legislators and their staffs. Such an informational rationale for delegation gives rise to the hypothesis that, "all else being equal, policy areas shrouded in uncertainty will tend to be delegated at higher rates" (Epstein and O'Halloran 1999a: 197; see also Bawn 1995; Huber 1998).

Second, legislative principals might face difficulties establishing the credibility of their commitment to specific policy choices over time. More specifically, the nature of politics as a game played over time points to two generic obstacles to credible commitment: time inconsistency, which occurs when a legislator's or government's optimal long-run policy differs from its short-run policy, so that these actors face a rational incentive in the short run to renege on their long-term commitments; and ill-defined political property rights, which occur when a group of legislators or a government faces the prospect of eventually being replaced in office by other actors with different preferences, who might then overturn their preferred policies. In both cases, legislators and governments may enjoy a rational incentive to delegate powers – and very substantial discretion – to independent bodies charged with the adoption and maintenance of certain policies, even in the face of pressures to renege from the principals or their successors. The classic example of such a disjunction between short-term and long-term preferences arises in the area of monetary policy, where legislators and governments may have a long-term preference for anti-inflationary monetary policies, but may find themselves unable to commit to such policies because of the short-term temptation to reduce interest rates and stimulate the economy on the eve of an election.

Problems of credible commitments also arise in specific issue-areas where policies generate diffuse benefits for the public at large but impose concentrated costs on potentially important constituents. For example, Congressional legislators may find it politically efficient to adopt a rigorous anti-trust policy against business cartels and concentrations or to close inefficient and expensive military bases, but in each case individual legislators would be tempted to be lenient faced with protests from concentrated interests in their own constituencies (Epstein and O'Halloran 1999a: 1–4). In this view, an independent regulator insulated from political pressures would enjoy greater credibility vis-à-vis political constituencies and markets, and legislators would benefit by delegating significant discretion to such non-majoritarian organizations. If this view is indeed correct, we should expect legislative principals to delegate powers, not only in issue-areas marked by relative uncertainty but also in issue-areas characterized by concentrated costs and diffuse benefits.

In recent years, this argument has been applied to the European Union by Andrew Moravcsik (1998: 73), who argues that member governments delegated powers in the various EU treaties primarily to establish the credibility of their mutual commitments by monitoring compliance and filling in the details of the treaties that form the central, but incomplete, contracts of the Union. Giandomenico Majone (2001) goes further, arguing that there are not one but in fact "two logics of delegation": one logic informed by the demand for policy-relevant expertise, in which principals delegate executive functions to agents within relatively constraining control mechanisms; and a second "fiduciary" logic, guided by the demand for credible commitments, in which principals deliberately insulate their agents – or "trustees" – so that the agents may implement policies to which their principals could not credibly commit. By and large, Majone argues, member states have delegated powers in EU treaties primarily for the purpose of establishing credible commitments, and therefore grant considerable if not complete discretion to supranational agents in those treaties. By contrast, the Council delegates implementing powers to the Commission in secondary legislation "to reduce the costs and improve the quality of decision-making in the Council," and accordingly design control mechanisms to limit Commission discretion (Majone 2001: 115).

The above claims from the American and EU literature can, for our purposes, be recast as hypotheses for empirical testing. Specifically, we can postulate that the net discretion of the European Commission will vary as a function of (H2) the demand for policy-relevant information in complex issue-areas and/or (H3) the demand for credible commitments among the member-state principals. In addition, following Majone, we will test the hypothesis (H4) that Commission discretion will vary strikingly between treaty-based fiduciary delegation to enhance credible commitments, and lower levels of discretion in secondary legislation designed to provide policy-relevant information.

Testing these hypotheses, however, requires an effort to operationalize both the dependent variables of delegation and discretion (see below) and especially the intangible independent variables of *uncertainty* and the demand for *credible commitments*. Measuring the inherent uncertainty, or informational intensity, of an issue-area is a difficult and contentious process since the actual complexity of an issue-area is impossible to measure directly, and the various proxies proposed by various scholars may in fact measure factors other than the issue-specific demand for information. In the various studies cited above, for example, a variety of measures of informational intensity, complexity, and uncertainty have been proposed, including the number of laws cited in a given bill (Krehbiel 1991); the number of Congressional committee meetings or hearings in a given issue-area (Epstein and O'Halloran 1999a: 206–11);

and, in the case of the EU, the length of a given piece of legislation (Franchino 2000), the number of provisions calling for the adoption of "detailed rules," the presence or absence of "action plans" in a given area, and the presence or absence of committees in a given piece of legislation (Franchino 2001). However, of these other measures a number are inapplicable in the context of the EU or risk-measuring factors other than information. For example, while Franchino's use of word count as an indicator of informational intensity seems plausible at first glance, it is striking that other studies of delegation (e.g. Huber et al. 2001) employ the same measure as an indicator of *discretion* on the equally plausible grounds that longer legislation is, *ceteris paribus*, more detailed and hence more constraining to an implementing agent than shorter legislation. Hence, attempts to measure informational intensity or uncertainty in quantitative terms invariably encounter a *proxy problem* in the sense that scholars are driven to rely on proxy indicators that provide precise numbers for statistical analysis, but at the risk of measuring something *other* than uncertainty.

For this reason, I resist developing quantitative proxies for uncertainty, relying instead on a broad classification of scientific and technical issues, together with foreign and defense policies, as the most likely to require extensive technical expertise.[4] If demand for policy-relevant expertise is an important motivation for member-state delegation to the Commission, we should see such delegation clustering in these issue-areas, and we should also see the member states allocating sufficient budgets and personnel to the Commission so as to provide this expertise. On the other hand, if delegation takes place largely outside these issue-areas, or if the member governments do not provide a sufficient budget and staff for the Commission to provide technical expertise in this area, then the informational rationale for delegation would not be supported.

Similar problems arise with the abstract concept of a demand for credible commitments, which is frequently invoked as an important motivation for delegation to domestic and international agents, but difficult to operationalize and measure independent of the act of delegation itself. In light of these difficulties, I employ two (imperfect) indicators of credible commitments, the first functional and the second based

---

[4] These policies, moreover, dovetail closely with Epstein and O'Halloran's (1999a: 206–11) classification of the most complex issue-areas based on committee hearings data.

on the distribution of costs and benefits by issue-area. With regard to the former, there is general agreement in the literature that certain delegated *functions* seem to be particularly associated with the alleviation of credibility problems. First, and most importantly, monitoring compliance with agreements is central to the credibility of any domestic or international agreement; although such delegation obviously includes an informational component, it should therefore count as evidence for the credible-commitments view. Second, the filling in of incomplete contracts by judicial rule-making or arbitration is another commonly cited means of increasing the credibility of a contract, which would otherwise be less constraining for the principals and should therefore also count as support for a credible-commitments motivation.

By contrast, the other two functions specified above may count in favor of either an informational or a credible-commitments rationale for delegation. With regard to legislative agenda setting, for example, Majone (2001) argues that member states delegated agenda-setting power to an integrationist Commission in order to increase the credibility of their common commitment to the European project; Nugent (2000) and others, however, have emphasized the Commission's informational role as an expert actor capable of producing legislative proposals that take into account the preferences and practices of all EU member states. Similarly with regard to regulation, the delegation of regulatory powers can be designed either to take advantage of agency expertise in the face of technical uncertainty or to insulate regulators from political pressures to increase the credibility of regulation – or both, since the categories of information and credible commitments are not mutually exclusive but overlapping. In sum, delegation of the first two functions – monitoring and enforcement and the filling in of incomplete contracts – represents support for the credible-commitments view of delegation; by contrast, delegation of agenda-setting and regulatory powers may provide support for either view, or both, requiring a closer analysis of the motivations of the principals.

A second means of analyzing the importance of credibility as a motive for delegation is to examine the pattern of variation across issue-areas. As noted above, a number of scholars have suggested that credible commitments should be particularly problematic for issue-areas or policies that impose concentrated costs and generate diffuse benefits. If this is the case, we should expect to see greater delegation of powers to agents, and greater discretion for those agents, in policies that impose concentrated costs and generate diffuse benefits – including most notably trade liberalization, anti-trust policy, environmental and consumer protection, and defense. By contrast, we should expect to see legislative principals retain regulatory powers for themselves in areas where benefits can be carefully targeted onto concentrated constituencies and costs are diffused, such as taxation policy, agriculture, and other pork-barrel spending programs. In the US setting, Epstein and O'Halloran find support for these hypotheses in their analysis of Congressional delegation. According to Epstein and O'Halloran (1999a: 201–203), "Legislators closely guard policy-making authority in those areas that afford them an opportunity to target benefits to particular constituents," such as taxation and social security. By contrast, legislators are more prone to delegate powers in areas where benefits are widely dispersed, making it hard to claim credit to individual constituents, and costs are concentrated, making delegation attractive as a means of shifting blame; examples include defense, foreign affairs, and selective service. Extending this analysis to the EU, we should expect to find member governments delegating the greatest degree of discretion in issue-areas characterized by concentrated costs and diffuse benefits (trade, anti-trust, foreign policy, environment and consumer protection) and least discretion in issue-areas with concentrated benefits and diffuse costs (taxation, agriculture, and other transfer payments).

DELEGATION TO THE EUROPEAN COMMISSION: THE EMPIRICAL RECORD

What powers, or functions, do the member governments of the European Union delegate to the European Commission? To what extent, and in what ways, do member governments attempt to curtail the discretion of the Commission through the use of various control mechanisms? Does such variation in delegation and discretion correspond to aspects of the political environment, such as uncertainty or the need for credible commitments? In this section, I seek to answer these questions through a detailed examination of the record of delegation and discretion to the Commission. The section first examines the record of delegation to the Commission in the EU's constitutive treaties, followed by a separate analysis of delegation in secondary legislation, concluding with analysis of the evidence in terms of the four hypotheses specified in the previous section.

Principal preferences, structure, decision rules, and private benefits

Delegation of functions to the Commission in the treaties

The European Union is a creature of the treaties that established and have subsequently amended its institutional provisions. Following the initial experiment of the European Coal and Steel Community (1951), the 1957 EEC Treaty was the founding "constitutional" document of the European Community, and has since been amended numerous times, most notably in three landmark treaties: the 1986 Single European Act (SEA), the 1992 Maastricht Treaty on European Union, and the 1997 Treaty of Amsterdam.[5] These treaties, incorporated into the *Consolidated Treaties* in 1997, lay out the basic institutional structure of the contemporary European Union, including the delegation of powers to supranational organizations such as the Commission, the Court, and the European Parliament. For our purposes, the treaties also provide an opportunity to assess the functions delegated to the Commission, the control mechanisms established to limit its discretion, and the pattern of cross-issue variation in that discretion.

The section of the *Consolidated Treaties* dealing specifically with the Commission comprises nine articles (Articles 211–19 EC) which describe the Commission's tasks and composition. The first of these (Article 211) begins with a non-exhaustive list of the Commission's functions:

In order to ensure the proper functioning and development of the common market, the Commission shall:

- ensure that the provisions of this Treaty and the measures taken by the institutions pursuant thereto are applied;
- formulate recommendations or deliver opinions on matters dealt with in this Treaty, if it expressly so provides or if the Commission considers it necessary;
- have its own power of decision and participate in the shaping of measures taken by the Council and by the European Parliament in the manner provided for in this Treaty;
- exercise the powers conferred on it by the Council for the implementation of the rules laid down by the latter.

---

[5] This chapter does not analyze the provisions of the Treaty of Nice (2001), which made no major changes in the delegation of powers to the Commission, or the Constitutional Treaty (2004), which has yet to be ratified by EU member states at this writing.

Clearly, these provisions, as supplemented by other articles in the Treaty, lay out a broad role for the Commission, which is called upon to participate in *setting the agenda* for the EC legislative process; *monitoring and enforcing* primary and secondary EC law; and *implementing* policies adopted by the Council. These functions, moreover, correspond closely to the functions spelled out by principal-agent models, including agenda setting, monitoring and enforcement, and the adoption of expert and credible regulation. Let us consider each, very briefly, in turn.

Agenda setting

With regard to agenda setting, the Commission has been granted the sole right of initiative for nearly all "first-pillar" or EC legislation, meaning that any legislation adopted by the Council, or by the Council and the Parliament, must proceed on the basis of a proposal from the Commission. This extraordinary delegation of powers to the Commission, Majone (2001) argues, represents a classic act of self-commitment to the project of European integration by member governments, on the plausible assumption that the Commission is a "preference outlier" with a strong preference for further integration, and can be expected to use its powers to pursue those aims.

The actual agenda-setting power of the Commission in any given area, however, depends not only on its right of initiative but also on the amendment rule and the voting rules for a given piece of legislation. Within the EC pillar of the Union, the treaties provide that a Commission proposal can be amended only through a unanimous vote of the Council of Ministers – an extraordinarily restrictive amendment rule which, while short of a "closed rule" requiring a straight up-or-down vote, presents a higher threshold to the adoption of amendments, and hence greater protection for the agenda-setter's proposal, than in most US Congressional legislation. The effect of this amendment rule, in turn, depends upon the voting rule governing the adoption of the legislation. Thus, in cases where unanimous agreement in the Council is required, the Commission's proposal enjoys no special status, in the sense that amendments can be adopted as easily as the Commission's original proposal. However, in those cases where the Council can adopt legislation by qualified majority, the Commission's proposal is much easier to adopt than to amend, and its agenda-setting power compares favorably to that of US Congressional committees. In a further complication, however, the co-decision procedure introduced by the Treaty of

Principal preferences, structure, decision rules, and private benefits

Maastricht weakens the Commission's agenda-setting power in favor of the European Parliament, by allowing the Parliament and the Council of Ministers jointly to amend Commission proposals (by an absolute majority in the former and qualified majority in the latter).

Monitoring and enforcement

In drafting and amending the treaties, member governments have devoted considerable attention to the problem of ensuring their own compliance with the provisions of the treaties, and for this purpose they have delegated extensive powers to both the Commission and the European Court of Justice to monitor and enforce member-state compliance with EC law. The most important treaty provision in this regard is Article 226 EC, in which the Commission is delegated the power to monitor member-state compliance with EC law and pursue infringement proceedings against member states before the Court of Justice for persistent non-compliance.

Initially, the power to initiate infringement proceedings did not include the right to impose specific penalties on member states; however, in the 1992 Treaty of Maastricht, member governments, faced with a sharp increase in non-compliance with ECJ judgments, amended the treaty to give the Commission the power to initiate infringement proceedings against member states for non-compliance with Court decisions, and to propose that the Court issue punitive fines against those member states. The fit between these provisions and the predictions generated by principal-agent analysis is clear enough to require little elaboration here. Clearly, the member governments of the original EEC delegated enforcement powers to the Commission to increase the credibility of their mutual commitment to the aims of the Community, and they have increased the Commission's enforcement powers subsequently for the same reasons. Furthermore, in delegating this power the member governments have also granted the Commission a significant element of discretion, allowing the Commission to initiate infringement proceedings on its own authority without seeking the approval of the Council.

Implementation and regulation

In addition to its role as a monitor and enforcer of EC law vis-à-vis the member governments, the Commission also plays a more direct role in the implementation of EU policies in certain areas. Unlike US executive departments or regulatory agencies, the Commission does not operate a parallel bureaucracy implementing EU policies "on the ground," a job left to the member governments, albeit under Commission supervision. Nevertheless, the Commission does play an executive role at the European level:

- adopting implementing regulations within the framework of Council and Parliamentary legislation;
- managing EC spending programs in areas such as agriculture, the Structural Funds, and research and technological development; and
- applying EC laws directly in certain issue-areas such as competition policy.

In addition, as we shall see presently, the EU member states have chosen to delegate further implementing and regulatory powers in secondary legislation, which remains the primary source of the Commission's regulatory authority.

In sum, the various provisions of the treaties delegate rather extensive and far-reaching powers to the Commission. More importantly, these powers fall neatly into three of the functions predicted by principal-agent analyses, lending strong initial support to H1. Consideration of these functions, however, tells us little about the actual *discretion* enjoyed by the Commission in the execution of its delegated powers, nor about the determinants of such discretion. It is to these questions that we turn in the next section.

The range of member-state control mechanisms

At first blush, the language of the Treaty suggests, in Article 213 EC, that the Commission is to be "entirely independent in the performance of its duties," and indeed the member states are enjoined "not to seek to influence the Members of the Commission in the performance of their tasks." However, the treaties, together with other provisions of secondary EU law, include a wide array of administrative procedures and oversight mechanisms that provide member governments with potential influence over individual Commissioners or the entire College of Commissioners as a body. These mechanisms include:

1. *Appointment and dismissal procedures*: The Commission and its president are appointed by the member governments, with a growing role for the European Parliament, allowing both sets of actors in

principle to influence the initial, or endogenous, preferences of the commissioners. By contrast, the treaties make only a highly restrictive provision for the removal, or "compulsory retirement," of individual commissioners, which may occur only by a decision of the European Court of Justice and only if the commissioner in question can no longer carry out her duties or has committed serious misconduct. Member governments, moreover, are forbidden to dismiss or even attempt to influence those commissioners in their duties, although in practice commissioners are naturally, and usefully, attuned to the political sensitivities of their own member states.

2. *Oversight procedures*: In its agenda-setting role, the Commission is required to place proposals before the member governments in the Council and to secure the requisite – and variable – majority or unanimous vote in favor of its proposals in the Council and, increasingly, the European Parliament. In terms of its implementing powers, the treaties allow the Council to set "conditions" for the exercise of the Commission's implementing powers. In practice, these conditions have developed into an arcane system of hundreds of "comitology" committees which oversee the Commission in a classic "police-patrol" fashion, examining Commission decisions and retaining the right to overturn those decisions by majorities that vary depending on the nature and sensitivity of the specific issue-area. Both quantitative and qualitative studies of comitology, moreover, have demonstrated clearly that the Commission, the Parliament, and the member governments in the Council have systematic and predictable preferences over the various types of comitology committees, and that the Council consistently employs more constraining comitology procedures in "sensitive" issue-areas and in issue-areas where the Commission's preferences are known to lie relatively far from the Council median (Dogan 2000; Franchino 2000; Pollack 2003a).

3. *Administrative law and judicial review*. The EU treaties themselves are nearly silent on the subject of administrative law, containing only a few broadly worded provisions such as the requirement in Article 253 EC that the Commission and other EU institutions "state reasons" for their actions. Nevertheless, the treaties do provide a broad framework for judicial review, most notably in Article 230 EC, which provides for the annulment of EC acts on a variety of grounds; and the European Court of Justice, together with various public and private plaintiffs acting as "fire-alarm" monitors, has developed these minimal requirements into an increasingly

elaborate and constraining system of administrative law. These developments, in turn, have had the effect of *legalizing* the principal-agent relationship between the Commission and the member governments (Goldstein et al. 2000), limiting the scope for extra-legal pressure from member states and making the Court the final arbiter of principal-agent disputes (Ward 2000; Pollack 2003a: 146–52).

4. *The budget*. In theory, legislative principals may use the budgetary process to control the staff and the resources available to their agents. Legislators unhappy with the behavior of a regulatory agency, for example, may reduce the resources available to the agency in response to shirking. However, as Terry Moe (1984) has noted, budgetary control is a rather blunt instrument, which may in practice reduce valuable agency outputs unrelated to the observed shirking and costly to the principals as well as the agents. Nevertheless, both the Council and the European Parliament have on occasion used their joint control of the EU budget to secure leverage on the Commission, either by cutting budgets for the Commission's favored programs or, in the case of the Parliament, by withholding the discharge of the annual budget.

5. *Institutional checks*. Finally, the Commission is also subject to additional institutional checks from two Community institutions, each of which has been established as an independent body with a clear mandate to monitor the behavior of the Commission and other Community institutions. The first of these, the European Court of Auditors, has a mandate to conduct an annual audit of the Community budget, and has issued a series of increasingly critical reports regarding the financial management of both the Commission and the member states. The second is the European Ombudsman, an independent official, appointed by the Parliament for a renewable five-year term, with a mandate to receive and investigate complaints of maladministration from individual EU citizens, companies, or associations.

Cross-sectoral variation in Commission discretion

Clearly, then, the delegation of power to the Commission has been accompanied by many of the classic control mechanisms used by political principals to control their executive agents in domestic political settings. One of the central predictions of principal-agent models of delegation

Principal preferences, structure, decision rules, and private benefits

Table 6.1. *Delegation and discretion of executive powers, Consolidated Treaties*

Issue-area	Delegation	Constraints	Discretion
1. Competition: Undertakings	33.33%	0	33.33%
2. European Social Fund	33.33%	.0833	30.55%
3. Competition: State Aids	28.57%	.0833	26.19%
4. Common Commercial Policy	22.22%	.1667	18.52%
5. Free Movement of Workers	14.29%	0	14.29%
6. Approximation of Laws	14.29%	0	14.29%
7. Transport	15.79%	.1667	13.16%
8. Agriculture	6.25%	0	6.25%
9. Social Provisions	4.55%	0	4.55%
10. EMU: Transitional Provisions	2.5%	.0833	2.4%

Source: Consolidated Treaties.

is that, in matters of delegation and discretion, "one size does not fit all," i.e. that member-state principals will vary the discretion of their agents across issue-areas as a function of the demand for policy-relevant expertise (H2) or credible commitments (H3).

In order to test these hypotheses, I coded the *Consolidated Treaties* as acts of delegation, measuring constructing a "delegation ratio," a "constraint ratio," and finally a "discretion index" for the Commission across each of the 35 issue-areas, following the coding rules laid down by Epstein and O'Halloran (1999a), and adapted to the EU by Franchino (2001), in order to determine whether EU member governments have tailored the discretion of the Commission as predicted by PA models of delegation.[6] Put simply, the delegation ratio for a given chapter of the treaties refers to the ratio of treaty provisions delegating executive powers to the Commission to the total number of provisions in the same chapter. Next, for each issue-area I calculate a constraint ratio, which is the number of types of control mechanisms that appear in a given chapter, over a denominator consisting of twelve possible control mechanisms listed by Franchino (2001). Third and finally, for each issue-area I derive a discretion index, which is defined as the delegation ratio minus the product of the delegation ratio and the constraint ratio. The results of this analysis are shown in table 6.1.

---

[6] For details of the methods followed in the collection of the data presented in this chapter, see Pollack 2003a: App. 1–3.

First, with regard to "delegation," I have adopted Franchino's (2001: 31) conservative rule about the coding of delegation, whereby "delegation is any major provision that gives ... the Commission the authority to move the policy away from the status quo." The results are shown in the second column of table 6.1. Using this rather restrictive index, the treaties delegate binding executive powers to the Commission in only ten issue-areas, most significantly in the areas of competition policy, where the Commission is delegated significant regulatory powers for the application of EC rules on cartels and concentrations and state aids; the common commercial policy, in which the Commission serves as the Community's negotiator on trade issues within the sphere of EC competence; and the European Social Fund, the relevant provision of which simply notes that "the Fund shall be administered by the Commission."

These functions, which are summarized in table 6.2, fall largely into two of the aforementioned categories: first, monitoring and enforcing compliance with EU competition rules (Articles 35, 75, 85, 86, 88) and/or policing member-state exceptions to such rules (Articles 76, 95, 134); and second, adopting implementing regulations (Article 39). The exceptions include Article 133, which authorizes the Commission to negotiate on behalf of the Union in international trade negotiations; and Article 147, which was adopted as part of the original Treaty of Rome and is the only treaty article to delegate to the Commission the power to implement a spending program.

Moving from delegation to constraints, Franchino (2001) lists twelve potential control mechanisms, above and beyond the horizontal provision for judicial review of Community acts, that member states might adopt to control the Commission. Following Franchino's method, a legislative provision featuring all twelve of these control mechanisms would have a constraint ratio of 1, while one with no control mechanisms would have a score of 0. A quick glance at the figures in the third column of table 6.1 and the more detailed analysis in the second column of table 6.3 reveals that the treaties do indeed employ a number of these issue-specific control mechanisms, above and beyond the horizontal controls discussed above.

Finally, if we calculate the initial delegation ratio, and then subtract a value which is the product of the delegation and the constraint ratios, we get a *discretion index*, which is reported in the final column of table 6.1 and roughly measures the total discretion allotted to the Commission in a given issue-area. Taken together, these figures suggest the treaties explicitly delegate executive powers and extensive discretion to the

Principal preferences, structure, decision rules, and private benefits

Table 6.2. *Executive powers delegated to Commission, Consolidated Treaties*

Issue-area	Powers delegated
1. Competition: Undertakings	Article 85 (1, 2) and Article 86 (3) empower the Commission to set down and enforce regulations dealing with cartels and with the abuse of dominant positions by firms.
2. European Social Fund	Article 147 provides that "The Fund shall be administered by the Commission."
3. Competition: State Aids	Article 88 (1, 2, 3) empowers the Commission to propose and to enforce rules regarding state aids to industry.
4. Common Commercial Policy	Articles 133 and 134 empower the Commission to serve as sole EU negotiator in the area of external trade.
5. Free Movement of Workers	Article 39 (3d) authorizes the Commission to draw up implementing regulations on the conditions for individuals to remain in the member state where they work.
6. Approximation of Laws	Article 95 (6, 9) delegates to the Commission the power to approve or reject national standards stricter than EU standards, and to bring such cases before the ECJ.
7. Transport	Article 75 (4) and Article 76 (1, 2) delegate to the Commission the power to monitor and enforce member state policies in the transport sector for conformity with the provisions of the common market.
8. Agriculture	Article 38 allows the Commission broad authority to fix countervailing charges where national policies distort competition among member states.
9. Social Provisions	Article 138 allows the Commission to initiate consultation with the social partners.
10. EMU: Transitional Provisions	Article 119(3) allows the Commission to "authorize the state in difficulty to take protective measures, the conditions and details of which the Commission shall determine."

Source: Consolidated Treaties.

Commission in a relatively small range of issue-areas, the most important of which are competition policy and the common commercial policy. Furthermore, since the latter are commonly characterized as issue-areas featuring concentrated costs and diffuse benefits, we can interpret these findings tentatively as support for the hypothesis that treaty-based

Delegation and discretion in the European Union

Table 6.3. *Types of constraint in executive delegation, EC and EU treaties*

Issue-area	Type of constraint
1. Competition: Undertakings	None specified
2. European Social Fund	*Consultation Requirements*: Advisory committee of member-state, trade-union, and employer's representatives
3. Competition: State Aids	*Legislative Action Possible*: Council can overturn Commission decision in Article 88(2) by unanimity
4. Common Commercial Policy	*Consultation Requirements*: Article 133 Committee *Legislative Action Necessary*: Final agreements must be approved by Council, by QMV
5. Free Movement of Workers	None specified
6. Approximation of Laws	None specified
7. Transport	*Rule-Making Requirements*: Measures must take into account the economic circumstances of carriers *Consultation Requirements*: Commission must consult an advisory committee for transport, and in some cases individual member governments *Exemptions*: Article 78 provides explicit exemption for the former East Germany
8. Agriculture	None specified
9. Social Provisions	None specified
10. EMU: Transitional Provisions	*Legislative Action Possible*: Council may overrule Commission decisions by qualified majority vote

Source: Consolidated Treaties.

delegation is motivated primarily by a desire to overcome problems of credible commitment.

Delegation and discretion in secondary legislation

By contrast with treaty-based delegation, EU member governments have delegated far more extensive executive powers to the Commission in secondary legislation – and they have accompanied this delegation with more, and more constraining, control mechanisms. Following an ambitious research design similar to Epstein and O'Halloran's (1999a) sampling procedure, Franchino has created a dataset of 158 pieces of major EC legislation, which he codes for delegation, constraints, and discretion according to rules broadly similar to those adapted for the treaties in the last sub-section. Despite some differences in terms of Franchino's coding of issue-areas and the differences in length and detail between primary and secondary legislation, his findings not only provide additional data with which to test hypotheses about delegation generally but also allow us to test H4, namely that member governments delegate broad discretion to the Commission in the treaties in order to ensure credible commitments, while delegating more mundane managerial tasks and less discretion to the Commission in secondary legislation.

Franchino's (2001) findings provide at best partial evidence for Majone's hypothesis. Specifically, Franchino's data reveal that member governments have delegated powers much more broadly in secondary legislation, including 71 of 158 pieces of legislation, and in 24 out of Franchino's 41 issue-areas, although the average discretion index across all legislation is a modest 4.4 percent. Clearly, then, member governments have been more willing to delegate executive powers to the Commission, and across a broader range of issue-areas, in secondary legislation than in the treaties, where the terms of delegation would be more difficult to change and shirking by the Commission more difficult to correct.

In terms of the issue-areas delegated, however, we find no clear, systematic differences in primary and secondary legislation, but a pattern of partial overlap. Specifically, Franchino (2001: 45) lists ten issue-areas with a discretion ratio of higher than 5 percent: (1) Competition – rules for undertakings (20.67 percent); (2) Monetary compensation amounts (15 percent); (3) Agriculture – organization of markets (14.74 percent); (4) Fishing – organization of markets (10.61 percent); (5) Competition – merger control (9.71 percent); (6) Commercial policy (7.37 percent); (7) Agriculture – financial provisions (6.90 percent); (8) Transport – market conditions (6.51 percent); (9) Agriculture – structural policy (6.33 percent); and (10) Regional policy (6.21 percent). As in the case of treaty-based delegation, we again find competition and commercial policy near the top of the discretion scale, suggesting that the aforementioned logic of commitments carries over from treaty-based to secondary delegation. In addition, however, we also find significant levels of discretion for the Commission in the management of EU spending programs, including agriculture, fisheries, and regional policy, despite the fact that these issue-areas do not appear to be characterized by either a high demand for credible commitments (since they involve disbursing concentrated benefits) or policy-relevant expertise (since none is mentioned in previous studies as an issue-area characterized by great scientific or technical complexity). In terms of hypothesis H4, then, the observed pattern of discretion suggests not two distinct logics of delegation (credibility and informal, respectively), but a partial overlap in these logics, which remains to be explicated.

Analysis

Returning to the four hypotheses put forward at the beginning of the chapter, the empirical evidence provides strong support for our first hypothesis (H1) regarding the nature of the functions delegated by EU member governments to supranational organizations. As we have seen, the Union's members have consistently delegated the functions of agenda-setting, adopting detailed regulations, and monitoring and enforcement, providing strong support to the functional theory of delegation put forward above.

Looking beyond the functions of the Commission to the patterns and determinants of Commission discretion in the treaties and in secondary legislation, the evidence examined above points to the importance of credible commitments (H3), the relative unimportance of informational concerns (H2), and the unexpected importance of speed and efficiency as an important transaction-cost motive for delegation.

If we look first at the pattern of delegation in the treaties, we find strong support for Majone's (2001) and Moravcsik's (1998) claims that treaty-based delegation seems to have been designed largely to increase the credibility of member states' commitment to their European obligations rather than to provide expert information in areas of technical complexity and uncertainty. The clearest evidence of this is the Commission's extensive discretion to bring infringement proceedings against member governments for non-compliance with EC law. The reasons for this are clear: in order to act as a credible enforcer, the Commission must be seen as independent of the demands and preferences of even the most powerful member governments, and this need for insulation and credibility is reflected in Article 226, which allows the Commission to initiate infringement proceedings on its own authority.

The Commission's power to set the legislative agenda might plausibly be interpreted as motivated either by credible commitments or by a desire to take advantage of the Commission's technocratic expertise. Such an informational motive for agenda setting, however, would not have required the specific provision in the original Article 149 EEC allowing

Principal preferences, structure, decision rules, and private benefits

the Council to amend Commission proposals only by unanimity. The significance of this provision, moreover, was clear to the drafters of the EEC Treaty, according to Pierre Pescatore (1981: 169), a participant in the negotiations. Recent archival research by Tsebelis and Kreppel supports Pescatore's account; they note, for example, that Paul-Henri Spaak, who introduced the unanimity provision in Article 149 as chair of the committee that drafted the Treaty, was aware of the power that it conveyed to the Commission, as was the German negotiator (and later first president of the Commission) Walter Hallstein (Tsebelis and Kreppel 1998: 59). There is, no doubt, a secondary informational component to the Commission's agenda-setting power, as the Commission might be expected to be uniquely aware of and sensitive to the concerns of all 25 member states; nevertheless, the bulk of the available evidence suggests that the original decision to delegate agenda-setting powers to the Commission was motivated by a desire by member governments to commit themselves by empowering a predictably supranationalist agenda setter.[7]

With regard to implementing and regulatory powers, finally, it is striking that the member governments did not delegate across-the-board regulatory powers to the Commission in the treaties, concentrating the Commission's treaty-based powers in a few issue-areas such as competition and external trade policy. As we have seen, both of these issue-areas are commonly recognized as imposing concentrated costs (typically on producers) in return for diffuse benefits, posing significant credible-commitments problems for national policy-makers; and both issue-areas are the subject of extensive delegation and discretion in other political systems such as the United States, where they remain the preserve of executive or independent regulatory agencies. Among the remaining issue-specific delegations, many of the Commission's powers combine a regulatory function with a monitoring and enforcement function, again consistent with the claim that member states delegate powers to enhance the credibility of their commitments. By contrast, the member governments have opted not to delegate extensive powers to the Commission in complex technical and scientific areas, providing little if any support to the informational hypothesis.

---

[7] By the same token, however, EU member governments later decided, in the light of experience with the terms of Article 149, to deny the Commission a similar monopoly of initiative in the politically sensitive areas of Justice and Home Affairs and Common Foreign and Security Policy – further evidence that governments have tailored the powers of the Commission by issue-area *and* in light of experience with existing provisions.

Delegation in secondary legislation displays greater variation in the issue-areas delegated and in the apparent motivation of the delegators, but here again the bulk of the evidence points to concern about credible commitments and away from informational rationales for delegation. In addition, however, EU secondary legislation also features a surprising level of delegation to the Commission in areas such as agriculture, fisheries, and regional policy that are classic pork-barrel policies distributing concentrated *benefits* to well-mobilized constituencies – a pattern diametrically opposed to the credible-commitments argument put forward above. Nor can this pattern of delegation be explained by member-state demand for policy-relevant expertise, since EU member governments possess large and expert bureaucracies in these areas, which are in any event not among the most scientifically or technically complex issue-areas of EU regulation. Rather, case-study analyses of these areas suggest that member governments are motivated neither by a demand for credible commitments nor by a need for policy-relevant information, but rather by a desire to reduce the workload of the Council and to increase the *speed and efficiency* of implementation, which is vital in the day-to-day management of agricultural and fisheries markets. Such concerns about the speed of decision-making play at best a minor role in most principal-agent models of decision-making; however, if we consider Epstein and O'Halloran's (1999a: 240) argument that the costs and benefits of delegation should be measured "relative to next best feasible alternative," the concern for speed in the EU context is not a trivial one. As any student of EU policy-making is aware, the European legislative process can be painfully slow, requiring months or even years to reach agreement in the Council of Ministers and, in certain issue-areas, a majority in the European Parliament. By contrast, delegation of executive powers to the Commission offers the prospect of speedy and efficient decision-making that would otherwise be impossible to achieve through the complex and super-majoritarian legislative procedures in place at the EU level.

With regard to hypothesis (H4), finally, we find at best partial support for Majone's (2001) notion of two distinct logics of delegation (fiduciary in the treaties, informational in secondary legislation). Instead, we find overlapping patterns and motivations across the two types of delegation, with credible commitments as a common concern in primary and secondary delegation, speed and efficiency a particularly important consideration in secondary delegation, and informational demands relatively insignificant as a motivator for either type of supranational delegation.

Principal preferences, structure, decision rules, and private benefits

THE ANOMALOUS ROLE OF THE EUROPEAN PARLIAMENT

Thus far, the evidence of delegation in the EU lends strong support to the principal-agent predictions that EU member governments delegate to the Commission to reduce the transaction costs of policy-making. In reviewing this evidence, however, we have paid rather less attention to one puzzling feature of EU delegation to the Commission, namely the repeated willingness of the EU governments to increase the role of the European Parliament in both the appointment and censure of the Commission. As we have seen above, the ability to appoint, remove, and reappoint agency personnel is one of the most basic control mechanisms in any principal-agent relationship. Simply put, the power of appointment allows principals to select agents whose preferences, they believe, will either approximate those of the median voter or produce the outcomes desired by the median voter. By contrast, the power of removal and the possibility of reappointment allow the principals to structure the incentives of agents by threatening either removal from or non-reappointment to office.

In the case of the Commission, EU member governments have granted themselves the central role in the nomination of the College of Commissioners and its president, who currently serve five-year terms of office; but they have only a highly constrained prospect of removing individual commissioners for serious misconduct, and are unable to dismiss the Commission as a whole from office during its five-year term. Put simply, the member governments retain sufficient control to appoint commissioners whom they believe will represent their interests, but allow the Commission sufficient independence during its five-year term to carry out its activities without fear of censure by the member states.

As Lyne, Nielson, and Tierney (this volume) point out, however, the situation is complicated by the growing role of the European Parliament, which can censure the Commission by a two-thirds majority of its members, and which also plays a growing role in approving the member states' nomination of both the Commission president and the full College of Commissioners. This supervisory role for the Parliament, alongside the member governments, presents two puzzles for the principal-agent approach: first, why have member governments delegated such powers to the Parliament; and secondly, what are the implications of this situation for the discretion and accountability of the Commission?

Delegation and discretion in the European Union

Why did they do it?

The delegation of supervisory powers to the European Parliament is puzzling in terms of traditional principal-agent models. To be sure, supervision of agents by legislative principals is commonplace in both theory and practice, as are institutional checks such as auditors and comptrollers. In the case of the European Parliament, however, the member states have delegated supervisory powers to a body whose preferences it cannot control – indeed, since members of the EP are directly elected in second-order elections that tend to take the form of protests against governments in power, the political complexion of the EP often runs counter to those of the governments in the Council of Ministers! Furthermore, by contrast with the European Court of Auditors or the European Ombudsman, the European Parliament has no special investigatory powers or expertise, yet it alone enjoys the right of censure over the Commission during its five-year term. The willingness of EU member governments to delegate such supervisory powers to a body with distinctive political preferences and without any special policy expertise therefore presents a puzzle for functional analyses of delegation.

By contrast with the functional, transaction-cost view of delegation put forward above, historically oriented scholars are nearly unanimous in their view that the framers of the various treaties created a European Parliament and endowed it with supervisory powers primarily to ensure the *democratic legitimacy* of this new layer of government, which they feared would otherwise be far removed from democratic control. In this regard, it is striking that even Andrew Moravcsik (1998: 276), whose liberal intergovernmentalist model strongly invokes the credible commitments view to explain most acts of delegation, concedes that EU member governments appear to have been motivated primarily by ideological motives, including a powerful belief in parliamentary democracy, in their decision to delegate powers to the Parliament. And indeed, the historical evidence of delegation to the EP supports the view that such delegation was motivated by concerns about the democratic character of EU institutions and policy-making, rather than by functionalist concerns about the reduction of transaction costs (Pollack 2003a: ch. 4). In the language of sociological institutionalism, the member states' repeated choice to replicate features of parliamentary democracy at the EU level represents a clear case of what DiMaggio and Powell (1991b) call "normative institutional isomorphism," in which an institutional form judged to be legitimate in one context is copied in another context.

Principal preferences, structure, decision rules, and private benefits

Nevertheless, to accept that member governments were motivated by normative concerns about democratic legitimacy is not to suggest that those member states were motivated solely by a "logic of appropriateness" nor that they ceased to pay attention to the likely consequences of delegation to the EP. Where the distributional implications of such delegation were unclear or unimportant, "federalist" states have pressed for, and reluctant states have accepted, an increased supervisory role for the Parliament. At the same time, however, the member states have repeatedly shown themselves unwilling to embrace fully the parliamentary model, for example by allowing the Parliament to nominate the incoming Commission. Indeed, there is no evidence that the member governments seriously considered renouncing their collective right to appoint the Commission president or their individual right to name "their own" commissioners – a right defended with equal vehemence by the traditionally intergovernmentalist British and French and by the traditionally supranationalist Benelux countries. If this interpretation is correct, it suggests that normative institutional isomorphism does occur in the EU, but it remains a marginal phenomenon, with member states embracing "legitimate" institutional templates only insofar as these templates do not risk compromising their substantive preferences.

Multiple principals?

The EU, then, is characterized by a hybrid system, in which the executive Commission is nominated by the member governments, who also remain the masters of the EU's constitutive treaties; yet the member states' nomination must be approved by the European Parliament, which also enjoys the unique ability to censure the Commission. For this reason, Lyne, Nielson, and Tierney (this volume) have suggested that the Commission is the agent of multiple principals, namely the member governments and the European Parliament.

The Parliament's supervisory powers over the Commission are indeed significant, both in terms of its role in the nomination process and in its use of the threat of censure. With regard to the nomination of the Commission, Simon Hug (2003) has correctly pointed out, the power of assent over the nomination of the Commission allows the EP to shape the endogenous preferences of the incoming Commission, whose preferences must be acceptable to an absolute majority in the EP as well as the collective position of the member states. At the same time, moreover, the EP has forcefully used its power of censure during the 1990s, most notably by precipitating the collective resignation of the Santer Commission in 1999, and this credible threat of censure by the EP means that the Commission must remain at least minimally responsive to the concerns of MEPs.

Despite these significant powers, it appears that the Parliament's relationship with the Commission falls short of Lyne, Nielson, and Tierney's requirement that multiple principles "can re-contract with the agent independent of the other principals" (this volume). If we look at the procedures for the appointment and dismissal of the Commission, we see that Parliament is capable independently of censuring the Commission, but cannot appoint a new Commission in its place, being limited instead to a straight up-or-down vote on the nominee of the European Council. In this sense, the Parliament is more akin to the US Senate, which can impeach the President by a two-thirds majority but does not thereby become the President's principal (Hawkins et al., this volume). Similarly, the Parliament can act as part of the Commission's *collective* principal when it delegates new powers to the Commission as part of the co-decision procedure with the Council of Ministers; the Parliament cannot, however, independently adopt or repeal such legislation without the agreement of the Council of Ministers, once again falling short of Lyne, Nielson, and Tierney's definition of multiple principals.

Nevertheless, while the EP falls outside the definitional boundary for a multiple principal set out by Lyne, Nielson, and Tierney, the authors are quite correct in pointing to the complex incentives facing the Commission within the EU's institutional structure, where the EU's member states remain collective principals for some purposes (e.g. treaty-based delegation), while the Council and the Parliament represent collective principals for other purposes (e.g. nomination of the Commission and delegation under the co-decision procedure), and the Parliament retains at all times an independent source of influence on the Commission through the prospect of censure. For this reason, modeling the Commission as the agent of a collective member-state principal does indeed present a misleading picture of the contemporary EU political system, characterized by a *dual accountability* of the Commission to the member states and the European Parliament.

CONCLUSIONS: COMPETING HYPOTHESES AND
COMPARATIVE STUDIES

This chapter set out to test, in the case of the European Commission, principal-agent hypotheses about the types of functions that member

Principal preferences, structure, decision rules, and private benefits

states delegate to the Commission (Why Delegate?) and the institutional form of such delegation (How Delegate?). In both cases, the empirical evidence provides strong support for the predictions of principal-agent models. Put simply, the EU's member states delegate to the Commission precisely the types of functions emphasized by the principal-agent literature, including most notably monitoring compliance with EU law, adopting efficient and credible regulations, and setting the legislative agenda in the Council of Ministers. In doing so, moreover, the same governments have designed administrative and oversight mechanisms to limit the discretion of the Commission, and they have employed these control mechanisms selectively and strategically across issue-areas as a function of their demand for credible or for speedy and efficient policy-making (but not for policy-relevant information, which can be provided easily by national governments themselves).

Nevertheless, in the context of the current project, it seems wise to end with two notes of caution. First, as we have seen, the delegation of supervisory powers to the European Parliament appears puzzling from the perspective of principal-agent models, and I have argued here that such delegation is best explained as an instance of normative institutional isomorphism (e.g. the transposition of domestic parliamentary models to the EU level). Hence, despite their secondary importance in the EU case, the sociological concepts of normative, mimetic, and coercive institutional isomorphism deserve to be taken seriously as rival hypotheses to explain the delegation decisions of states in international politics. Similarly, while principal-agent models stress factors such as asymmetric information and statutory discretion of agents as the primary resources of IOs vis-à-vis governments in world politics, these hypotheses should be tested self-consciously against the competing constructivist hypothesis that IOs command other resources, including morality authority and legitimacy, that may grant them greater influence than traditional PA analyses would suggest (Barnett and Finnemore 1999; Hawkins and Jacoby, this volume).

The second point concerns the generalizability of our findings beyond the EU to other international contexts, including the various regional and global IOs studied by other contributors to this project. Even in the absence of a systematic comparative survey, it is clear that the EU is at or near the far end of the continuum in terms of delegation to executive, judicial, and legislative agents. Indeed, no other international executive enjoys the regulatory and agenda-setting powers of the European Commission; no other international court reaches so comprehensively into

Delegation and discretion in the European Union

the legal orders of its member states as the European Court of Justice; no other international assembly enjoys the legislative powers of the European Parliament; and no other international (or indeed domestic) financial institution enjoys the statutory independence of the European Central Bank. Principals' motives for delegation also appear to vary across organizations: witness the contrast between the EU case, where informational concerns appear at best secondary, and other organizations such as the IMF and the UN Security Council, where informational concerns appear to have been a central motivation for delegation (Martin, Thompson this volume).

For this reason, a full account of international delegation should seek not only to demonstrate in parallel the utility of principal-agent models in explaining principal-agent interactions *within* IOs – although that is certainly useful – but also and more ambitiously to explain variation *across* IOs, including the fundamental question of why the EU has so far outpaced other international organizations in the delegation of powers to supranational agents. Perhaps most importantly, we should be alert to the possibility that the observed variation is driven by variables (a) external to traditional PA analysis and (b) across which the EU provides little or no variation. If this is the case, then a comparative analysis of delegation in international politics may need to look beyond the traditional PA literature, paying more attention to the *international* side of delegation in international politics, and engaging in *comparative* cross-institutional studies.

While space precludes a systematic presentation of such a comparative theory of delegation, my point here can be illustrated with reference to three variables that are largely absent from traditional PA models, and across which the EU provides little variation, but which we might expect to be important in explaining variation in delegation across international organizations. First, while PA models are not inconsistent with and can accommodate *power* differentials among collective principals, such models generally assume that such differentials are reflected in the voting rules of political institutions – a naïve assumption in terms of IR theory. Just as importantly, traditional PA models do not engage with the possibility of a hegemon among the collective principals, yet as Lyne, Neilson, and Tierney (this volume) point out, the existence of a hegemon within a collective principal can in theory have profound effects on principal-agent interactions and hence (through backwards induction) on the decision to delegate powers to international organizations. In this regard, it is striking that the European Union has no hegemon but rather a mix of large and small states, while most of the rest of the IOs studied in this project are (or have been) dominated by a hegemonic United States, the importance of which requires further study.

Second, traditional PA analyses tend to assume that delegation takes place within a domestic rule of law, and that principal-agent interactions will be structured by a legally binding contract between principal and agent. Similarly, the EU witnessed an early and far-reaching *legalization*, with the European Court of Justice emerging as the authoritative interpreter of EU law and the authoritative arbiter of principal-agent disputes. More specifically, legalization in the EU has increased the importance of formal/legal rules – which are therefore formulated with extreme care by member governments, who recognize them as binding and not simply as "cheap talk" – while decreasing the scope for informal pressure on the Commission from member governments. By contrast, most other international organizations studied in this project are more weakly legalized, which in turn leaves greater room for (a) "cheap talk" in legally non-binding acts of delegation and (b) informal political pressures on agents from their member-state principals.

Finally, because of the early delegation of powers in the EU, states in other international organizations have delegated powers to their agents in the shadow of the EU's example, raising the possibility that delegation decisions have been influenced by *social learning* from the EU. Such learning may, as sociological institutionalists argue, take the form of normative or mimetic institutional isomorphism, with states in new IOs emulating legitimate or successful templates from the EU, as in the case of the recently created African Union which replicates at least the generic structure of EU institutions. By contrast, however, states may also learn from the mistakes of EU member states, which have incurred some agency losses as a result of the partial independence of the Commission, Court and European Parliament, and therefore *resist* delegating powers or discretion to supranational bodies; anecdotal examples here include EU member states' own reluctance to delegate new powers in recent treaties, as well as the grudging acts of delegation to IOs in NAFTA and Mercosur. Hence, the EU may provide the occasion for social learning in other IOs, but whether it serves as a model or anti-model remains, as yet, unclear.

PART III

Variation in agent preferences, legitimacy, tasks, and permeability

7

How agents matter

DARREN G. HAWKINS AND WADE JACOBY

In spite of the growing sophistication of the principal-agent (PA) literature, it still contains a remarkably thin view of agent behavior. That is, PA theorists have made surprisingly few *direct* claims about agents. Almost twenty years after it was written, Williamson's (1985: 30) pithy formulation – that agents are "self-interest seeking with guile" – remains the classic statement, and most current formulations do not go far beyond it.[1] Mainly, the field has focused on what principals can do to control such agents. These controls – including detailed rules, screening and selection, monitoring and reporting requirements, institutional checks, and sanctions, as detailed in the Introduction – give us an *indirect* picture of agents as seen through the eyes of principals. While the indirect picture reinforces Williamson's original notion of potentially troublesome agents, it also suggests that principals have many tools to control these agents.

Scholars have paid less attention to the strategies that agents use to try to circumvent these controls. Agents often do more than just attempt to hide their information and their actions, as discussed in the Introduction. In fact, as we discuss below, some agent strategies are not very hidden at all. Other strategies are indeed hidden, but agents use different

---

We thank David Lake, Daniel Nielson, Michael Tierney, Andrew Cortell, Lisa Martin, Rachel Cichowski, Karen Alter, Jay Goodliffe, Mark Pollack, Kelly Patterson, Scott Cooper, Jon Pevehouse, Rachel Epstein, Ed Page and many others who commented during a series of presentations. Camille Jackson and Anna Sanders provided invaluable research assistance.

[1] For example, Bergman et al. (2000: 257) note that "delegation is often problematic. Agents may have different interests from their principals . . . and/or the principal may be unable to observe the agent's actions on his behalf."

Agent preferences, legitimacy, tasks, and permeability

methods to cover their tracks. Though scholars have made great efforts to articulate and describe a range of principal control strategies, as summarized in the Introduction, a parallel effort needs to be made to understand agent strategies. Moreover, a focus on principal control mechanisms privileges the ways in which principals design the contract governing agent behavior, essentially directing attention to moments of institutional creation. What happens between the creation moment and subsequent outcomes can depend on agent behavior and strategies. Of course principals can later recontract, yet such recontracting is often quite difficult due to collective action problems among principals (Nielson and Tierney 2003a). If scholars are to successfully analyze the interaction between principals and agents, they need to understand agents in greater detail. Other chapters in this volume identify agent characteristics as important explanatory factors – heterogeneity of preferences for Thompson, professional versus political staffing for Cortell and Peterson, and the particular nature of international courts for Alter – while we focus on agent strategies.

Our central point is that principal preferences and control mechanisms alone cannot fully explain which agents principals end up hiring or how those agents act once hired. More specifically, independent agent *strategies* can influence a *principal's decision to delegate* and the *agent's level of autonomy*. Theorists who see agents as simply trying to hide information and action are likely to miss important strategic interactions that alter PA outcomes. Our arguments are relevant not only to the PA approach but also to broad theoretical debates about international institutions. Much of the institutionalist literature is focused on theorizing *state preferences and design* of IOs (Abbott and Snidal 2000; Koremenos et al. 2001). We focus theoretical attention on IOs as *strategic actors with agency*. IOs matter not only because states have designed rules to resolve problems, but because those IOs are themselves independent actors that interact strategically with states and others. While few might disagree with this contention, scholars have not yet – with a few exceptions (Barnett and Finnemore 1999, 2004) – theorized the strategies of those actors and how they influence international outcomes. We share with Barnett and Finnemore (2004) a concern with taking IOs seriously as agents. Unlike them we focus not on the social knowledge that endows IOs with authority (and that takes them beyond a principal-agent approach) but rather on the particular strategies that IOs pursue in their relationship with states.

How agents matter

Most of us know intuitively that agent strategies differ, and popular culture constantly reminds us. Forrest Gump is the perfect agent because he always does exactly what he is told with total commitment (and surprising competence). When his drill sergeant asks Forrest what he thinks, Forrest shouts, "Whatever you tell me to think, sir!" To the sergeant, Forrest is a "@!%@! genius." To us, Forrest is an agent who has no strategies that would trouble his principal. But Forrest is unusual. Much more common are what we might call the George Castanza agent. Like his *Seinfeld* namesake, this agent is shiftless, marginally competent, and always on the take. Screening and selection having already failed, close monitoring of this agent is a must. Principals do get some work out of this kind of agent – otherwise they would terminate the contract – but it's always a close call on whether the costs outweigh the benefits. PA theorists hardly expect to find many Forrest Gump agents – though like the sergeant, they know how to appreciate them when they see them – but they often describe George Costanza agents, with whom the principal is never satisfied, but also not quite ready to abandon.

More neglected in PA analysis is the kind of agent exemplified by the Man with No Name, made famous by Clint Eastwood. In *High Plains Drifter*, the Man with No Name is hired by a town's leading citizens to protect them against the outlaws who terrorize them. In *A Fistful of Dollars*, he is hired by each of two warring families to help in their fight against the other. Whether splitting principals (the town fathers) or playing them off against one another (the two families), this agent is a nightmare: he hides the way his preferences diverge from those of his principals, he waits for moments of maximum principal vulnerability to clarify contract terms, he embraces all the autonomy granted by the principals, and then uses his power to take more. Self-interested with guile, indeed. The point of the analogy is not to supplant negative stereotypes of IO officials as feckless and incompetent with equally cartoonish pictures of them as ruthless and deceptive. The point is that agent strategies vary greatly and are likely to have some influence on outcomes. Scholars may know this intuitively, but consideration of that variation has played little role in either PA or international institutions theory to date.

Agent strategies are likely to influence both principal delegation decisions and agent autonomy, and we adopt the Introduction's definition of both concepts. We argue that agent strategies can entice potential

Agent preferences, legitimacy, tasks, and permeability

principals into delegating authority and then often increase the agent's own autonomy once that authority has been delegated. While a whole range of agent strategies are worthy of examination, we focus on four: interpreting principal mandates and other rules prior to delegation, reinterpreting those rules once states have delegated, expanding permeability (to non-principal third parties) and buffering (creating barriers to principal monitoring of agents). Our point is *not* that principals are too dumb to anticipate these strategies and to devise counter-strategies. Rather, given that all controls impose costs on the principals who use them and that as a result principals may not employ control mechanisms vigorously, we wish to identify the strategies that agents use to exploit these difficulties in order to secure delegated authority and to increase autonomy.

For every endogenous aspect of the contract designed by principals, we stress an exogenous complement that can result from agent strategies. All principals propose a mandate and a set of rules for agent behavior. As we show below, however, potential agents do not always wait patiently for principal delegation but seek to convince principals through principal-friendly interpretations that they will be excellent agents. On the other hand, once principals delegate more authority, agents can openly attempt to reinterpret these mandates and rules in ways that increase their autonomy. Similarly, principal monitoring through agent communication is a normal, endogenous part of most agency contracts. Yet agents can develop strategies to buffer such monitoring, sometimes by creating fairly elaborate organizational structures to raise the monitoring costs. Finally, principals and agents exist in a broader political context, and principals may well allow agents to be permeable to certain third parties that can influence agent decision-making (Gould 2003). Since permeability is a potential aid to principals – through the well-known mechanism of "fire alarms" (McCubbins and Schwartz 1984), it is often endogenous to the agent contract. But agent strategies can also increase permeability in ways that let them serve third parties rather than principals.

The chapter has three sections plus a conclusion. First, we specify the scope conditions under which agent strategies will matter most. In the second section, we analyze the ways in which agent strategies may affect both delegation and autonomy. Finally, we offer a case study of the European Convention on Human Rights. We show that the European Human Rights Commission and Court first helped convince states to delegate to them and then used three distinct strategies to gain greater autonomy.

When do strategies matter? Agency costs and pool size as scope conditions

For agent strategies to matter, agents need leverage. In particular, the costs of creating new agents must be high compared to the costs of delegating to existing agents, and the pool of existing agents must be limited (see table 7.1).[2] This argument underpins all of the subsequent analysis and sets scope conditions on the arguments to come. Where the cost of creating new agents is low or where the agent pool is large, agent characteristics and strategies are less likely to matter.

Principals incur two types of costs in creating new agents: contracting costs and uncertainty costs. Contracting costs include the time and resources required to negotiate with other potential principals and to set up new agents and new control mechanisms. Although states delegating to existing agents must also pay contracting costs, we assume these are typically lower than for new agents. Principals that create new agents must negotiate fundamental agent characteristics, decision rules, funding methods, broad competencies, and decision-making structures. Such features are already established for existing agents so that contracting costs are limited to negotiations over the task at hand. Additionally, principals often minimize these costs by writing rules at the moment of agent creation about how new delegation should proceed (Gruber 2000).

Uncertainty costs multiply these contracting costs for new agents. When creating new agents, principals are uncertain about whether those agents will operate in practice as they do on paper, whether the control mechanisms will work, whether other principals might have hidden

Table 7.1. *Scope conditions: When agents matter*

	High costs of creation	Low costs of creation
Small pool of agents exists	Agent characteristics and strategies are crucial.	Agent characteristics and strategies matter less because Ps can create new agents.
Large pool of agents exists	Agent characteristics and strategies matter less because Ps select from among existing agents.	Agent characteristics and strategies do not matter.

---

[2] On the high costs of creating new agents, see Keohane 1984 and Weber 1994.

agendas in agent creation, and whether and how the prospective agent will benefit the principal. With existing agents, principals have more information about the agent's preferences and abilities, as well as the nature of the political interaction among principals or between principals and agents. As a result, principals have higher confidence in the predicted outcomes and – provided their preferences are sufficiently aligned – are more likely to delegate due to the lower risks.

Where the cost of creating new agents is relatively high, a limited pool of existing agents further increases the importance of agent characteristics and strategies. Where agent pools are large, screening and selection can work well as a control mechanism. As pools diminish in size, however, screening and selection become increasingly irrelevant, and the characteristics of existing agents loom increasingly large. In both international and domestic politics, the number of available institutional agents is generally quite small; only a few bureaucracies or IOs with the needed expertise are available for any given problem, and principals often lean on existing agents to take on new tasks. Small pool size can also adversely affect other control mechanisms. Sanctions, for example, are less effective when agents know that principals have few other options. Endless US delays in UN budget payments would undoubtedly have been more effective in bringing reform if the United States could credibly threaten to use its money to employ other agents. The UN monopoly in so many issue-areas makes its existing characteristics both more important and more difficult to change. Moreover, agent strategies are likely to matter more in politics than in economics because the typical agent output is public policy, which is usually a monopoly good and rarely priced. This makes it difficult or impossible for principals to compare alternative providers and measure efficiency.[3]

Our argument so far suggests that limited agent pools can make agent characteristics and strategies more important to PA outcomes. This position echoes an early sympathetic critique of PA theories, which observed that political bureaucracies are likely to be more difficult to control than economic agents and that political contexts work differently than economic ones (Moe 1984). Few have followed up this insight, despite the fact that a fair number of empirical studies have now shown that many political agents have more autonomy and slack than standard PA theories would suggest (Eisner and Meier 1990; Hill and Weissert 1995; Krause

---

[3] We thank David Lake for helping us make this point.

1996; Rourke 1976; Wood 1988). Our approach also resonates with sociological approaches to organizational behavior, which have long emphasized the important role that organizational structure can have on political outcomes (Perrow 1986; Pierson 1996; DiMaggio and Powell 1991a; Barnett and Finnemore 1999).

HOW AGENT STRATEGIES INFLUENCE DELEGATION AND AUTONOMY

Scholars in both PA and international institutionalist traditions have focused on *principal preferences* to explain *delegation* and *control mechanisms* to explain *autonomy*. Invoking PA theory, Pollack (2003a) argues that states delegate to IOs to reduce transaction costs and gain credibility. Abbott and Snidal (2000) utilize institutionalist theory to reach a similar conclusion that states delegate to IOs to reduce transaction costs, strengthen credible commitments, and resolve problems of incomplete contracting. Although based on a different approach, Moravcsik (2000: 1997) also points to the importance of government (not state) preferences when he argues that governments delegate to IOs to gain domestic policy lock-in. With respect to autonomy, Pollack (2003a) echoes mainstream principal-agent explanations by arguing that state control mechanisms determine the scope of IO autonomy. Nielson and Tierney (2003a) agree, but add that unresolved collective action problems among principals can provide agents greater autonomy.

Without at all denying that principal preferences and control mechanisms are important, in this section we explain what happens when we reverse the causal arrows to treat *agent strategies* as independent influences on principal delegation and agent autonomy. We cover four such strategies: agent interpretation of potential mandates prior to delegation, agent reinterpretation of their mandates once delegation has occurred, agent efforts to increase their permeability to third-parties, and agent efforts to buffer principal monitoring. These agent strategies can expand their autonomy and/or persuade principals to delegate more authority to them. These strategies also can be used to circumvent principal control mechanisms. The strategies vary in interesting ways. Interpretation and reinterpretation address ex ante principal controls (rules, screening, and selection), while increasing permeability and buffering seek to circumvent ex post efforts (monitoring, sanctions) (Strøm 2000). Interpretation and reinterpretation are done openly, while buffering is generally hidden, with expanding permeability often a mix of overt

Agent preferences, legitimacy, tasks, and permeability

and covert action. Principals do not always rebuff agent strategies for a variety of reasons, including a lack of information on the extent to which their control structures have been challenged, the judgment that it is too costly to redesign or rebuild control structures, difficulties in reaching agreement within collective principals, or even the conviction that the unexpected agent behavior actually suits their interests.

Agents interpret and reinterpret rules

Although the use of particular rules is a control mechanism in its own right, all of the control mechanisms developed in PA theory are based on rules, in a broader sense. Monitoring and reporting requirements require rules – usually formalized and written down – about how much information agents must report and when and how to report it. Institutional checks and balances rely on rules about which agents have which powers at what points, which parties must approve of an agent's action, what constitutes approval, and how agents achieve that approval. No set of rules can be completely precise nor cover all contingencies; thus, there is always room for interpretation. Principals of course have the capacity to interpret the rules to their advantage, but so do agents. Agents can decide, for example, whether particular events fall within their mandates for action.

Early in a delegation relationship, agents are likely to mirror principal interpretations of the rules. Principals rarely delegate all at once to new agents but rather delegate only limited tasks or for a limited time. In the international arena, states commonly create new agents by treaty when only a limited number of states have ratified that treaty. The remainder of the states are likely to carefully monitor the agent's behavior before delegating authority through ratification or other methods. In particular, principals are concerned about the agent's interpretation of its overall mandate: the cases in which it can act, the powers it possesses, the nature of the desired outcomes. Agents seeking additional delegation are likely to interpret the rules in principal-friendly ways in order to receive that delegation.

Once substantial delegation occurs – in the international arena, once sufficient numbers of states have ratified a treaty or otherwise accepted an IO agent – agents are less likely to demonstrate their deference for the benefit of less important principals that have not yet joined. As a result, longstanding agents are more likely – depending on the agent's preferences – to openly reinterpret their mandate and other rules in ways

How agents matter

that are at odds with principal preferences. We thus distinguish between interpretive strategies that precede delegation and reinterpretive strategies that follow it, sometimes many years later. Reinterpretations occur as circumstances or agent preferences change. Of course, agents cannot simply reinterpret mandates in unrestrained fashion. In addition to principal threats, agents are constrained by their desire for good reputations, their commitment to professional norms, and their desire to have others adopt their interpretation, points made by Alter in this volume.

Agents can pursue a variety of reinterpretive methods that increase the costs of principal control mechanisms or that decrease the probability that principals will override such reinterpretations. Four mechanisms stand out.[4] First, agents can reinterpret the rules in gradual ways that, though visible, do not give principals enough incentives to overturn the reinterpretations and that allow the principal time to adapt to the new interpretations. Those incremental steps can then sum in substantial ways. Second, agents can reinterpret rules in ways that split collective principals and make it unlikely that they will act to overturn the ruling. Third, agents can behave in ways that accord with the substantive preferences of principals but that develop procedural innovations. If principals are eager to embrace the substantive decision, they will often prefer not to raise concerns about the procedural innovation at that point, but then may find that agents invoke such procedures as precedents in later decisions. Then, especially if a collective principal is split, it is difficult to restore the original procedural guidelines. Finally, agents can ask principals to formalize a practice that agents have developed informally. Principals may hope that formalizing such changes will end agent innovation, but if agent preferences have grown out of sync with those of the principal, formalization may simply solidify their foundation for further efforts to change the contract. As always, principals can end the contract, but agent access to large amounts of data and expertise enables them to pursue and defend independent reinterpretations with vigor. We illustrate these points in our case study.

---

[4] Barnett and Finnemore (2004: 7) point out that agent interpretation can actually "create social reality" by "defining meanings, norms of good behavior, the nature of social actors and categories of legitimate social action." We agree, but see these as long-term processes with diffuse and unpredictable outcomes that are also shaped by principal interpretations. We remain focused on the medium-term and more discrete dependent variables of principal delegation and agent autonomy.

Agent preferences, legitimacy, tasks, and permeability

Agents increase their permeability to third parties

Principals and agents do not operate in a vacuum but rather interact in political contexts that include other actors. While these non-principals have no share in the formal voting rights that control agents, they can be highly relevant to agent behavior. In international relations, important social groups have mobilized around almost any issue where states have delegated resources and authority to IO agents, including security, economic, environmental, gender, and human rights issues. Recent scholarship has emphasized that social groups in different countries have increasingly joined together through networks or organizations and have succeeded in many cases in altering the agenda and behavior of IO agents (Keck and Sikkink 1998; Risse et al. 1999). In some cases, the causal arrows can even become reversed as non-principals influence agents who then influence principals (Tsebelis and Garrett 2000).

Agent permeability refers to institutional features of agents that allow non-principals to access an agent's decision-making process. Principals may have many reasons to make permeability endogenous to the contract, but perhaps the most commonly cited is the desire to enlist non-principals in monitoring the agent, the so-called fire alarm mechanism (McCubbins and Schwartz 1984). In this view, as Lake and McCubbins make clear in the Conclusion, third parties use permeability structures exclusively to provide information to principals. We argue that agents may also be able to influence their own levels of permeability and that third-party actors not only provide information to principals but also try to influence agents.

Permeability can be determined by examining institutional rules and practices regarding access. At the low end of the scale, principals and agents regularly close their deliberations to outsiders. Central banks, NATO, and the UN Security Council are probably among the least permeable agents in the world, routinely meeting in secret. In highly permeable agents, on the other hand, non-principals can file grievances against principals with adjudicatory agents and directly argue their case on equal footing with principals before impartial judges. In between the high and low ends of the scale, non-principals can lobby agents, help fund them, participate in debates, or simply observe. Where agents face election, it is axiomatic that interest groups and other non-principals can of course be enormously influential. Where agents are appointed, non-principals can utilize persuasion, shame, information or symbols to influence decision-making (Keck and Sikkink 1998). Many UN agencies fall in this middle range and have often become more permeable over time. Other global organizations like the World Bank also stand as intermediate cases in which non-principals can participate within important limits (Fox and Brown 1998; Nelson 1995).

Increasing permeability is likely to influence agent preferences as non-principals use incentives and persuasion to push agents in their preferred direction. While third parties undoubtedly provide information to principals, as Lake and McCubbins point out in this volume, they also attempt to influence the agent directly. Agents are likely to be responsive to third parties when their preferences align, when third parties have information or other resources the agents need to complete their job, or when agents are attempting to gain the compliance of third parties and it is costly to coerce that compliance. Agents are also likely to be responsive to third parties when they share basic understandings, norms, or professional commitments and hence are open to persuasion. At a minimum, permeable agents will be pushed toward decisions favoring powerful non-principals yet within boundaries set by principals. At a maximum, non-principals will push agents to transgress these boundaries. This is especially likely when permeability favors non-principals whose preferences differ from those of principals.

Agent permeability is not a fixed characteristic and not all permeability is endogenous to the PA contract; rather, permeability can be manipulated by strategic agent action. It is difficult for principals to design autonomous and permeable agents and yet control access to those agents, especially in limited agent pools where third parties have few other choices for action. Agents designed with limits on their permeability, can, over time, expand the range of actors with whom they interact or expand the depth of their engagement with third parties. Agents facing budget or personnel cuts can seek to rally non-principal support. Bureaucracies can structure public input and information gathering in such a way as to favor outsiders with similar preferences. In the United States, voters have repeatedly instructed their agents, the legislators, to design laws restricting the access of large donors like corporations or unions (both non-principals) to those same agents. Despite repeated attempts, non-principals persist in finding ways to access those agents, who are extremely permeable. Congress experiences the same problem in designing bureaucracies to work with non-principals, which then seek to capture those agents. In the international arena, the European Court of Justice expanded its permeability by empowering individuals to raise violations of European law in the

Agent preferences, legitimacy, tasks, and permeability

national courts and encouraging those courts to send them the cases (Alter 2001).

Agents buffer principal monitoring using dualism and ceremonialism

Organizational sociologists have long been fascinated with aspects of organizations that seem not to make direct contributions to organizational efficiency. Some of these insights are ripe for extension to the PA relationship. Buffering refers to an organization's attempt to resist monitoring. We identify two forms of buffering: dualism and ceremonialism. Dualism is the creation of a loose coupling between an organization's core tasks (what it actually does) and those practices that please other powerful players in their institutional environment (what others want it to do) (DiMaggio and Powell 1991a; Meyer and Rowan 1991). Ceremonialism is the superficial reporting of an organization's activities designed to satisfy monitors without revealing too much information. Where interpretation is a response to ex ante controls such as screening and selection, agents use buffering to mitigate the intrusiveness of ex post monitoring of their behavior. Interpretation and reinterpretation are overt activities, but buffering is often more covert. Agents can compartmentalize monitoring by promoting "dualist" features in their own organization; the part of their organization that is most pleasing to outsiders is then developed publicly while the other part remains more hidden. Agents can ceremonialize monitoring by getting principals to accept incomplete or even symbolic information or by making monitoring purely formal and superficial.

Increasing permeability can facilitate agent buffering. When conflicting demands on agents from principals and third parties grow, agents may develop dualist features (DiMaggio and Powell 1991a). That is, over time, non-principals' influences may come to be reflected in the agent's structure: one part works for the principal, perhaps as originally contracted, while another part works for other constituencies. For example, UNICEF receives roughly half its budget from non-state actors, and it was a pioneer in setting up NGO consultative committees, both in national offices and at headquarters. It has now become pro forma for IOs to have NGO consultative committees to engage certain external actors (e.g. the NGO Liaison Office at the UN, World Bank Consultative Committee). IO consultation also extends to private firms as well as NGOs (especially at UNDP and the UN generally). Agents may thus reconfigure themselves so that principal controls affect only a portion of the agent's activities. Since agents attractive to principals are likely to be attractive to others as well, principals may not be able to stop their agents from moonlighting on behalf of others' causes, especially if the organization had a long history prior to being contracted by the principal. Thus, permeability can create the incentive for dualism, and dualism creates the possibility for more permeability and, indirectly, more autonomy.

Both forms of buffering – dualism and ceremonialism – raise the costs of real monitoring for principals. Rather than be subject to police patrols (auditing by principals) or fire alarms (various forms of decentralized tattling), strong agents may offer principals a kind of structured self-reporting, which might permit the principal's desire for reassurance, but attenuate any potentially intrusive aspects. This latter possibility is heavily tilted in favor of agents, for they may well get to sign off on all the parameters of what monitoring does occur. The examples of Enron and WorldCom are illustrative: principals (shareholders) assumed themselves to be operating under various mixes of police patrols and fire alarms (the proliferation of such systems implying effective redundancy rather than ineffective chaos); meanwhile, the actual monitoring more closely approximated structured self-reporting in which the agents had first internalized, and then thoroughly ceremonialized the monitoring. When principals select monitoring and reporting requirements as their key mechanism for controlling agents, they can run large risks, and as in the corporate scandal examples, they may also not discover this until it is too late.[5]

Thus, dualism is a strategy that both results from agent permeability and may generate more permeability over time. It allows some agents to serve multiple constituencies (principals and third parties) and still expand their own autonomy. This is a neat trick in and of itself. Under the right conditions, dualism can also be a license to steal from principals, who find their monitoring costs continually on the rise. Of course, principals could monitor the *outcomes* agents produce and forget about trying to monitor agent *behavior*. This move simplifies matters for the principal, but it may not improve things much because if agents provide

---

[5] Our reading is consistent with the fact that voter anger prompted a legislative response in the form of mandated "real" monitoring. That the Sarbanes-Oxley Act will cost US firms billions underscores a real dilemma about the clumsiness of principal controls: because shareholder/principals at some firms failed to control their agents, voter/principals have essentially levied a massive tax on themselves as consumers. The biggest winners are all the surviving accounting firms.

Agent preferences, legitimacy, tasks, and permeability

truly valuable services for principals, they may be able to skim off extraordinary amounts and still return a "profit" to their principals.

Two basic claims flow from the discussion above: First, principals are more likely to delegate to agents who employ *interpretive* strategies designed to convince principals that agent preferences are close to their own. Second, agent autonomy is likely to be greater when agents employ strategies to *reinterpret their mandates and other rules, expand their permeability, and buffer principal monitoring*. These two claims are sequenced over time; agents must first convince principals to delegate more authority, and only once principals have committed themselves can they try to carve out greater autonomy. The alternative arguments, drawn from the existing literature, are that delegation is driven by principal needs and that agent autonomy is determined by principal control mechanisms (see Pollack 2003a).

Why don't principals simply alter their control mechanisms to counteract these agent strategies? In some cases, they do. We make no general claim that principal efforts to check agents are ineffective; indeed, we are impressed with the extravagant lengths to which principals will go to clip agent wings. But in calling attention to possible agent strategies that drive the strategic interaction of principal and agent, we see five reasons why principals may not always root out agent strategies designed to produce greater autonomy. First, principals sometimes can be fooled into believing that they are monitoring something real and important about the agent. Second, the costs to principals of better control mechanisms sometimes exceed the benefits gained from reining in agents, especially when the costs to agents of improved evasion are low. Thus, agents may be able to actually drive up the control costs for principals. Third, principals may change their preferences, perhaps under agent influence, and come to agree that even though the agent is utilizing strategies designed to give it greater autonomy, it is also accomplishing something of real value. Fourth, principals may not be able to agree among themselves on whether and how to change agent behavior. Fifth, the principals may still be relatively better off than without the agent (and so continue the contract), even when it is also plain that they are relatively worse off than they would be with more effective monitoring instruments.

HUMAN RIGHTS AGENTS

We demonstrate the plausibility of the above arguments by applying them to the European Convention of Human Rights (ECHR) and its two main institutions, the Commission and the Court. Why did states delegate significant authority under the Convention? Once that authority was delegated, to what extent did the Commission and the Court expand their autonomy? Why? We make four analytical claims:

1. Principals are more likely to delegate when agents use strategies of interpretation designed to convince principals that agent and principal preferences align.[6]
2. Once states have delegated authority, agents can use buffering strategies to covertly increase their autonomy.[7]
3. Once states have delegated authority, agents can use strategies to increase their own permeability to third parties and thereby increase their autonomy.
4. Once states have delegated authority, agents can use reinterpretation strategies to openly increase their autonomy.

These claims go beyond the existing arguments in the literature, which suggest that principal preferences explain decisions to delegate and that principal control mechanisms determine agent autonomy – a perspective represented in this volume in chapters by Martin and Pollack. If our arguments are correct, we should see states (potential members of a collective principal) observing agent preferences before delegating. We should also see the Commission and Court (the agents) attempting to convince states to delegate by interpreting rules in ways consistent with state preferences and by behaving in ways that diminish the need for careful state monitoring. Once high levels of delegation occur, we should see the agents utilizing the three strategies just indicated to increase their autonomy. If the existing theoretical explanations are correct, we should observe states deciding to delegate without considering agent preferences, and we should witness a strong relationship between control mechanisms and agent autonomy, regardless of agent strategies.

---

[6] This claim refers to marginal, not absolute levels of delegation. The distinction is crucial. We assume many principals understand the generic risks of reinterpretation, permeability, and buffering and that this awareness likely depresses absolute levels of delegation. In any given set of principal choices, however, agents that openly interpret their mandates in principal-friendly ways should induce more principal delegation than agents or potential agents who do not.
[7] As will be clear, "covert" refers not to cloak and dagger operations by legal bureaucrats, but rather to their preference for making initial changes quietly and below the radar of busy state officials.

Agent preferences, legitimacy, tasks, and permeability

The ECHR constitutes a good case for our theory because the Commission's and Court's strategies varied over time, as did the level of delegation they received and their autonomy. In this volume, Alter argues that principals have few contractual mechanisms for checking a court's authority. While control mechanisms may be limited and courts may care deeply about their reputations, the ECHR institutions are still agents because states created them in the first place and can withdraw authority from them at any time, either individually or collectively. The ECHR also provides a helpful case for theory building because different analytical perspectives suggest different outcomes. From a perspective that emphasizes state sovereignty, states should be reluctant to delegate authority on human rights issues or allow much autonomy for human rights IOs because delegation would invite external meddling in internal affairs (Kissinger 2001). Yet from a domestic politics perspective, human rights IOs might help guarantee domestic stability and some states should therefore be eager to delegate authority and autonomy (Moravcsik 2000). A functionalist principal-agent approach would expect judicial bodies to exhibit high levels of autonomy due to state need to make their commitments credible (Pollack, this volume). The ECHR offers a rich empirical domain in which to explore these competing predictions.

Although the ECHR is not particularly well-known, it is an increasingly important institution. A recent comprehensive survey of 32 of its member states found that every single state had to change important domestic policies, practices, or legislation in response to Court rulings (Blackburn and Polakiewicz 2001; see also Shelton 2003). Nor are these rulings limited to a few prisoners in a local jail cell. Rather, they affect domestic policies and institutions with broad scope. For example, the Court has required Great Britain to reform laws banning gay sex, to allow gays in the military, to curtail wiretapping and other police powers, and to ban corporal punishment in public schools (Stiles forthcoming). In Turkey, the Court has ruled repeatedly against the government's security policies with respect to Kurds, including a March 2003 ruling that Abdullah Öcalan – the well-known Kurdish guerrilla leader – received an unfair trial. Despite Court rulings against states in increasingly important and contentious issue-areas, state compliance is so routine that top legal scholars argue that the Court has "almost uniform respect and obedience rendered to judgments" (Janis et al. 1995: 8).

European states created the Court through the European Convention on Human Rights, which was signed in 1950 and went into effect in

1953 when a sufficient number of states had ratified the Convention.[8] The Convention committed states to human rights principles defined chiefly in terms of civil liberties and political rights, excluding social and economic rights. The Convention created a Commission, which began operating in 1954, that processed complaints about human rights violations, weeded out those that did not meet the criteria for admissibility, gathered information about the cases, attempted to reach friendly settlements between the disputants, published reports and recommendations, and forwarded unresolved disputes to other decision-making bodies.[9] In 1959, a Court was established when a sufficient threshold of states accepting its jurisdiction was reached. To the Court, states delegated the ability to decide if the Convention had been violated and to pass binding judgments requiring states to alter their practices. When European states disbanded the Commission in 1998, they transferred its functions to the Court as well.[10]

From the beginning, states were cautious about delegating this authority and so created a two-step delegation process. The original mandate in the Convention did not allow the Commission to receive complaints from individuals unless individual states expressly authorized it, nor did the Convention grant jurisdiction to the Court unless individual states expressly authorized it. Thus, for states to delegate authority they first had to ratify the Convention and second had to accept – in writing – the principle of individual petition and binding Court jurisdiction (possibly accepting one without the other). Without *both* individual petition and Court jurisdiction, the Convention could not realistically be enforced (Moravcsik 2000). Without individual petition, cases would have to be submitted by other states – an unlikely occurrence because any state submitting a complaint could have a complaint submitted against it in retaliation. Without binding Court jurisdiction, states would not participate in Court proceedings and would be unlikely to implement principles the Court articulated in other cases. Hence, states ratifying the Convention without accepting these optional clauses in fact delegated very little authority. Together, individual petition and compulsory

---

[8] Useful overviews of the European institutions include Merrills 2001; Ovey and White 2002; Janis et al. 1995.
[9] Convention for the Protection of Human Rights and Fundamental Freedoms (hereafter, "European Convention"), *American Journal of International Law*, 1951, 45 (2), Supplement: Official Documents, 24–39, Articles 25–32.
[10] European Convention, as amended by Protocol 11, at http://conventions.coe.int/Treaty/EN/cadreprincipal.htm, accessed Sept. 8, 2003.

Agent preferences, legitimacy, tasks, and permeability

jurisdiction constitute a significant transfer of sovereignty, as individuals could essentially sue their state for human rights violations in an international court with binding decision-making authority.

In the 1950s and 1960s, the Commission and the Court knew that several states were reluctant to delegate authority to them. Our theory suggests that the IOs could receive substantial authority only by persuading principals to delegate to them through a strategy of interpreting their mandate in a restrained manner that was fundamentally deferential to state preferences. A close review of the agents' actions suggests they were quite restrained indeed. Of the more than 1,500 individual petitions submitted to the Commission in its first eight years, it only found 11 admissible (Weil 1963a, 809). Some of the cases it rejected would have undoubtedly brought substantial attention to the Commission, yet it was quite deferential to states, refusing to accept petitions from well-known former Nazis such as Rudolph Hess and disallowing any petition on *any* grounds from the German Communist Party, which had been dissolved by the German government (Weil 1963a: 810–11). The Court, for its part, made only ten judgments in its first ten years and did not rule against a state on a substantive issue until 1968, nearly ten years after its creation and 18 years after states first adopted the Convention. This record of deference to states included the Court's much-watched first case, *Lawless*, in which the Court decided that Ireland had indeed denied due process rights to an alleged member of the outlawed Irish Republican Army, but that this denial was lawful and consistent with the Convention because Ireland had first implemented a state of emergency (Robertson and Merrills 1993: 66–67, 184–89). From their earliest cases, both the Commission and the Court articulated a doctrine of a "margin of appreciation," which recognized that governments have important interests in maintaining law and order and that governments are better positioned to judge those interests than international judicial bodies (Yourow 1996: 15–21).

The Commission and Court remained cautious throughout the 1970s, as illustrated in table 7.2. The Commission admitted only 2 percent of its cases through 1979, and the Court ruled against states only 25 percent of the time. This pattern of caution within the Commission and Court is exactly what we would expect given that some key democracies delayed delegating full authority to them until the mid-1970s or even later. The apparently comprehensive membership in the ECHR by 1981, however, seems to have emboldened the Court. Once France, Italy, Portugal, Spain, and Switzerland accepted the optional clauses in the

Table 7.2. *Court and Commission permeability and autonomy, 1955–2004*

Year	Decisions taken on admission[a]	Percent admitted	Number of court rulings	Percent against states
1955				
1956				
1957				
1958				
1959				
1960			0	
1961			5	0
1962			0	
1963			0	
1964			0	
1965			0	
1966			0	
1967			0	
1968			7	29
1969			4	25
1970			1	0
1971			9	22
1972			0	
1973			0	
1974			0	
1975			4	50
1976			29	7
1977	7341	2	0	
1978	731	2	11	36
1979	280	9	14	57
Subtotal 1960s–70s	8352	2	84	25
1980	341	6	7	43
1981	430	5	10	40
1982	425	10	16	56
1983	436	7	18	39
1984	582	9	27	63
1985	582	12	14	5
1986	511	8	28	29
1987	590	5	39	62
1988	654	7	33	42
1989	1338	7	41	51
Subtotal 1980s	5889	8	233	49
1990	1216	12	39	69
1991	1659	13	73	63
1992	1704	11	90	69
1993	1765	12	59	56

(continued)

Agent preferences, legitimacy, tasks, and permeability

Table 7.2 (continued)

Year	Decisions taken on admission[a]	Percent admitted	Number of court rulings	Percent against states
1994	2372	25	65	52
1995	2990	27	70	56
1996	3400	18	115	44
1997	3777	19	139	47
1998	4420	17	168	58
Subtotal 1990–98	23,303	18	818	56
1999	4251	17	173	86
2000	7862	14	566	83
2001	9728	8	827	83
2002	18,450	3	897	87
2003	18,034	4	883	86
2004	21,181	4	1005	84
Subtotal 1999–04	74,775	6	4351	85

Source: Columns 2–3: for 1955–1990, European Commission of Human Rights, Secretary, 1998, "Information Note," Strasbourg: Council of Europe; for 1990–2004, *Survey of Activities*, European Court of Human Rights, online at http://www.echr.coe.int/ECHR/EN/Header/Reports+and+Statistics/Reports/Annual+surveys+of+activity/, accessed July 2005.

Columns 4–5: for 1960–1994, Gomien 1995; for 1995–98, *Judgments and Decisions* and *Reports of Judgments and Decisions*, European Court of Human Rights; for 1999–2004, European Court of Human Rights, "Judgments and Decisions," at http://www.echr.coe.int/Eng/Judgments.htm, accessed July 2005.

[a] No yearly breakdown is available for Commission decisions from 1955–76; 1977 entries represent the cumulative total for all years between 1955 and 1977.

1970s, only the odd triumvirate of Greece, Turkey, and Cyprus was left outside both the Communist bloc and the ECHR. In the context of the Cold War, it may not have seemed that there were many potential new members left outside. Indeed, 1982 was the first year that as many as 10 percent of Commission decisions were admitted to the Court, and it showed the leading edge of a sustained jump in Court rulings and rulings against states (see table 7.2).

Substantial evidence shows that states watched closely the Commission and Court, especially as the states debated whether to accept the optional clauses that would represent real delegation. Denmark and Ireland were the first to accept the optional clauses (1953) but each attached significant strings – Denmark used sunset clauses for both optional clauses, accepting them for only two years at a time, and Ireland's high court initially limited the applicability of ECHR judgments

(Golsong 1958). The next cluster of states to accept the optional clauses came in the period 1955–60, and their actions allowed the Court to be established. The debates in each of these states – Austria, Belgium, Germany, Iceland, Luxemburg, and the Netherlands – revealed substantial attention to the track record of the new Commission (Partsch 1956/1957). For example, the Dutch government admitted initial fears the Commission would make political decisions, but that "after the Commission had been established, it became clear that it had no political structure" and that abuse of its authority was non-existent (Council of Europe 1958–59: 562). And when the German opposition wondered why the Chancellor had not accepted the two optional ECHR clauses, the government argued that there was "no rush" and refused to commit Germany to the clauses for another 18 months.[11]

In the next phase between 1961 and 1966, another group of cautious states – Norway, Sweden, and the United Kingdom – accepted the optional clauses. Though an early ratifier of the ECHR, Sweden's government was long unwilling to pay the sovereignty costs in the subsequent step of mandatory Court jurisdiction until "experience has shown that there is a practical need of the Court."[12] In the early 1960s, under pressure from other states and some domestic politicians to accept the Court's jurisdiction, Sweden (and Norway) officially declared in 1960 that they "needed to experience how the Court functioned practically by observation" before deciding whether to delegate.[13] Only in 1966 (two years after Norway), did the Swedish government approve automatic Court jurisdiction, noting that "experience has so far shown that the Court's operations are limited."[14] The Court had handed down no judgments from 1963–66, and the Swedish government noted that all pending cases dealt with "language issues in Belgium." Thus, Sweden delegated fully only after its six-year observation of the Court's preferences revealed nothing troubling.

Britain also waited until 1966 to fully delegate to the ECHR. The Conservative government of Clement Atlee had actively opposed a strong Convention and insisted on the optional clauses for individual petition and Court jurisdiction (Moravcsik 2000; Stiles, in press). Declassified

---

[11] *Bundestag Drucksache* 174/53 of January 12, 1954. Translated by author.
[12] "His royal majesty's government bill No. 165 of 1951." March 2, 1951. Translated by Lotta Andersson, 14.
[13] "His royal majesty's government bill No. 33 of 1966," January 27, 1966, 4. Translated by Elena Gismarvik.
[14] Ibid., 4.

Agent preferences, legitimacy, tasks, and permeability

executive branch documents show that when the Labour government took power in 1964, it began dealing with objections to British delegation – objections that centered largely on thorny colonial issues. For example, in response to worries about the potential effect of Court decisions on immigration from former colonies, the Lord Chancellor argued that, "past experience shows how very few cases go to the Court," and the Foreign Office's legal advisor chimed in that, "The approach of the Commission to this problem has in my experience been reasonable. I do not see why we should expect less of the Court, which is composed of even more eminent men than the Commission" (Lord Lester 1998: 249). In this and other debates, the main arguments within the British government revolved around the preferences of the Court. Even once thus reassured, the government notified the Commission that it would accept the right of individual petition for only three years so that Britain might terminate its acceptance if problems arose. Of the last remaining major European democracies, Italy and Switzerland delegated fully to the Court in 1973–74 while France delayed until 1981.[15]

We now turn to the question of autonomy. We measure autonomy as the percentage of rulings against states, a measure consistent with the definition of autonomy in this volume and with the literature on judicial politics (Larkins 1996, 1998; Helmke 2002). Our unit of analysis is a Court finding of a violation or non-violation of a substantive Convention article, where each judgment may have more than one finding.[16] Looking at judgments ("cases") as a whole presents serious aggregation problems: If the Court rules against states on one of three substantive issues in a given judgment, does the judgment count as for or against states? Hence, it makes more sense to disaggregate the judgments and to look at individual findings reported by the Court. As the last column in table 7.2

---

[15] Outside the communist states, Spain, Portugal, and Greece were authoritarian systems, and Finland did not join the Council of Europe until 1989.

[16] In an effort to get at the core issues concerning Court rulings on human rights violations, we do not count procedural issues, friendly settlements, and cases struck from the Court's docket for other reasons. This probably results in an undercounting of the Court's autonomy, in large part because the Court quite frequently rules against states on procedural issues. States are almost exclusively responsible for raising procedural issues as a way to avoid substantive rulings. We code cases where the Court decides a complaint is inadmissible as a finding in favor of the state. These are relatively rare because most cases have been previously screened for inadmissibility, but they include cases where, upon further and more extensive review, the Court decides the application cannot proceed and hence these rulings favor states.

demonstrates, the Court ruled against states 25 percent of the time in the 1960s and 1970s, but this increased to around 50 percent in the 1980s and then 85 percent since 1998. These contrary rulings cannot be dismissed as a simple matter of the Court ruling against states in obscure and isolated cases, especially because the increase in negative rulings came at the same time as a dramatic increase in the number of cases decided. Moreover, the European Court is increasingly exercising its authority in key public policy issues, including security issues and hot-button social issues like gay rights.[17]

What drives this increase in agent autonomy over time? Pollack (2003a and this volume) argues that principal control mechanisms determine the range of agent autonomy. Where agents, such as the European Court of Justice, have enormous autonomy, it is because principals have designed control mechanisms that way in order to resolve information and credibility problems facing the principals. In this view, the range of agent activity depends on principals. This argument constitutes a useful starting point for analyzing the Court. States imposed few control mechanisms on the Court, suggesting that they intended it to enjoy substantial autonomy. The most important control concerned procedural rules governing access to the Court. States attempted to limit individual access to the Court in a variety of ways, including the opt-in clauses for individual petition and Court jurisdiction, Commission screening of individual applications, and measures allowing only the Commission or states to take cases to the Court. Of equal importance, individuals had no standing before the Court and no way to represent themselves there even once the Commission referred their case to the Court. States instructed the Commission to bring complaints to the Court but then to act not in the interests of the individual but rather as the "defender of the public interest." States did not even make provisions to inform individuals of proceedings before the Court in which they were the chief complainant (Robertson and Merrills 1993: 303–10).

The largest problem with an explanation focusing on control mechanisms is that the Court's autonomy increased substantially *before* states altered the control mechanisms to allow individuals greater access to the Court. Under Protocol 9 that went into effect in October 1994, states amended the Convention to allow individuals – in addition to the

---

[17] For overviews of the Court's expanding jurisprudence, see Janis et al. 1995; and Harris et al. 1999.

Agent preferences, legitimacy, tasks, and permeability

Commission or to states – to bring a case to the Court and to receive copies of the Commission's reports on their cases. Prior to this protocol states had amended the Convention several times, but never altered the rules governing individual access or other key control mechanisms. By the time states adopted Protocol 9, however, the Court's rulings against states were typically running between 70 and 80 percent each year, much higher than the 50 percent in the 1950s and 1960s. As a result, the growth in autonomy cannot be explained by principal decisions to change the control mechanisms governing individual access.

We argue instead that the Commission and Court increased their autonomy by using the strategies outlined above. First, the Commission gradually developed a *dualist* structure that served the interests of individual complainants in addition to the public interest mandated by states. From their earliest days, Commission members felt they had a stronger duty to individual applicants than the Convention allowed. In the first case the Commission referred to the Court, *Lawless v. Ireland* case in 1960, the Commission communicated its findings to the applicant and invited his comments, which it then intended to present to the Court (Robertson and Merrills 1993: 305–306). At first, this dualist structure was rather crude. In the *Lawless* case the Commission representative literally voiced first the Commission's opinion and then, where it differed, the applicant's opinion (Weil 1963b: 155). Over time, the procedures became more sophisticated. In 1970, the Commission invited the assistance of the applicant's lawyer in proceedings before the Court (Robertson and Merrills 1993: 307). By 1982, the Commission had created a large number of procedural rules allowing the applicant direct access to the Court. As two close observers of the Court put it: "After these changes it was apparent that everything which could be done to improve the applicant's position, short of amending the Convention, had been done" (Robertson and Merrills 1993: 307). It would take states another 14 years to ratify these agent-led changes by amending the Convention with Protocol 9.

While the Commission's *dualism* was not exactly hidden, neither was it particularly well-known or well-advertised, in part because it concerned procedural issues rather than substantive outcomes and in part because the Commission utilized the normative cover of the needs of justice. As a result, most states monitoring the Court missed their importance. Sweden's government, for example, chiefly monitored the types of cases referred to the Court and the substantive outcomes of the Court's decisions. If it had probed more deeply, Sweden would have discovered a

Commission that was beginning to set important procedural precedents that allowed individual citizens greater institutional access than states initially intended. But even the most effective opponent of Sweden's entry, the Foreign Minister Osten Undén, failed to report on the subtle procedural changes introduced by the Commission cases. Instead of probing deeply into these details, he summarized his monitoring of the ECHR system by noting that the Court ruled on "interesting cases but hardly of the sort that they are examples of the practical need for extensive legal investigations" (Undén 1963).

What Undén and others missed was that both the Commission and the Court operated in *professional* environments that gave great weight to individual complainants. Moreover, the Convention had tasked the Commission and Court with upholding individual rights against state abuses, and Western norms of justice deem that all parties deserve to be heard in court. The Commission's normative commitment to justice and the broader normative environment favoring due process led it to press for more individual access to the Court. This behavior is consistent with the dualist hypothesis, which suggests that agents will adapt to their environments in ways that reflect all of the demands placed on them and not just principal preferences.

The Commission's dualist activities helped the Court gradually increase its own *permeability* to individual petitioners. Over time, the Court issued a series of rulings that largely confirmed the Commission's efforts to grant individuals more access to the Court. In 1961 in *Lawless*, the Court argued that, "The Court must bear in mind its duty to safeguard the interests of the individual" (quoted in Janis et al. 1995: 67). At this time, the Court was mindful of state concerns and so required the Commission, rather than the individual complainant, to present the applicant's views. Ten years later in the *Vagrancy* cases, the Court went farther by allowing the applicant's lawyer to assist the Commission in the presentation of the case before the Court. Still in its cautious mode, the Court insisted that the lawyer only be able to act when called upon by the Commission to assist it and thus did not grant the lawyer an independent voice (Robertson and Merrills 1993: 307). In 1982, the Court took the final step by amending its own rules of procedure to allow individuals to represent themselves directly.

At least partially as a result of these rulings, the Court's permeability – as measured by the number and percent of complaints admitted by the Commission – increased dramatically (table 7.2). In the 1950s and 1960s the Commission admitted only 2 percent of the applications it received, a

Agent preferences, legitimacy, tasks, and permeability

number that grew to 8 percent in the 1980s and 18 percent from 1990–98. Throughout this period, the number of applications rose steadily; by 2004, the Court was reaching admissibility decisions on more than 21,000 cases a year. This increase in permeability has undoubtedly facilitated the Court's growing autonomy. States are likely to refer only a few carefully selected cases that they think they will win. The Commission's willingness to refer more cases after 1980 was crucial because it allowed the Court a greater range of possibilities in which to exercise autonomy. An applicant's ability to present his/her own case also boosts Court autonomy by increasing the chances the Court will be persuaded by the applicant's arguments.

After dualism and permeability were at least partly in place, the Court issued some landmark judgments that *reinterpreted* the nature of the Convention and the Court's own mandate. One basic question typically facing courts is whether they are dealing with rules intended as contracts between two parties or with law-making rules having an "object and purpose" that should be defended and elaborated through rulings. Courts that interpret rules as a contract are likely to rule in a more conservative fashion that is deferential to the wishes and understandings of the contracting parties, while courts who believe the rules have a teleological purpose that should be advanced are more likely to rule in activist ways. Beginning with *Wemhoff v. FRG* in 1970 and reaffirmed in *Golder v. United Kingdom* in 1975, the Court explicitly adopted the latter approach: "Given that it [the Convention] is a law-making treaty, it is also necessary to seek the interpretation that is most appropriate in order to realise the aim and achieve the object of the treaty, and not that which would restrict to the greatest possible degree the obligations undertaken by the parties" (Harris et al. 1999: 7; Ovey and White 2002: 34–39). A minority of judges complained, to no avail, against this approach, arguing that because the Court was treading on sovereignty, "a cautious and conservative interpretation" was in order.

The Court followed up by issuing several rulings interpreting the Convention in light of changing social standards, not by the standards or intentions of the drafters of the Convention in 1950. In a 1978 decision, *Tyrer v. UK*, the Court declared that the Convention is "a living instrument which, as the Commission rightly stressed, must be interpreted in the light of present day conditions" (Harris et al. 1999: 8). The Court has reaffirmed its authority to use evolving social standards in many subsequent cases and has sometimes expanded the scope of rights granted in the Convention as a result. For example, in a case in 2002, the Court found that destroying property could constitute "degrading treatment" and thus violate the human rights Convention (Shelton 2003: 126–27 and footnotes). It justified this expansive interpretation of the Convention by arguing that "the increasingly high standard being required in the area of the protection of human rights and fundamental liberties correspondingly and inevitably requires greater firmness in assessing breaches of the fundamental values of democratic societies" (cited in Shelton 2003: 126–27). In 1979, the Court began restricting the "margin of appreciation" that it gave to national governments in determining their own needs for law and order. As one thorough review summarized it, Court judgments after 1979 "more carefully supervised margins of national discretion, and are more assertive in defense of claimants' rights" (Yourow 1996: 56).

We do not argue that the Court, in 1960, strategically charted a course whereby it would, 40 years later, enjoy much higher autonomy. Yet the evidence suggests that Commission and Court officials played an active role in securing state delegation and in expanding their own autonomy. In the early years, the Commission accepted few cases and sent even fewer to the Court, which usually did not rule against states – all of which resulted in more state delegation to the Commission and Court. At the same time, the Commission began creating a dualist structure to accommodate its commitment to individuals, and the Court aided this process by increasing its own permeability through precedent-setting rulings. After a large number of states committed to the regime, the Court reinterpreted the Convention in broad fashion and began issuing rulings against states on an increasing number of rights of ever-broader scope. As one observer put it, "the interpretive tools of the European Court of Human Rights permit it to conduct all battles, and in the way it wants" (quoted in Carozza 1998: 1221). States may tolerate the Commission's and Court's path and even benefit from it (whether they do is an open question), but it seems clear they did not originally intend or chart that path, which has been blazed by the agents themselves.

SUMMARY AND CONCLUSION

The goal of principal-agent theory, according to two leading scholars, "is to develop theories about how particular institutional forms can be used to increase the likelihood of compliant behavior by bureacrats" (Huber and Shipan 2002: 27). PA theorists of course recognize the potential for agency losses, but most have generally argued that principals can minimize *actual* losses through control mechanisms designed into the PA contract. The result, by implication, is a world in which principal characteristics and strategies determine the level of agent autonomy, an approach adopted by Martin and Pollack in this volume. As Huber and Shipan (2002: 27) put it, principal-agent studies "correctly emphasize that [agent] discretion is often *deliberate*. It is purposefully granted by politicians to bureaucrats because doing so is the best strategy for achieving desired policy goals."[18] More specifically, they view the level of discretion offered to agents as the result of conflict between principal and agent preferences, the ability of principals to write detailed rules, the absence of conflict among collective principals, and the absence of alternative principal means of influencing agents (Huber and Shipan 2002: 215).

We agree that PA theorists have focused on principal control mechanisms to explain agent autonomy, and we have sought to draw attention to agent strategies instead. The central claim of this chapter is that agents possess a variety of strategies that PA theorists have not yet explored and that can substantially influence both principal decisions to delegate and agent autonomy. We do not argue that principals are unaware of these strategies or unable to answer them with strategies of their own. Rather, we argue that agents are often able to increase their levels of autonomy when they utilize these strategies, given the costs that principals face in implementing control mechanisms. Agents are also able to strategically limit their own autonomy (or signal their intention to do so), thus inviting the principal to delegate more authority to those agents. We emphatically do not argue that agent autonomy is the result of "helpless abdication" by principals, the alternative position articulated by Huber and Shipan (2002: 17). Rather, autonomy is at least partially the result of rational, strategic calculations undertaken by agents. Principals of course counter agent strategies with some of their own, but for a variety of reasons may have only limited success.

The fact that PA theorists generally have understood agents to be prior constructions of principals may lead to a bias in the theory. When PA theory makes agents endogenous (e.g. subject to principal design), then

---

[18] Emphasis in original.

even if agents do drift away over time, they remain basically agents of the masters who initially built them. Carpenter (2001: 11) has noticed a similar problem in studies of American bureaucracies; namely, that scholars "study bureaucracy only through the legislation that creates agencies, the Presidents who govern them, or the court decisions that check or enable their decision making." The big problem with this approach is that "it reduces political development to institutional *creation*, to the neglect of institutional *transformation*." As this study clearly demonstrates, IOs can and do evolve considerably over time, often at the initiative of the IO itself. Scholars who fail to examine agent strategies in detail are unlikely to be able to explain changes over time in the extent of agent autonomy.

We have identified four strategies that agents use to influence the PA relationship: interpretation, reinterpretation, building permeability, and buffering, which can in turn be broken down into ceremonialism and dualism. We have illustrated the ways in which the European Commission and Court of Human Rights used those strategies to first persuade states to delegate more authority to them and then to expand their own autonomy. The effort to lay out agent strategies and illustrate their influence only constitutes a first step in the research process. The next step is to identify which agents are more likely to use those strategies and the conditions under which they are likely to be successful. Moreover, agent characteristics are likely to vary substantially across time, issue-areas, and institutions and are likely to interact with agent strategies in ways that influence PA outcomes.

Showing how agent strategies matter is likely to enrich PA theory. For example, a key issue might be the inducements that potential agents give to principals to "choose us" (or that existing agents give to get new "business" from principals who already hire them for other jobs). To what extent could a critical mass of potential high-quality agents be a contributing factor to secular trends toward increasing delegation? The natural extension of a theory of agent inducement would then be to formalize the conditions under which agents could not only induce principals to hire them but also to change contract terms ex post. All of the strategies noted in this paper would be plausible starting points for such a discussion.

Finally, a more robust theory of agent characteristics and strategies might help the field connect the collective action problems of principals to agent behavior more directly than we have done. Lyne, Nielson, and Tierney (this volume) emphasize the way that agency costs often reflect

Agent preferences, legitimacy, tasks, and permeability

problems among multiple and collective principals.[19] Given the turmoil they note, agents employing the strategies we have emphasized could try to bribe or offer excludable side payments to some members of their own collective principal in order to get them to set the terms the way the agent wants them set. Of course, there are limits to this strategy. If free-rider problems within collective principals are substantial, then even small agent-source problems might lead principals to end their delegation at the first future opportunity. This logic should act as a check on the troublesome agents introduced early in the chapter: after all, a housekeeper who loafs is bad, one who steals is worse, but one who sows dissension between the principals in the household will be the last housekeeper those principals ever hire.

[19] And as Martin (this volume) suggests, as coordination costs rise, agencies also gain discretion.

8

Screening power: international organizations as informative agents

ALEXANDER THOMPSON

INTRODUCTION

The 2003 military intervention against Iraq inspired numerous commentators to lament the failure of the United Nations (UN) Security Council during the episode. Supporters of the Bush Administration policy argued that the Council's unwillingness to explicitly endorse military action amounted to a failure to confront threats to international order and exposed the organization as weak, or even "irrelevant" and "impotent."[1] Less predictably, some members of the international law community offered a critique on legalistic grounds. The Security Council, they argued, did not stop the United States from intervening unilaterally, thereby failing to fulfill its role as defender of international law and promoter of international peace. In a talk before the American Society of International Law, for example, Richard Falk (2004: 2) judged the Security Council "deficient" with respect to the "war prevention goals of the Charter." In a more sweeping critique, international law scholar Michael Glennon (2003: 16) laments the "rupture of the UN Security Council," which failed "to subject the use of force to the rule of law."

I would like to thank the editors of this volume, as well as Kenneth Schultz, Peter Gourevitch, and participants in the conference on Delegation to IOs at the University of California, San Diego, for very helpful comments on earlier drafts. Portions of this chapter appeared previously in the journal *International Organization* (Thompson, 2006).

[1] President Bush himself warned in his September 2002 speech before the General Assembly that failure to deal emphatically with Iraq would render the UN "irrelevant." Conservative columnist Charles Krauthammer (2003) pronounced the UN "impotent" for its failure to effectively disarm Iraq, and predicted the organization's demise. See also Perle 2003.

Agent preferences, legitimacy, tasks, and permeability

These criticisms can be challenged on their own terms: After all, the Security Council did not endorse the war, and its mandated inspections appear – especially in retrospect – to have been very useful in containing and defanging Iraq. But they also rely on a narrow and largely inaccurate view of the Security Council's role in coercive military intervention. The notion of failure only makes sense in relation to some metric for defining success, and the above critiques depend on certain (often implicit) assumptions about the primary functions of the Security Council. In particular, both sets of critiques rely on a vision of the body as a coherent actor whose job is to maintain peace by enforcing rules and dictating the behavior of states. This is a literal interpretation of the Security Council's role – as responsible for identifying threats and applying military force against them if necessary – envisioned in the Charter.[2]

Treating almost any international institution in this way, as quasi-governmental, is unrealistic; it sets too high a bar for judging success. This chapter provides a more fundamental defense of the Council's actions in the recent Iraq war by offering a different perspective on its role, and the role of other international organizations (IOs), in episodes involving the use of force. As Darren Hawkins, David Lake, Daniel Nielson, and Michael Tierney (Hawkins et al.) note in the introduction to this volume, principals have incentives to delegate to agents when the latter specialize in performing certain tasks. Powerful states, not IOs, specialize in applying military force, and thus the international community must typically rely on them to deal with collective threats. However, the international community – including both leaders and their domestic publics – faces uncertainty when it comes to "hiring" these coercive agents to act on their behalf. This uncertainty creates an important role for IOs. I argue that in the context of a potential military intervention, IOs specialize in providing information about the coercing state's intentions and the likely consequences of its policy, information that helps the international community decide whether to support the intervention. This specialization creates an incentive for the international community to rely on IOs as their agent to "screen" interventions worthy of

---

[2] Chapter VII of the Charter endows the Security Council with the power to identify threats to international peace and security, to respond with diplomatic and economic sanctions, and if necessary to mandate military action. While the framers of the Charter realized that the Security Council would be largely dependent on member states for military forces, they viewed these forces as being at the disposal of the Security Council (Articles 45 and 47). In practice, however, the Security Council does not perform a command and control function.

international support from those which are not. Thus the international community, as a collective principal, relies on two sets of agents: powerful states to apply coercion and IOs to screen these coercers.

The screening function also provides an incentive for states to subject themselves to the constraints of an IO – as an alternative to working unilaterally or with an ad hoc coalition – when they pursue the use of force. The international support that results from the screening process is desirable for even a powerful coercing state since it determines the political costs of a given policy and in some cases affects the policy's long-term success. Absent the information generated by IO approval – that is, when the policy is rejected by an IO or when an IO is not involved – the international community is less likely to respond favorably. It is important to note that, in such cases, the IO agent has succeeded equally well in performing its screening function.

Once a coercing state is authorized to carry out an operation, the international community typically has little control over its actions; the potential for slippage and undesirable outcomes is high. This is the same problem faced by employers, who, upon hiring a new employee, may find it difficult to dismiss the employee even if performance is poor (Spence 1973: 356).[3] Therefore, ex ante efforts at screening and selection are of paramount importance, and problems of adverse selection rather than moral hazard and commitment are the primary focus of this analysis.

This chapter addresses several arguments raised in the editors' introduction. Two are worth highlighting from the start. First, Hawkins et al. draw attention to screening and selection issues but provide a limited view of the possibilities. They argue reasonably that states want to avoid delegating to IOs that will not faithfully carry out the intended tasks and will therefore invest in choosing IO agents that are "sympathetic" in terms of their leadership and preferences. The problem of asymmetric information between principal and agent is obviously central to my argument, although in my account potential coercing states, not IOs, are the relevant agents with hidden information, with IOs playing an intervening role as screening mechanisms. Thus with respect to the screening hypothesis, my findings are consistent with the framework chapter, although refinements are required in the context of the substantive issue I investigate.

---

[3] The authority granted by IOs to coercing states is revocable, although IOs and other states have few mechanisms of ongoing control once an intervention has begun.

Agent preferences, legitimacy, tasks, and permeability

My argument also complements the discussion of preference heterogeneity by Hawkins et al. They argue that a set of heterogeneous states are less likely to delegate to an agent than are like-minded states, an insight that helps explain why endorsement of interventions by certain IOs might be especially important. Precisely because IOs with a heterogeneous membership are less likely to agree on whether and how to authorize intervention, their successful decisions to do so are more informative and meaningful. Building from informational theories of legislative committees, I argue that IOs with a diverse membership are able to send more information to the international community regarding a potential coercer and its policy than are more homogeneous institutions, such as regional organizations and ad hoc coalitions. In the spirit of the Hawkins and Jacoby chapter, I thus focus explicitly on variation in the characteristics of IO agents.

This chapter proceeds by presenting the theoretical argument on how IOs serve as informative agents of the international community in the context of military coercion. The third section presents a case study of the 1990–91 Iraq conflict, which serves to illustrate the screening function of IOs. I then extend the logic of the argument to shed light on how coercing states "forum shop" across institutional alternatives. Among other implications, the relevant tradeoffs demonstrate why the Security Council is uniquely effective as a screening agent. The concluding section returns to theoretical themes raised in this volume.

THE SCREENING FUNCTION OF IOS

Across the range of international institutions, formal IOs uniquely have the capacity to act independently of state interests and influence.[4] It is the *neutrality* of IOs, in particular, that allows them to serve as informative agents of the international community, supplying information that an individual state – in our case, a potential coercer – could not credibly supply. Because they cannot be controlled by individual states, and because they are standing bodies with (more or less) diverse member interests, they have two advantages as information generators: first, they are able to impose constraints on a coercer, making signaling of limited ambitions possible, and second, they act as representatives of the

---

[4] Abbott and Snidal 1998. For further conceptualization of IO independence, see Haftel and Thompson 2006; Thompson and Haftel 2003; and various chapters in this volume, including the introduction, Alter, Cortell and Peterson, and Hawkins and Jacoby.

international community, allowing them to generate information on policy consequences that is regarded as neutral and thus credible. Both types of information are important to leaders and their publics as they assess the coercer and its intervention policy, in other words, as they attempt to overcome their adverse selection problem.

To help us understand what makes IOs informative, we can conceptualize them in the same terms as legislative committees, one function of which is to supply information to the legislature (their principal). Like these committees, comprised of legislators, IOs are composed of a subset of states in the international system. Driven mainly by the works of Thomas Gilligan and Keith Krehbiel, informational theories of legislative organization propose that committees are designed to serve as sources of policy-relevant information for the legislature as a whole (Gilligan and Krehbiel 1989, 1990; Krehbiel 1991). The most important design feature is their composition in terms of member preferences, which largely determines how informative the signals sent by committees are. Specifically, a committee that is heterogeneous (that is, whose membership is diverse and "bookends" the median preference of the floor) sends more information than a homogeneous committee; and a committee composed of "preference outliers," whose membership has extreme preferences relative to the floor median, is less informative than one with a more moderate composition. Only when they are diverse and representative can committees transmit information that is seen as credible and therefore informative to the legislature as a whole.

These principles of information transmission by institutional agents can be usefully applied to the realm of international institutions. It is instructive to consider the properties of IOs in comparison to the primary multilateral alternative in the context of coercive interventions: ad hoc coalitions. Whereas IOs are standing bodies, multilateral coalitions are by definition composed of like-minded states, as the phrase "coalition of the willing" reflects. In the language of the legislative signaling literature, they are homogeneous and composed of preference outliers. Because the ideal point of the median member of such a coalition is likely to be very close to the ideal point of the coercer with regard to the question of intervention, the coalition is not likely to impose substantial constraints and support from the coalition is not informative to the median member of the international community. Among the most robust findings in theories of strategic information transmission is that actors with more similar preferences can send more informative signals to each other (Crawford and Sobel 1982; Lupia and McCubbins 1994b: 368; Krehbiel

1991). Therefore, by itself, multilateral support of a coercer conveys little information to the international community.

As informative agents, IOs send two types of information to the international community, one directed at state leaders and the other at publics. In the remainder of this section, I outline these information transmission mechanisms in more detail.

Information on intentions and policy consequences

I assume that state leaders are relatively well informed about policy alternatives and consequences and that IO member states do not have a meaningful information advantage over other states in terms of expertise or knowledge about an issue. Other leaders do, however, lack information regarding the intentions of the coercing state's leadership and are concerned that the coercer, in confronting a collective threat, will pursue a policy that is more aggressive or ambitious than the international community prefers. Such behavior is a form of agency slack (in the form of "slippage") that might undermine the interests of other states by producing undesirable outcomes.

Both the international community and states considering coercion are faced with a dilemma. In a use of force context, it is difficult for powerful states to reassure others that their goals are limited and unthreatening. And yet the international community must rely on such states as agents to intervene militarily when there are genuine collective threats. An IO with neutral preferences can send a highly informative signal because it imposes costs on a coercer that a more aggressive state (i.e. one with intentions that threaten third-party states) would be unwilling to pay. The IR literature certainly recognizes that international institutions impose costly constraints on states, usually in the context of credible commitment arguments, but conceptualization and identification of these precise costs is not well developed (Lake 1999; Martin 1992a). At least four overlapping costs may be imposed when coercion is channeled through an IO.

First, a state's freedom of action is almost always limited when a policy is channeled through an IO, thereby reducing the discretion of a coercing agent. Other member preferences contribute to defining the limits of possible coercive measures and a coercer is accepting these limits when it chooses to work through an IO. Indeed, once a state chooses to act through an IO, it is faced with generating some support and is thus constrained to bring a limited and defensible set of goals to the table. For example, early US drafts of Resolution 1441 – which eventually re-established an inspections regime in Iraq and threatened "serious consequences" in the absence of cooperation – were watered down to eliminate provisions that would have been rejected by other Security Council members, such as a more specific authorization of "enforcement" and a provocative requirement that any Permanent 5 state could send representatives as part of an inspections team (Blix 2004: 76–79).

Second, coercers face organization costs – including the costs of communicating, bargaining, and reaching common positions – when they work through an IO (Olson 1965: 47). These are a form of transaction costs. Any multilateral approach to foreign policy increases the costs of decision-making and of implementing policy. These are compounded by political factors and "influence costs," as each actor seeks to shape the organization's decision to his own benefit.[5] For years in Bosnia, the Europeans and United States struggled to implement a coherent plan as each government sought to shape the policy in its own interests. In the end, as one analyst of the bargaining concludes, "U. S. administrations typically compromised with or accommodated the Europeans, adopting policies at odds with their own policy preferences" in order to retain NATO's imprimatur (Papayoanou 1997: 92). Side-payments may be another cost of organizing consensus in the context of an IO.

The third type of cost, delay, is partly a product of the first two. In contrast to a less formal multilateral approach, IO approval involves votes and a structured decision-making process, which require a willingness to engage in diplomacy and wait for approval of the policy. Fourth and finally, working through an IO increases the level of scrutiny to which an intervening state is subject. Since IOs increase transparency and require a more public accounting of actions, the international community is able to track the behavior of a state that chooses to work under their auspices, as they both prepare and conduct an intervention. Moreover, the exchange of information and discourse that takes place within an IO tends to reveal information about states' preferences and intended actions, leading to more effective monitoring and higher-quality signaling at the international level (Wallander 1999; Keohane 1984). The diversity of IO members is key. Unlike a unilateral effort or an ad hoc coalition with similar interests, most IOs include states with disparate

---

[5] On "influence costs," see Milgrom and Roberts (1990: 58).

Agent preferences, legitimacy, tasks, and permeability

interests who will be watching the coercer with a critical eye. This scrutiny almost axiomatically leads to more sincere signaling (Lupia and McCubbins 1994b: 368).

These various costs, which I refer to generally as the *costs of constraint*, allow the coercer to send a meaningful signal when it chooses to work through an IO. The coercer has shown restraint and a willingness to cede some control, something a more threatening "type" would not be willing to do. This reassures third-party states, which are in turn less likely to retaliate politically and to oppose the intervention.

However, even if other state leaders determine that supporting the coercive policy is in their national interest, they may face domestic barriers to doing so; they must convince their own publics that supporting another state's use of force is justified. IO approval helps overcome this additional obstacle by sending policy-relevant information to domestic publics abroad.

While IR scholars have paid increasing attention to how domestic publics influence state interests and policy,[6] the role of domestic publics *abroad* is not well understood and should be considered as an important strategic player. Members of publics are poorly informed relative to their leadership. They have uncertainty regarding the reasons for a given policy and the relationship between the policy and potential consequences. In the context of coercion on the part of another state, they do not know if the policy is justified and serves multilateral interest or whether it involves selfish goals with undesirable international consequences. Because international issues often lack salience, and because each individual has negligible influence on foreign policy, members of the public have little incentive to gather information on foreign affairs and to engage in careful calculation regarding international events. It is perfectly rational, therefore, for individuals to remain largely ignorant of international policy matters.

Ignorance, however, does not imply indifference. Publics are looking for "information shortcuts" to assess international issues, and IO endorsements can perform this function (Popkin 1991). Since the claims of IOs are more neutral and representative of the international community than claims of individual governments, or of ad hoc coalitions, the signals they convey regarding a policy are more credible and thus more informative. This is the fundamental principle behind the informational

---

[6] For a good example in the context of coercion, see Schultz 2001.

rationale for committee heterogeneity in legislatures: "In the presence of uncertainty," write Gilligan and Krehbiel (1989: 463), "diversity of interests on the committee promotes informational efficiency." Individual citizens, like legislators, respond to new information they receive about the reasonableness and effects of policies, and they update their beliefs in sensible ways (Shapiro and Jacobs 2000: 224).

Through this process of information transmission, which helps domestic publics identify intervention policies worthy of support, IO approval makes it easier for leaders to offer support. As one Canadian diplomat notes, "The average Canadian doesn't know the details and the nittygritty [of foreign policy]. It comes down to symbols. With IO approval, you hardly need to make the case [for supporting an intervention]."[7] In the language of the two-level games literature, the information transmitted to domestic publics by the IO agent increases the size of the domestic "win-set" for leaders throughout the international community by minimizing domestic opposition (Putnam 1988). More generally, this information logic may provide an alternative to standard norm-based explanations for why publics favor multilateralism – especially centered around an IO – over unilateralism.

THE SECURITY COUNCIL AND IRAQ, 1990–1991

The 1990–1991 Persian Gulf conflict serves to illustrate the screening function of IOs during episodes of military intervention. Following the Iraqi invasion of Kuwait in August of 1990, the United States went to great lengths to work through the UN in order to apply pressure and ultimately to expel Iraq from Kuwait, seeking Security Council resolutions at every stage. Resort to force came only after 12 resolutions condemning Iraq's behavior and imposing sanctions, including the passage of Resolution 678, which authorized UN member states "to use all necessary means." In the end, support was widespread and the United States suffered no serious diplomatic setbacks as a result of the war. Thirty-seven countries contributed personnel to the coalition and about twenty provided military hardware. Financial contributions of $54 billion were also made to the United States.[8]

---

[7] Author's interview with a senior Canadian diplomat, November 14, 2003 (location withheld to preserve anonymity).

[8] On military contributions, see Lake (1999: 208–10); Matthews (1993: 313–15). On financial contributions, see Terasawa and Gates 1993, and Freedman and Karsh (1993: 358–61).

Agent preferences, legitimacy, tasks, and permeability

Most observers of Gulf War diplomacy agree that by turning to the Security Council and acting with its approval the United States was able to achieve greater legitimacy and support for its use of coercion. But this observation begs important questions. Why and how was the UN able to perform this function? Why did UN involvement in what was fundamentally a US-led effort change how other states perceived and reacted to events? The logic of screening and information transmission helps us address these questions.

During the early stages of the episode, the international community did indeed face an adverse selection problem and was uncertain about whether it should "hire" – that is, offer tacit or direct support to – the United States as its coercive agent. Initially, most governments and publics were deeply torn on the question of American intervention. Many Arabs viewed Saddam as a hero, and Arab public opinion loathed the idea of Western troops entering the region (Lesch 1991; Heikal 1992: 225–26). Even King Fahd of Saudi Arabia, who faced the most immediate threat of continued Iraqi aggression, was highly reluctant to accept US help, as Mohamed Heikal makes clear: "Never in his eight years on the throne had King Fahd faced a decision as difficult.... Saudi instincts rebelled against pressure to accept American help" (Heikal 1992: 213). Non-Arab leaders were no more eager. Gorbachev faced strong domestic opposition to supporting the United States and told Bush during Desert Shield that he "was nearly as eager to get U. S. troops out of Saudi Arabia as he was to get Iraqi troops out of Kuwait" (Beschloss and Talbott 1993: 262). France had been Iraq's foremost Western ally and, like many other countries, faced substantial losses due to the cessation of trade and the oil embargo (Terasawa and Gates 1993: 182–83).

In sum, it was not at all obvious to leaders and publics that potential US military action was in the interest of the international community. The case shows that the Security Council process imposed costly constraints on the United States that served to diminish concerns over US ambitions among foreign leaders, and that UN approval helped overcome domestic opposition in various countries, facilitating their governments' support of the intervention.

Screening US intentions

As the United States contemplated the use of coercion to push the Iraqi army out of Kuwait, it had to take into account probable reactions to the introduction of the only superpower's military might into a politically sensitive region of the world. States in the Gulf region had a genuine concern for their sovereignty and the encroachment of US military influence, and states outside of the region were worried about the precedent being set and their own interests in the Gulf. For many leaders, American muscle flexing was inherently threatening and undesirable. When the United States sought approval and relinquished some decision-making to the UN, this sent a strong signal to the international community that the United States had the limited, status quo goal of reversing the Iraqi invasion.

By channeling its coercion through the Security Council, the United States suffered costs that helped to signal its intentions. Aside from the operational and logistical difficulties that arose from putting together a multinational force, American political and military leaders faced a number of very real constraints in the form of policy changes and delays, as well as in the extent of the coercive goals pursued. US behavior was also subject to a high level of transparency and scrutiny. All of these limitations were generated or enhanced by working through the UN. The Bush Administration was constrained by the Security Council and the slow and methodical decision-making process that resulted from seeking approval during each phase. As one senior Bush administration official lamented, "When you try to bring people on board, you have to listen to them" (*Newsweek*, October 1, 1990: 20). This reflects the influence costs of seeking IO approval.

At two stages in particular US policies were delayed and modified in order to mollify the Security Council: the decision to enforce the initial embargo on Iraq and the decision to launch Desert Storm. Resolution 661, passed on August 6, imposed a trade embargo on Iraq. But the first enforcement measures did not take place until August 31. Though the United States – and Britain, whose navy was also actively patrolling the Persian Gulf – was willing and able from the start to enforce the UN embargo on shipments to Iraq, these ships were allowed to pass through the naval blockade for several weeks. US decision-makers faced a dilemma, as National Security Adviser Brent Scowcroft describes:

The question was, do we move unilaterally to stop them, or do we wait and try to get additional authority from the UN? We had lengthy discussions with the British about it and of course [Margaret] Thatcher said go after the ships . . . [James] Baker was insistent that we wait. He convinced the President we would lose the Soviets (who were still adamantly opposed to using force) and perhaps the chance for a positive vote in the Security Council on enforcement if we went ahead unilaterally. (Bush and Scowcroft 1998: 351–52)

Agent preferences, legitimacy, tasks, and permeability

Colin Powell and Dick Cheney agreed that, for political reasons, they should wait for UN approval (Woodward 1991: 284). The French and Soviets had argued that 661 alone could not be used to authorize enforcement; the latter in particular were a major obstacle and delayed a new resolution approving force (*Toronto Star*, August 25, 1990: A1). Ultimately, this approval came in the form of Resolution 665, passed by the Security Council on August 25, which authorized the use of force to disable ships destined for Iraq that refused to stop for inspection.

Waiting for UN endorsement in order to enforce the embargo was costly for the United States, apart from the fact that supplies were getting through to Iraq in the meantime. To begin with, there was a credibility issue, as hesitation might raise questions about US resolve (Freedman and Karsh 1993: 147). Moreover, waiting for another resolution raised the prospect that the United States and Britain would lose flexibility, a fear expressed by Thatcher that proved well founded (Thatcher 1993: 821). Afraid that US enforcement actions could trigger war, China, the Soviet Union, and France insisted on strict wording for the resolution that did not simply state that "minimum use of force" could be used – the Americans' preferred syntax, which had almost unlimited interpretations – but rather spelled out that only measures "commensurate to the specific circumstances as may be necessary" could be employed. Moreover, there is some evidence that these three countries explicitly sought Resolution 665 as a way to imposed limits on the American use of force.[9] As one journalist noted at the time, "the Soviet Union wanted to get as many constraints as possible on U.S. military action in the Gulf" (*The Independent*, August 27, 1990: 7).

For US decision-makers, the next great debate – and delay – was over the launching of Desert Storm. Once again, Thatcher argued to Bush that going back to the UN was too risky; she worried that it would constrain the United States and Britain unduly. In seeking a further resolution, she argued, "We risk amendments," therefore it was preferable to "go to war on our own terms" (Bush and Scowcroft 1998: 384). In the end, the United States waited four months from the date of the invasion until Resolution 678 authorized the use of force on November 29. Considerable diplomacy and consultations took place before the United States could even propose language for a resolution. Though Shevardnadze and Baker had agreed on acceptable wording for the resolution

---

[9] For more on the passage of Resolution 665, see Freedman and Karsh (1993: 143–50).

as early as November 8, and though Gorbachev told Bush at a November 19 meeting that he would vote in favor of the resolution, the Soviets insisted on more time for diplomacy throughout the month (Freedman and Karsh 1993: 230–32). Even when a date for a Security Council vote was settled, while the United States hoped to set a relatively prompt deadline for Iraqi withdrawal, the Soviet Union and France insisted on a "pause for peace" as a condition of the Resolution's passage. The Soviets asked for a January 31 deadline; the French compromise of January 15 was selected. The very idea of an "announced" war represented a constraint, as US policy-makers had preferred a more flexible approach (*New York Times*, November 14, 1990: A1).

Delay was costly for US military planners and policy-makers for two reasons. First, it allowed Saddam to prepare for hostilities. Bush expressed his concern very clearly in early January, worrying that, "Each day that passes, Saddam's forces also fortify and dig in deeper into Kuwait. We risk paying a higher price in the most precious currency of all – human life – if we give Saddam more time to prepare for war."[10] Though part of this waiting period was needed by the US military to move troops and equipment into position, its duration probably exceeded by weeks the optimal length of time. The second potential cost of delay came in the political realm. The anti-war movement was rapidly developing momentum in January, including within Congress. Thus delay was the last thing Bush wanted from a domestic political standpoint, and it almost cost him dearly (Mueller 1994: 59–60). Internationally, some feared that it would be hard to maintain a coalition over time. In a *Washington Post* editorial, Henry Kissinger warned that the "psychological basis" for war would wane over time as the initial emotion over Iraq's invasion faded, and that the extensive diplomatic efforts that were taking place would "undermine the military option by consuming time" (*Washington Post*, November 11, 1990: B7).

Nevertheless, the wait was politically important: It satisfied European countries that hoped to further explore diplomatic solutions and it allowed Arab leaders to investigate "Arab solutions." It also signaled that the United States was willing to be constrained and was approaching the conflict in a manner that accommodated the interests of others.

When the United States declared a cease-fire on February 28, reactions were mixed. Saddam was still in power and another day or two of

---

[10] George W. Bush, Radio Address to the Nation on the Persian Gulf Crisis, January 5, 1991. Available at <http://bushlibrary.tamu.edu/research/papers/1991>.

fighting would have led to the destruction of far more Iraqi equipment and the capture of thousands more Iraqi troops. These signs of failure led to postwar accusations that the coalition had not even succeeded. US leaders limited their goals in this way partly because they felt constrained by the UN mandate and did not want to risk forfeiting it. Bush knew it would be costly to adhere to the UN mandate, as prewar polls showed a strong public desire to remove Saddam (Mueller 1994: 41–42, 545). According to Bush: "I firmly believed we should not march into Baghdad. Our stated mission, as codified in UN resolutions, was a simple one – end the aggression, knock Iraq's forces out of Kuwait, and restore Kuwait's leaders. To occupy Iraq . . . would have taken us way beyond the imprimatur of international law bestowed by the resolutions" (Bush and Scowcroft 1995: 464). George W. Bush confirms that his father felt constrained by the resolutions only to force Saddam from Kuwait (Woodward 2002: 329). To shed the aegis of the UN by pursuing more ambitious goals would have been to risk alienating states around the world, and a more expansive set of goals – which were considered early on but rejected when the UN pathway was chosen – would have been interpreted as aggressive and threatening.

UN involvement, and the signal it sent, was important in different ways to different third-party states. Arab leaders, who were especially preoccupied with US and Israeli influence following the end of the Cold War, reacted to the prospect of Western intervention with "deep fear and suspicion of ulterior motives,"[11] including the exploitation of local resources and a desire to strengthen political dominance in the region.[12] As David Lake points out (1999: 235–36), those states most immediately affected, such as Kuwait and Saudi Arabia, were being asked to forfeit an independent foreign policy and to effectively submit to protectorate status for the duration of the American military presence. Moreover, war aims that included the overthrow of Saddam were entirely unacceptable to other Arab regimes. Self-imposed restraint and limited aims were thus key for the United States to avoid a political backlash by states in the region.

States outside of the region were concerned for somewhat different reasons. The French hoped that Saddam's regime would remain in power

---

[11] Khalidi (1991: 167). See also *Los Angeles Times*, August 31, 1990: A6.
[12] Azzam (1991: 481). For example, Saudi Arabia's King Fahd suspected the United States of wanting to establish additional military bases (Heikal 1992: 212).

and that Iraq would not be unduly weakened so that their trading relationship could ultimately remain intact. After losing Europe to the West, the Soviets had genuine political and strategic apprehensions over US motivations and long-term goals in the Middle East, a major Cold War battleground (Alexandrova 1991: 233–34). As one Foreign Ministry official complained early in the standoff, "There are no guarantees that the United States will leave Saudi Arabia after the crisis is over" (*New York Times*, August 31, 1990: A13). The United States thus granted the Soviet Union considerable control over decision-making, via direct diplomacy and especially the Security Council (Baker 1995: 396–410). Forfeiting some autonomy to the Security Council sent an important signal to the broader international community that US preferences made it a trustworthy coercive agent.

Overcoming public opposition

From the time American troops began arriving to defend Saudi Arabia, leaders throughout the international community faced tough domestic political questions in deciding whether to support a potential US-led invasion. By November, all of the US's European allies (except the UK), Canada, and all Arab members of the emerging coalition had made a Security Council resolution a condition for supporting the use of force. This would help them "sell" support of the war to their own domestic audiences. It is clear that US policy-makers had foreign publics in mind when they chose to work through the Security Council. Scowcroft believed that the UN "could provide a cloak of acceptability to our efforts and mobilize world opinion behind the principles we wished to project" (Bush and Scowcroft 1998: 491).

Domestic audiences were most skeptical in the Arab and Muslim world. Western military involvement in the Middle East was a sensitive issue, stimulating memories of colonialism and drawing attention to the Arab–Israeli conflict. This made it very difficult for many Middle East leaders to openly support US intervention. Indeed, even before the initial invasion, as Iraq amassed troops on the Kuwaiti border, Arab leaders pleaded with the United States to take a low profile. They feared that the relatively strong US reaction would only inflame the situation (Freedman and Karsh 1993: 51). Following the Iraqi invasion, no Arab regime dared to call publicly for Western assistance; even Kuwait's desperate call for international help was qualified with an explicit preference for an "Arab solution."

Agent preferences, legitimacy, tasks, and permeability

Among the Arab public, even those who disapproved of Iraq's invasion saw the US role as a separate matter and were strongly opposed (Heikal 1992: 239). "For many Arabs," explains one regional expert, "the prospect of a U. S. military presence shifted the political argument from the issue of Iraqi aggression to the issue of Western neocolonialism" (Lesch 1991: 37). Equally important for Arab leaders was the mobilization of opposition groups, mostly Islamist in orientation, whose position was initially strengthened by US involvement (Azzam 1991: 478–79). Saddam fanned these sentiments by portraying the struggle as anti-American and anti-Israel. Arab leaders who were convinced that US intervention did not pose a threat and hoped to offer support were therefore torn between international and domestic politics. A study of Arab public opinion during the Gulf War concludes that Arab governments were in fact constrained by domestic attitudes and calibrated their policies accordingly (Pollock 1992).

Nevertheless, despite significant opposition, "predictions that the presence of Western forces in the Gulf would set the 'Arab street' ablaze largely fizzled" (Lake 1999: 243, fn. 173). Once a few key Arab states, such as Egypt, Syria, and Saudi Arabia, decided that the risks to the region of a belligerent and even more powerful Iraq were too great to countenance, and that Western intervention was sufficiently unthreatening, their leaders followed the American lead and launched a "coordinated information campaign" centered around the multilateral nature of the intervention (Telhami 1993: 194). UN cover allowed Egyptian President Hosni Mubarak to argue to his citizens that Saddam "is one man against the world," and his policy of supporting the intervention was supported by 84 percent of the population.[13] Pro-coercion governments were able to prevent Saddam from imposing his own interpretation of events – as an Iraq versus US conflict. Notably, even those governments that supported Saddam throughout most of the crisis still endorsed UN sanctions and welcomed UN involvement.

The domestic political challenges facing leaders outside the region were qualitatively different but no less important. The Soviet Union, in particular, was a key partner – indeed, it may have been the only country whose consent was absolutely required for the United States to proceed.

---

[13] *New York Times*, November 8, 1991: A1; "Poll Shows Majority Egyptians Back Government Policy," Xinhua Overseas News Service, January 20, 1991 (accessed via Lexis-Nexis), citing a poll conducted by the American Chamber of Commerce in Cairo.

And yet Gorbachev and his Foreign Minister, Eduard Shevardnadze, faced myriad domestic challenges, leading them to insist that any decisions on possible military action be taken by the Security Council (*Washington Post*, November 9, 1990: A1). Gorbachev was under immense pressure from the right to dissociate Soviet policy from the appearance of excessive US influence (Fuller 1991: 58). The prospect of supporting military coercion against Iraq also triggered a fierce debate between the Arabists in the Soviet foreign policy establishment and Shevardnadze, who was portrayed by them as pro-American (see Alexandrova 1991: 232–33; Fuller 1991: 58). Especially since the Soviet Union and Iraq had been close allies during the Cold War, the Soviet public was not convinced that an invasion of Iraq was in their national interest, and diplomatic efforts by the United States to get the Soviet Union on board were frustrated as much by domestic opposition as by any international factor (Baker 1995: 282; Beschloss and Talbott 1993: 247). Speaking to Baker, Gorbachev put a fine point on the problem: "You are asking the Soviet Union to approve the use of American force against a long-time ally of the Soviet Union."[14] The bottom line was that no group in the Soviet Union could envisage supporting an "American" military campaign.

In the end, Gorbachev and Shevardnadze were able to maintain just enough domestic support by pointing to Security Council approval and by framing the operation to the public as a collective mission. The UN became the focal point of Soviet policy. For example, almost as soon as Desert Shield was announced, the Soviet Foreign Ministry spokesman observed that: "The experience of many years shows that the most correct and sensible way of acting in conflict situations is through collective efforts and the utmost use of UN mechanisms. . . . We are for the Security Council to tackle this most urgent issue [of the Iraqi invasion of Kuwait] now" (quoted in Freedman and Karsh 1993: 125). Framing the coercion of Iraq in reference to the UN helped mitigate domestic opposition by showing that collective interests were at stake, thus enabling a key state to support the policy.

Various Western leaders also relied on the UN to make support politically possible. According to one observer, "France would not have been drawn into the Gulf except under the aegis of the UN" (Connaughton 1992: 106–107). Though Mitterrand felt that Article 51 should

---

[14] BBC Television, Washington Version, January 17, 1992, quoted in Freedman and Karsh (1993: 231).

have been sufficient from a legal perspective, he did not feel that it could justify coercion to his domestic audience. "Article 51 doesn't mind public opinion," he explained to Baker. "Fifty-five million French people are not international lawyers. We need that resolution [to authorize the use of force] to ensure the consequences it will entail" (Baker 1995: 315). Germany and Japan both faced cultural and constitutional barriers to supporting military action. In order to justify their support of the coalition, in terms of both law and public opinion, their governments framed the intervention as a collective effort under the aegis of the UN.[15]

A useful comparison of international public opinion can be made to the 2003 Iraq war, conducted with no Security Council mandate. While 70 percent of Western Europeans supported intervention in the first Gulf War,[16] only 19 percent of Europeans polled in January 2003 supported the second.[17] UN authorization seems to have been a key variable in the latter case. When asked if the United States should intervene militarily in Iraq without UN approval, a plurality in only one European country (Slovakia) out of 30 agreed. When asked if their country should participate in a military intervention *with* Security Council approval, the number of pluralities jumps to 15.[18] A Gallup International poll also conducted in January 2003 showed that few populations were in favor of war. When asked if their country should support a war, majorities in only the United States and Australia responded positively; in the remaining 37 countries there was not majority support. The prospect of UN authorization, however, raised favorable attitudes toward the war by 30–50 percent in most EU countries, and by 46 percent in Canada, 56 percent in Australia, 52 percent in New Zealand, 29 percent in India, and 35 percent in Nigeria.[19]

In both wars, even when government leaders had decided that supporting the intervention was in their country's interest, they often faced domestic opposition. As one newspaper characterized the situation in Europe in late August 1990, while unanimous condemnation of Iraq was unprecedented, "domestic political difficulties and wariness about jumping aboard a U. S. bandwagon are still causing division on the issue

---

[15] *The Daily Telegraph*, September 10, 1990: 12; Purrington and A. K. (1991: 318).
[16] Gallup poll conducted in October 1990, summarized in the *Washington Post*, October 25, 1990: A31.
[17] EOS Gallup Europe, "International Crisis Survey," available at <www.eosgallupeurope.com/int_survey>.
[18] Ibid.
[19] "Iraq Poll 2003," available at <www.gallup-international.com/surveys.htm>

International organizations as informative agents

of military action outside a UN umbrella" (*The Independent*, August 25, 1990: 7). The Security Council's imprimatur was the most powerful tool for convincing these publics that the coercive policy was justified and worthy of support. As one Turkish government official notes, contrasting the 2003 Iraq war with the first, "a resolution gives us something to work with domestically; we just didn't have that in the second case."[20]

The passage of various UN resolutions in the 1990–91 episode allowed leaders to portray the intervention to publics around the world as a reasonable response to a common threat. The heterogeneity of the Security Council – the non-permanent members at the time were Canada, Colombia, Ethiopia, Finland, the Ivory Coast, Cuba, Malaysia, Romania, Yemen, and Zaire – allowed Bush to credibly point out that "diverse nations are drawn together in common cause" (State of the Union speech, January 29, 1991). Other state leaders used the same themes in their public statements and publics reacted to this information by offering widespread support for using force against Iraq. By lending its neutral approval, the Security Council helped publics screen a desirable intervention policy from an undesirable one.

INSTITUTIONAL VARIATION AND FORUM SHOPPING

Of course, the international community has little control over whether a potential coercing state chooses to work through an IO at all – the coercer may operate unilaterally or with a coalition of the willing. Moreover, the coercer sometimes has a choice among IOs. These choices by themselves send information and have implications for the ability of the international community to screen coercive policies. In this section I extend the logic of the theoretical argument to address two questions. First, under what conditions will a potential coercing state choose to operate through an IO? Second, when IO-based action is chosen, how do coercers choose among the available organizations?

I have so far described formal IOs as possessing some neutrality from state interests, which explains their ability to act as informative agents. However, we can more accurately think of institutional neutrality as varying across all institutions, including among IOs themselves. While there are clearly other important variables, including voting rules, bureaucratic autonomy, and informal sources of leverage by states, I define institutional neutrality in terms of the distribution of preferences among

---

[20] Author's interview with a Turkish diplomat, New York, November 13, 2003.

Agent preferences, legitimacy, tasks, and permeability

Institutional neutrality

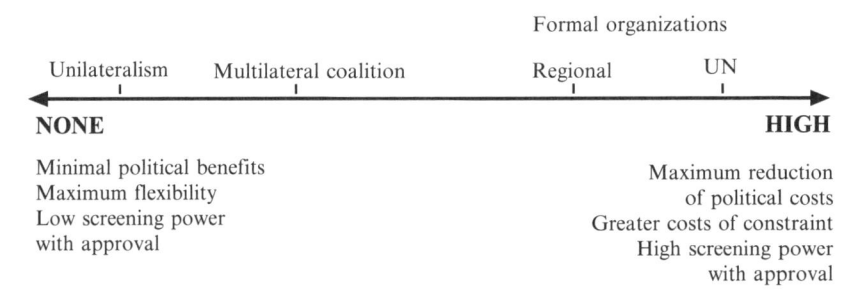

```
                                           Formal organizations
   Unilateralism    Multilateral coalition    Regional      UN
◄——————|——————————————|——————————————————|——————————|——————————►
   NONE                                                    HIGH
   Minimal political benefits              Maximum reduction
   Maximum flexibility                      of political costs
   Low screening power              Greater costs of constraint
   with approval                         High screening power
                                                with approval
```

Figure 8.1. Implications of variation in institutional neutrality

its membership. I argue that the screening power of an institution during episodes of military coercion depends importantly on its independence with respect to the interests of the potential coercing state, on the one hand, and how representative it is of international community interests, on the other.

From the perspective of the coercing agent, as the neutrality of institutions increases, so do the constraints – the policy is more likely to be delayed, modified, or blocked altogether. These costs are mirrored commensurately by political benefits: The greater the neutrality of the institution, the more informative is that institution to the international community principals and the lower are the political costs of using force. Variation among institutions in terms of preference distributions thus helps answer the additional question of forum shopping, with each institutional choice offering a mixture of costs and benefits (here I treat multilateralism as an informal institutional form).

Figure 8.1 portrays the tradeoffs associated with achieving authorization from institutions that are more or less neutral, with unilateralism representing a complete absence of independent authorization. Unilateralism allows a coercer to retain full autonomy but does not help reduce international political costs since the choice to go-it-alone tells the international community that the coercive policy is motivated by selfish goals. This can be thought of as a *negative* screen. Thus, we expect to see unilateralism either when coercing states require maximum flexibility or when they anticipate the international political costs of coercion to be low, or both. Ad hoc multilateralism is a middling strategy: Like-minded states do not constrain the coercer as much and are not viewed as impartial representatives of the international community, thus "coalitions of the willing" produce only modest political benefits. Formal IOs are most neutral due to their standing memberships and are therefore the most informative institutions with respect to the international community. They are the most effective *positive* screening agent. From the coercer's perspective, involving formal IOs reduces international political costs but (and largely because) it also imposes constraints.

These tradeoffs are captured in two *ceteris paribus* propositions that establish the more general conditions under which coercers will seek IO approval over other options. First, *the lower the value they place on flexibility (i.e. the less sensitive they are to the costs of constraint), the more likely coercers are to turn to IOs.* Second, *the higher the anticipated international political costs, the more likely coercers are to turn to IOs.* When both conditions are met, states are most likely to channel policies through IOs. Two examples – the 1989 Panama invasion (conducted *unilaterally* and without IO approval) and the 2003 Iraq war (conducted *multilaterally* and without IO approval) – illustrate this logic and provide contrasting cases to the 1990–91 Gulf War.

Unilateralism in Panama can be explained by the high value that was placed on flexibility and the modest concern over political costs. Turning to an IO or a multilateral coalition would have been too costly given strategic objectives – to arrest Manuel Noriega, retrieve an imprisoned CIA operative, and overwhelm the Panamanian Defense Force before it could organize – that required surprise and rapid action. Secrecy was of paramount importance, making diplomacy and deliberation impractical (Woodward 1991: 178; Powell 1995: 428). Moreover, the most obvious IO option, the OAS, had proven slow to move. While it had passed a resolution condemning the May 1989 elections, which were marked by fraud and then nullified by Noriega, the organization could not succeed over the next several months in pressuring Noriega to step down and ultimately could not agree on more concrete action (Felton 1989: 2223). The cost of these constraints was simply too high to countenance. In any case, the United States expected reactions to its intervention to be relatively muted. Outside the region, most governments were content to let the United States operate with a free hand in its own sphere of influence.[21] Latin American countries reacted negatively

---

[21] In general, US policy-makers operate on the assumption that intervention in the Western hemisphere will be less politically costly. Author's interview with a State Department official, Washington, DC, January 11, 2000.

to the intervention but were too dependent on the United States to retaliate in a meaningful way. As one scholar notes, "the Bush Administration was prepared to weather the inevitable protests since the complainants were either unable or unwilling to make Washington pay any tangible price" (LeoGrande 1990: 619).

The Middle East, on the other hand, is a more sensitive region for the United States. In the lead-up to the 2003 war, policy-makers were indeed concerned about an international backlash and spent months trying to achieve an explicit Security Council endorsement. However, the United States was not willing to forgo flexibility – in terms of delay and limits on its goal to overthrow Saddam – and this made Security Council approval impossible in the end. The aversion to IO-imposed constraints likely came from two sources. First, there was the lesson from the most recent prior intervention, Kosovo, where NATO members bickered constantly and lowest-common-denominator policies were consistently chosen (ICISS 2001: 59). Second, the effect of the September 11, 2001, attacks was to heighten the US sense of vulnerability. As David Malone notes, "This led to greater hostility in Washington towards attempts at the UN and elsewhere to constrain US power" (Malone 2003: 76). Even in Afghanistan, the Bush Administration had declined an explicit Security Council authorization to intervene "in order to retain as much freedom of action in its response as possible" (Malone 2003: 76). While the concern over international political reactions was still high, as they were at the time of the Gulf War, the United States was not willing to sacrifice flexibility. Unwilling to achieve an IO mandate, the White House focused its efforts on building a coalition and stressing its size and involvement in order to achieve some political cover.

As figure 8.1 illustrates, choices among IOs themselves, at the right end of the continuum, represent a microcosm of the tradeoffs confronted across the continuum. Building again on theories of committee signaling in legislatures, figure 8.2 graphically presents three variations in IO member composition. Assuming that the coercing state is more pro-intervention than the median member of the international community (whose preferences are shown distributed in a roughly normal fashion), the coercer's choice among IOs will determine how much information is sent to foreign leaders and publics. Figure 8.2a represents a situation where the IO membership is both heterogeneous and representative, reflected in a median preference that matches the median preference of the international community. In security matters, the Security Council best matches these characteristics. The distance between the IO's median

International organizations as informative agents

a. Heterogeneous IO with representative (moderate) preferences

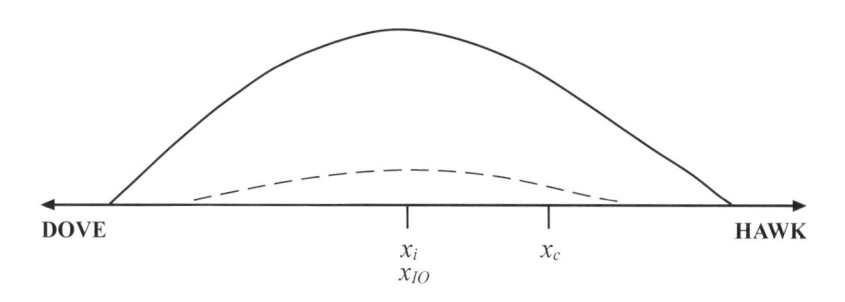

DOVE — x_i, x_{IO} — x_c — HAWK

b. Homogeneous IO with outlier (hawkish) preferences

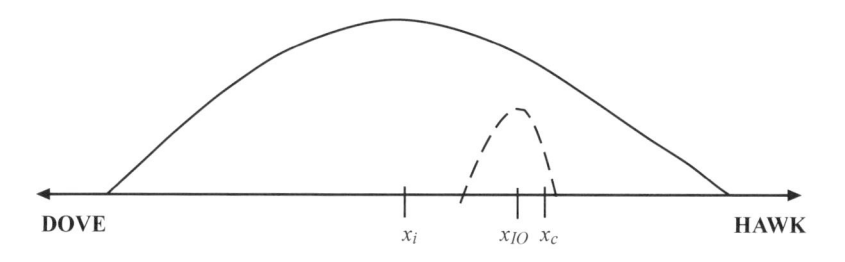

DOVE — x_i — x_{IO} x_c — HAWK

c. Homogeneous IO with outlier (dovish) preferences

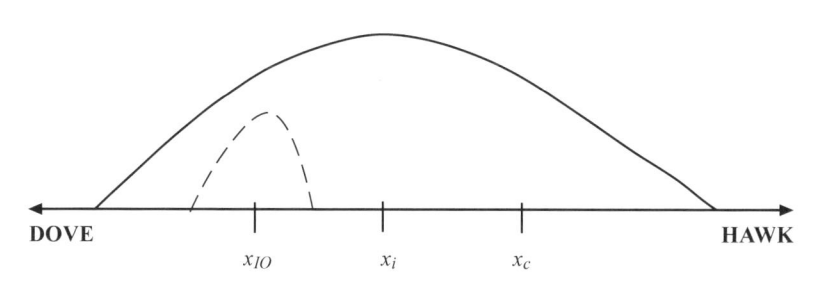

DOVE — x_{IO} — x_i — x_c — HAWK

——— International community   − − − IO membership

x_i = ideal point of median member of international community
x_{IO} = ideal point of median member of IO
x_c = ideal point of the coercing state

Figure 8.2. Preference distributions regarding military intervention

Agent preferences, legitimacy, tasks, and permeability

preference and the coercer's ideal point suggests that the IO is independent with respect to the coercer; the proximity of x_{IO} and x_i implies that information transmission to third parties is efficient, that is, that the IO serves as an informative agent of the international community. Channeling coercion through this IO will likely entail costly constraints – including the possibility of having the policy blocked altogether[22] – but will also produce high quality information regarding intentions and policy consequences. In short, the coercer is relinquishing the most authority in return for the greatest political benefits resulting from the IO's screening power.

Figure 8.2b represents another typical case. The IO membership is relatively homogeneous and, though they are less hawkish on average than the coercer, their median preference is much closer to the coercer's than to the median principal's.[23] Because they are less neutral and representative than the IO in figure 8.2a, the coercer is able to retain more flexibility and is more likely to achieve an outcome closer to its ideal. While some information will be transmitted to the international community if coercion is channeled through such an IO, this choice of forum is less effective as a mechanism for lowering international political costs. This explains why regional bodies, such as the OAS and NATO, have a limited ability to legitimize US interventions (Slater 1969). Authorization of the 1983 Grenada invasion by the obscure Organization of East Caribbean States did not prevent widespread condemnation of the action by US allies and through a General Assembly vote. As the Kosovo example shows, regional IOs tend to be chosen when a coercer cannot achieve Security Council approval, when the anticipated political costs are quite low (the humanitarian goals of the Kosovo intervention provided a widely accepted justification), and when a relevant IO is available.

Finally, figure 8.2c represents an unusual (but plausible) case and an exception to the rule regarding committee composition. In the context of legislatures, Krehbiel recognizes the possibility that a homogeneous

---

[22] Indeed, even the United States, the Council's most powerful member, has been blocked by vetoes or threats thereof on multiple occasions, most recently in Kosovo and Iraq. In the latter case, the United States also would not have achieved the nine-vote threshold for a resolution to pass, a reflection of the body's diversity and independence.

[23] A graphic representation of a multilateral coalition would look most like the IO in figure 8.2b, though with less variance in preferences and an ideal point closer to the coercer's.

committee composed of preference outliers might make a claim that goes against expectations. In this case, the signal is exceptionally informative and the potential to screen effectively is very high. For example, if an agriculture committee proposes to reduce subsidies or if a defense committee proposes to cut military spending, this sends clear information to the floor that these policies are reasonable (Krehbiel 1991: 83). An analogy in IR might be a case where the Arab League endorses intervention against an Arab state.

The coercer's choice among institutional alternatives – from unilateralism, to ad hoc multilateralism, to a choice among IOs – is ultimately determined by its goals and the circumstances of the case, which influence how sensitive the coercer is to the costs and benefits outlined above. It is important to note, however, that the coercer may be constrained by the limited availability of appropriate IOs in a given case.[24] Given the alternatives available, a coercer will seek to work through an institution that is as neutral *as necessary*, but no more.

CONCLUSION

The central political role for IOs during episodes of military intervention is to act as a screening mechanism for leaders and publics around the world. IOs act as an agent of the international community whose function is to transmit information about coercing states and their proposals to use force. I have offered a theoretical argument for how this information transmission works and for why, and under what conditions, powerful states channel their coercive policies through IOs – as an alternative to unilateralism or ad hoc multilateralism – despite the costs of doing so.

With respect to their informative properties, a key institutional feature of international institutions is their membership composition. IO memberships that are heterogeneous and broadly representative are able to provide information that is viewed as more credible to the international community, allowing them to perform the screening function more effectively. Regional organizations and coalitions of the willing, by contrast, are not as neutral and therefore not as informative. These agent characteristics help explain the widely observed phenomenon that the

---

[24] Hawkins et al. (this volume) make a similar point when they note the paucity of IO agents from which state principals can choose.

Security Council plays a uniquely powerful role as a "legitimizer" of state policies involving the use of force (Voeten 2005; Hurd 2002; Thompson 2006). As my case study demonstrates, by working through the Security Council in the 1990–91 conflict with Iraq, the United States was able to send information regarding its intentions to other state leaders and to send policy-relevant information to publics abroad, information that increased international support for the intervention.

Applications of principal-agent theory to international organizations have tended to focus on a few "usual suspects" in the landscape of IOs, many of which are represented in the contributions to this volume – e.g. European Union institutions, the World Bank, the IMF, and certain UN agencies. These organizations are intrinsically important and clearly worthy of study, but they are not representative insofar as they have unusually large and influential bureaucracies. Hawkins et al. explicitly argue that IOs are best understood as bureaucracies.[25] And in most treatments of IOs as informative agents – including Lisa Martin and Mark Pollack's contributions to this volume – their ability to supply information depends on the expertise of an independent staff. However, as this chapter illustrates, we need not focus on bureaucracies to understand IOs as agents. This is an important point since many IOs have no meaningful staff, let alone an autonomous bureaucracy. My theoretical discussion of membership composition and preference heterogeneity points to different sources of IO influence and should serve to broaden our theoretical understanding of delegation to IOs.

---

[25] On bureaucracies as a source of IO autonomy, see Barnett and Finnemore 1999.

9

Dutiful agents, rogue actors, or both? Staffing, voting rules, and slack in the WHO and WTO

ANDREW P. CORTELL AND SUSAN PETERSON

These days, IOs seem to have few friends and many critics. Their detractors alternately portray them as witless tools of the United States and other powerful states (Mutume 2005; Oatley and Yackee 2000) or as rogue actors who, in escaping the control of the states that created and comprise them, threaten national sovereignty (Miller 2005). Like most of the chapters in this volume, we reject such oversimplifications. The institutional design of some IOs allows them to engage in behavior undesired by their member states, while others are highly constrained and incapable of such independence. Nevertheless, even those agents capable of slack usually act as their principals intend. In 2003, the World Health Organization (WHO) took the unprecedented step of directly warning travelers away from countries with significant outbreaks of Sudden Acute Respiratory Syndrome (SARS). Both before and after this radical step, however, and for much of its history, the WHO staff eschewed actions that violate its contract with its members. In recent years, similarly, the World Trade Organization's (WTO) Appellate Body (AB) granted non-state actors standing in the WTO dispute settlement process, despite clear evidence that the member states saw the IO as overstepping its authority. Like the WHO actions, however, WTO behavior proved the exception to the rule; the WTO most often carries out its delegated functions in much the way its members intend.

We thank the editors and other participants in the project and especially the following colleagues: Karen Alter, Martha Finnemore, Erica Gould, Darren Hawkins, Wade Jacoby, David Lake, Lisa Martin, Jonathan Mercer, Daniel Nielson, Heather Scully, and Michael Tierney.

Agent preferences, legitimacy, tasks, and permeability

Under what conditions do IOs engage in slack? That is, what factors determine when an IO's administrative element – its "supportive administrative apparatus" (Abbott and Snidal 1998: 4) comprising the personnel appointed to facilitate member state coordination and implement the organization's mandate – takes independent action undesired by the principal? Recent applications of PA theory to IOs suggest that the agent's institutional design influences its autonomy and the likelihood that it will engage in slack. As Hawkins, Lake, Nielson, and Tierney note in the introduction, principals use various mechanisms of control – the initial grant of discretion, monitoring and reporting requirements, screening and selection mechanisms, institutional checks, and sanctions – to structure agents' incentives and ensure compliance with principals' preferences. Our analysis supports this general approach but suggests that many PA applications fail explicitly to theorize one or both of two crucial analytic steps in their arguments.

First, whether an agent engages in slack depends largely on its preferences. PA approaches generally take agents' preferences as given and assume they will conflict with those of the principals. As Michael Barnett and Martha Finnemore (1999: 705–706) note, however, this is a problematic assumption since "IOs . . . are often created by the principals (states) and given mission statements written by the principals. How then, can we impute independent preferences a priori?"[1] PA theory's focus on screening and selection suggests an answer: an IO's staffing rules influence its preferences. In particular, international or independent staffs – as opposed to staff seconded from and assigned to represent the interests of their own states – are likely to form preferences independent of those of their members.

Second, PA theory correctly acknowledges that whether an agent can engage in slack depends on the extent of agreement among principals. When significant preference heterogeneity exists, an agent can exploit disagreement to advance its own preferences (Kiewiet and McCubbins 1991: 26–27; Nielson and Tierney 2003a: 249). The existence of preference heterogeneity alone, however, does not identify whether or how such differences matter. Structures of control or voting rules

---

[1] Barnett and Finnemore's (1999) analysis may produce the same error they criticize. They contend that IOs' divergent preferences and dysfunctional behavior flow from defining features of modern bureaucracies and internal, bureaucracy-specific traits. To the extent that all IOs share characteristics common to modern bureaucracies, however, they all should seek to escape the control of their creators.

Staffing, voting rules, and slack in the WHO and WTO

influence agents' autonomy by reconciling preference heterogeneity and conditioning principals' use of oversight mechanisms.

In this chapter, we explain when IOs can engage in slack and speculate on when they actually do. We begin our analysis with the grant of discretion in the delegation contract. When states grant IOs significant discretion, rather than specifying detailed rules to the agent for carrying out its responsibilities, slack is possible. Discretion is a necessary, but not sufficient condition for slack, however. IOs may slip the control of their principals only when two other conditions apply. First, an IO's administrative element must have preferences that are distinct from those of the principals. This is most likely when the IO is staffed by international personnel, rather than appointees seconded from national governments. At the same time, independent staff that form a kind of epistemic community are unlikely to want to see their organizations, and thus the success of their mission, torn apart. For this reason, international staffs also may, and often do, restrain themselves and advocate preferences similar to their principals'. Second, whether an IO with independent preferences is able to translate them into slack depends, in large part, on the voting rules governing relations among the states. In general, voting rules that empower relatively few states enhance principals' control and limit slack; rules that empower numerous states make agreement among principals difficult and therefore generally enhance IO autonomy.

We present, in short, a two-step approach in which staffing explains preferences and, in IOs with independent preferences, voting rules explain the ability of the administrative elements to implement them. Only IOs with international staffs and voting rules that disperse decision-making authority across at least a majority of the members are capable of slack. Even those IOs, however, may be unlikely to engage in behavior undesired by their members because of fear of the consequences of such action for their mission and reputation.

The chapter proceeds in two parts. In part one, we present our argument. After briefly discussing the importance of the grant of discretion in the delegation contract as a necessary condition for slack, using the example of the North Atlantic Treaty Organization (NATO), we examine the impact of staffing procedures and voting rules. In part two, we apply the argument to two IOs with favorable staffing and voting rules – agents, in other words, that are most likely to engage in slack – the WHO and the WTO. In both cases the administrative elements are able to act in ways undesired by the principals, but they did so infrequently. The very factor that gives the administrative element preferences for change, the presence of an international professional staff, also discourages it from rocking the boat.

INTERNATIONAL ORGANIZATIONS AND SLACK

Discretion, "often the most prominent feature of the [delegation] contract" (Hawkins et al., this volume), is a necessary condition for autonomy. If principals do not delegate any discretion to their agent, of course, the IO lacks the ability unilaterally to defy the wishes of its members. If states grant discretion, slack may emerge, but it need not. After briefly discussing the importance of discretion as a prior condition, we focus on the two explanatory variables, staffing and voting rules, which determine whether IOs that have been granted discretion are able to use it in ways undesired by states.

The opportunity for slack first emerges when member states write discretion, a grant of authority that specifies the principals' goals but not the particular actions the agents must take to achieve those goals, into the delegation contract. Such discretion may include the scope of the issues the agent is authorized to handle, the policy instruments available to it, and the procedures an agent must follow to use its policy instruments (McCubbins and Page 1987: 411–13). The grant of discretion creates the opportunity for slack; different types of IOs – i.e., courts, banks, regulators, or bureaucracies – will provide states with recourse to different control mechanisms and supranational institutions with different strategies to advance their agendas (Cox and Jacobson 1973; Tallberg 2000). To the extent that it is possible to generalize about the initial grant of authority, one aspect appears paramount: whether IOs have the authority to fulfill their mandate without the specific, prior approval of the members. If they do not, there is little chance that the agent can engage in behavior undesired by the principal.

NATO illustrates this point nicely. States delegated limited authority to their agent, particularly on core military issues, choosing instead to create a system of rules for how the agent is expected to do its job. Most important, NATO's administrative element does not decide when force will be employed; states do. In practice, the states, individually or through the North Atlantic Council (NAC), NATO's highest decision-making body, retain tight and continuous control of these decisions by requiring NATO commanders to seek approval for targeting and other decisions (Clark 2001). Principals gave NATO's secretary general the authority to use his good offices to resolve disputes and to raise issues for consideration by the NAC (Jordan 1967: ch. 2; NATO 2001: ch. 10), but he cannot act on his recommendations without NAC approval. Staff assist with force development, standardization, and infrastructure development, studying issues, facilitating the exchange of information, and identifying common standards and collective needs. In all these areas, certainly, NATO's administrative element may influence principals' preferences and behavior, but it has limited autonomy. All staff recommendations come back to the states, which administer funds, enter into agreements with each other, and transfer funds directly to other states (Kay 1998: 42).

It should be no surprise, then, that NATO has little room for independent action, since its creators designed it this way. Consider the contrast between NATO and the WHO and WTO, discussed below. States have delegated to the WHO the authority to study public health threats and publicly disseminate information without requiring approval for specific recommendations. The WTO, similarly, has the authority to adjudicate trade disputes among members and to set its own procedures for doing so. That agents like the WHO and the WTO have a wider range of independent action available to them than NATO tells us little more than that the principals wanted these IOs to enjoy greater autonomy. To achieve this goal, states deliberately built discretion into the delegation contracts. The interesting question then becomes, when can IOs that have been granted significant discretion actually engage in slack? The answer lies in two other elements of institutional design, which are less easily manipulated by the principals.

First, *staffing rules*, the procedures affecting the type of personnel hired for the IO's administrative element, determine whether and to what extent IOs develop preferences distinct from those of the member states. These rules vary between two general forms: either personnel are seconded from states or they comprise an international civil service.

Staffing procedures affect the degree to which an IO will hold independent preferences.[2] National representatives are unlikely to form preferences independent of the principals, but an international staff composed of officials instructed to represent the IO is likely to develop

---

[2] Staffing rules also may influence the IO's capacity to implement its preferences. Individual states should find it easiest to screen seconded officials. Sanctions are likely to be more credible, moreover, against seconded officials who identify their primary professional interests with advancement in the national government than civil servants whose promotion hinges on advancing the IO's objectives.

distinct preferences. This is true for at least two reasons. First, international staff are more likely to be experts in their particular field, such as public health or international trade. Staff who share a common professional identity are likely to focus on the knowledge- or problem-based aspects of the IO's mission and to develop a similar "logic of appropriateness" (March and Olsen 1998) as their professional roles become the lenses through which they view the IO's mandate (Alter, this volume). The logic of appropriateness associated with serving a particular international social purpose or normative value leads the IO to understand its job in ways that may run counter to states' preferences. The staff may see itself not simply as the states' agent, but also as a member of an international community delegated the responsibility of overseeing the community's values. Staff at the WHO, for example, might come to see themselves as trustees for public health for the world and the international jurists in the WTO's AB are protectors of fair and free trade.

Second, international civil servants, unlike national representatives, have bureaucratic incentives to advance the IO's mission. The job security and prospects for advancement of an international civil servant depend on criteria associated with the IO and not with member states. Such internally generated evaluations – as well as the organizational cultures that are likely to develop – increase the inward focus of staff members, producing independent interests that may conflict with states' preferences. Representatives of member states, in contrast, tend to be interested in maximizing their state's national interest or concerned with domestic or electoral politics, concerns that are absent for unelected IO bureaucrats. Even when national representatives share specialized knowledge and professional norms, as in NATO's military staff, they possess multiple interests, any one of which may take precedence over an IO's mandate.[3]

At the same time that international staffs have both epistemic and bureaucratic incentives to develop independent preferences, they face at least two sets of countervailing pressures. First, international staff who share a common social purpose are likely to be acutely aware of the extent to which they are dependent on states for the agency's existence

---

[3] This does not mean that a purely seconded staff cannot form independent preferences. As the officials' tenure lengthens and their prospects for future employment outside the government increase, even seconded staff may develop preferences independent of the member states (Keohane et al. 2000: 460).

and resources. They therefore will tend to avoid advocating positions that jeopardize the IO's existence or resources. Second, an international staff will be wary of behavior that may tarnish its reputation in the eyes of member states and the international public (Johnston 2001). In both cases, international staffers are not unlike national representatives, whose preferences are unlikely to diverge from their principals' because of fear of sanctioning. International staff will share this fear when survival or reputational concerns loom large. Threats to the IO's resources and reputation also threaten the staff's shared international social purpose and normative values and therefore temper the staff's tendency for independence. In short, the IO staff simultaneously may be pulled to form independent preferences and pushed to conform to states' preferences. Which set of dynamics takes precedence in any given case remains a task for empirical investigation.

IOs cannot engage in slack unless their administrative elements have preferences distinct from those of their member states, but not all IOs with independent preferences are equally capable of achieving them. Understanding the conditions that enable the staff to achieve its preferences, then, requires a focus on the *structure of control* or *voting rules* governing states' attempts to oversee the administrative element. These rules structure the resolution of preference heterogeneity among the members of a collective principal (Lyne, Nielson, and Tierney, this volume) and determine members' ability to approve IO behavior, sanction their agent, or reach consensus on a new delegation contract (Pierson 1996; Pollack 1997).

The structure of control varies along a continuum measuring the distribution of voting authority across states. On one end is a highly dispersed structure characterized by unanimity or consensus, in which all states must agree and any one can reject a proposed action. The midpoint is majority rule, while super-majorities disperse authority to a greater extent because they accord an equal role to a larger number of states. A slightly more concentrated structure of control emerges when a minority or a committee can oversee the IO's actions. The most concentrated structure comprises a single state, which exercises de jure authority over the IO, most likely through heavily weighted voting rules.

Contemporary IOs illustrate this range. In the WTO, control is highly diffuse since decision rules are primarily based on consensus among its 148 members. In other IOs, a less than unanimous majority oversees the organization's actions. The WHO uses a majority or super-majority voting system, depending on the issue, and the European Union (EU)

Agent preferences, legitimacy, tasks, and permeability

employs a qualified majority voting system for its members' relationship with the Commission. No contemporary IO approximates a concentrated structure. Those that come closest – the International Monetary Fund and the United Nations Security Council – concentrate veto power in a minority of members, but disperse authority for approval of an action across a majority of members.

The voting rules structuring the relationship among the principals influence an IO's ability to implement its preferences and engage in slack (Alter and Lyne, Nielson, and Tierney, this volume). In general, voting rules that empower relatively few states enhance principals' control and limit slack, because it is relatively easy for the states to overturn unwanted actions. Under such conditions, slack is minimized because "agents rationally anticipate the preferences of principals and the high probability of sanctions . . . and adjust their behavior accordingly" (Pollack 2002: 202). A structure of control that empowers numerous states, in contrast, generally enhances agent autonomy because it makes it difficult for principals to halt or overturn undesired IO behavior. In such situations agents recognize that their principals lack the political consensus to sanction them. In effect, the structure of control determines whether and to what extent there exists a credibility gap regarding principals' capacity to execute their threats against agents who slack.

Our argument expects that only IOs characterized by a specific institutional design should be capable of slack. A grant of discretion creates the opportunity for slack, but only those IOs like the WHO and WTO with international staffs and relatively dispersed structures of control actually can engage in slack. Figure 9.1 summarizes this argument.

At the same time, IOs that are capable of acting in ways undesired by the states that created and comprise them rarely do. For much the same reason they form independent preferences – because they comprise an international staff charged with representing the IO, not their home governments – the staff are unlikely to want to engage in behavior that might jeopardize their resources and mission.

CASES

An ideal research design would test the argument across a range of cases, corresponding to the types depicted in figure 9.1, but that is not possible in a single chapter. Instead, we examine two cases in which slack is most likely, where the IO's administrative element comprises an international staff and voting rules disperse authority. We explore the WHO and WTO

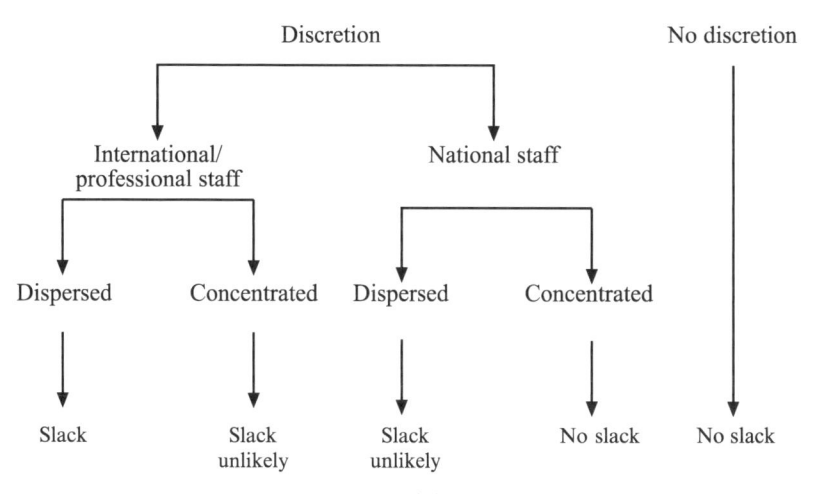

Staffing, voting rules, and slack in the WHO and WTO

```
                        Discretion                    No discretion
                   ┌────────┴────────┐
            International/        National staff
         professional staff
         ┌──────┴──────┐         ┌──────┴──────┐
      Dispersed   Concentrated  Dispersed  Concentrated
         │            │            │           │            │
         ▼            ▼            ▼           ▼            ▼
       Slack        Slack        Slack      No slack     No slack
                   unlikely     unlikely
```

Figure 9.1. Institutional design and IO slack

over time and across different aspects of their mandates, providing many more observations than cases. The interesting tasks, given the most likely case selection, are to trace the process by which the independent variables produce slack and ask why slack does not occur even more often than it does. The following case studies explore these two issues in depth after briefly examining the principals' grants of discretion to their agents and measuring the two independent variables, staffing and voting rules.

The World Health Organization

Established in 1948 as the "directing and coordinating authority on international health work," the WHO seeks "the attainment by all peoples of the highest possible level of health" (WHO 1948: Preamble). To fulfill this ambitious mandate, the member states delegated to the IO significant information-gathering and other responsibilities and created a staff composed of medical and public health professionals who were likely to develop independent preferences based on their shared expertise and commitment to the WHO's mission. The founders instituted a two-thirds majority-voting rule, making agreement among the principals relatively difficult. Together, the staffing and voting rules suggest an agent capable of escaping the control of its principals with relative impunity. Indeed, WHO staff have engaged in slack, most notably on SARS, but this outcome has been rare, since the staff's shared expertise and bureaucratic commitment often induce caution. In one case, in fact, the staff reversed itself in response to a member's criticism, despite the state's inability to overturn the WHO's decision.

Article 2 of the WHO constitution outlines the significant functions of the WHO in the health arena: coordinating international health work among state and non-state actors; eradicating disease; promoting health in a wide range of areas; providing technical assistance and aid to member governments to strengthen health services; developing and promoting international health standards; maintaining epidemiological and statistical services; "propos[ing] conventions, agreements, and regulations and mak[ing] recommendations with respect to international health matters"; "promot[ing] and conduct[ing] research in the field of health"; studying and reporting on "administrative and social techniques affecting public health and medical care from preventive and curative points of view"; "provid[ing] information, counsel and assistance in the field of health"; and "assist[ing] in developing an informed public opinion among all peoples on matters of health" (WHO 1948: Art. 2).

Originally, the structure of the WHO secretariat reflected the two broad types of activities delegated to the staff, information-gathering and technical assistance.[4] Today, the secretariat is organized by substantive issue-areas, and the individual departments, each of which is headed by an assistant director-general, retain responsibility for research, surveillance, health promotion, training, coordination, and other tasks.[5] In short, the WHO staff gather and disseminate information, issue recommendations, publish expert reports, and provide technical advice across a wide range of health issues, often with very little direct oversight by the member states. Expert committees, for example, must consent to any changes in their reports. Like many other less formal WHO documents, reports require only the director-general's approval to be published (Jacobson 1973: 202). These reports guide WHO personnel and medical professionals worldwide and, because they usually are reported in the media, reach a wider public (Jacobson 1984: 124).

---

[4] Each activity had its own department. The Central Technical Services was responsible for information-gathering, while the Advisory Services provided expert consultants and trained specialists to countries requesting assistance (Berkov 1957: 30–31).

[5] Departments include: HIV/AIDS, TB and Malaria; Communicable Diseases; Non-communicable Diseases and Mental Health; Sustainable Development and Healthy Environments; Health Technologies and Pharmaceuticals; Family and Community Health; Evidence and Information for Policy; External Relations and Governing Bodies; and General Management.

Staffing, voting rules, and slack in the WHO and WTO

The WHO's founders delegated these responsibilities to an administrative element – including the director-general, secretariat, and executive board – comprised largely of doctors and other public health experts. The World Health Assembly (WHA), the WHO body of member state representatives, elects the executive board, which includes 32 technical experts whose role is to advise and facilitate the WHA's work. According to WHO doctrine, members of the board serve as individuals, not as national representatives. The executive board nominates and the WHA appoints the WHO's director-general.

The director-general, in turn, oversees a secretariat of 3,500 health and other experts. These officials staff the IO's office in Geneva and six regional offices, as well as thirteen laboratories in ten countries. Early in the WHO's history, the principals sought to insure a high level of scientific proficiency among the staff by issuing temporary, rather than permanent contracts. The founders believed that staff who stayed too long would become too deeply immersed in the WHO bureaucracy and lose their scientific edge. Writing in 1973, however, Jacobson noted that "[t]his policy prevails in de jure though not completely in de facto terms" (Jacobson 1973: 199).

In addition to the permanent and temporary staff members in the secretariat, the director-general also appoints expert advisory panels, expert committees, and scientific groups to monitor and study a number of international health concerns. These bodies include individuals with relevant scientific, medical, and technical expertise. Members of expert advisory panels report on developments within their fields, while expert committees and scientific groups study specific issues (Jacobson 1973: 202).

The founders established a majority or super-majority voting rule, depending upon the issue under consideration, to govern relations among states and between the principals and their agent. The 192 members are represented within the WHA, the IO's highest policy-making body, on a one-state, one-vote formula. Most WHA decisions are taken by majority rule, although "important questions" – regulations, resolutions, and amendments to the constitution – require a two-thirds majority of members present and voting (WHO 1948: Art. 60). Attempts to rein in or reprimand runaway staff would require the support of two-thirds of the WHA, and such a majority might be difficult to assemble. The recipients of WHO technical assistance – African, Asian, and Latin American states – are likely to side with an activist staff's attempts to enlarge the IO's budget or expand its mandate into new operational activities.[6] After 1960, in fact, the developing states constituted a two-thirds majority within the WHA.

In practice, WHO staffers allied with developing states in the WHA on numerous occasions, taking the WHO into new health areas like pharmaceuticals (Mingst 1992: 216–18), breast-milk substitutes (Sikkink 1986; Mingst 1992: 216–17), and tobacco control (Lazurus 2003; Williams 2003). The so-called "politicization" of the WHO provides another example of this phenomenon. In the 1970s, parts of the administrative element sometimes encouraged WHA members to assert themselves on a number of explicitly political issues, usually over the objections of some of the largest donor states. Despite US complaints that the issues were outside the WHO's mandate, the WHA endorsed expert reports on the dangers of nuclear weapons and the epidemiological effects of the Vietnam War (Jacobson 1973: 187; Williams 1987: 63). Expert reports and WHA resolutions voiced IO preferences in the Middle East conflict, criticizing Israeli policy for its effects on Palestinians' health, demanding WHO visits to the occupied territories, and supporting the Palestinians' right to self-determination as a means of improving health conditions (Jacobson 1973: 187; Mingst 1992: 223; Williams 1987: 64). In each case, the administrative element's reports and recommendations explored new areas not envisioned by the founders, but policy change occurred only when a two-thirds majority of the principals voted to move the organization in these new directions. The staff did what it was supposed to do – identify, study, and respond to health threats – even if some states, including some very powerful ones, objected to the particular threats identified or the solutions advocated.

Although these cases do not constitute slack, they highlight the conflicting influences – both epistemic and bureaucratic – on staff preferences. Their medical, scientific, and public health training and expertise often push WHO staffers to advocate that the IO branch out into new areas of health and wellness. At the same time, their medicalized view of the WHO's role often pushes them to exclude more political issues. As former Director-General Gro Brundtland put it, "We can set standards in areas where there is a reasonable agreement about facts and technical medical content. But on the more political front about how to finance healthcare, or what part of the gross domestic product should go to

---

[6] If, in fact, the preferences of the administrative element and the bloc of developing states diverge, it would be relatively easy for the WHA to overturn the staff's actions.

health – all of these issues are deeply political and they certainly are not decided, in any way, by an international institution with just under 4,000 people" (Global War 2002: 26).

The staff's shared commitment to the survival and prosperity of the agency reinforces this caution. In 1983, for example, then Director-General Halfdan Mahler warned developing states in the WHA:

If we allow ourselves to be lured astray into fields beyond our constitutional competence I am afraid we will find ourselves in those very minefields that we have been trying to avoid in the interest first and foremost of the health of the deprived peoples living in the Third World. None of us would want to blow up our Organization nor would we want to lose the tremendous prestige we have gained as an Organization of 160 member states, able to cooperate with one another for the health of people everywhere without distinction of race, religion, political beliefs, social or economic development – indeed, what our very Constitution demands of us. (Williams 1987: 63)

In 1989, similarly, then Director-General Hiroshi Nakajima negotiated a compromise when recognition of the Palestinian Liberation Organization (PLO) threatened to rend the organization. The United States promised to withhold its contribution, one-quarter of the WHO's annual budget, if the PLO's membership application were approved. Nakajima brokered a compromise by lobbying WHA members to put the health of the agency before politics (Lewis 1989; Randal 1989). In both cases, the WHO's staff acted as a brake on the kind of change it advocated in other cases.

Both epistemic pressures for change and bureaucratic incentives for caution battled in another area – communicable disease surveillance and response – where the WHO staff ultimately chose to slack. In this area, the WHO operates within the confines of the International Health Regulations (IHR). Originally adopted in 1959 as the International Sanitary Regulations and renamed in 1969, the IHR are designed to "ensure the maximum security against the international spread of diseases with a minimum interference with world traffic" (WHO 1983: Foreword). The regulations required member states to notify the IO of outbreaks of three diseases: cholera, plague, and yellow fever. If invited into the affected country, WHO staff could then study and recommend responses to the outbreak and provide assistance to the national governments. The limited notification requirement was intended to form "the backbone of WHO's international surveillance activities on the diseases subject to the IHR" (Fidler 2004: 33). Yet states had no legal obligation to report any other diseases, and the WHO staff had no authority to disseminate information obtained by any means other than the required disease reporting by governments.

The staff has exceeded this authority on several occasions. Their concern with the public health consequences of a disease outbreak led staff to form preferences at odds with the intentions of the principals, while the dispersion of voting authority among the principals meant that it would have been difficult to rein in the staff. The administrative element had long struggled to operate within the IHR and fulfill its mission to "stimulate and advance work to eradicate epidemic, endemic and other diseases" (WHO 1948: II, 2g). With the approval of the WHO Committee on Communicable Diseases and the executive board, Director-General Marcolino Candau in 1970 exceeded the IO's authority by reporting an outbreak in Guinea of cholera, a disease covered by the IHR, without official notification or permission from the Guinean government. The government had ignored repeated appeals by the director-general and refused to report the outbreak, so Candau took matters into his own hands and publicly disseminated information from other sources. In making the public announcement, Candau acknowledged that he was acting outside the IHR but claimed that his actions were necessary to fulfill the IO's functions as outlined in Article 2 of the WHO constitution (Fidler 2004: 64). Other parts of the administrative element – the Committee on Communicable Diseases and the executive board – condoned the director-general's actions. Although there was little fallout from this action, the staff exercised caution and never again exceeded the IHR in this manner.

The staff's preferences for change in the terms of the delegation contract remained strong. The WHO took a beating in the 1980s and 1990s by states and non-state actors for its increasing irrelevance on issues like AIDS (Godlee 1994a, 1994b). The staff was becoming increasingly frustrated, moreover, by the IHR's restrictiveness and ineffectiveness: only three diseases required notification; states routinely violated the regulations by failing to report cases of these diseases; and the IHR proved irrelevant to the growing HIV/AIDS pandemic (Fidler 2004: 35–41). In response, WHO staff began lobbying member states to revise the health regulations. The staff's arguments about the need for IHR revision resonated with many member states, which had long agreed that the existing IHR were inadequate. In 1995 the WHA instructed the director-general to undertake revisions to the IHR (WHA 1995). The administrative element sought to augment disease reporting by national governments with epidemiological information acquired from non-state sources, acquire the authority to report on "public health emergencies," rather than just specific diseases, and establish a dispute settlement mechanism to settle disagreements arising under the IHR (WHO 2002; Fidler 2005: 21–24).[7] Initially, the revisions were to be complete by 1998, but the target date was delayed four times to May 2004 because of technical issues and member state resistance to the dispute settlement mechanism and a subsequent WHO proposal that the IHR identify the required capacities of national disease surveillance systems (Fidler 2005: 26–30). Before the revisions were complete, in 2001 the WHA bowed to encroaching technological capabilities and formally approved the gathering of epidemiological information from non-governmental sources.

While the process of revising the IHR inched forward, the WHO administrative element acted outside the existing contract on several occasions. First, the administrative element defied the principals by collecting and using epidemiological information from non-governmental sources. In 1994 a non-governmental organization (NGO) initiated an internet-based reporting system, the Program for Monitoring Emerging Diseases, which was designed to provide early warnings of infectious disease outbreaks. In 1997 the WHO began using an NGO network, the Global Public Health Intelligence Network to search non-governmental sources for evidence of disease outbreaks, including many diseases not covered by the IHR. In 1998 the IO began operating its own Global Outbreak Alert and Response Network (Fidler 2004: 63, 66–67). In short, from 1998 to 2001, when the WHA approved the gathering of information from non-governmental sources, the administrative element was engaging in slack often without member state knowledge, never mind approval.

In this context, in February 2003 the WHO was alerted to the outbreak of a new disease, SARS, which gave rise to a second and more egregious example of WHO slack. The IO's behavior in this case constituted a significant break with prior patterns in at least two ways. First, on the basis of non-governmental information suggesting both that the

---

[7] As Fidler (2005: 23–24, n. 125) explains, "This dispute settlement provision would apply to all disputes, not just those involving measures that restrict international trade. The Committee of Arbitration proposal seemed clearly designed to address the problem of unwarranted and excessive measures because the problem of failure to notify was remedied by WHO's ability to gather non-governmental sources of surveillance information."

epidemic might have originated in the Guangdong province of China and that it was continuing unabated, and in the face of the intransigence of Chinese officials, WHO staff repeatedly and publicly accused the Chinese government of denying them access to the province (Ying and Savadore 2003). According to David P. Fidler (2004: 96–97), "[i]n an unprecedented move, WHO went on the offensive against China," which was under no obligation to report cases of a disease not subject to the IHR. "WHO's public criticism of the Chinese government represented a radical break with the traditional diplomacy that characterizes relations between the Organization and member states."

Second, under Director-General Brundtland's leadership, on March 12 the WHO issued a rare global health alert. Later in March and in April, the IO issued a series of unprecedented emergency alerts warning travelers to avoid Hong Kong, Toronto, Taiwan, and parts of China in an effort to curb the spread of the disease. WHO officials imposed conditions for lifting the travel advisories, which were widely perceived to injure tourism and trade in affected countries and which provoked loud complaints from China and Canada. The WHO was acting not just outside the existing delegation contract, but, as Fidler (2004: 139–40) concludes, its actions went "well beyond the authority it was proposing to write into the revised IHR. . . . [T]he most radical of all the WHO recommendations – the geographically-specific travel advisories – were directed at travelers not WHO member states. For the revised IHR, WHO proposed that it would issue 'recommendations for actions by Member States.'"

As was true when some staff and developing states sought to expand the WHO's mandate into political issues, staff preferences reflected conflicting pressures. For most staff, their role as health professionals compelled them to advocate strong action, in clear violation of the terms of the existing delegation contract, to bring the burgeoning SARS epidemic under control. When asked where the WHO's mandate for this action came from, the current Director-General J. W. Lee replied, "[I]n a sense our mandate is . . . the truth" (NPR 2003), not the delegation contract between the principals and their agent. Some staff objected, however, to the decision to issue the travel alerts. If they were wrong about the severity of the crisis, they reasoned, the IO's legitimacy would suffer (Cohen et al. 2003: A6). In fact, WHO staff exercised caution, at the same time they clearly were operating outside the delegation contract. In response to protests by the Canadian government, the WHO lifted its travel advisory against Toronto after only six days, despite an original timetable under which the WHO would revisit the need for the advisory after three weeks, or twice the incubation period for SARS (Fidler 2004: 92).

The WHO's administrative element ultimately succeeded in changing the organization's procedures and mandate, gaining post hoc member state approval for what it had already done (WHA 2003). Prior to May 2003, however, the IO engaged in slack in both the SARS and the earlier cholera epidemics, as well as in its information-gathering activities between the two cases. This slack emerged because of the WHO's institutional design. The IO's professional staff of medical and public health advocates sought to do what was necessary to stem the epidemics of infectious disease, not to follow the political dictates of its principals. It would have taken a highly concentrated voting rule to overturn the administrative element's actions, which violated the terms of the delegation contract and which some – but not two-thirds – of the states clearly disliked. Alternatively, it would have taken a secretariat of political appointees, rather than health professionals, to create an organization in which the staff did not advocate independent preferences on infectious disease surveillance and control. At the same time that we see significant slack in the area of communicable disease, the WHO cannot be described as a rogue actor. The very institutional feature that generates independent preferences, a professional staff, also produces caution among public health professionals, who fear the possible consequences of acting outside the delegation contract for the legitimacy and financial health of their organization.

The World Trade Organization

Established in 1995, the WTO seeks to liberalize trade among its large (148 by July 2005) and growing membership. To fulfill this mandate, the member states delegated to the IO dispute resolution responsibilities and nominal informational roles. They also created a staff of international economic professionals, whose shared expertise and commitment to the WTO's mission are likely to generate independent preferences. The members traditionally employ a consensus voting rule for most issues, which makes it difficult to reach agreement or change the status quo. Together, these staffing and voting rules suggest an agent capable of forming its own preferences and escaping the control of its principals, at least with respect to the dispute settlement system. In fact, the AB, the highest element of the WTO's dispute settlement system, has taken at least two significant actions that amount to slack, both of which influenced the standing of non-state actors in the organization's dispute settlement system. At the same time, the AB's concern for its standing in the eyes of member states has led it to exercise caution, going so far as to reverse one of these actions even though the displeased members were incapable of overturning it.

The WTO comprises two central administrative organs, a secretariat and a dispute settlement system. The secretariat enjoys no independent decision-making power. Its 22 divisions primarily provide expert information to the members, public, and media, organize and support the members in their meetings and negotiations, and provide technical assistance to developing country members (WTO). The staff of about 630 civil servants includes mainly trade economists, international trade lawyers, other specialists in international trade, and translators, and is headed by a director-general. Gregory Shaffer (2001: 56) likens the professional staff to an epistemic community, since its members share similar beliefs about the validity of neo-classical economics and the importance of trade liberalization. The secretariat staff may express these preferences, but it finds it difficult to act on them since it plays only a supportive role. As Shaffer (2001: 56) observes, "[o]n the basis of their reputation for impartiality, inside information, and close contacts with trade diplomats, Secretariat members can, at least at the margins, help shape knowledge, frame issues, identify interests, facilitate coalition-building, and thereby affect outcomes."[8]

The members delegated significantly greater discretion to a two-tiered dispute resolution body. These bodies are expected to offer an independent interpretation of members' compliance with their treaty obligations and are empowered to recommend how members can make their trade practices compatible with their WTO obligations. The first tier comprises three-person dispute resolution panels constituted for individual disputes. Panels independently determine whether a member's actions conform to WTO rules. Their rulings may not change the rights the trade agreements grant to members (see WTO 1994: DSU).

The second tier comprises a standing seven-member entity, the AB. The AB is assisted by its own small secretariat, comprising a director and about

---

[8] In this capacity, secretariat officials assist the dispute settlement panels. According to one former member of the AB, "it is thus safe to assume that the influence of these officials on the work of individual panels can be considerable" (Ehlermann 2003: 473).

a dozen lawyers. The AB is delegated authority only when the parties to a dispute do not agree with a panel's ruling. Based on the WTO's Dispute Settlement Understanding (DSU, Art. 17.13), The AB can only uphold, modify, or reverse a panel's findings and may rule only on elements of the panel's legal interpretation appealed by one of the parties. It lacks the power to remand a case to the relevant panel. AB members, like panelists, may seek information from outside experts and are expected to interpret the trade treaty "in accordance with customary rules of interpretation of public international law" (WTO 1994: DSU, Art. 3.2). Like the panels' decisions, the AB's rulings may not change a member's treaty obligations. In addition, the treaty calls on the AB to develop its own working procedures for appellate review, thereby enhancing its autonomy. The AB works out these procedures with the chair of the Dispute Settlement Body – the member state council – and the WTO director-general, although the latter two officials' approval is not required. In fact, only a single, one-sentence article (WTO 1994: DSU, Art. 17.9) is devoted to this authority, which has come to encompass a wide range of technical details regarding the appeal process as well as other procedural issues on which the members failed to act (Steger 2002). The AB has the greatest autonomy, and thus the most potential for slack, in this area.

Panelists are drawn on an ad hoc basis from a small group of officials, many of whom represent member states, yet serve in their individual capacity. Put otherwise, panelists serve on a part-time, case-by-case basis and continue in their full-time jobs, whether in the public or private sectors. A recent EU report found that "panelists do not have time to develop expertise in the procedural or technical aspects of the dispute settlement system" (quoted in Miller 2005). Members created screening and selection mechanisms to reduce unintended outcomes at this level: members select the pool of potential panelists and may reject a panelist chosen for a dispute involving them; and panelists may not be nationals of the parties to a dispute unless the disputants agree. Moreover, disputants can screen a panel's report in an "interim review" and comment on its findings and conclusions. Perhaps most significantly, disputants can automatically appeal undesired panel decisions to the AB, the second tier of the dispute settlement system.

The AB's members are "persons of recognized authority, with demonstrated expertise in law, international trade and the subject matter of the covered agreements generally. They shall be unaffiliated with any government" (WTO 1994: DSU, Art. 17.3). These officials serve four-year terms, renewable once, and are chosen to be "broadly representative"

Agent preferences, legitimacy, tasks, and permeability

of the membership. As Karen Alter (2003: 795) notes, "the politics of appointment is focused primarily on the geographical distribution of judicial appointees," thereby reducing the ability to screen potential AB members. The members of the AB possess heterogeneous backgrounds, including prior experiences in government, IOs, private law firms, and academia.[9] Nevertheless, they possess a shared professional focus on international economic and legal issues.

According to James Bacchus (2002: 1030), an original member of the AB who served from 1995 to 2004, AB members' shared professional interests have helped them to develop a common goal.

From the beginning, I have been joined. . . . by distinguished international jurists of the very highest order. They have, each and all, been legal thinkers and legal craftsmen of the very highest quality. They have been students of history and philosophy as well as students of economics and jurisprudence. They have been seekers of the better world that yet can be – if we succeed in our shared efforts to secure the international rule of law.

In this regard, the AB members' professional focus led them to recognize that their "shared goal from the very start was the establishment of an independent, quasi-judicial institution that would serve all the Members of the WTO equally and effectively" (Bacchus 2003: 7). Yet Bacchus also points out that the meaning of "members" of the WTO is not limited to only the states.

Our "range of duty" is to the entire population of all of the 146 Members of the WTO. Five billion people are with us whenever we sit together at our table. . . Their needs, their longing, their passions, their aspirations for a fuller and truer humanity – their fondest hopes for freedom – are all ever with us as we reason together in our efforts to help the Members of the WTO clarify and uphold their international treaty obligations. We believe that, by reasoning together, we can best serve all their hopes for freedom (Bacchus 2003: 7).

These two roles – agents of the member states' governments and representatives of individual citizens – are not inherently incompatible. Nevertheless, giving priority to the interests of the international public can lead to slack.

Claus-Dieter Ehlermann (2003: 478), another original AB member who served from 1995 to 2001, concludes that this shared identity and outlook also have been cultivated by the structures and processes of the

---

[9] See www.wto.org for complete biographical information of the current members as well as those previously serving.

AB itself, noting that the members create their own procedures for carrying out the responsibilities delegated to them. Ehlermann emphasizes the AB's "working procedures," which he concludes have "contributed to the independence of the Appellate Body, both in an objective and subjective sense." Its "system of exchange of views" has "contributed greatly to consistency and coherence of decision making" and "to the high degree of collegiality among . . . members." In fact, while the treaty enables individual AB members to offer dissenting opinions, to date the AB has made decisions by consensus in its 70 or so rulings.

A General Council, comprising official representatives from each member state, oversees the organization's secretariat and the dispute settlement process. Its decisions are taken by consensus, meaning that no state present objects to a decision. The organization identifies situations requiring voting, which is based on the principle of one state, one vote. Changes in the organization's central principles demand unanimity. Although authoritative interpretations of individual aspects of the IO's treaty require a three-quarters majority,[10] standard practice has been to reach decisions by consensus. Members approve panel and AB decisions using a reverse consensus procedure; a panel's and the AB's decisions take effect within 60 and 30 days respectively, unless states decide by consensus not to adopt the ruling (WTO 1994: DSU, Arts. 16.4, 17.14). It is possible, then, for members to vote separately on specific parts of the AB's reports (Ehlermann 2003: 479).

The structure of control further enhances the AB's autonomy in creating working procedures. Existing voting rules make it difficult for members to overturn undesired procedures: three-quarters of the members are required to reverse the AB's interpretation of the treaty, or the members can amend the treaty by consensus. This voting rule leads

the balance [to tip] in favor of the Appellate Body because it is very difficult for the WTO members to make a collective decision. The decision-making process in the WTO under Article IX [which requires a three-quarters majority to adopt interpretations of the agreements] reflects a major structural deficiency in the WTO system, because it lacks provisions to provide a flexible "legislative response" to Appellate Body's decisions, regardless of whether they are considered to be wrong or right (Joergens 1999: 213).

The AB then has a large potential for slack. First, members delegated a wide range of discretion, particularly in the procedural area. Second,

---

[10] Some actions require a two-thirds majority, including submissions of amendments for members' consideration.

Agent preferences, legitimacy, tasks, and permeability

professionals who have developed their own identity and operate on the basis of internally generated procedures staff the AB. Thus, it is likely to form an understanding of appropriate actions that conflict with member states' ideas. Third, voting rules make it difficult for members to reverse the AB's decisions. Taken together, these three characteristics indicate that the AB's members possess the capacity to produce slack.

Yet a perusal of the ten-year history of the WTO indicates that slack is rare, since AB members recognize that their ability to create an efficient international judicial body hinges on the willingness of states to participate in it. The historical record indicates that the AB has taken many decisions that have displeased some states. In doing so, however, the AB has acted as members intended: to determine whether defendants have passed domestic laws or regulations that contravene their treaty obligations. Similarly, the AB has affirmed some members' understanding of appropriate procedures even though there was no consensus about their appropriateness. For example, it agreed (WTO 1997) that member states could use private counsels to represent them in the dispute settlement system. Although "this was the first time in the fifty years of experience under the GATT, and then the WTO, in which a country had been represented by private counsel," Bacchus (2001: 957) observes, the AB "concluded that it was not for us to second-guess a member of the WTO on who that member wanted to include in its delegation in an Appellate Body proceeding. So we let in the lawyer." In effect, the AB has taken actions that are not universally supported, but these actions do not constitute slack since the AB was doing what it was intended to do. There are two exceptions to this pattern.

Both cases of slack emerge with respect to the AB's decisions regarding the standing of NGOs. The participation of NGOs had been debated during the Uruguay Round negotiations, but a majority of members opposed the inclusion of friend-of-the-court (*amicus*) briefs in the treaty. Hence the treaty is silent on their role. Nevertheless, the AB ruled that the treaty grants it and panels the discretion to accept *amicus* briefs from NGOs (WTO 1998, 2000a). This action reflected the AB's sense of commitment to the wider population affected by the WTO. As Bacchus (2004: 4; also Ehlermann 2003: 484) subsequently explained, "[t]he opportunity to submit *amicus* briefs can give those from the wider world the chance to have their say – without in any way undermining the essential intergovernmental nature of such proceedings. *Amicus* briefs can provide an additional and valuable point of view – as they do for judiciaries throughout the world." A vast majority of states opposed this decision, noting that the AB's actions altered members' obligations and that the matter was outside the AB's jurisdiction. The representative from Mexico voiced the position of many developing states:

When the D[ispute] S[ettlement] U[nderstanding] provisions were being negotiated in the Uruguay Round, there were already proposals that panels should be able to receive *amicus curiae* briefs. If such a possibility had not been included in the DSU provisions, it was because WTO members had decided that it was not appropriate. In other words, Members were not faced with a situation where they had accidentally created a legal lacuna as a result of not having foreseen that this kind of problem might arise in the future. Members had deliberately decided not to include that possibility in the DSU. (WTO 2000c: 14)

There was not unanimous opposition to the AB's action, as several states, including the United States, supported NGO participation. Those members opposed to the AB's unilateral decision to modify the treaty consequently did not reverse the action.

A different outcome emerged in November 2000, when the AB established a process for the submission of friend-of-the-court briefs for the Asbestos case (WTO 2000b). The AB division's secretariat posted the procedure on the IO's website and the secretariat's External Relations Division sent "an email . . . to the subscribers of the NGO bulletin as per established procedure" (WTO 2000c: 9). The AB claimed authority for this action from the WTO's treaty and justified its decision "in the interests of fairness and orderly procedure in the conduct of this appeal," the empowering language of the working procedures (WTO 2000b: 1; 2003a). The secretariat explained its action by reference to "its own procedures for increasing the knowledge and understanding of interested individuals and institutions" about the IO (WTO 2000c: 3). These actions occurred after the 1999 Seattle demonstrations and increasing complaints about the institution's lack of transparency and distance from non-state actors, which the procedures were envisioned to help satisfy. Most members considered both entities to have overstepped their competencies, however, by entering into procedural areas reserved for states.

A special session of the General Council convened to address the matter. Based on members' negative reaction, the chair of the Council instructed the AB to "exercise extreme caution in future cases until Members had considered what rules were needed" (WTO 2000c: 28). This constrained response reflected the consensus voting rule for amending the DSU, which made it difficult for members to overturn the AB's action, since a minority of members supported it. The AB nonetheless

Agent preferences, legitimacy, tasks, and permeability

subsequently rejected all 17 *amicus* briefs that followed its new procedures (WTO 2001).

One explanation for the AB's reversal reflects the ongoing review of the DSU and the possibility that the members would fix loopholes in the DSU to rein in the AB. Yet since a minority of members welcomed the participation of NGOs, the consensus voting rule makes such reforms unlikely.[11] A more persuasive explanation emerges, in Ehlermann's (2003: 484–85) words, from the fact that "this decision had given rise to a major diplomatic row" and, in doing so, affected the legitimacy of the AB and the WTO itself. In a revealing reflection written after the episode, Bacchus (2002: 1035) voices similar concerns about the strength of the dispute settlement system: "[I]t is neither my role nor my place to make suggestions to the Members of the WTO about their rule-making... It is for the Members of the WTO to decide how best to establish an effective system for making new rules."[12] Member state criticism then became a more significant determinant of the AB's actions than the body's internally generated desire to bring procedural clarity or increase the rule of law.

The WTO's institutional design enables the IO's AB to pursue actions outside the delegation contract. The AB is well positioned to advance independent preferences thanks to the voting rules in place. As Ehlermann (2003: 485) points out, "nobody can – or should – expect the Appellate Body to change its interpretation of the DSU" until three-quarters of the members agree to change the treaty. Yet throughout the WTO's ten-year history, only two cases of significant slack have emerged. The same institutional feature that generates independent preferences – a professional staff – also inhibits slack by the seven jurists, who fear the consequences of member state opprobrium for their capacity to develop an effective and legitimate international judicial process. In this respect, concrete and large-scale member state interest in institutional reform, as difficult as it is to achieve due to the consensus voting rule, may still be a powerful inhibitor of slack.

---

[11] In fact, members remain at odds over appropriate reforms and recently postponed the deadline for revisions. See WTO 2003b.

[12] He continues (2004: 4) to believe in the need for such rules as he explained in a speech following his departure from the AB: "The participation of *amicus curiae* in dispute settlement proceedings ... can – and should – be governed and controlled in a reasonable way by reasonable rule – as it is in judiciaries throughout the world. The rule used by the Appellate Body several years ago in the asbestos case is a good place for the Members of the WTO to start in addressing this issue."

CONCLUSION

This chapter explores when IOs can engage in slack and speculates on when they actually do. PA approaches provide a useful starting point: the design of the delegation contract, particularly whether the IO is granted significant discretion to fulfill its mandate, identifies the agent's autonomy. Yet this permissive condition does not explain whether an agent will want to use its autonomy in ways undesired by its principals or whether it can succeed in doing so. To fully understand an IO's propensity to engage in slack, we need to examine characteristics of both the agent and the principal.

Like Hawkins and Jacoby (this volume), first, we argue that agent preferences matter. Those preferences are, in large part, a function of staffing procedures. An IO's administrative element is most likely to develop independent preferences that conflict with member states when it is staffed by international personnel, rather than seconded national appointees. WHO and WTO staff are appointed to represent the IO, not their home governments, and each forms a kind of epistemic community whose preferences often diverge from the principals'.

Not all international staffs are equally capable of achieving their preferences, however, often for reasons having little to do with the agent. For this reason, like Lyne, Nielson, and Tierney (this volume), we focus on a second variable: the voting rules governing relations among the members of a collective principal. In general, voting rules that empower relatively few states enhance principals' control and limit slack; rules that empower numerous states, such as those characterizing the WHO and WTO, make agreement among principals difficult and enhance agent autonomy. Our two-step argument, in short, explores the effects of both agent and principal characteristics on the likelihood of slack.

Being capable of slack, however, does not mean that an IO will engage in slack. In contrast to PA approaches' emphasis on oversight mechanisms as the primary means by which principals control their agents, we argue that staffing procedures may create incentives for self-restraint. An independent staff that has a professional commitment to advance its mandate is unlikely to want to see its organization and mission undercut by loss of legitimacy or financial support. Together, the WHO and WTO cases show staffs that sometimes opposed expansions of their organization's mandate, exceeded their authority only rarely and cautiously, and reversed their actions despite the inability of their member states to overturn them.

Agent preferences, legitimacy, tasks, and permeability

Our focus on staffing procedures overcomes an omission in rationalist approaches, identifying the origins of IOs' preferences, as well as a shortcoming in constructivist perspectives, why IOs' organizational cultures do not produce more frequent demands for slack. It also explains why the same IO may appear to be both rogue actor and dutiful agent. Further research on agent preferences is needed to establish the scope conditions that lead the IO to opt for one or the other behavior at any given time. This work should couple a focus on agent preferences with an appreciation of the internal dynamics of the collective principal. Delegation under anarchy has great potential for slack because states guard their sovereign rights and create voting structures that distribute authority across the membership.

10

Delegating IMF conditionality: understanding variations in control and conformity

ERICA R. GOULD

INTRODUCTION

States delegate to international organizations (IOs) all of the time. Activities ranging from weapons-inspecting to peacekeeping to monitoring exchange rate practices and free trade arrangements have all been delegated by states to international organizations. International relations scholarship tends to be dominated by two basic interpretations of the outcomes of this delegation. According to one, IOs are perfect handmaidens of state principals and IO activities conform directly to state preferences. According to the other, IOs are independent bureaucracies governed by their own interests or culture; IO activities are not closely related to state preferences at all. However, empirical reality seems to fit neither model. International organizations and specific international organizational activities vary along a continuum of conformity with state instructions. Some IOs and their activities closely reflect state wishes, whereas others seem to be determined by other factors. What explains this variation?

The principal-agent framework (PA) addresses these issues directly and offers an explanation of why certain IOs or particular IO activities conform more closely to state directives, while others do not. This chapter focuses on the delegation of a particular activity to a particular IO – the design of conditional loan arrangements to the International Monetary Fund – and considers how well PA theory explains the variations in IO conformity with state preferences.

I thank Judith Goldstein, Miles Kahler, Barbara Koremenos, Lisa Martin, Jon Pevehouse, Kenneth Stiles and the editors for incisive, detailed comments on earlier drafts and the International Monetary Fund archives for access crucial to the completion of this research.

Agent preferences, legitimacy, tasks, and permeability

In particular, this chapter focuses on the extent to which the PA framework helps us understand the relationship between state preferences and IO activity – or between the principal and the agent – once the initial delegation has taken place. States may initially delegate conditionality for a variety of reasons (Milner, this volume). My main focus is how well principals are able to control the IO agent once conditionality has already been delegated. To what extent can a PA model explain these variations? Fund conditionality is a particularly puzzling and apt focus for this study because original empirical material suggests that there is wide variation in agency slack, or agent conformity with principal preferences. In addition, the Fund's activities (as compared to other IOs) are particularly influential; as a result this variation has been a source of controversy. As the US congressionally appointed Meltzer Commission report stated, Fund conditionality "has given the IMF a degree of influence over member countries' policy making that is unprecedented for a multilateral organization" (IFIAC 2000). Fund conditionality thus offers an interesting case: why has state control over the design of Fund conditionality agreements varied?

In short, this chapter suggests that the PA framework has particular strengths and weaknesses in explaining ongoing IO activity and the variation in principal control. In terms of strengths, the PA framework offers insights to explain the variations in IO conformity with state principal preferences by focusing on both the agent's and the principal's cost-benefit analysis. In the case of Fund conditionality, there is a good deal of variation in Fund conformity with state principal preferences. The PA framework helps explain the broad patterns of conformity or deviation: elements of Fund conditionality programs that are *less* costly for principals to monitor end up conforming *more* to principal preferences. Similarly, those elements of Fund conditionality programs that are *more* costly for principals to observe and enforce tend to conform *less*.

However, this chapter also highlights some limitations of the PA approach, as defined by this volume, for explaining and predicting IO activity.[1] While the PA approach was able to explain some broad trends in Fund activity – namely, variations in conformity with principal preferences – it could not explain or predict *actual* agent activity when

---

[1] Hawkins et al. (this volume) define the PA relationship narrowly as a contractual one in which the principal can "terminate" the agent. Dixit et al. (1997: 753) define principals more broadly as any actor that "influences" or "pressures" another. See also Bernheim and Whinston 1986.

Understanding variations in control and conformity

the agent deviates from principal preferences or explain variations in conformity *within* a specific activity type. These deficiencies have serious consequences for scholars interested in explaining actual IO activity. While the PA approach may help scholars determine how much "autonomy" (or potential slack) an IO may be able to take advantage of, it cannot necessarily indicate whether the agent will actually take advantage of that autonomy and, if so, whether and how they will deviate from principal preferences.[2] Will Fund conditionality become stricter or more lenient if principals find it too costly to monitor the IMF closely?

The chapter will proceed as follows. First, it will briefly review the existing literature on IMF agency slack, which consists mainly of two dominant perspectives with nearly diametrically opposed interpretations of the empirical landscape. The chapter then introduces the key features of the PA framework employed here: the models of the principal and the agent, the measures of collective principal preferences and agent activity, and the nature of delegation. The fourth section is largely empirical. Using new measures of IMF conditionality and principal preferences (both gleaned directly from the IMF archives), I assess variations in the IMF's agency slack with respect to the design of Fund conditionality agreements. The pattern of agency slack that emerges is complex: certain design features tend to conform more to principal preferences than others; certain programs seem to conform more to principal preferences than others. The fourth section is largely analytical. Conventional explanations do not provide a convincing explanation for this pattern of agency slack. To what extent does the PA framework, which is directly concerned with agency slack, explain this variation? In short, I argue that PA does explain the broad trends in conformity across design features, but that it does not provide an explanation for actual IO activity outcomes. The conclusion offers some suggestions to remedy this weakness.

Existing literature on the IMF's agency slack

Different theoretical approaches point scholars to different questions. The PA framework usefully points us towards asking three general questions: Why do principals delegate? How do principals try to control agents? And what are the consequences of that delegation (or how well

---

[2] See Hawkins et al. (this volume) for definitions of agency slack and autonomy.

Agent preferences, legitimacy, tasks, and permeability

does agent behavior conform with principal preferences)? This chapter focuses mainly on the second and third questions regarding the ongoing delegation relationship and the consequences of delegation.

Surprisingly, IR scholarship to date has largely ignored these questions. Instead, most IR scholarship tends to be dominated by two basic interpretations of international organizations. For one, IOs are perfect handmaidens of state principals. Much of the academic and popular literature on the International Monetary Fund falls in this camp. For instance, Miles Kahler has argued that the US has exercised strong control over Fund conditionality, and has generally pushed for the increases in conditionality that we have observed (Kahler 1990). Strom Thacker has similarly argued that Fund lending decisions, although not specifically Fund conditionality, are driven strictly by US interests (Thacker 1999). For the other model, IOs are independent bureaucracies governed by their own interests or culture. For instance, Michael Barnett and Martha Finnemore argue that international organizations are often "dysfunctional." The "dysfunctional" activities of IOs are driven by the IOs' cultural environment, not by the IOs' state principals (Barnett and Finnemore 1999: 707). In the case of the IMF and conditionality, Barnett and Finnemore argue that the Fund staff's expertise gave them a great deal of latitude to develop and adjust certain intellectual models, which in turn justified the expansion in Fund conditionality. They argue that the failure of Fund programs may drive the expansion in Fund conditionality, but that the staff's expertise determines the content of that change (Barnett and Finnemore 2004).[3]

However, empirical reality seems to fit neither of these models. Instead we observe IOs, including the IMF, acting against the interests of their state principals in some instances, and we observe IOs strictly controlled by states in others. In the case of Fund conditionality agreements, we have observed examples of Fund agreements that seem tailored to the interests of the Fund's biggest donor, the United States. Russia in 1998 and Mexico in 1995 are two favorite and oft-used examples. Similarly, we have observed examples of arrangements where the US explicitly stated opposition to a program or loan, which was nonetheless passed, for instance India in 1957 and 1981 and the UK in 1969 (Memo from G. L. L. de Moubray, January 17, 1957; James 1996: 333–34; Interview 4

---

[3] Martin (this volume) offers another perspective: states vary the delegation of authority to the IMF based on distributional conflicts and the "demand for information."

with author, February 2000).[4] Thus individual cases could be used to support either or both of the dominant, yet conflicting, interpretations of international organizations. The PA framework offers more of a middle ground, suggesting that agency slack may vary across different agents, across different agent activities, and across time. However, the existing literature on Fund conditionality provides only limited empirical data and thus has not allowed scholars to adjudicate between these competing interpretations of reality (Guitàn 1981, 1995; Polak 1991; Horsefield 1969: vol. 1; Dell 1981; Williamson 1983; Kahler 1990; Barnett and Finnemore 2004).

PRINCIPALS, AGENTS, AND THE DELEGATION OF CONDITIONALITY

Gauging agency slack

Fund conditionality agreements – agent activity – have changed significantly from their original design. However, it is not immediately

---

[4] The author conducted 16 interviews between September 1999 and May 2002 in Washington, DC, San Francisco, and New York. Each interviewee was asked a list of open-ended questions about the process of constructing, influencing, and revising Fund conditionality programs, about the role of being an executive director or staff member (depending on the interviewee), and about the role of the Fund in the international system. From this starting point, conversations veered in different directions depending the interviewee. Interviewees largely preferred to remain anonymous; as a result references to these interviews are general. The interviews conducted and consulted by the author are: Interview 1: Executive Director or member(s) of Executive Director's office, September 14, 1999; Interview 2: Executive Director or member(s) of Executive Director's office, February 8, 2000; Interview 3: Executive Director or member(s) of Executive Director's office, February 8, 2000; Interview 4: High-level fund staff member, February 9, 2000; Interview 5: Executive Director or member(s) of Executive Director's office, February 10, 2000; Interview 6: High-level fund staff member, February 10, 2000; Interview 7: Executive Director or member(s) of Executive Director's office, February 10, 2000; Interview 8: Executive Director or member(s) of Executive Director's office, February 11, 2000; Interview 9: Executive Director or Member(s) of Executive Director's office, February 11, 2000; Interview 10: Executive Director or member(s) of Executive Director's Office, February 14, 2000; Interview 11: Executive Director or member(s) of Executive Director's office, February 15, 2000; Interview 12: Executive Director or member(s) of Executive Director's office, February 15, 2000; Interview 13: Executive Director or member(s) of Executive Director's office, February 17, 2000; Interview 14: High-level fund staff member, August 30, 2000; Interview 15: Commercial bank executive, October 3, 2000; Interview 16: Former high-level fund management, May 28, 2002.

Agent preferences, legitimacy, tasks, and permeability

apparent how to interpret this change since the delegation "contract" has been revised, and principal preferences over conditionality may have also evolved.[5] Scholars have found the degree of agency slack – the degree to which agent activity deviates from principal directions – to be particularly difficult to measure (e.g. Pollack 2002). How does one know when Fund conditionality is truly conforming to principal directives and when it is not?

Weingast and Moran (1983) have suggested that scholars observe how often the principal (here embodied by the Fund's EB) disciplines or corrects the agent as an indicator of agency slack. All Fund conditionality programs need to be approved by the EB, which acts as a final veto player. By that logic, one could record instances when the Board rejects a program and disciplines a transgressing agent. Interestingly, the EB rarely revises, much less vetoes, particular Fund arrangements (Interviews 2 and 4 with author, February 2000; Southard 1979). There are only a few instances in the Fund's entire history of the EB turning down or even modifying a request for a conditional loan arrangement.[6] For Weingast and Moran (1983), this observation suggests perfect agent conformity: EB controls are so effective that IMF activities always reflect EB preferences. However, there are two reasons why this interpretation appears doubtful. First, there is the general problem of observational equivalence: scholars who argue that principals perfectly control the agent and scholars who argue that agent activities are relatively autonomous may both predict EB inaction (Nielson et al. 2003). Second, in the particular case of Fund conditionality, interviews with numerous EDs and their staff, in addition to the texts of the EB meetings, suggest that principals frequently disagreed (albeit with varying intensity) with individual Fund program designs, and yet programs are still approved.[7] As a result, analyzing EB meetings or votes does not appear to be the best way to assess agency slack.

---

[5] Martin (this volume) focuses on the early development of staff–EB relations and some of the early changes, like allowing staff to negotiate loan agreements in borrowing state capitals, which she argues resulted in a "shift of authority to staff was not evidence of a runaway agency or lack of attention on the part of the principals, but an intentional choice determined by the need to tradeoff direct control for high-quality information."

[6] One example was the proposed 1979 Sierra-Leone stand-by arrangement, which was reduced, but not denied. E-mail correspondence from James Boughton, December 1998; Kapur et al. (1997: 496).

[7] The author conducted interviews with EDs, or members of the EDs' staff, from 10 of the 24 ED offices in February 2000. See also fn. 5.

Understanding variations in control and conformity

By contrast, Kiewiet and McCubbins (1991) suggest that comparing principal preferences with subsequent agent activity is one of the most useful and direct ways of assessing agency slack. Such a suggestion requires both a measure of principal preferences and of agent activity. This chapter follows Kiewiet and McCubbins' (1991) suggestion. The following two sections discuss how the principal and agent are conceived, and the measures of principal preferences and agent activity utilized in this chapter.

The principal

According to Hawkins, Lake, Nielson, and Tierney in the introduction to this volume, a principal is "an actor who grants conditional authority to an agent." In this case, the IMF's principal is a collective one (Lyne, Nielson and Tierney, this volume; Nielson and Tierney 2003a: 247). The EB is a body of state representatives that delegated the task of designing conditional loan agreements to the IMF's management and staff in 1952. Since then, the terms of this delegation have been revised several times.

According to the collective principal concept, decision rules that aggregate preferences within the collective principal are primary (ibid.). Famously, IMF EDs have different "weighted" voting power when voting on certain decisions. Many decisions also require super-majorities that further accentuate the power of EDs with relatively high voting power. However, in the case at hand, the very well-known weighted voting system *does not* actually govern conditionality agreements. Instead conditional loan arrangements are formally approved by the simple majority of votes cast, not the majority or super-majority of voting power (Article XII, Section 5c).

How should one measure principal preferences over Fund conditionality design? Scholars often simply assume principal preferences. Alternatively, principal preferences are inferred either from explicit statements regarding preferences over agent activity or from principal behavior in a related area (Nielson and Tierney 2003b). In this chapter, I rely mainly on the Conditionality Guidelines, which are explicit instructions on conditionality debated at length and passed by the EB at irregular intervals according to the same decision rule (majority of votes cast) used to approve individual conditionality agreements (e-mail from James Boughton, August 19, 2003). While the Guidelines may not be perfect reflections of collective principal preferences, they do offer a unique, and I would argue relatively accurate, measure of principal preferences when few others exist. However, in order to increase confidence in the accuracy of this measure, I supplement this proxy with additional sources of evidence – including statements from Fund staffers and insiders and careful case studies completed by other scholars – which provide further support that these Guidelines are useful estimations of the collective principal's preferences. In order to gauge the agency slack, I compare those instructions (or stated preferences) with subsequent agent activity: did the IMF conform to collective principal instructions?

The agent

The other half of a PA model is naturally the agent, in this case the IMF. Scholars also often assume certain agent interests, for instance that the bureaucracy wants to "maximize their budget, their staff and their independence" (Vaubel 1996: 195; Niskanen 1971). In this case, I employ a more inductive model of the IMF and its interests. As I have argued previously, the Fund itself is comprised of an international staff of economists, most trained at a few select US and Western European universities (Gould 2003; Gould 2006; Clark 1998: 182 cited in Kapur 2001: 33; Evans and Finnemore 2001 on the homogeneity of the staff). Despite their diverse national backgrounds, new staff and management join the Fund with remarkably similar shared assumptions and principles influenced by their education (Chwieroth 2003: 9). Both the Fund's staff and its management have been trained as economists and want to be successful economists, influencing the direction of the international economy at large and the economies of individual borrowers by applying theoretical principles. The failure of an implemented Fund program damages not only the reputations of the individual staff members who designed it, but also the organization's reputation and the credibility of the principles that have been applied. As a result, I assume that the Fund – that is, the staff and management – want Fund programs to succeed in measurably improving the economies in which they intervene.

Some stress the differences between the Fund's management, some of whom are political appointees, and the Fund's staff, most of whom are careerists. This distinction between staff and management is not emphasized here. Certainly the PA relationship is not simply EB–Fund. The chains of delegation extend in both directions. While each step in this delegation chain may be important and lead to increases in agency slack, for the purposes of this chapter, I am most interested in, and limit myself to, the basic delegation from states (the EB) to an international organization (the IMF's staff and management).

Until recently, access to Fund programs, or measures of Fund activity, have been limited. For this chapter, I rely on a recently constructed dataset of 249 Fund conditionality agreements (SBA, EFF, SAF, and ESAF) from 20 countries between 1952 and 1995, the Conditionality Dataset, as a measure of agent activity. An observation is a unique conditional loan arrangement, in other words a unique country-loan-year. True random sampling, while methodologically preferable, was not viable given the organization and resources of the Fund archives. Consequently, I selected representative countries and then, data and access permitting, included all relevant agreements for that country between 1952 (when conditionality began) and 1995 (after which many arrangements remained classified at the time of data gathering). The 249 cases came from the following 20 countries: Argentina, Bangladesh, Bolivia, Brazil, Central African republic, Côte D'Ivoire, El Salvador, Ghana, Haiti, Korea, Mali, Mexico, Morocco, Niger, Philippines, Romania, South Africa, Turkey, United Kingdom, and Yugoslavia. Despite this atypical case selection method, the 249 cases are generally representative, both by region and arrangement type (Gould 2003; Gould 2006).

The Conditionality Dataset codes each loan agreement according to its terms as stated in the original loan agreement, including the letter of intent, attachments, and the resulting press release. A typical Fund loan agreement includes a letter from the borrowing country requesting a loan and detailing an extensive policy program concerning many different sectors of the economy and government. The arrangement itself generally outlines more policy proposals and the program's schedule of reviews, and often in the penultimate paragraph specifies which conditions are binding. Binding conditions trigger the suspension of the Fund loan if they are violated. Each case was coded according to 31 separate criteria questions and 52 different binding conditions.

Predictions of the principal-agent model

The PA framework focuses on the principal's and the agent's cost-benefit analysis (Hawkins et al., this volume). The principal will delegate when the benefits of delegation exceed the costs. Likewise, the agent should also comply with principal directives to the extent that the benefits of compliance exceed the costs of non-compliance. Principals clearly have a variety of control techniques at their disposal: monitoring and reporting requirements, screening and selection procedures, institutional checks and balances and sanctions (Kiewiet and McCubbins 1991). However, perfect monitoring and enforcement of an agent is too costly. As a result, principals employ these control techniques as long as their benefits (associated with improved compliance) exceed their costs (e.g. resources and time expended). If monitoring and enforcement were costless, presumably agency slack would be reduced to zero. However, the divergence of interests between the principal and agent, the costs of monitoring and the informational asymmetry between principal and agent result in agency slack. Some degree of uncertainty about agent activities or some acceptance of deviations from principal preferences will likely be optimal according to the principal's cost-benefit calculus because of the cost function of monitoring. The general hypothesis derived from the PA framework is:

If control and monitoring are more (less) costly, then agent behavior should conform less (more) to principal preferences, assuming divergent interests and that other variables remain constant.

Enforcement should be more or less costly under specific circumstances. For instance, agents with ideal points located relatively closer to the principal's (on a hypothetical unidimensional policy space) should be less costly to control than agents with ideal points that are situated further away, all else equal. As a result, principals often try to "select" agents with similar preferences to their own. In the case at hand, different aspects of the conditionality agreements (length, number of conditions, etc.) are designed by the same agent (the IMF), so agent type should not account for variations in agency slack. More promisingly, the PA framework highlights the importance of the nature of delegated activity. Certain activities may require a much greater investment of the principal's energy and resources in order to achieve the same degree of compliance as a less complicated or opaque activity.

Monitoring and enforcement of any given activity for a fixed agent will be more costly if that activity is less observable, less measurable, and more dependent on agent expertise (Bawn 1995: 697; Epstein and O'Halloran 1994: 716; Huber and Shipan 2002; Bendor et al. 2001: 244; Kiewiet and McCubbins 1991: 17). When agent activities are not easily observable or measurable, then the principal must expend energy and resources in order to collect information about agent activities, and hence the degree of agency slack. As a result in these cases, the principal often relies on agent-dispensed information, which is less costly but may compromise the assessment of agent activity. By contrast, when agent activities are easily measurable and observable, the principal can collect independent data on agent activities easily and sanction the agent when their activities deviate without excessive costs. Similarly, when agent activities rely heavily on agent expertise, agency slack should increase for at least two reasons. First, agents are more likely to have an informational advantage; as informational asymmetries increase, so should the costs of monitoring and enforcement. Second, when agent activities require expertise and there is uncertainty surrounding the delegated activity, principals may face a tradeoff between "circumscribing wayward bureaucrats and giving them the latitude to react to unforeseen contingencies" (Bawn 1995: 697; Kiewiet and McCubbins 1991: 17). Bawn and Epstein and O'Halloran have argued that as the "technical uncertainty" surrounding an issue increases, principals will grant the agent greater discretion (Epstein and O'Halloran 1994: 716; Huber and Shipan 2002; Bendor et al. 2001: 244). This greater discretion allows the agent greater opportunity to slack.

MEASURING AGENCY SLACK: THE CASE OF IMF CONDITIONALITY

In order to gauge agency slack, this section compares the Fund's activity, as measured by the Conditionality Dataset, with the collective principal's preferences, as measured by the EB-generated Conditionality Guidelines. The EB issues policy directives that are intended to guide and constrain future Fund activity, including Fund conditionality arrangements. Thus I consider: how well do Fund activities conform to these basic directions and rules of activity? This section reveals that since at least the late 1960s, there has been a particular pattern of compliance: certain directions have been closely followed, whereas others have been largely neglected by the Fund's staff and management.

Delegation of conditionality

State representatives established the International Monetary Fund in Bretton Woods, New Hampshire in 1944 in order to help maintain international monetary stability by monitoring and maintaining the Bretton Woods exchange rate system. Initially the discretion to design, negotiate and offer conditional loan agreements was not delegated to the International Monetary Fund (Dell 1981; Horsefield and Lovasy 1969; James 1996; Gold 1979; Martin, this volume; Gould 2006). It was not until 1952, after a protracted struggle between members of the executive board (EB), that states formally delegated the authority to design and negotiate conditional loan agreements to the IMF. The Fund's first conditional lending facility, the stand-by arrangement (SBA), is an agreement between a member country and the IMF that stipulates that the country can be assured that it will be able to draw (or borrow) a certain specified amount of Fund resources automatically within a certain window of time, as long as the country commits to, maintains, or implements certain agreed-upon policies. The EB set specific instructions regarding these agreements for the staff. SBAs were initially envisioned to be short-term assurances of automaticity, and require little if any change in a country's policy (SM/52/5, January 22, 1952; SM/52/57, October 1, 1952).[8] The decision that established the SBA instructed that these agreements would be limited to six months in length, 25 percent of a country's quota and would not be automatically renewable (EBD No. 155 (52/57); SM/52/49, July 31, 1952; Aufricht 1964; Horsefield and Lovasy 1969: 403).

During the first few years after the establishment of the SBA, the practice and policy of Fund conditionality evolved. Both the Fund's staff and the EDs seemed to be willing participants in many of these early changes. Soon after the October 1952 decision was passed, Fund staff began deviating from it (Gould 2006: ch. 4). However, principal preferences also appeared to develop and change quickly, during this period as well (Martin, this volume; Hawkins and Jacoby, this volume). For instance, in December 1953, the EB officially changed its instructions to the staff regarding the length, stating that stand-bys could extend longer than six months, "if this appears warranted by the particular payments problems of the member making the request" (Aufricht 1964: 64). Next, the staff began adding binding conditions to Fund conditionality agreements; countries were required to implement certain policies or meet certain targets in order to maintain free access to the specified stand-by amount for the full period of the loan. IMF staff began dividing conditional loans into installments and eventually conditioning disbursement of each installment on different criteria. The staff initially developed each of these new practices, largely without state guidance. However, many of the existing practices were codified in 1968 through the First Amendment to the Articles, which stipulated that smaller "gold tranche" drawings would be approved virtually automatically, whereas larger drawings would be subject to conditionality, generally under a one-year

[8] These and subsequent IMF documents are located in the IMF archives.

SBA, which would be phased and require the borrower to meet certain binding conditions (SM/66/14, January 24, 1966, 1–2; Gold 1979: 70).

First Conditionality Guidelines

While some staff practices were codified by the First Amendment in 1968, others were criticized. The EB's first major attempt to provide the Fund staff and management with clear instructions to change their design of conditional loan agreements came with the First Conditionality Guidelines. EDs thought there was not enough uniformity across programs, and also that Fund conditionality had become too stringent (EBM/68/122–123, August 14, 1968; EBM/68/128, September 6, 1968; EBM/68/131-2, September 20, 1968). In the debates preceding the 1968 decision, nearly all EDs, including the US ED, advocated less stringent conditionality and fewer binding conditions (EBM/68/122–23, August 14, 1968). According to the Fund's own estimates, the number of performance criteria (or binding conditions) included in Fund programs had more than doubled – from 2 to 5.1 – in less than a decade (SM/68/128, Supplement 3, September 4, 1968). By 1967, even the relatively small first credit tranche (FCT) SBAs required countries to meet 2.1 binding conditions on average. The EB passed new rules for guiding staff activity on Fund conditionality on September 20, 1968.

This EB decision included two main instructions. First, in contradiction with guidelines the staff had developed for themselves in 1963, the EB stipulated that FCT SBAs would not be phased and not include binding conditions. However, all arrangements beyond the FCT would be phased and would require both binding conditions and consultation clauses. "Exceptional cases" would not be required to be phased. In other words, the EB tried to establish some uniform design criteria for loan programs that were in and above the FCT. Second, while the EB instructed the staff to include binding conditions and consultation clauses for all larger upper-credit tranche (UCT) SBAs, the EB agreed that binding conditions had "proliferated" in previous SBAs and hereafter should be limited to those "necessary to evaluate the implementation and achievement of the objectives of the program" and "keep the number of criteria [or conditions] to the minimum necessary, for the success of the program" (SM/68/128, Supp.4, September 13, 1968). In short, UCT SBAs were to be phased, require binding conditions, and require consultation clauses.[9]

[9] FCT SBAs versus UCT SBAs are calculated using the Conditionality Dataset, where FCT SBAs are SBAs where the amount of the loan is equal to 25 percent or less of

Agent preferences, legitimacy, tasks, and permeability

The First Conditionality Guidelines offered clear instructions for the IMF management and staff. However, only some of these instructions were heeded. Fund programs did become more uniform in some respects, but not in others. For instance, before 1968, FCTs and UCTs required phasing for a somewhat similar proportion of agreements (66 percent for UCTs and 80 percent for FCTs), with three or four phases on average per agreement (where one phase equals no phasing; the loan is delivered in one installment). After the First Conditionality Guidelines, the design of FCTs and UCTs diverged with respect to the use of phasing. FCTs did not abandon phasing all together, but they did include phasing much less frequently after 1968 than before it. Seventy-three percent of the FCT programs sampled between 1969 and 1978 did not require any phasing, whereas UCTs consistently required phasing after 1968, as instructed by the Guidelines. Ninety-seven percent of UCT agreements sampled between 1969 and 1978 required phasing, with an average of 4.2 installments per agreement (see table 10.1).

With regard to the requirement of binding conditions, the First Conditionality Guidelines stipulated that FCT SBAs should not require binding conditions, whereas UCT SBAs should consistently require binding conditions but limit the number to "the minimum necessary." Prior to these Guidelines, FCTs were actually more likely to require binding conditions (80 percent) than UCTs (73 percent). After the Guidelines, both FCT and UCT SBAs became more likely to require binding conditions (96 percent and 100 percent, respectively). As a result, the UCT SBAs moved in greater compliance with EB preferences for greater uniformity, while the FCT programs actually moved away from the EB's stated preference of no binding conditions for these smaller programs. In fact, only one FCT SBA (of 23 sampled between 1969 and 1978) did not include any binding conditions, as instructed by the board.

Through the First Conditionality Guidelines, the EB also instructed the Fund's management and staff to limit the number of binding conditions. However, even during the 1970s when, according to many scholars, competition from low or no conditionality lending vehicles forced the Fund to offer easier terms, the number of conditions actually continued to increase. According to the Fund's own research, the average number of binding conditions required by an upper credit tranche between 1969 and 1977 was 5.8. Recall that the Fund staff estimated the

the country's quota, and UCTs are all SBAs above that amount. This assignment of status closely, but not perfectly, correlates with Santaella (1995: table 10.1).

Table 10.1. *Conformity with First Conditionality Guidelines: phasing, number of binding conditions and uniformity*

	1968 guidelines	Before 1968	1969–1978	Greater conformity?
FCT SBA	No phasing	Mean = 3.5 phases 80% with phasing	Mean = 1.7 phases 27% with phasing	Yes
	No binding conditions (B. C.)	Mean = 3.4 B. C. 80% with B.C	Mean = 4.8 B. C. 96% with B.C	No
UCT SBA	Phasing with limited exceptions	Mean = 3.7 phases 66% with phasing	Mean = 4.2 phases 97% with phasing	Yes
	B. C. required	73% with B.C	100% with B.C	Yes
	Limit # of B. C. to only those "necessary"	Mean = 3.5	Mean = 6.9	No

Source: Conditionality Guidelines.

average number of binding conditions between 1965 and 1967 was 5.1, indicating a modest increase during the decade between the first and second conditionality reviews. According to the Conditionality Dataset, the average number of binding conditions in a SBA also increased during this period, from an average of 5.6 in 1968 to an average of 8 in 1978. The Fund's own data – collected in preparation for the Second Conditionality Guidelines debate – suggested that UCT SBAs were far from uniform. Between 1969 and April 1977, on average SBAs for Asian countries required 7.6 binding conditions, whereas SBAs for African countries required only 4.1 conditions. Fourteen "fiscal" binding conditions were required for all SBAs during that period, 12 of which were included in Western Hemisphere (Latin American and Caribbean) and European SBAs (SM/77/128, June 6, 1977, tables 10.1–10.6).

Second Conditionality Guidelines and conformity assessment

The EB resurrected the discussion of conditionality guidelines in the late 1970s. During the debates preceding the Second Review of Conditionality decision in 1979, as with those preceding the 1968 decision, EDs spoke passionately about the need for Fund staff members to stick to broad macroeconomic targets as binding conditions, rather than specific (e.g. fiscal) policies and the need to reduce the number of binding conditions. The elected ED from Australia diplomatically articulated a sentiment shared by many other EDs when he stated:

> Requirements had been made of countries to reduce subsidies, or to raise the prices of government services, change the structure of taxes, and so on. While no doubt appropriate from an economic point of view, it might have been better if those requirements had not been raised to the status of performance criteria [binding conditions], but left on the level of well-intentioned advice.
> (EBM/78/82, June 5, 1978, 4)

Related to this preference for less structural and fewer binding conditions, many EDs emphasized the need for the Fund to stick to short-term balance of payments financing, as its mandate instructed, rather than its drift into longer-term development lending. For instance, the US ED argued that "the Fund should confine itself to the shorter range ... in order not to blur the distinction between it and other institutions" (EBM/78/82, June 5, 1978, 15; Garritsen de Vries 1986: 504; International Monetary Fund 1983: 20–23). A broad consensus emerged in the EB that several of the staff developments on conditionality practices had gone too far, and did not reflect principal preferences.

The Second Review of Conditionality was passed by the EB in 1979 and again provided new guidelines for IMF conditionality. Three of these instructions are noteworthy in their attempt to define and constrain future Fund activity. First, reiterating the 1968 review, the Second Review emphasized uniformity across loan programs, this time stipulating that phasing and binding conditions would be omitted from FCT SBAs, and included in all others. Second, the decision provided the staff with instructions about the length of these intendedly short-term loan programs. The permitted length of Fund programs was extended to reflect the then-current practice, but an explicit limit was set. By 1979, the average conditionality program was about 11 months.[10] Most new arrangements were now supposed to last around 12 months and at most three years (SM/78/296, Rev. 1, Supp. 3, March 5, 1979; Gold 1979: 17). Third and finally, the Guidelines returned to the question of how many and what type of binding conditions (or performance criteria) should be included in Fund programs. The First Review had instructed staff to limit the number of binding conditions, but those instructions had generally

---

[10] This is the average of the sampled stand-by arrangements in the Conditionality Dataset. This is not the actual length of the arrangements, but rather the length specified in the conditionality agreement itself.

not been heeded. Through the Second Review, the EB instructed the staff to limit the inclusion of binding conditions in both number and type. Binding conditions should "normally be confined to (i) macroeconomic variables, and (ii) those necessary to implement specific provisions of the Articles or policies adopted under them" (SM/78/296 Rev. 1, Supp. 3, March 5, 1979; Gold 1979: 30). Binding conditions should also be limited to only "those that are necessary to evaluate the implementation of the program" – and type – to macroeconomic, not structural conditions. In short, these Guidelines attempted to limit the increase in conditionality by reducing the "number of performance criteria, insisting on their macroeconomic character, circumscribing the reasons for reviews and keeping preconditions to a minimum."

These Guidelines have been ineffective at restraining conditionality. In fact Jacques Polak wrote, "these restraining provisions [from the 1979 decision] have not prevented the intensification of conditionality in every direction that the guidelines attempted to block" (Polak 1991: 53–54). Polak's quote appears to be a bit of an overstatement: conformity with the guidelines actually varied depending on the particular term. For instance, the EB had instructed the Fund to design uniform SBAs, and in certain ways uniformity did increase after the 1979 Decision. Of the 66 UCT SBAs in the Conditionality Dataset from 1980 to 1995, only one did not include phasing and all of them required binding conditions. However, the number of binding conditions and the amount of phasing continued to vary widely across SBAs even after the 1979 decision. Between 1980 and 1995, the average number of binding conditions for a UCT SBA was 10.6, but ranging from 6 to 17. The average number of phases was 5.7, ranging from 1 to 15. Second, Fund arrangements did continue to get longer on average, but only moderately so. According to the Conditionality Dataset, the average SBA between 1968 and 1978 was 11.7 months by design, whereas the average SBA between 1979 and 1995 was 15.5 months by design. While 40 of the 73 SBAs sampled between 1980 and 1995 were longer than 12 months (which was the targeted ideal length), no SBAs were longer than three years (which was set as the firm upper limit). Third, the number of binding conditions did continue to increase substantially.[11] According to the Conditionality Dataset in 1979, the average number of binding

---

[11] Polak (1991: 14) has also provided averages in the number of performance criteria for several time periods that indicated that performance criteria have proliferated.

Table 10.2. *Conformity with 1979 Second Conditionality Guidelines*

	1979 guidelines	1969–1978	1980–1995	Greater conformity?	2002 guidelines
Phasing	None for *FCT*	Mean = 1.6 77% no phasing	Mean = 6 N = 1	Unclear	None for *FCT*
Phasing	Phasing for all *UCT*	Mean = 4.2 4% no phasing	Mean = 6 2% no phasing	Yes	Phasing for all *UCT*
Length	Approx. 1 year, with 3 years as upper limit	Mean = 12 months Max = 24 months	Mean = 16 months Max = 36 months	Yes	12–18 months, up to 3 years maximum
Number of B. C.	All *UCTs* require B. C., but limit to "those necessary"	100% required B. C. Mean = 7	100% required B. C. Mean = 11	No	Use conditions "parsimoniously"
Type of B. C.	"normally . . . macroeconomic conditions	64% required no procedural conditions	27% required no procedural conditions	No	"Normally . . . macroeconomic and structural measures"

Note: Only sampled SBAs were included from the Conditionality Dataset.
Source: Conditionality Dataset.

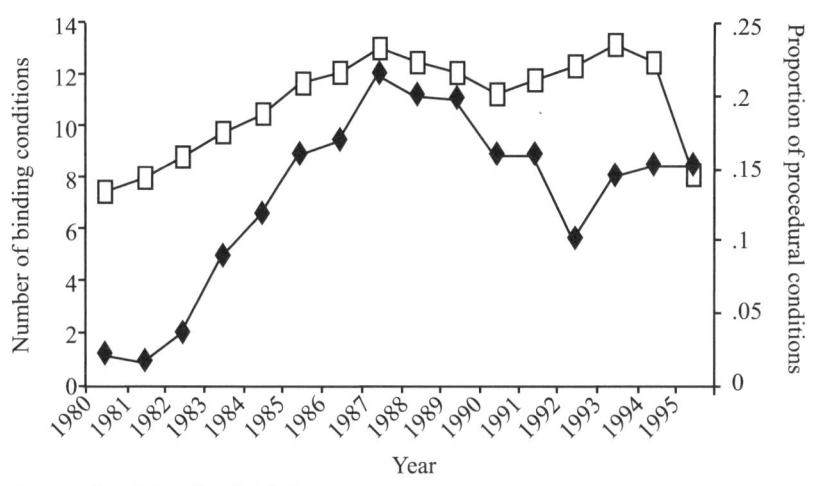

Understanding variations in control and conformity

Source: Conditionality Guidelines.

Figure 10.1. Change in the number and type of binding conditions, 3-year moving average

conditions for a SBA was 7.2 and by 1994, it was nearly double the 1979 average at 13.5. Fourth and finally, the types of binding conditions also continued to change and become more structural in nature, despite EB instructions to the contrary. Table 10.2 indicates the decrease in the percentage of SBAs requiring no procedural conditions after the 1979 decision (and particularly after 1982). Figure 10.1 depicts the three-year moving average of the change in the number (top line, left axis) and type (bottom line, right axis) of binding conditions for all arrangements sampled between 1980 and 1995.

Third Conditionality Guidelines

In the wake of the recent debates on the appropriateness of Fund conditionality, the EB approved new Guidelines on Conditionality and a related decision on SBAs on September 25, 2002. This new decision replaced the Second Review of Conditionality Guidelines, which had officially instructed staff activity since 1979. As with the EB's previous Guidelines on Conditionality, these emphasize uniformity and attempt to rein in the increases in conditionality. They also include some new features, like an emphasis on country "ownership" of programs and Fund-recommended reforms. However, it is noteworthy how many of the instructions appear to reiterate points from the First and Second Guidelines.

Four main instructions are worth highlighting. First, the EB encouraged the staff to strike a balance between "maintaining the uniform treatment of members" and "paying due regard to the domestic social and political objectives, the economic priorities, and the circumstances of members" (sic). Second, the EB instructed the staff to apply "program-related conditions . . . parsimoniously." However this time, the EB engaged in ex post recontracting and "parsimony" was itself parsed out, giving Fund staff less room to maneuver. According to the EB's decision, conditions should be feasible ("reasonably within the member's direct or indirect control") and "either (i) of critical importance for achieving the goals of the member's program . . . or (ii) necessary for the implementation of specific provisions of the Articles [of Agreement]." Conditions should also "normally consist of macroeconomic variables and structural measures that are within the Fund's core areas of responsibility," which are specifically delineated. Third, an accompanying decision on SBAs reiterated the EB's preference for limits on the length of SBAs. It stated that the "normal period for a stand-by arrangement will range from 12 to 18 months . . . [and] may extend beyond this range, up to a maximum of three years." Fourth, and consistent with previous decisions, the EB specified that SBAs or drawings within the FCT should not be subject to phasing or binding conditions, but that "they will be included in all other stand-by arrangements."

In many ways the 2002 Guidelines repeat preferences stated explicitly in 1968 and 1979 by the EB – instructions regarding the inclusion of conditions, the "scope" and number of conditions, the uniformity and length of programs – and consistently not followed by the staff. In short, according to this measure, principal preferences do not seem to have changed substantially since the 1968 and 1979 EB decisions. If this measure is accurate, then the changes in agent activity – in Fund conditionality – since 1979 do not seem to be driven by a change in collective principal preferences.

Additional evidence of principal preferences

But is this an accurate measure? Are the statements passed in the Conditionality Guidelines a reliable measure of collective principal preferences, or is it "naïve" to take states at their word? Conventional wisdom suggests, contrary to the discussion and measure employed here, that the

Fund's state principals actually prefer more and stricter conditions, rather than fewer, less constraining conditions. The claims and evidence marshaled by those articulating the conventional wisdom – that the state principals generally preferred more and stricter conditions – as well as two additional types of evidence – statements by Fund insiders and case studies conducted by another scholar – are considered briefly, and provide further support for the accuracy of the measure employed here (see Gould 2006, Chapter 4, for a more detailed discussion).

The conventional wisdom suggests that powerful creditor states, like the US, have disproportionate power in the EB and have pushed for increases in conditionality. Often scholars will use individual and non-representative cases to substantiate this claim. Alternatively, scholars have focused on two general periods in the Fund's history: the initial delegation of conditionality in the 1950s or the Reagan Administration period. Since this study is more concerned with *ongoing* collective principal control, not the moment of delegation, the 1950s is less pertinent for this study. However, to the extent that the Reagan Administration did push successfully for increases in conditionality, as argued for instance by Kahler, the collective principal preferences indicated by the Conditionality Guidelines would appear to be inaccurate (Kahler 1990: 104). To the contrary, however, the Reagan Administration did not push in any consistent way for increases in conditionality, and data from actual Fund agreements indicate that conditionality did not abruptly increase after 1980, as suggested by Kahler and others.[12] The Reagan Administration's public rebuke of reputedly lax programs in its first year in office (e.g. Grenada, India, and Pakistan in 1981) did not last long.

---

[12] Kahler (1990: 104–105) considers Williamson's (1982) evidence "convincing" that the Reagan Administration successfully increased Fund conditionality. While this argument is plausible from the data gathered by Williamson, US pressure is just one of several explanations that Williamson (1982: 48–52) considers to explain what he perceived as an abrupt change in conditionality around 1980. Williamson does not conclude that US influence was decisive; Kahler does not test his argument against the competing ones raised by Williamson. Regardless of the analytical argument one may make to explain changes in conditionality, the evidence from Williamson (1982) has since been somewhat discredited. As Boughton (2001: 563) states, "Williamson was working with one hand tied behind his back, in that he did not have access to data on performance criteria in the Fund's lending agreements. His often-cited study therefore relied on two indirect indicators, neither of which provides unambiguous information." Subsequent data gleaned from actual Fund conditionality agreement – the Conditionality Dataset – indicates that there was not an abrupt change in conditionality around 1980.

Agent preferences, legitimacy, tasks, and permeability

Soon enough, the Reagan Administration earned more of a reputation as pushing for weaker, rather than tighter, Fund conditionality.[13]

If the Conditionality Guidelines reflect stated collective principal preferences and thus the EB has preferred decreases in conditionality (at least since 1969), then we should observe evidence of the EB's opposition to increases in conditionality in other realms. Statements from Fund insiders should indicate this pressure from the EB and key powerful states to weaken conditionality. While few leaks from the Fund make their way to the public ear, statements by (former) staff members do indicate that (powerful) states have pushed for decreases in conditionality when they have intervened. For instance, Anne Krueger, currently the deputy Managing Director of the IMF, has written that "the United States has supported lending to countries whose policy reforms were clearly insufficient, suggesting even to casual observers the loans could not be used productively" (Krueger 1993: 99–100). Similarly, C. David Finch, a Fund staffer for 37 years, "abruptly resigned" in 1987 in "protest over what he judged to be political interference with the evaluation of proposed stand-by arrangements" (Boughton 2001: 1046–47). Finch objected to the US and other creditor states pressuring Fund staffers to weaken Fund conditionality. As Finch wrote in 1988, "In many cases, creditors' interests lay in short-term order, not in long-term reform. As a result . . . they reacted by pressuring the IMF to accept weaker economic reforms" (Finch 1988: 126).

If the EB has pushed for decreases in conditionality, then careful case studies conducted by other scholars should also note state pressure to decrease conditionality. While many scholars have assumed US (or other creditor state) influence in one direction or the other, Randall Stone (2002) is unique in his use of diverse methods and sources of evidence to substantiate his claims. Stone focuses his study on the enforcement, not the design, of Fund conditionality agreement. He argues that when the US weighs in, it pushes for easier terms and easier enforcement for its allies. As he writes, summarizing his model and empirical results, powerful states "urge the Fund to be lenient toward their favored clients" (Stone 2002: 18). Stone substantiates these claims through large-N empirical analyses and case studies of post-communist countries in the

---

[13] As one *New York Times* article (Farnsworth 1987) on the 1987 World Bank–IMF Annual Meetings wrote, "Delegates from the third world welcomed the willingness of Treasury Secretary James A. Baker 3rd to . . . soften often-crushing I. M.F. loan conditions."

1990s. For instance in the case of Russia's 1992 loan agreement, Stone writes that IMF negotiators initially demanded a strict program; however, the US "urged the IMF to soften its usual requirements" (Stone 2002: 119–120 and 124 citing *New York Times*, March 27, 1993: I, 1). Several other cases discussed by Stone similarly support the assumptions employed by this study: that creditor states and the EB have actually pushed for decreases in conditionality.

In short, an array of evidence – including the EB's Conditionality Guidelines, statements by Fund insiders and case studies – suggest that powerful states and the EB have urged a reduction, not an increase, in Fund conditionality.

A pattern emerges from comparing the collective principal's instructions (Conditionality Guidelines) with subsequent agent activity (measured by the Conditionality Dataset). In general certain instructions have been more closely followed than others. Fund conditionality does not perfectly conform to principal instructions. The number and types of conditions deviate from principal instructions, while the phasing of Fund conditionality programs conforms more and the length of Fund conditionality programs conforms quite closely. These trends mask even greater variation. Within a particular year, Fund programs vary considerably in terms of the length, number of conditions, and amount of phasing. If the collective principal has preferred more uniform agreements with fewer conditions, why do certain arrangements continue to diverge, requiring more and different conditions? Why have the collective principal's preference that arrangements remain short – and within certain month limits – been respected, but their preferences regarding the number and type of conditions have not?

EXPLAINING VARIATIONS IN CONTROL AND CONFORMITY: THE STRENGTHS OF THE PRINCIPAL-AGENT APPROACH

The patterns of agency slack do not correspond with the predictions of the two conventional wisdoms about IO activity. State-centric approaches would expect a near-perfect correlation between state instructions and subsequent IO activity. Clearly that is not the case. While individual cases of Fund agreements vary in the degree to which they conform with state instructions, the broad trends are that the length of Fund agreements and phasing appear to conform to state instructions, while the number and type of conditions largely do not. Bureaucratic explanations would expect international organizations to be governed

Agent preferences, legitimacy, tasks, and permeability

by their own logic, generally removed from state principal instructions. However, this is also not the case. Certain elements of the Fund program, like the length, and also particular individual programs, conform quite closely to state principal instructions.

As suggested earlier, the PA model predicts that if control and monitoring are more costly, then agent activity should conform less to principal preferences, assuming divergent interests and that other variables remain constant. Certain IOs (or agents) may be more costly to monitor or control than others. Several factors suggest that the IMF may be a particularly costly agent for the state principals to control. For instance, the technical nature of the Fund's activities, the quick expansion in the amount of Fund activity, and the related extension of the Fund's hierarchy (or "delegation chain") make diligent monitoring an increasingly costly activity, while the secrecy surrounding Fund activity prevents reliance on procedural third-party enforcers (Barnett and Finnemore 2004; Martin 2002; Nielson and Tierney 2003; Lyne, Nielson, and Tierney, this volume; McCubbins and Schwartz 1984). However, this chapter is less concerned with comparing the IMF to other IOs, than comparing different aspects of IMF activity. Just as international organizations can be plotted along a continuum from more to less difficult to monitor and control, similarly IO activities can be plotted along such a continuum.

Certain IO activities may also be more costly to monitor and control than others. As discussed earlier, if agent activities are less observable, less measurable, and more reliant on agent expertise, then principal costs of monitoring and enforcement should increase and hence agency slack should increase, all else equal. This chapter discusses variations in conformity of four elements of the Fund conditionality agreement: the length of the agreement, the number of phases, the number of binding conditions, and the types of binding conditions. These elements also vary in terms of how observable, measurable, and reliant on agent expertise they are, and hence how costly they are for principals to monitor. The *length* of the agreement is the most easily observable and measurable. Length is measured in month increments, and there is little room for interpretation. The EB does not need to rely heavily on the staff's expertise or privileged knowledge to develop an opinion about the appropriate length of a particular Fund program. EDs also find *phasing* easily observable and measurable; proposed Fund programs include clear schedules of loan disbursements and EDs can easily keep track of these disbursements. However, the EB relies more on the IMF staff and management's expertise to determine how many phases – or loan installments – are optimal for a particular borrower. In short, neither length nor phasing are particularly costly elements of the Fund conditionality agreement for the EB to monitor and enforce; however, phasing appears to be somewhat more costly to monitor and enforce, due to the board's reliance on Fund staff expertise to determine the appropriate number and schedule of phases.

By contrast, the *number* and *type of conditions* are much more costly for the Fund's collective principal to monitor and enforce than both length and phasing. The design of the actual reform program – which at its heart consists of the number and type of conditions – is not a formulaic process. There is still a great deal of uncertainty surrounding the design of the conditionality agreement, and particularly the recommended reform program. In fact, 50 years after the creation of the SBA, the unfortunate consensus is that the Fund still has not mastered the design of conditionality programs. Assessments of the success of Fund programs frequently argue that Fund programs may actually have a detrimental effect on Fund borrowers (particularly their economic growth) (Ul Haque and Khan 1998; Stone 2002: ch. 3). Nevertheless, the EB relies heavily on the Fund staff's expertise, including their experience negotiating with government, their experience with and knowledge of a particular borrower and its economic circumstances, and their specialized training, to determine the appropriate reform program for each particular case. While the EB – time and again – has articulated clear general principles regarding the design of Fund programs, the EB also relies on staff expertise to help them determine whether individual cases are exceptions and require bending the rules.

In addition to being more reliant on Fund expertise, the number and type of conditions are less observable and less measurable than length and phasing. First consider the simple observability, using Haiti's 1976 stand-by agreement as an example. The agreement includes two documents: the SBA itself and an annexed letter from Haiti's National Bank President and Minister of Finance and Economic Affairs. The length is clearly stated in the fourth paragraph ("a period of *one year* from August 2, 1976"), as is the schedule of phasing: loan disbursements should not "exceed the equivalent of SDR 3.491 million *until October 31, 1976*, the equivalent of 3.88 *until January 31, 1977*; the equivalent of SDR 4.88 million *until April 30, 1977*, and the equivalent of SDR 5.88 million *until June 30, 1977*. . ." (EBS/76/317, Supp. 1, August 3, 1976; italics added). By contrast, Haiti's proposed reform program is described in the five-page annexed letter, and not all of these proposed reforms are considered binding conditions. In other words, only some of those reforms, if violated, would cause the Fund loan installments to be withheld. For instance, some of the binding conditions are circuitously identified as "the intention stated in the last sentence of paragraph 7 of the annexed letter" or "any of the intentions stated in the last two sentences of paragraph 8 of the annexed letter" in a particular paragraph in the SBA (EBS/76/317, Supp. 1, August 3, 1976, 1). From this cryptically worded paragraph, it is not immediately apparent how many different conditions are being required of Haiti (seven, according to the Conditionality Dataset's methodology), much less whether that number was being kept to the "minimum necessary, for the success of the program," as instructed by the 1968 Guidelines.

In short, length and phasing are more observable, measurable, and less reliant on agent expertise than are the number and types of conditions. As a result, the PA framework suggests that the least amount of agency slack should be associated with length; there should also be limited agency slack with respect to phasing; however, one should observe a good deal more agency slack with respect to both the number and type of conditions.

The broad trends are consistent with the predictions derived from the PA framework. The length of the agreements and the amount of phasing, two features that are easily observable and less reliant on expertise, should be less costly for the principal to monitor and enforce. Those features conform closely to principal directives. By contrast, the design of the Fund program, including the number and types of conditions required, relies heavily on agent expertise and is less easily measurable and observable. As a result, PA suggests that it would be more costly for the principal to monitor and enforce its preferences over the design of the policy program itself. Consistent with this prediction, the number and type of conditions deviate from principal preferences, particularly when compared to the relative conformity of the length and phasing.

WHAT EXPLAINS VARIATIONS IN INTERNATIONAL ORGANIZATIONAL ACTIVITY? THE WEAKNESSES OF THE PRINCIPAL-AGENT FRAMEWORK

While the PA framework seems to provide a convincing explanation for the broad trends in agency slack, at least three deficiencies raise questions about its utility for scholars interested in studying international organizations.

First, while the basic predictions derived from the PA framework are observed, basic implications of this framework are not. Most notable is the lack of principal re-contracting in the face of agent non-compliance. Stated otherwise, if the number and type of conditions consistently violate EB preferences, why has the EB not begun vetoing agreements or developing new rules to monitor its wayward agent? In recent years, the EB has taken steps to review Fund conditionality agreements before negotiations are completed (and effectively *fait accompli*) in order to increase compliance with its preferences; a third set of Conditionality Guidelines has also been passed. These late-coming and relatively meager efforts may be taken as evidence in support of the PA framework and its expectation of principal re-contracting. However, what is far more notable is how limited re-contracting has been over the last few decades. This observation confounds the expectations of the PA framework.

Second, this chapter considered to what degree variations in agency slack across activity type were consistent with the expectations derived from the PA framework. In short, they conformed well. However, the PA framework does not provide a ready explanation for the equally significant cross-sectional variations in agency slack. In other words, why do certain programs seem to comply with principal preferences regarding the number and type of conditions more than other programs? Why did Morocco's 1982 EFF seem to conform more to principal preferences than the Philippines' 1984 SBA?[14] Typical principal control mechanisms (like screening and selection, monitoring and reporting, institutional checks and balances, and sanctions) do not explain this variation in conformity and slack. In other words, the PA framework (at least as it has been utilized here) offers blunter predictions of variations in agency slack across activity type and seems hard-pressed to explain finer variations in state control across cases.

Third and relatedly, the PA framework may predict or explain broad patterns of agency slack, but that does not mean it explains or predicts actual agent (in this case, IO) activity. Since many scholars are interested in actual IO activity, not theoretical variations in state control that may or may not manifest themselves as variations in IO activity, this deficiency strikes me as the most serious. To be clear, the PA framework portends to explain both variations in state control/agency slack and

---

[14] Conditionality Dataset. Morocco's 1982 EFF required eight binding conditions and no procedural conditions, whereas the Philippines' 1984 SBA required 15 binding conditions and two procedural conditions.

Agent preferences, legitimacy, tasks, and permeability

variations in agent activity. Agent preferences differ from the principal's; thus agent activity should be predicted by the principal's preferences and control mechanisms (or costliness of enforcement), in combination with agent preferences.

However, in the case where agent autonomy (or potential agency slack) is relatively wide, one's assumptions about agent preferences strongly determine predictions about agent activity or policy outcomes. This heavy reliance on agent preferences is problematic for two distinct reasons. First, much work in the PA tradition employs relatively thin assumptions about agent interests – budget maximization, task expansion, "slack" maximization – and from those general assumptions, specific preferences over agent activity would presumably be derived (Barnett and Finnemore 1999: 705).[15] Scholars utilizing the PA framework certainly may take agent interests and preferences more seriously and develop their assumptions through more in-depth analysis. However, in the latter case, scholars are likely reaching outside of the PA tradition to develop agent preferences. Thus another set of tools or another theoretical tradition would be doing much of the explanatory work.

Second, scholars utilizing the PA tradition are exclusively interested in two actors: the principal and the agent. However, in the case of agency autonomy – when the agent has room to maneuver – agent interests, though not agent preferences over their activities, may determine ultimate agent activity. Take the example of a principal who is a storeowner and an agent who is her employee. The owner is often away from the store and provides the employee with a good degree of autonomy. What the employee does with his autonomy (or potential slack) may not be determined by his preferences over his own activity (often assumed to be working less), but instead by a third-party actor that appeals to his interests (earning money). A local couple may pay the employee extra money to close the store temporarily and deliver groceries to their home. In other words, the agent's interests may allow his activities to be influenced by third-party actors when slack is possible.

For the case of the IMF, I have made a similar argument regarding the role of third-party actors appealing to an agent's interests (Gould 2003;

---

[15] Many assume agency preferences as exogenously given (Niskanen 1971; Vaubel 1983, 1986, 1991) or endogenously defined by procedural constraints (Bawn 1995; McCubbins et al. 1989), with some underlying assumption about what the agency is trying to maximize.

Gould 2006). I have argued that a class of actors – dubbed supplementary financiers – influence the design of Fund conditionality agreements because they appeal to the IMF's particular interests. The Fund (staff and management) want their programs to be successful in the short-run; this success preserves their negotiating authority and power. Supplementary financing is often crucial for the short-run success of individual Fund programs because the Fund provides only a fraction of the amount of financing necessary to correct the payments imbalance and implement the Fund program. Both the Fund and the borrower rely on this outside financing to supplement the Fund loan. This reliance gives the supplementary financier a degree of leverage over the design of Fund programs. This is just one example of how agent interests (not preferences) and third-party actors may explain what an IO agent actually does with its slack, and thus be a necessary ingredient if the goal is explaining actual IO activity.

CONCLUSION

This chapter is a preliminary attempt to apply the insights of the PA approach to the study of IMF conditionality. IMF conditionality is an intriguing puzzle for the PA approach. Agency slack varies depending on the particular feature of a Fund conditionality agreement. Certain elements of the Fund agreement – like the number and type of conditions – appear to deviate from principal preferences on a more regular basis than other elements, like length and phasing. Most state-centric accounts (and in fact many PA accounts, which tend to overemphasize the effectiveness of principal controls) would expect the Fund's state principals to exercise greater control over the staff's activities. This investigation of the delegation of conditionality to the IMF suggests certain benefits and certain limitations from the PA approach.

Applying the PA approach to the study of international organizations is useful for a variety of reasons. Perhaps most important, it focuses our attention on an important set of questions. Does IO activity conform to state preferences? How effective are states in controlling IOs? Are there certain characteristics of IO activity that allow IOs greater autonomy? This chapter suggests that state principals may not always be able to perfectly control international organizational agents. In order for the PA approach to be useful to scholars, it needs to be able to explain variations in the dependent variable: agency slack. Critics have rightly noted that (too) much of the work in the PA tradition focuses on explaining a constant dependent variable: constrained agent activity. This chapter therefore tries to demonstrate the utility of the PA tradition, not only in explaining responsive, constrained agents, but also deviant ones. The PA approach can provide a framework for understanding IO activities or IOs themselves on a continuum of conformity.

However, applying the PA framework to the study of international organizations may have some drawbacks, which are also highlighted briefly here. While PA may do a good job of explaining why principals adopt certain mechanisms of control and predicting what the range of agent activity will be, it does not necessarily do a very good job of predicting actual agent activity, in this case IMF conditionality. While PA models may tell us something about why Fund activities deviate from principal instructions, they tell us little about the ultimate outcome: which point in the range does the agency choose and why? Why do they deviate to *these* activities? The clear downside of exclusively applying the PA approach to the study of IOs is that we may therefore understand that the agent is able to exercise a certain degree of autonomy, but have little idea what the agent will do with that autonomy.

To remedy this problem, future work in the PA tradition can follow one of two avenues. First, scholars could develop and adopt more nuanced assumptions regarding agent preferences over their activity (and when to expect them to diverge from the principal's) in order to offer more accurate predictions of agent activity.[16] Alternatively, future work may broaden the focus beyond simply the influence of formal principals and agents over agent activities. If agents maximize certain interests (e.g. Fund staff maximizing short-run success of Fund programs), there is no logical reason why third-party actors cannot manipulate agent incentives and influence agent activity, just as formal principals often do. The eventual policy or point within the equilibrium range, in this case the design of Fund conditionality agreements, may reflect the influence of third-party actors, for reasons that PA theorists will not find surprising. Third-party actors, not only formal principals, may be able to manipulate agent incentives and thus agent activity. Therefore, within the range of autonomy specified by PA insights, the actual form of activity may be specified by either the agent's preferences over its own

---

[16] For instance, this suggests a possibility for fruitfully combining approaches. Work in the sociological institutionalist and historical institutionalist traditions often focuses on the basis for the divergence of preferences between staff and states, or between agents and principals. See Cortell and Peterson (2004: 7–8).

activities or by a third-party appealing to the agent's natural incentives and interests.

In short, the PA approach is very useful in highlighting agency slack and understanding how the agent is manipulated by its principal. However, those employing the PA framework will need to either develop more nuanced theories of agent preferences over activity or broaden the PA relationship in order to explain actual international organizational activity, not "simply" the potential ranges of IO activity and mechanisms of state control.

11

Delegation to international courts and the limits of re-contracting political power

KAREN J. ALTER

International courts (ICs) clearly fit the paradigm of delegation examined in this volume. States operating as a collective principal create ICs through a revocable delegation contract; appoint IC judges; and can write or rewrite the mandate and laws that ICs interpret. Principal-agent (PA) theory expects courts to be among the more independent "agents," intentionally so. As Giandomenico Majone argues, in delegation to enhance the credibility of a principal the "Fiduciary Agent" is made independent because "an Agent bound to follow the directions of the delegating politician could not possibly enhance the commitment" (Majone 2001: 110). Thus intentionally principals allow judges to be fired only for egregious acts unbecoming to their office, and judicial salaries are protected. Still, PA theorists expect states to have substantial tools of control because international judicial terms are short (4–8 years), because international judges may worry about their professional futures including whether or not their term is renewed, and because states can sanction ICs through rewriting their mandate, legislating to reverse their rulings, or through non-compliance.

This chapter has generated interest and comments from so many people, I am sure to forget some. I would like to thank Judy Goldstein, Brian Hanson, Lawrence Helfer, Ian Johnstone, Mona Lyne, Jide Nzelibe, Helen Milner, Jon Pevehouse, Eric Posner, Paul Stephans, David Steinberg, and the participants in PIPEs at the University of Chicago for comments on earlier versions of this paper. Special thanks to Robert Keohane who defended me against a highly critical onslaught, to Jonas Tallberg, Darren Hawkins, Dan Nelson, David Lake, and Mike Tierney, who while enthusiasts of PA theory engaged my work constructively in numerous reads, and to Richard Steinberg. This paper has benefited tremendously from the sustained challenges from participants in the project on Delegation to International Institutions and the later sharp critiques at the "Transformations of the State" Sonderforschungsberich 597 at the University of Bremen.

While these expectations are shared by most PA theorists, studies employing PA theory to analyze ICs have offered contradictory predictions about whether and when we should expect IC autonomy. Geoffrey Garrett and Barry Weingast have argued that the European Court of Justice (ECJ) has far less autonomy than national courts because the ECJ fears re-contracting. They assert that ECJ decisions mainly select among the range of outcomes the most powerful states implicitly want (Garrett and Weingast 1993: 201). In a later co-authored article Garrett argues that when the ECJ is interpreting the provisions of European treaties that require unanimous support to change, ECJ autonomy is high but when the ECJ is interpreting directives or regulations that can be changed by a lower voting threshold, ECJ autonomy is lower (Tsebelis and Garrett 2001). Yet elsewhere Garrett argues that the ECJ will have greater autonomy when there is greater clarity in the law (because the ECJ can use the clarity for political cover) and when its case law is well established (Garrett et al. 1998). Mark Pollack and Jonas Tallberg argue that the ECJ is actually quite autonomous, even more autonomous than national supreme courts, because the rules to legislate over an ECJ decision make re-contracting extremely difficult and unlikely (Tallberg 2002b; Pollack 2003a: 201). Paul Stephan predicts that ICs – and especially the ECJ and WTO – will be far less independent than domestic courts to the point that "one should not expect ambitious, systematic, and comprehensive law coming from an institution endowed with the authority to develop unified law on an international level" because IC judges can be replaced after a short term in office (Stephan 2002: 7–8).[1] These arguments are not logically inconsistent; rather authors are drawing conclusions from different institutional rules that point in opposite predictive directions. But with these various arguments any PA claim can be made and pointed to as an "explanation" of an independent or dependent IC behavior.

Adjudicating the conflicting claims is likely impossible because of the fungibility of state preferences, difficulties measuring slippage, and overdetermination problems. Because state interests are fungible, a single ruling can be interpreted as evidence for contradictory claims. For

---

[1] This prediction cuts against international law scholars who expect the ECJ and the WTO to be among the more autonomous ICs because they have compulsory jurisdiction and the ECJ has private access (Helfer and Slaughter 2005; Posner and Yoo 2004).

Agent preferences, legitimacy, tasks, and permeability

example, Garrett and Weingast use the ECJ's *Cassis de Dijon* decision[2] to support their claim for low ECJ autonomy arguing that the ECJ was influenced by powerful Germany which had a long-term interest in open markets (Garrett 1995: 174–75). Karen Alter and Sophie Meunier argue that Germany lost in the *Cassis* ruling, not only because the German government's argument as the defendant in the *Cassis* case was rejected by the ECJ, but also because as a high standard country Germany wanted either high European level standards or the ability to impose its standards on products produced outside of Germany (Alter and Meunier-Aitsahalia 1994: 539, 542). Bernadette Kilroy tests whether the ECJ appears to give preference to the interests of the most powerful states, finding that the ECJ responded more to the threat of noncompliance than the threat that states might sanction the ECJ (Kilroy 1995, and 1999). Mark Pollack assesses Kilroy's analysis, finding that despite her efforts Kilroy cannot rule out other explanations of ECJ decision-making – such as the argument that the ECJ decides the case purely on the basis of law, without varying its rulings according to the power or intransigence of member states, or the likelihood of state compliance (Pollack 2003a: 200). If we cannot use as evidence the positions governments articulate in the cases themselves or in public afterwards (because politicians may be acting strategically rather than sincerely), and we cannot agree on what states' interests actually are (in which case we should also wonder how an IC judge is supposed to ascertain "state interests"), then concepts like relative slippage, autonomy, or retreat will remain variable depending on the analyst.

Instead of trying to adjudicate claims about relative autonomy, this chapter focuses on whether "re-contracting politics," meaning the principal's ability to screen agents during the appointment process, to replace agents because of principal displeasure, or to otherwise change the delegation contract as a form of sanction, appears to be the tool of state political leverage PA theory expects it to be. States surely have re-contracting power in that they make appointments decisions and they can change the contract. But I argue that this power is not a significant tool of political leverage over ICs, and thus states do not have special powers over ICs by virtue of being part of the collective principle.

I offer two complementary reasons for why re-contracting politics are not the axis around which states and ICs seek to mutually influence each

---

[2] *Rewe Zentral AG v. Bundesmonopolverwaltung für Branntwein* (*Cassis de Dijon*), ECJ case 120/78, [1979] ECR 649.

other. Section one makes an empirical argument, explaining the political and institutional factors undermining the effectiveness of recontracting tools as means to influence IC decision-making. The analysis implies that principal control tools may actually be weaker at the international level compared to the domestic level. Offering my own explanation for the puzzle of why states would design ICs that are in some ways less subject to influence than their domestic counterpart, I argue that the outcome of weak re-contracting tools is partly unintentional (negotiators, mimicking domestic delegation, likely do not realize the extent to which their re-contracting tools will be ineffective) and partly a result of the fact that concerns about international power politics essentially trump principal concerns about controlling ICs. In locating the source of the weak re-contracting tools in international political factors, this section contradicts the claim of the introduction and conclusion that the consequences of delegation to international entities, like ICs, are similar in the domestic and international realms.

Section two moves away from the PA categories defined in the introduction of the volume, using the categories international law scholars use to explain variation in the ability of states to influence ICs – including whether or not states must first consent to an IC's jurisdiction and who has access to ICs. Law scholars' arguments suggest that states essentially pick their poison in delegation to ICs, choosing from the beginning to create more or less independent ICs with the knowledge that there is a relationship between the independence and the effectiveness of ICs. While the factors law scholars identify as important are part of the contract design, they do not give rise to re-contracting politics because they are not subject to re-contracting threats. In other words, once the poison is picked, different types of state-IC politics follow from the choice.

Section three draws together the arguments of the chapter and their implications for the themes of this volume. Rejecting the central role of re-contracting politics does not mean that states do not influence ICs, or that ICs are not subject to political influence. Nor is the claim that ICs can never be held accountable – no political actor is beyond sanction and reproach should it stray beyond what others will tolerate. Rather, the analysis suggests that being a member of the collective principal is not a meaningful source of state power, and that other modes of influence likely matter more than re-contracting power. For cases that make it to court, states use rhetorical and legitimacy politics to try to influence ICs. To the extent that rhetorical and legitimacy politics matter, other actors besides states may be actively involved. States also use fully legal avenues such as refusing to consent to jurisdiction, or settling out of court, or shifting dispute resolution to more controllable political venues in order to navigate around the fact that they do not want slippage yet beyond rhetorical influence they cannot control IC decision-making. While these arguments are not inconsistent per se with PA theory, the analysis suggests that PA theory itself will not be very useful in studying the dynamics influencing variation in international judicial decision-making across cases or even across international courts.

(RE-)CONTRACTING POWER AND STATE INFLUENCE OVER ICS

A number of scholars have argued that constitutional courts are more like trustees than they are traditional agents, and thus that the variables PA theory relies on are less likely to be helpful in understanding delegation to courts (Alter 2005; Grant and Keohane 2005; Majone 2001; Stone Sweet 2002).[3] But to say that some courts are more like trustees is not to say that states have determined to simply trust that ICs will exercise their discretion prudently. States are concerned about slippage, meaning they are concerned about international judges interpreting the rules of the collective principal in ways that were not intended and that the collective principal does not want and would not have agreed to. But here the problem of collective principals, discussed in greater detail in the chapter by Lyne, Nielson, and Tierney, manifests itself. The ICs interpretation may not be what the collective would agree to, but it likely does represent what a sub-set of states actually prefer. Thus IC slippage is really about ICs awarding victories in politically contested cases that state-litigants could not win in negotiations, and thus essentially rewriting through interpretation the law that states have agreed to. Because some actors actually prefer the new interpretation, returning to the status quo ante may be politically impossible. Even if a state-litigant chooses to ignore the IC ruling, the legal ruling itself can shift the political context by changing the status quo of what the law means in the eyes of others; by labeling a state's extant policy "illegal" popular support for the policy can be undermined. If one considers the thousands of international legal rulings that have been issued compared to the relatively small number of polemical rulings, it would seem that slippage is fairly rare. Despite

---

[3] These authors refer in passing to courts as "fiduciary agents" or "trustees." In a separate article I develop this category further (Alter 2005).

its rarity, one need only consider the Bush Administration's concerns about the International Criminal Court to know that states care greatly about this slippage risk, even if 999 times out of a thousand states are happy with the job ICs are doing.

Thus the question emerges: even if courts are trustees, can the collective principal use the contracting tools – their power to appoint, power of the purse, or power to relegislate – that they exclusively hold to shape how the international judiciary exercises its discretionary decision-making authority? If re-contracting tools were effective, then principals would have a source of power that other actors could not access, and thus a special leverage to wield vis-à-vis ICs. This section focuses on each of the traditional PA tools identified in the introduction to this volume, with the exception of monitoring tools and checks and balances,[4] reviewing the scholarship on whether or not re-contracting tools influence ICs. The best evidence we have suggests that these re-contracting tools provide little to no political leverage states can use vis-à-vis ICs. The question then is why do states have decision-rules that directly undermine their ability to sanction or influence wayward IC agents?

Screening and appointment processes as tools of principal control

Scholars and politicians expect that judicial philosophy will influence how judges approach opportunities for interpretive discretion so that by selecting for certain types of judges, the principal may be able to influence judicial decision-making. There is some evidence to support this expectation. Max Schanzenbach convincingly shows that in the United States, Republican-appointed judges exercise their discretion regarding prison term lengths differently than do Democrat-appointed judges (Schanzenbach 2004). Eric Posner and Miguel de Figueiredo find that ICJ judges tend to vote with their countries 80 percent of the time, more than the 50 percent they expect if legal decision-making were random (Posner and De Figueiredo 2004). And Erik Voeten finds that European

---

[4] Monitoring and reporting is not really a tool of control for courts; courts openly publish their rulings, not so much to help states monitor them but because publication of rulings is the best way to create political pressure for compliance. Also, I fold what might be considered a discussion of checks and balances into the sanctioning/re-contracting discussion since relegislating (traditionally considered a "sanction") would also be the way ICs might be "checked" or "balanced" by political bodies.

Agent preferences, legitimacy, tasks, and permeability

Court of Human Rights (ECHR) judges vote with their country 74 percent of the time (Voeten 2004). But whether the appointment process serves as a tool of control is another matter. Indeed none of these authors links their findings to arguments about principal control.

In the domestic context, Schanzenbach can show that appointment decisions affect legal outcomes because in his case a single judge is able to decide on the term length of the convicted criminal. But at the international level, judicial decision-making involves more than one judge. While one could imagine that screening effects could radically change US Supreme Court jurisprudence, which often turns on a single vote, it is harder to make the case that screening influences IC decision-making. Posner does not actually claim that legal outcomes are affected, though he does imply that judicial voting is biased in that votes are not randomly distributed across cases. But Posner includes in his count cases where the ICJ in whole or by majority sided with a particular country, not controlling for whether or not legal reasoning could explain a judge's vote equally as well. Erik Voeten rectifies these deficiencies, focusing on split decision cases where it is clear that legal factors are not determinative (otherwise the ruling would not be split) and controlling for when judges were part of a majority in finding for a legal violation—in which case the facts and law may matter more than the nationality in influencing judicial decision-making (Posner cannot use these controls because his "N" is already too small to generate statistically solid conclusions). With these controls, Voeten is able to identify only 31 rulings out of the larger sample of 5,010 rulings where a country won its case by one vote and where its judge was in the majority, thus where in theory national selection effects of appointment could have shaped the legal outcome. Controlling for other factors shaping judicial decision-making, Voeten identifies 11 occasions where a state likely escaped sanction due to the strategic behavior of a country's judge (Voeten 2004). The cases of potential national selection effects are not particularly noteworthy, so it is not that these 11 cases are the most important rulings the ECHR has made. Overall Voeten's findings suggest that where there is sufficient legal ambiguity to generate a split decision (800 of the 5,010 ECHR judgments sample, thus 16 percent of ECHR cases), there is less than a 2 percent chance that selection effects could shape the legal outcome. It is also interesting to note that Voeten found no correlation between whether ECHR judges were appointed by left or right national governments and how judges voted in split decisions. Instead, the largest predictive factor of whether or not judges were "activist" in their votes was whether the country appointing the judge was also a member of the European Union.

Of course judges could also amplify their influence by persuading their colleagues to support their view. Indeed states seem to intend for this to occur, to ensure that national positions are represented in judicial deliberations. Thus regional organizations intentionally provide a space for a judge from each country, and de facto allow countries to select their judge, accepting whomever is nominated. Also, the ICJ has provisions to appoint special judges to ensure that each country has a national voting on their case. But by ensuring that both parties have national representation within the legal body, the effect can cancel itself out. The canceling effect is why showing national voting does not per se show court bias.

It is not surprising that judicial screening tools are more effective at the domestic level compared to the international level. In the United States there is a politicized process for judicial appointments, one that allows the dominant majority to screen appointees based on their ideology. Given the effort political parties have invested in the judicial appointment process, it would indeed be surprising if selection politics did not have an influence. But at the international level there is no controllable international political process to shape who gets to nominate international judicial positions – rather each state has unilateral control over who they nominate. Sometimes powerful countries can veto nominations at the point that judges are being selected from a pool of potential candidates, and this is where politics of international judicial appointments occurs. Indeed there can be intense politics surrounding the choices for international judicial appointments, where there are choices to make (Steinberg 2004; Gordon et al. 1989). However, for regional ICs (e.g. the European Court of Justice, the Inter-American Court of Human Rights, and the European Court of Human Rights) one judge from each member state will be selected and states accept whomever a country nominates. Permanent members of the Security Council also get to select their own judge for the ICJ. Each country may well have specific criteria to screen for the type of judicial candidate they nominate. But there is no evidence that states coordinate their efforts, or that the result of these efforts is a bench with a philosophical slant that can be linked to appointment politics.

The ways ICs decide cases also blunt the effectiveness of the appointment process as a tool of control. While IC decisions are made based on a majority vote, it is not always possible to tell how different judges voted. The ICJ, International Tribunal for the Law of the Sea, the Inter-American Court of Human Rights, and the European Court of Human Rights regularly publish dissenting opinions. But the ECJ and the WTO Appellate Body never publish dissents, and the International Criminal Tribunals for Yugoslavia and Rwanda rarely publish dissents. (It is not yet clear what the ICC will do regarding dissents.)[5] Even where dissents are allowed, many IC rulings are actually made by small panels of judges and states generally have no control over which sub-set of judges will hear their case.[6] This means that to influence a court using the selection tool states would have to "correctly" influence the vast majority of international appointments – not just their own appointee – in a context where the nominees are put forward by the nominating state and not through a collective process.

It is even less likely that a fear of not being reappointed shapes judicial decision-making. Often IC judges are not reappointed, but rarely if at all is it because of the decisions they made on the bench. IC judges on universal legal bodies are regularly rotated out to create geographic representation on the court. Even where there is a permanent national seat international judges are regularly rotated out because each new national leadership wants a chance to appoint their own judge. While IC judges could in theory still worry about their life after they serve their term, in practice the international judges I have interviewed have not been very worried about this. There is no international judicial career trajectory because the pool of international judicial appointments is simply too small[7] and many IC judges are near retirement or see an appointment to an IC as a short-term professional experience in any event. While there may well be isolated examples where a person did not get a job they wanted because of their association with an IC (though I know of no examples), whether a judge could anticipate these situations, let alone moderate their behavior to avoid the situation, is highly

---

[5] The Rome Statute of the ICC says that there will be one decision but it "shall contain the views of the majority and the minority"; it is not yet clear how this will be handled in practice.

[6] This is not true for the panel stage for the WTO where states can select panelists, but the AB does not allow for state selection of judges. Also for ICJ cases where states have not consented to compulsory jurisdiction, states can participate in selecting the sub-set of judges who will hear their case. (Art. 31 Statute of the International Court of Justice describing the appointment of ad hoc judges.)

[7] There are 21 courts, with about 200 appointees from around the world who could be described as being "international" judges and 191 states belonging to the United Nations (Alvarez 2003: 2).

questionable. Even Richard Steinberg, who believes that the United States and Europe veto AB judges whom they suspect will be activist, does not argue that the concerns about reappointment lead judges to follow the wishes of the United States or Europe (Steinberg 2004: 264).

Thus while there are selection politics at the international level, they do not appear to give rise to an international judiciary with a particular philosophical slant let alone a judiciary that needs to worry that their actions on the bench will create personal limitations on their future professional achievement. The possible exception to this argument would pertain to the role of the prosecutor in an international criminal tribunal, a role that will be far more visible than that of a single judge on an international court. As I will discuss later, one way states seek to limit IC slippage is to keep cases from international judicial bodies. Criminal prosecutors decide which cases to investigate, and whether and how to plea-bargain outside of court. There is only one chief prosecutor, and the chief prosecutor will be able to tell those below him or her what to do. States that can control the selection of the ICC prosecutor may be able to influence which cases are taken to the ICC for resolution and perhaps even the arguments the prosecutor pursues in the cases, though not per se what the judges then do with the arguments raised.

Control of the budget as a tool of principal control

In order to protect judicial independence, principals often limit their ability to use the budget as a tool of influence. Thus we often find statutory limits on the ability of legislators to cut judicial salaries. In the international context, the way international legal processes work also limits the ability of principals to use budgets as a tool of control. For most international litigation the greatest costs are borne by the parties who hire lawyers to assemble the case and assemble all of the factual material needed to support their position, and provide some of the "costs" supporting the legal process. The IC's budget covers translation, and support staff. To cut an IC's budget would mainly slow down the legal process and the multilingual and timely accessibility of rulings, which may make the legal process even less appealing but will not per se control how IC judges deal with the cases before them.

International criminal courts are again different in that the office of the prosecutor shares the international criminal court's budget. Cases can only go forward to the ICC when the prosecutor has a preponderance of evidence to support a conviction. By manipulating the prosecutor's budget and helping or hindering the prosecutor, states can influence which crimes are investigated and whether or not the prosecutor can assemble a winnable court case. While the budget probably does not "control" how the IC judges interpret the law, it likely does affect the cases and the evidence brought to the court in the first place.

Clear rules as a tool of principal control

States fight over every word in international legal agreements, yet winning these fights does not ensure that state interests are protected over time. Not only can courts interpret even clear rules in ways states never intended, they regularly fill in where rules are vague, and on their own set the "standard of review" – the burden of evidence that will be required by judges for a finding in favor of a plaintiff. Many legal cases turn on the standard of review. For example, though WTO member states drafted clear rules on when safeguards are legal, the WTO appellate body added a standard of review that the damages had to have been "unforeseen" before safeguard protections would be legal, using this standard to find against safeguard protections by the United States and Argentina.[8]

Because writing more precise rules is no insurance against IC slippage, states often try to mitigate international judicial slippage by writing explicit caveats into the law itself. For example, the Danish wrote into the Maastricht Treaty a protocol that allows them to limit Germans from buying vacation homes in Denmark and the Irish wrote a protocol stating that nothing in the EU treaties can overrule Ireland's constitutional provisions regarding abortion.[9] Caveats like these abound, but they require states to select at the time of negotiation a small handful of issues to champion since international negotiators will want to limit the number of caveats they agree to. Where other negotiating parties will

---

[8] Argentina – Safeguard Measures on Imports of Footwear WT/DS121/AB/R Report of the Appellate Body, December 14, 1999. WTO Appellate Body Report: United States – Safeguard Measures on Imports of Fresh, Chilled or Frozen Lamb Meat from New Zealand and Australia AB-2001-1, WT/DS177,178/AB/R (01-2194), adopted by Dispute Settlement Body, May 16, 2001. These cases are discussed in Alter 2005.

[9] See the Protocol on the Acquisition of Property in Denmark in the Treaty on a European Union and the very last Protocol Annexed to the Treaty on European Union and to the Treaties Establishing the European Communities the High Contracting Parties in the Treaty on European Union.

not agree to a caveat in the law, states often note with their ratification a "reservation" that asserts for the country an exception to the treaty. The number of reservations a country asserts is also politically limited lest one anger fellow signatories who will not feel that the agreement is actually reciprocal. Also, while states can assert reservations, courts will not per se accept them as legally valid. Indeed the legal effect of "reservations" on binding obligations is far from clear (Swaine 2005).

The thing to remember is that even with caveats and reservations, as time evolves new governments and interests arise, interpretations of the caveats can change, and thus many state interests can become unprotected over time. For example, when states agreed to the EC's Equal Treatment directive they added Article 2(2) that said: "This Directive shall be without prejudice to the right of Member States to exclude from its field of application those occupational activities and, where appropriate, the training leading thereto, for which by reason of their nature or the context in which they are carried out, the sex of the worker constitutes a determining factor."[10] At the time this caveat was negotiated, British and German law explicitly allowed derogations to the requirement of equal treatment for the military.[11] These caveats did not stop the ECJ from later asserting its authority to oversee the limits of excluding women from military positions. The ECJ ultimately upheld UK exclusions of a female cook from the Royal Marines because the presence of a woman could undermine group cohesion in an elite unit, but it found Germany's constitutional ban on woman in combat-related roles to be too comprehensive and therefore discriminatory.[12] Germany embraced

---

[10] Council Directive 76/207/EEC of February 9, 1976 on Equal Treatment for Men and Women in Employment, OJ [1976] L 39/40.

[11] Article 85(4) of the United Kingdom's 1975 Sex Discrimination Act states: "nothing in this Act shall render unlawful an act done for the purpose of ensuring the combat effectiveness of the naval, military or air forces." In Germany women were only allowed to serve in the band, or in the medical services, and by a provision in the German constitution (the Basic Law) were explicitly prohibited from "render[ing] service involving the use of arms" (German Basic Law Article 12 a (4)). These exceptions were arguably consistent with Article 2(2) of the Equal Treatment Directive, and were never challenged by the European Commission as a violation of European law probably because the realm of the national security remained firmly a national issue and a policy area where sex discrimination had long been accepted as the norm.

[12] *Sirdar v. Army Board*, Case C-273/97, 1999 E. C.R. I-7403, [1999] 3 C. M.L. R. 559 (1999). *Alexander Dory v. Federal Republic of Germany*, Case C-186/01 judgment of March 11, 2003. *Tanja Kreil v. Bundesrepublik Deutschland*, Case C-285/98, 2000 E. C.R. I-69.

Agent preferences, legitimacy, tasks, and permeability

the ECJ's outside pressure, changing its constitution and actively integrating women in a number of roles in the military (Kuemmel 2003; Liebert 2002). But one must only look at the efforts to exclude the ECJ from foreign policy issues to know that states did not and would not have agreed to let the supranational European court rule on *any* issue related to how they organized their national militaries if they had been given the choice.

Empirically speaking, there is little solid evidence that more precise rules limit IC autonomy. Indeed Geoffrey Garrett, Daniel Keleman and Heiner Schulz actually expect greater precision to facilitate ECJ independence because the court can use the precise wording as political cover (Garrett et al. 1998). While a special edition of *International Organization* hypothesized about a relationship between the level of precision of a legal rule and its influence in general, the volume as a whole was unable to substantiate the link (it did not try to link precision to slippage) (Goldstein et al. 2001). Instead in that volume Karen Alter found that a number of factors unrelated to rule precision shaped whether or not the ECJ comes to influence domestic policy (Alter 2000) and Kathryn Sikkink and Ellen Lutz found in Latin America that more legalized and precise rules regarding torture had actually less influence than less legalized rules regarding disappearances and democracy (Lutz and Sikkink 2000).

Sanctions through rewriting the delegation contract as a tool of principal control

Legislative bodies always retain the right to change the law if they are unhappy with how it is being applied or interpreted by judges. Geoff Garrett has argued that the threat that states might go back and rewrite a rule helps mitigate judicial slack (Garrett 1995; Garrett et al. 1998; Garrett and Weingast 1993; Tsebelis and Garrett 2001), but the empirical support for this claim is far from conclusive. One can find plenty of examples of politicians playing to their political base by condemning the actions of "unaccountable judges." Yet compelling examples of serious threats on courts, like President Roosevelt's threat to "stack" the US Supreme Court, or Charles De Gaulle's threat to eliminate the French Conseil d'Etat (Parris 1966), are very rare. Even attempts to legislatively reverse a court – such as the Republican Congress's recent effort to overturn judicial decisions in the Terry Schiavo case – are surprisingly rare.

Why are these cases so rare, and why are the examples all domestic? It is only really possible to relegislate over a legal ruling when one political party has commanding control over the legislature so that a populist political attack can become a political reality. At the international level no one actor or party has commanding control over the legislative process, and states tend to disagree about which policy is best, making them unable to unite behind an alternative interpretation. Thus developing country outrage at a WTO appellate body ruling regarding *amicus* briefs has led to blocked efforts to reform the WTO dispute resolution mechanisms, but not a reversal of the *amicus* brief ruling, in large part because the United States and Europe are happy with *amicus* briefs being allowed (Schneider 2001). US anger at the ICJ's Nicaragua ruling[13] led to the withdrawal of the United States from the ICJ's compulsory jurisdiction, but no change in international law regarding the use of force.

The most likely venue one might find international relegislation to counteract an IC decision is the European Union, since the EU produces copious legislation that sometimes requires only a qualified majority vote. Yet despite Garrett's claims of ECJ re-contracting threats, and despite widespread public disenchantment with European integration, Damian Chalmers could identify only four examples of legislation intentionally added to counteract an ECJ decision, examples that were not per se "sanctions" in light of undue activism (Chalmers 2004: 15, nn. 55–56).[14] The most well-known example was the "Barber Protocol" adopted because many European countries were unhappy about the costs of the ECJ's *Barber* ruling equalizing the retirement ages of men and women. Yet this protocol only limited the *Barber* ruling's retrospective

---

[13] ICJ judgment of 26 November 1984 – Jurisdiction of the Court and Admissibility of the Application. ICJ Judgment of 27 June 1986 – Military and Paramilitary Activities in and against Nicaragua (*Nicaragua v. United States of America*) – Merits.

[14] (1) The Barber Protocol is discussed in this paragraph. (2) A protocol was added to the Treaty on the European Union saying that nothing in the EU treaties could undermine Ireland's constitutional provisions regarding abortion. Yet this provision did not reverse the ECJ's *Grogan* ruling challenging Irish policies that limited women from traveling to Britain to get an abortion. *Grogan* stands; Ireland no long tries to restrict women from traveling to the UK to get an abortion; and abortion services remain legally classified as falling under EU rules regarding the free movement of services. (3) When the ECJ ruled against a German affirmative action policy (in the *Kalanke* ruling) on the basis that the EC directive disallowed such policies, states corrected the directive. (4) Two declarations were added to the organization of German, Austrian, and Luxembourg public credit unions to counteract an ECJ ruling regarding competition law.

effects; the decision itself was not reversed. Nor could Mark Pollack link this "sanction" to any change in ECJ behavior: "[I]ndeed one might argue that the Court's post-*Barber* jurisprudence, rather than constituting a generalized retreat, represents a return to the pre-*Barber* pattern in which the Court generally, but not always, opts for a broad interpretation of Article 141, most often over the objections of one or more . . . member governments" (Pollack 2003a: 200).

Judges will tell you, perhaps in a fit of denial, that they consider the separation of powers to mean that legislatures write laws, and judges interpret laws. Since it is always the prerogative of the legislature to change the law, they argue, relegislation is not a political or social sanction that undermines their reputation. But we do not have to take judges at their word to believe that relegislation is not a sanction. That we find so little serious discussion of relegislation viewed as a political sanction implies either that judges do not slip, that they slip yet there is not support to relegislate, or that others do not see the well-being of judges as adversely affected by legislatures changing legal texts.

Arguably ICs hesitate to aggressively apply legal principles that generate great controversy, but the law in question and the legal interpretations remain on the books to be dusted off when political tempers cool or in a less contentious political context. Institutions change over time through reinterpretation of statutes, by shifting the emphasis from one provision in a statute to another, or by seizing on and giving new life to moribund yet latent statutes and roles (Pierson 2004; Thelen 2004). Indeed the US Supreme Court's famous *Marbury v. Madison* ruling remained a dead letter for years. Only through time did the *Marbury* ruling come to be seen as a defining moment when federal judicial authority was established, changing the course of US constitutional and judicial history forever.

Why are principal re-contracting tools so weak?

It is not impossible that principal tools of control can work, nor is it the case that a belief in the sanctity of judicial independence is stopping states from using the tools they have – after all, governments show little compunction about using their re-contracting tools to influence domestic judiciaries. The question is why have states chosen appointment rules and relegislation rules at the international level that undermine their ability to credibly threaten or influence international judicial actors? The analytical problem in answering this question is the difficulty involved in interpreting what has not happened. Some would read the lack of state sanctions against ICs as a revealed preference, arguing that the reason principals neither use nor change their control tools is that ICs do not slip in ways principals care about. Brian Marks has shown the flaws of this answer. Using game theoretical modeling, Marks shows that even when a majority of legislators oppose a judicial ruling, and the voting rule allows for the majority to change the legislation, the majority may not relegislate. Marks concludes that "inaction is neither a sufficient nor necessary condition [to signal that something is acceptable to] a majority of legislators. Nor can we conclude that the absence of legislative reaction implies that the court's policy choice leads to a 'better' policy in the view of the legislature" (Marks 1989: 6).

Since we cannot rely on revealed preferences, we need theory to fill in the rationale behind the perplexing behavior we observe – in this case principal delegation to international courts that are in many ways even less subject to principal influence than their domestic counterparts. Let me suggest an "isomorphic mimicry meets international politics" explanation of why we find such weak principal control tools at the international level.[15]

Governments likely delegate to ICs for the same reasons they delegate to domestic courts – to have courts fill in contracts, resolve disputes, and to use legal mechanisms to help monitor compliance (McCubbins et al. 1989; Milgrom et al. 1990; Weingast and Moran 1983). But in undertaking delegation for these reasons, likely neither negotiators nor the national legislators who ratify international agreements have fully thought through how the international context is in fact quite different from the domestic context. The context is different in a number of ways.

First, changing international agreements is far harder than changing domestic agreements, and in this respect international agreements are more similar to constitutions than they are to domestic statutory law. The difficulty in changing rules stems both from the heterogeneous interests of states at the international level and from international voting rules shaped by power concerns rather than legislative efficiency and principal control objectives. Voting rules in international institutions tend to be designed to allow a small number of powerful states to block the legislative will of the majority, and a large number of weak states to block the

---

[15] For a similar type of isomorphic argument where domestic institutions are imported to the international level, see McNamara 2002.

will of the powerful. Such rules make it difficult to get agreement on anything, and especially difficult when it comes to reversing slippage – a "joint decision-trap" context (Scharpf 1988) where few may like the status quo yet no one can agree to a new status quo (Alter 2001: 195–98).

Second, international law differs from domestic law in that the subjects of domestic law are generally private actors where the subjects of international law are sovereign states. PA models of delegation to the judiciary which Weingast et al. build on are administrative and civil courts models.[16] In domestic administrative and civil law contexts, the interests of the government and the courts are aligned; in the words of Martin Shapiro, courts are branches of the state itself, working in tandem with the government to advance state social control over the population (Shapiro 1981: 17–28). Only in a constitutional review role do the interests of courts and states not align since in constitutional review courts are checking legislative power. This difference between constitutional review and other judicial roles is why rational choice scholars like Jon Elster and Giandomenico Majone create separate concepts and categories for delegation to constitutional courts, which they see as "self-binding" as opposed to "other-binding" (Majone 2001; Elster 2000).[17] While most of the functional tasks that are delegated to ICs are very similar to the administrative review and dispute resolution roles given to domestic courts (Alter 2006a), because ICs will be issuing rulings vis-à-vis state actors, they will inherently be constraining the exercise of national sovereignty, just as constitutional courts limit the exercise of legislative sovereignty. This means that delegating the exact same functional monitoring or filling in tasks to an international court will be different compared to the domestic context. Add to the difference in legal subject that often international law has a "supreme" status over conflicting domestic or local laws. Thus even if states do not intend to create constitutional international courts, and think they have only asked IC to interpret the rules they collectively agreed to, in fact states often get ICs that end up practicing constitutional review over sovereign states.

---

[16] Even in administrative contexts rational choice scholars find that factors other than principal interests are of greater influence on administrative decision-makers. See Weingast and Moran 1983; Caruson and Bitzer 2004.

[17] Note that Stone Sweet's and Majone's trustee model is based on constitutional courts in a domestic context (Stone Sweet 2002; Majone 2001). Keohane and Grant extend the trustee category to courts in a discussion of the overall of accountability of IOs in world politics (Grant and Keohane 2005), and Alter to ICs in specific (Alter 2005).

Differences in the international compared to the domestic context cut two ways. To the extent that states delegate to ICs with an expectation that their government will have the same tools of influence over courts internationally as they do domestically, they are likely relying on a false analogy. But there is a third relevant difference between the international and domestic context: exit through non-compliance carries fewer political liabilities for international law compared to domestic law. Governments have a big stake in maintaining the political sanctity of the "rule of law" at home. Their internal legitimacy as well as external financial attractiveness for foreign capital depends on private actors having faith that their lives and investments will be safe because legal rules will be respected and enforced. Governments do not have as big a stake in maintaining the "international rule of law," and they are advantaged compared to other international actors when it comes to convincing their population that national interests should trump (Alter 2003: 792–96). Because "non-compliance" with IC rulings is not too politically costly, delegation to ICs comes with a built-in insurance policy. No matter how bad the slippage, governments can walk away from an IC sanction with relatively little pain.[18]

The empirical support for this "isomorphic mimicry meets international politics" explanation is best revealed through detailed historical analysis of particular delegation decisions. In my book *Establishing the Supremacy of European Law*, I historically establish the very clear and open intent that states had in delegation to the ECJ – states saw themselves as creating an international administrative review court for the European Coal and Steel Community's High Authority, and they intentionally modeled the ECJ directly on the French Conseil d'Etat. When the Treaty of Rome was drafted, the ECJ's role was slightly transformed, though states never agreed to make European law supreme to national law or to elevate the Treaty of Rome into a constitutional document. Instead the ECJ itself asserted the direct effect and supremacy of EC law, transforming the Treaty of Rome into a form of constitution (Stein 1981; Weiler 1991), and states ended up with a court that was fundamentally different than what they intended (Alter 2001: ch. 1).

---

[18] WTO rulings can create real financial costs, but rich states especially can find these costs bearable so that compliance becomes a choice they can buy their way out of. For some, the inability of the WTO system to provide meaningful pain for rich countries is a flaw in the design of the WTO system (Pauwelyn 2000).

Agent preferences, legitimacy, tasks, and permeability

Short of historical accounts for all existing courts, there is suggestive evidence for this "isomorphic mimicry" explanation that is more broadly generalizable. If states assumed that international courts would be like their domestic brethren, we could understand why states were in many cases willing to delegate to ICs the drafting of their own procedural rules for decision-making. We could also understand the apparent lack of concern for controlling ICs that went into the design of international judicial appointment processes. And we can understand the legitimacy problems ICs face, since states did not think they signed up for having ICs rule national policies illegal or shift the meaning of international agreements.

The question remains as to why states have not learned that uncontrollable ICs present dangers they do not like, adjusting their behavior accordingly. On the one hand, they have learned. The United States was once a great champion of international courts, and it has turned into the chief opponent of delegating authority to ICs. Also, whereas in the past the statutory rules regarding ICs were drafted in small committees, and pretty much adopted by the larger plenum wholesale,[19] the far more detailed and contested debates over how and what power was delegated to the ICC reveal that states are trying to involve themselves more in decisions regarding delegation to ICs. European citizens are also clearly paying more attention to the substance of their delegation in the European Union. Still, we can find the model of international delegation to highly independent ICs replicated for newly created ICs, since the historic independent IC is the model championed by states who want to limit the ability of the most powerful states to influence ICs.[20] Indeed while there was great haggling over the design of the ICC, the United States ultimately lost in its efforts to create an ICC with a Security Council veto.

Perhaps the larger reason we do not see states act to improve their "tools of control" is because the potential solutions have greater

---

[19] For discussions of the negotiations of the ECJ and Andean Court statutes, see Pescatore 1981; Keener 1987. In the WTO context as well, it appears that larger battles in the Uruguay Round involved substantive trade issues and that the design of the dispute resolution mechanism was not a subject of sustained negotiation by state parties.

[20] The various ad hoc criminal courts follow similar models, and the proposals for new regional trade and human rights courts in Africa appear to be drafted based on boilerplate texts about the European Court of Justice and the European Court of Human Rights.

downsides than the benefit of a more controllable IC. Perhaps states *have rejected* suggestions aimed at creating a more controllable IC because they do not want the strongest countries to have even more influence over ICs, nor are they willing to create any precedent for external interference in national choices about who represents them in ICs. Perhaps they also fear that efforts to control the ICs would undermine the legitimacy of these fragile legal institutions, undermining the benefits of delegation to independent ICs. These reasons could explain Richard Steinberg's assessment that even though concern about judicial lawmaking has been raised 70 times by representatives of 55 WTO member states in the last ten years (Steinberg 2004: 256), and a number of political reforms for the WTO legal process have been offered, these reforms "are untenable politically" and unlikely to be adopted (Steinberg 2004: 273–74).

Giandomenicao Majone argued that in delegation to fiduciary agents, the "agent" is purposely designed to be independent (Majone 2001). Certainly the difficulty in dismissing judges mid-term and of cutting their salaries is by design, to help protect the independence of judges. But the difficulty of using the appointment process to shape IC decision-making, the unwillingness of states to cede their voting rights to facilitate relegislation, and the unwillingness of states to subject IC decisions to a veto by some version of qualified majority, are probably artifacts of international power politics and the apprehensions states have about subjecting the international legal process to more of these politics.

WHAT DOES SHAPE WHETHER INTERNATIONAL COURTS ARE MORE OR LESS INDEPENDENT?

Law scholars generally do not use the language of principal-agent theory to think about judges as strategic or politically influenced decision-makers, knowing that the factors driving judicial strategy have less to do with re-contracting concerns than with achieving the judicial goals of influencing policy and the behavior of other actors (Murphy 1964; Epstein and Knight 1998; Murphy et al. 2002). International law scholars also generally do not use PA theory to hypothesize about what makes ICs independent or effective,[21] yet they are very interested in

---

[21] An exception is a recent article by Lawrence Helfer and Anne-Marie Slaughter. What they call the "formal/structural" mechanisms correspond in part to the mechanisms identified by PA theory. Ex ante structural tools include writing

whether states control ICs and how state control relates to IC effectiveness. Recently Eric Posner and John Yoo contrasted "dependent courts," where the parties to the dispute are allowed to select arbiters, with "independent courts," where IC judges are selected in advance of the dispute. Lawrence Helfer and Anne-Marie Slaughter offer many challenges to Posner and Yoo's finding that dependence is associated with effectiveness (Helfer and Slaughter 2005), yet they largely accept the notion that certain ICs are more independent than others. The debate highlights that there is variation in the design of ICs that occurs below the radar screen of traditional PA variables, variation that shapes the extent to which ICs can be more or less independent actors.

Yoo, Posner, Helfer, and Slaughter agree that courts with compulsory jurisdiction are more independent, as are courts with access for non-state actors because states are less able to control which cases make it to ICs. Courts where parties can choose their judges and where consent to jurisdiction is required are less independent because the judges must please the parties or the states won't appoint them again or bring them cases in the future. How independence relates to effectiveness is contested. Yoo and Posner want to find that independence is bad, but their argument that independence makes courts less effective uses compliance levels as the measurement of whether or not ICs are effective. We know that compliance and effectiveness are two separate issues (Raustiala 2000), and that high levels of compliance do not per se mean that regimes are effective (Downs et al. 1996). Slaughter and Helfer criticize Yoo and Posner for this, but they also call into question some of their empirical measurements and interpretations. Without wanting to take sides in the debate, I should say Yoo and Posner are relative outliers as most scholars either associate the factors that contribute to IC independence with effectiveness (Helfer and Slaughter 1997; Keohane et al. 2000; Helfer

---

precisely defined legal rules, defining methods and standards of review that allow deference to states, allowing state reservations when legal obligations are adopted, allowing reservations or requiring state consent for an IC to have jurisdiction in the case, limiting access to the IC, and screening tools used in the original appointment. Ex post structural tools include relegislation of international legal rules to "correct" an IC interpretation, renegotiation of the tribunal's jurisdiction, refusal to reappoint judges, delaying implementation of a decision, or unilateral withdrawal from a tribunal's jurisdiction (Helfer and Slaughter 2005). They do not test whether these tools are effective, and one should consider that these arguments are offered as a retort to Eric Posner and John Yoo's argument that independent ICs are bad in and of themselves (Posner and Yoo 2004).

and Slaughter 2005) or consider the ICs with the qualities associated with independence (the ECJ, ECHR, and WTO) to be among the more effective ICs in terms of their ability to make rulings on important issues and to have their rulings respected.

More important is the common ground in the arguments which suggests that principals "pick their poison" in the design choices for ICs. If states want to really bind themselves and others to comply with an agreement, they design ICs to maximize their enforcement capabilities – agreeing to compulsory jurisdiction, wider access, and sanctions that can be associated with IC decisions. When principals are more wary about delegating authority to an IC, they require consent to jurisdiction and make IC rulings purely declaratory to make non-compliance less costly. If these scholars are right, we have two more reasons for why re-contracting politics do not seem to be at play. First, the decisions to consent to compulsory jurisdiction and the access rules for ICs add an element of endogeneity to explaining delegation, suggesting that states pick the type of delegation they want in the first place, either choosing independent or dependent courts. (This endogeneity argument holds, however, only so long as the principal gets the court it chose.) Second, after the design is set, the delegation decision is fixed. Even if states should change their mind, independent courts are not amenable to ongoing re-contracting politics.

An interesting yet puzzling footnote to this debate is that increasingly ICs are designed with compulsory jurisdiction and non-state actor access (Alter 2006a; Romano 1999). What is driving this turn to enforcement through international courts, and towards private access and compulsory jurisdiction, is a real puzzle. Principal-agent explanations of why states "delegate" to international courts cannot really explain why delegation is more common today compared to the past. Those who do focus on the timing of the trend mainly offer observations that surely are correct: the end of the Cold War likely facilitated the creation of many of the new international courts; the proliferation of regional trade agreements has contributed to a proliferation of international courts operating within specific regions (Romano 1999; Brown 2002). Such explanations do not explain the design trend or really explain the delegation. The closest we come to an explanation of the design trend is the work of James McCall Smith who argues that delegating enforcement to more legalized third-party dispute resolution bodies is associated with deeper trade agreements with more specified obligations and a greater desire by parties to have compliance with the agreement (Smith 2000).

Agent preferences, legitimacy, tasks, and permeability

Elsewhere I show that certain design choices are associated with the delegation of certain judicial roles, suggesting that a functional intent for the court drives judicial design choices (Alter 2006b). But while this "functional explanation" can account for the variation in observed design, the possibility of judicial roles morphing across roles suggests that any delegation to courts is subject to unintended consequences, and the puzzle of why states seem to repeatedly and increasingly be creating ICs they can't control remains unanswered.

HOW STATES LIVE WITH INDEPENDENT INTERNATIONAL COURTS: MOVING BEYOND PRINCIPAL-AGENT THEORY

This chapter offers two separate yet complementary reasons for why recontracting politics will not be the central axis through which states seek to influence ICs. (1) International political factors have led states to create decision rules that make re-contracting tools especially ineffective at shaping international judicial decision-making. (2) The elements of contract design that influence the extent to which ICs will be independent from states do not themselves give rise to re-contracting politics, meaning they are not amenable to re-contracting threats.

Let me add a third argument which I develop in more detail elsewhere (Alter 2005): delegation to trustee-agents may simply be fundamentally different than delegation to agents, giving rise to a different sort of politics. Trustee-agents are defined by three factors.

1. While trustee-agents are empowered by a revocable delegation decision, they are selected because the principal wants to harness the personal reputation or professional norms associated with the trustee-agent. Because trustees value their reputation, they will be guided more by professional norms than by concerns about principal preferences, sometimes dying on their sword rather than be seen as caving to political pressure. This element of trustee behavior helps us understand why the ICJ condemned Ronald Reagan's Nicaragua policy even though it knew the decision would be ignored and that the United States would respond by withdrawing from the ICJ's compulsory jurisdiction.[22]

---

[22] For a discussion of this case, see Alter 2005.

2. Trustees also differ from traditional agents in that they are granted independent decision-making discretion and thus are not expected by others to act as the agent of the principal (Grant and Keohane 2005). Indeed the trustee may in fact be deemed not just more efficient but actually a superior decision-maker, so that efforts cast as "political interference" or exceeding state or principal authority can alienate the trustee's constituency and members of the principal whose support is needed for re-contracting.

3. Trustees have a putative third-party beneficiary who is different from the principal. Because both the trustee and the principal are vying for the political support of the beneficiary, neither the trustee nor the principal can be exclusively focused on what they or each other may most want. I argue that this difference between delegation to agents versus trustees makes re-contracting politics less effective and forces states instead to use rhetorical and legitimacy politics to try to influence ICs (Alter 2005). This trustee argument is consistent with the chapter of this volume by Darren Hawkins and Wade Jacoby who suggest that the selection of an agent is itself important because agents can behave differently from each other even if they are situated in the same re-contracting environment, meaning even if the rules for appointment, reappointment, monitoring, and sanctioning are basically the same.

None of this implies that ICs are not influenced by states, that states are unconcerned about independent ICs, or that ICs are not political actors. The larger point is that re-contracting politics, a privileged tool only the principal can employ, is not where state–IC relations are likely to play themselves out. A number of implications follow from these arguments.

Factors other than principal control tools likely matter more in determining IC independence. While the factors PA theory expects to generate variation (decision rules and informational contexts) may not shape the relative independence of ICs, international law scholars expect access rules and whether or not there is compulsory jurisdiction to be related to IC independence. This list in itself is certainly too narrow if one considers that the European Court of Justice and the Andean Court of Justice are by design institutionally identical yet play very different political roles within the legal common market systems they inhabit (Alter 2006b). Also, the arguments about the greater ability to use appointment and budgeting tools vis-à-vis the ICC suggests that different sorts of legal processes may be amenable to different sorts of political tools – namely that criminal courts may simply be different than ICs that are primarily involved in dispute resolution. Together these arguments suggest that viewing ICs as a single category may in itself be fundamentally flawed. Instead, the political contexts, legal rules themselves, and legal processes themselves may vary by IC and case, and these factors may shape the extent to which ICs can act independently from states.

Because states cannot control ICs, states need other mechanisms to make slippage less problematic. States clearly do care about IC slippage. Thus the question really should be how do states live with the potential for slippage, given that their re-contracting tools provide little protection? I have offered a few suggestive answers to this question. First, states acccpt that exit through non-compliance is an insurance policy for their concerns. Viewing exit as a built-in insurance mechanism can in itself provide insight into the construction of international legal rules and international legal mechanisms.[23] Second, there is a large politics aimed at trying to keep important cases away from ICs, so that ICs do not have an opportunity to issue rulings states do not want. For example, we see the United States going to considerable lengths to negotiate special agreements to try to keep countries from cooperating with any ICC investigation of Americans (Kelley 2005). This politics in no way suggests a lack of IC influence. Rather, states are bargaining in the shadow of the court, negotiating to settle cases outside of court. There is much to suggest that bargaining in a court's shadow (as opposed to in court itself) may present the best prospect of using ICs to influence state behavior (Busch and Reinhardt 2000).

Legitimacy politics may be how states and ICs try to mutually influence each other. Because ICs do not have coercive enforcement powers, they must rely on legitimacy politics as their principal tool of influence. Meanwhile, IC dependence on other's perceptions of their reputation and authority makes international judges subject to legitimacy politics being used against them. A number of implications follow. First, PA theory focuses on the issue of principal control. Once we enter the world of legitimacy politics, we should expect that principals can easily lose control (Hurd 1999, 2005; Risse et al. 1999). Second, the means and

---

[23] Joost Pauwelyn sees this option as part of the WTO dispute resolution system itself, present in the system's reliance on reciprocal sanctions as the main tool of enforcement and also visible in many aspects of WTO law (Pauwelyn 2000, 2005).

modes of legitimacy politics are rhetorical rather than material (Schimmelfennig 2003; Johnston 2001; Müller 2004). Third, in legitimacy politics there may be actors other than states and ICs that may invoke and use these politics. For example, Jonas Tallberg (2002) and Susannah Schmidt (2000) have shown how the EU's Commission employs the EU legal system to influence states; Ian Johnstone (2003) has shown how the UN General Secretary uses international law as a tool of political influence; Ian Hurd (2005) has shown how Libya used the United States' own norms against it; and Margaret Keck and Kathryn Sikkink (1998) have shown how transnational advocacy networks can use legitimacy politics as a tool of influence.

To the extent than these arguments are right, starting from PA theory to understand judicial behavior may be simply unhelpful. PA theory mainly looks at the decision rules for appointments and recontracting and informational disparities to generate variation in the independence of actors, and it expects more independent actors to slip more. Both of these expectations may be wrong. There may be other contextual factors far more important than decision-rules that account for variation in agent behavior (Alter 2000), and even independent actors may have reasons not to aspire to "slip." PA theory as an analytical orientation tends to generate exaggerated expectations about the role of re-contracting politics and about the influence of principals as political actors. Also, precisely because PA theory tries to connect insights about domestic institutions to insights about international institutions, the theory itself may obscure our ability to discern how the nature of international context generates different behavior, leading similar institutional actors to behave differently than their domestic counterparts. While one could try to model ideas like trust, reputation, or concerns about non-compliance into PA models, it is not clear that the framework itself – inspired by the insight of delegation – is the best means toward this end. Indeed there are many ways to make institutions accountable (Grant and Keohane 2005). Why should an analyst privilege re-contracting politics just because delegation takes the form of a revokable contract?

The promise of delegation to ICs, or perhaps the nightmare of some, is that ICs will create a legal and political space where regular politics and the power disparities in the world do not shape outcomes. If delegation to ICs succeeds in creating this space, IC interpretations of international rules will be more authoritative than states auto-interpreting the rules

Agent preferences, legitimacy, tasks, and permeability

to suit their interests, bringing with it a loss in state latitude and autonomy. This is the intent behind delegation to ICs, but it is not an intent or context that PA theory best elucidates. Yet this intent and outcome is important because delegation to ICs changes the international political context. ICs do influence state behavior, and states cannot control ICs. For this reason, the realm which ICs and states share creates an alternative venue in which politics plays itself out, attractive to litigants precisely because states do not control this venue.

PART IV

Directions for future research

12

The logic of delegation to international organizations

DAVID A. LAKE AND MATHEW D. MCCUBBINS

States now delegate substantial policy authority to a host of international organizations (IOs). The chapters in this volume describe patterns of delegation by states to the multilateral development banks (MDBs), the International Monetary Fund (IMF), the European Union (EU), United Nations Security Council (UNSC), the World Trade Organization (WTO), World Health Organization (WHO), and the European Court of Human Rights (ECHR), the European Court of Justice (ECJ), and others. Many of these agents have been delegated greater authority by states – or have carved out greater autonomy for themselves – and are deeply integrated into the structure of global governance.

This chapter does not summarize the preceding chapters, but briefly highlights several themes. We conclude that delegation to IOs is remarkably similar in cause, structure, and effects to delegation within states. Principal-agent (PA) theory, which has proven useful in understanding patterns of delegation in the domestic arena, is equally applicable and powerful in explaining delegation to IOs. Most of the chapters in this volume focus on the design and efficacy of institutions to control agent opportunism; this is largely internal to the relationship between principals and agents. Incorporating the role of third parties (TPs), including the many NGOs that now make up global civil society, is the research frontier. We highlight the role of NGOs as potentially important actors in providing information that is essential to the success of international delegation. Thus, this chapter is an unusual conclusion for a collaborative volume. Rather than looking backwards at the preceding chapters and synthesizing their findings, we mostly look forward and outline the route we believe future research on delegation to IOs ought to follow.

We thank the other editors of this volume for helpful comments.

Directions for future research

DELEGATION, AGENTS, AND AUTONOMY

The Introduction to this volume posits six motives for delegation: (1) specialization and expert knowledge possessed by agents; (2) the presence of policy externalities affecting many states; (3) paradoxes of collective decision-making that can be resolved by granting agenda-setting power to agents; (4) resolving disputes between principals; (5) enhancing policy credibility by yielding authority to agents with more extreme preferences; and (6) locking in policy by creating an autonomous agency. The subsequent chapters do not present systematic tests of these incentives, but adapt the several factors to the problem of delegating to IOs and offer novel extensions tailored to the specific issues or relationships they examine. Nonetheless, these six factors are fundamental to the decision to delegate: without one or more of these attributes, there is little reason to delegate anything to anybody.

A recurring theme of the preceding chapters is that states delegate to IOs, in one form or another, to bolster state credibility. States delegate to IOs to tie their hands and enhance their credibility in the international community (Thompson, Pollack, this volume) and with their domestic publics (Milner, this volume). The other factors appear less prominently across the chapters, but are no less important. Specialization, and especially the need for expert knowledge, is key to the IMF (Gould, Martin, this volume), whereas the EU has received greater authority to cope with policy externalities, disputes, and problems of collective decision-making (Pollack, this volume). Although direct comparisons are not undertaken, the motives for delegation to IOs appear to be similar to those for delegating to other agents in other political arenas.

Like all agents, IOs possess varying autonomy and potential for agency slack. It is impossible to measure slack directly. Indeed, if observable indicators of slack existed, principals – who typically have far more at stake than outside observers – would make sure and rapid use of this information. Nonetheless, it appears that agency autonomy is relatively low in the IMF and MDBs (Broz and Hawes, Martin, Gould, this volume), confirming charges that these IOs are frequently pawns of the developed states. The glaring exception is illustrated by Lyne, Nielson, and Tierney (this volume) where the US attempted to contract bilaterally (rather than through established multilateral channels) with the Inter-American Development Bank. In short, the Bank wasted a large amount of money and the US responded with increased oversight and slashed the budget – both responses consistent with expectations of principal

The logic of delegation to international organizations

behavior when faced with a shirking agent. Agency autonomy appears relatively high in international courts and other dispute resolution bodies (Hawkins and Jacoby, Cortell and Peterson, and Alter).[1] Martin and Gould in separate chapters show how the executive board of the IMF, representing its state principals, has repeatedly altered rules and oversight procedures to ensure staff compliance with their wishes. This is more effective in the areas of loan duration and phasing, Gould finds, because it is easier to monitor staff in those areas than in negotiating conditions. Even Alter, who argues that international courts are highly insulated from their principals, finds a variety of instruments used more or less effectively by states to limit the autonomy of courts. Controlling agents is always imperfect and often difficult, of course. But the analyses in the several chapters above demonstrate clearly, as PA theory would expect, that when IO agents slack member states periodically attempt to improve oversight of and performance by their agents.

Some agency slack is to be expected in all delegation relationships. As Hawkins and Jacoby argue in extending this basic insight, opportunistic agents can use their current autonomy to create greater autonomy for the future. The same factors (see above) that make delegation rewarding for principals also create opportunities for agents to develop autonomy and act against the interests of their principals. Indeed, the greater the gains from delegation, the greater the agency losses principals will tolerate before reverting to unilateralism or international cooperation (see figure 1, ch. 1). In delegating to IOs, as elsewhere, "no pain, no gain."

In turn, some measure of agent autonomy is a prerequisite for states to enhance their credibility, lock-in favored policies, overcome collective decision-making problems, or resolve disputes through delegation. If agents are directly and wholly controlled by their principals, they cannot be used to create commitments, for instance, to policies that their principals might prefer in the long run but not in the short run. Nor can wholly controlled agents settle disputes between their state principals; at the very least, wholly controlled agents would be immobilized between conflicting principals. In our view, the trusteeship status that Alter attributes to courts and claims as outside PA theory is, in fact, fully expected

---

[1] PA theory is a framework, of course, and does not itself specify general propositions about what the agents will do with the autonomy they possess; this depends upon the specific theory used by the analyst to explain observed behavior in the issue area they are examining.

by the theory and follows from the need for substantial autonomy to perform the tasks for which courts are responsible.

Perhaps most distinctly in an international context, the collective decision-making procedures of the principals are central to what gets delegated and to the level of agent autonomy. Unlike the domestic arena where agent actions need only a simple (or occasionally a super-) majority to survive, the international arena is more frequently characterized by weighted super-majority or unanimity voting.[2] This makes it harder to delegate authority to an IO in the first place, since any one country (or group of countries) can veto a change from the status quo, but it also makes it harder to rein in agents once they are duly authorized, as any one beneficiary of the agent's actions can veto proposals by the others to punish the agent or to re-contract (see Hawkins and Jacoby, Cortell and Peterson). The peculiar institutional rules for collective decision-making in many IOs offer important new venues for studying how institutional design, delegation, and autonomy interact.

Overall, it appears that delegation is delegation, whether within states or between states and IOs. The motives, problems, and effects are much the same, with apparent differences being generated by different values of common variables rather than by fundamentally different processes – despite many claims in the extant literature to the contrary.[3] There is little evidence in the chapters above to suggest that problems of agency slack between states and IOs are uniformly more severe than in other delegation relationships. Although it has its limitations, especially the inability to make general claims about what agents do with the autonomy they possess (Gould, Alter), PA theory applies equally well to international delegations as it does to domestic delegations. Delegation "under anarchy" appears to be pretty much the same as delegation in other political forums.

WHEN DOES DELEGATION SUCCEED?

A key issue in all delegation relationships is how principals can know or learn about the actions taken by their agents. Given the ubiquity of

---

[2] Lyne, Nielson, and Tierney (this volume) find that, even under weighted voting, small countries can prove decisive in collective principals.
[3] Waltz (1979) makes the clearest case for the separate "worlds" of domestic and international politics. Mearsheimer (1994) argues that international institutions are fundamentally different.

The logic of delegation to international organizations

agency slack, and indeed the need for agent autonomy for some purposes, when and how can principals decide whether delegating authority to opportunistic agents is "worth it"?

The chapters in this volume emphasize factors internal to the agency relationship in explaining agency slack and success. In some cases, the characteristics of the principals matter: greater agent autonomy typically arises as a consequence of multiple, conflicting principals (Lyne, Nielson, and Tierney, Martin) and consensus decision-making (Cortell and Peterson, Hawkins and Jacoby). Similarly, agent characteristics are also important. Agents are likely to possess greater autonomy when they are limited in number and costly to create de novo (Hawkins and Jacoby), professional (Cortell and Peterson), and possess greater expertise and more information (Martin, Cortell and Peterson). In other circumstances, it is the relationship between principals and agents that is determining, especially the costs of monitoring and control (Gould). Yet, in nearly all instances, these factors are limited to the principal, agent, and their interaction.

In other delegation settings, particularly in the domestic political arena, scholars have recognized that principals have available a larger repertoire of information sources. Just as agents can adapt to their principals, a point stressed by Hawkins and Jacoby, principals can, in turn, anticipate their agent's adaptations. Central to this larger repertoire are TPs who are additional actors and, sometimes, additional agents who can advise principals on the proposals offered by their original agents. Under some circumstances, illustrated in this volume by Thompson's analysis of the UNSC (in this case, another agent), TPs can provide meaningful information on whether actions by an agent improve the welfare of the principal or not, and thus reduce the chances of delegation failure.

In the remainder of this chapter, we sketch out the broader repertoire of strategies available to principals and identify the conditions necessary for them to make welfare-improving choices.[4] To anticipate our conclusions, principals can identify, will choose, and will actually benefit from delegation when:

1. There exist alternative policies that both the principal and the agent prefer to the status quo;

---

[4] This is a reduced form of the arguments developed in Lupia and McCubbins (1998).

2. The agent has an incentive (either because it values a policy more than the status quo or will be sanctioned by the principal otherwise) to propose an alternative that the principal prefers to the status quo; and
3. The principal can distinguish between better and worse alternatives, either because (a) it possesses the knowledge itself necessary to judge the agent's proposed action or (b) it can acquire knowledge (be "enlightened") from some TP; and
4. The principal can acquire knowledge from a TP when (a) the TP is perceived as knowledgeable, (b) the principal perceives a common interest with the TP, (c) external forces (costly effort, verification, or penalties for lying) lead the principal to perceive the TP as trustworthy, and (d) conditions (a) and (b) or (c) are true.

When these conditions are met, there is at least one alternative (or set of alternatives) the principal prefers to the status quo, the agent will propose that alternative (or one from the set of preferred alternatives), and the principal knows enough to accept it. In this case, the delegation occurs and improves the principal's welfare. As a shorthand, we call this a case of "successful" delegation.[5] Given some current status quo, the principal is better off delegating than not and, knowing what she now knows, would make the same choice again in the same circumstance. This is, obviously, a relative standard of success. It does not imply that the principal receives her first best outcome, or that the agent does not slack. Absolute standards are unrealistic. Judging how much slack principals can tolerate or how many costs are imposed on the principal before an act of delegation is deemed "unsuccessful" requires analysts to reach conclusions about preferences, costs, uncertainty, and so on that the parties themselves often cannot measure. All that our definition implies is, given what it knows ex post about the delegation action, the principal would make the same decision again. This conforms with most common language meanings of the term "success." When delegation is successful, we similarly conclude that agents are accountable – that is, they have done, at least in part, what their principals want them to do. In turn,

---

[5] Success is obviously a shorthand here for "improves the principal's welfare relative to the current status quo, net of transactions costs." Transactions costs incurred by principals in delegating authority to agents can be important (Alchian and Demsetz 1972; Jensen and Meckling 1976; Spence 1974; Kiewiet and McCubbins 1991; Laffont and Tirole 1993). Lupia and McCubbins (1998: 91–92) show that the theorems presented in this chapter are robust to including transaction costs.

The logic of delegation to international organizations

delegation fails and agents are not accountable when an agent's actions *reduce* a principal's welfare relative to the status quo.

Common features of delegation relationships

While the chain of delegation must differ from one context to the next, especially from domestic to international political arenas, we argue that all delegations share common features and these features affect the consequences of delegation. As a result, it is possible to draw general conclusions about how *all* acts of delegation work and when they can succeed – including delegations to IOs.

Our theory provides a simple representation of a delegation act to make transparent critical insights about the dynamics common to each link in the chain of delegation. The foundation of our theory is the premise that at least three features are common to each link in the chain of delegation. First, as discussed in the Introduction to this volume, every act of delegation involves a *principal*, the person or actor making a contingent grant of authority, and an *agent*, the person or actor to whom that authority has been granted. Second, as also discussed in the Introduction, every act of delegation contains *the possibility of conflicting interests, asymmetric information (hidden action or hidden information), or both*.

Third, and the point we emphasize here as central to future research on delegation to IOs, principals may be able to adapt to agency problems. When skeptics of delegation proclaim that agents are not accountable, at either the domestic or international levels, they argue implicitly that principals cannot adapt to their limited information (see Barnett and Finnemore 1999, 2004). And although Hawkins and Jacoby are correct to point out that agents can adapt to their principals, and that principals condition their strategies on what they can learn about their agents, they nonetheless fail to consider that principals can anticipate agency adaptations (see Nielson and Tierney 2003a). It is important to recognize that the skeptics reach their conclusions by *assuming* that principals are incapable of (further) adaptation. These claims, as well as other common conjectures about the consequence of delegation, depend on the assumption that principals have no alternatives to ignorance. But principals often can adapt. Given uncertainty about how an agent's actions translate into observable outcomes, discussed in the Introduction, a principal has three ways of obtaining information about her agent's actions: *direct monitoring* of an agent's activities (the principal gathers information herself), attending to the *agent's self-report* of his activities, or attending to *third-party testimony* about the agent's actions. Although each of these options can provide a principal with the knowledge she needs, each option also has serious drawbacks.

Direct monitoring is typically very costly. In this form of police-patrol monitoring, principals are constantly overseeing the actions of their agents (see McCubbins and Schwartz 1984). For a collection of countries to monitor the World Bank, for instance, one or more of its members may need to construct its own agency with expertise in international development lending, dedicate some portion of the staff in that agency to observing the Bank and evaluating whether its programs could be carried out more effectively, and then reporting back to the collection of states on its findings. The observers in this case would be a "shadow" World Bank conducting many of the same studies and evaluations that the Bank itself does in order to determine the efficacy of its lending practices. As discussed in the Introduction to this volume (Hawkins et al.), direct monitoring reduces the gains from specialization that underlie delegation in the first place. Since principals typically have many responsibilities to attend to, direct monitoring of any or all of their agents is often prohibitively costly. Therefore, a principal who wants greater knowledge has a strong incentive to rely on the oral or written testimony of others.

Relying on an agent's self-report is equally problematic because that agent may be reluctant to reveal what he knows (see Lupia and McCubbins 1994a). The problem of hidden information which permits agency slack to arise in the first place cannot be solved simply by mandating the agent to tell the principal all that he knows. In turn, constructing incentives for the agent to reveal his information is difficult, precisely because the principal can never be sure that the agent is, in fact, being truthful. The problem here is analogous to selling knowledge between firms, which is typically subject to profound "market failures" which can only be resolved by internalizing the transaction within a single organization (Caves 1982; Williamson 1985). As long as principals and agents remain distinct and have possibly conflicting interests, problems of asymmetric information are difficult to resolve between the parties themselves.

If direct monitoring is prohibitively costly and agents have no incentive to share expertise, then a principal who wants greater knowledge can get it only from the testimony of a TP.[6] When a principal relies on

---

[6] In this context, a TP (or sometimes below, speaker) is equivalent to an "endorser" in Milner (1997).

third-party testimony, she does not have to pay (directly) the cost associated with direct monitoring. In addition, she may not face the same interest conflicts that keep an agent from revealing what he knows. However, third-party testimony is not a panacea. TPs and principals may also have conflicting interests (e.g. the principal is liberal and the TP is conservative). The TP and principal may, of course, contract to align their incentives more closely.[7] Nonetheless, if the TP has expertise that the principal does not, and if the principal cannot adapt to the TP's advantages, then the principal cannot obtain knowledge from the other party.

These three common factors form the basis of a theory of delegation. We use this theory to identify conditions under which conflicting interests and information asymmetry cause delegation to fail. In the process, we argue that common claims about the failure of delegation, i.e. unaccountability, must be re-evaluated. While we agree with the premise that agents and principals may have conflicting interests, and the premise that agents have information advantages that principals do not, we challenge the claim that principals lack any means for coping with these dilemmas – including principals delegating to IOs. Instead, we find that if a principal has access to the testimony of others and possesses the ability to identify enlightening testimony, then delegation can succeed, i.e. can improve the principal's welfare over the status quo, even if the dilemmas of delegation are present. In sum, the task is to derive, rather than assume, when the ubiquitous conflict of interests and information asymmetries do, and do not, lead delegation to fail.

A model of delegation

Our model of delegation requires three actors – a *principal*, a *TP*, and an *agent*. We represent the agent's actions as the proposal of a single alternative, $x \in [0,1]$, to a commonly known status quo policy, $sq \in [0,1]$. The alternative x is an analogy, for example, to an international agency's formal proposal to change a particular policy, a commission's stance on an issue, or any agent's unspoken plan of action. The principal either accepts the agent's proposal or rejects it in favor of the status quo. One can think of the principal as a collection of states who must decide whether to accept or reject a proposal from an IO to change a particular

---

[7] As long as the wage contract for the TP is independent of the wage contract with the agent, successful delegation may be possible.

Directions for future research

policy, a voter choosing which candidate to vote for, or anyone who must judge the actions of another to whom they delegate.[8] Before the principal makes this choice, the TP provides information about the relative attributes of x and sq. TPs common to domestic political contexts include friends, relatives, co-workers, media organizations, interest groups, political candidates, political parties, bureaucrats, and others. In international contexts, TPs may include other states and national level interest groups, other international organizations, and transnational non-governmental organizations (NGOs). Unless otherwise stated, and we will state otherwise, we assume that all elements of this interaction are common knowledge.

The theory consists of five basic assumptions. We sketch these assumptions here – Lupia and McCubbins (1998) provide a more detailed description.

Assumption 1: The agent, TP, and the principal are goal-oriented.

Each player has an ideal point on $[0, 1]$ and a single-peaked utility function. We assume that each player prefers that the principal chooses the alternative, x or sq, that is closest to its own ideal point.

Assumption 2: The principal is uncertain about which alternative is better for her.

We assume that the principal has beliefs about, but may not know, whether x or sq is closest to its ideal point. Specifically, it knows the location of sq and its own ideal point, p. However, it is uncertain about the location of x.

Assumption 3: The TP makes a statement and can lie.

The TP can make one of two statements to the principal – "the agent's proposal is *better* for you than the status quo" and "the agent's proposal

---

[8] We focus on the case where the principal chooses one of two alternatives because it is simple and common to politics. To see how common this case is, consider the following facts. Parliaments vote many government bills up or down without amendment. Most jury decisions are a choice between one of two litigants or one of two legal points of view. Regulatory decisions often entail simple acceptance or rejection of a single proposal to change the regulatory status quo (for surveys, see Joskow and Noll 1981; Kahn 1988). Of course, voters sometimes choose from three or more alternatives. However, even here binary choice is a good analogy as even here voters could characterize their choice as "candidate A" versus "the other candidates," or "the incumbent" versus "any alternative" (see Simon 1955; March and Simon 1958). In the case of IOs, principals decide whether to authorize the use of force, or not (Thompson), create an international court and give it standing on a particular issue, or not (Alter), and so on. Even where the delegation decision is actually continuous, as in the choice of how much aid to give bilaterally versus multilaterally, the modeling decision is often treated in dichotomous terms (Milner).

The logic of delegation to international organizations

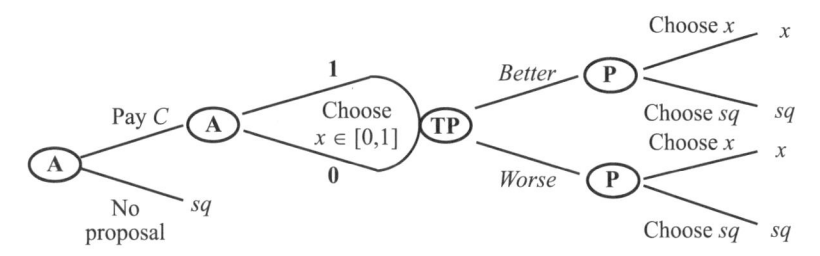

Figure 12.1. Delegation with communication

is *worse* for you than the status quo." The TP need not make a truthful statement.

Assumption 4: The sequence of events.

Figure 12.1 depicts the sequence of events.[9] First, the agent (A) can propose a single alternative, x, to the status quo. Proposing is costly. To make a proposal, the agent must pay the exogenously determined cost, $C \geq 0$ (e.g. conduct a study of x, other possible alternatives, and sq). If the agent does not pay C, then the game ends and each player's payoff is determined by the spatial distance between sq and their own ideal point; the bigger the distance, the smaller the payoff. Second, if the agent pays C, then he proposes x and the game continues.[10] Third, the TP makes its statement (depicted as *Better* or *Worse* in figure 12.1). Fourth, the principal (P) chooses x or sq. Then, the game ends. Each player's payoff is determined by the distance between the alternative that the principal chooses, x or sq, and their own ideal point. The agent's payoff is reduced by C if he makes a proposal.

Assumption 5: The TP has two types: persuasive or not persuasive.

In Assumption 5, we apply the lessons of previous research on learning and communication to define two TP types, called *persuasive* and *not persuasive* (Lupia and McCubbins 1998). When the TP is persuasive, the principal believes his signal and may be able to learn what she needs to know about the agent's proposal. When the TP is not persuasive, the

---

[9] Not pictured is a preliminary stage of the game in which Nature determines the game's initial conditions (i.e. we the analysts learn what the principals and agents want as well as what common knowledge the principal and agent share about their interaction).

[10] Our results are robust without a loss of generality to the case where the agent is uncertain about the consequences of his actions. That is, the effect of communication has the same type of effect on the agent's incentives regardless of whether he knows or is uncertain about the consequences of his actions.

principal ignores the signal. Underlying this definition of the TP's type, are two conditions required for persuasion.

The conditions for persuasion. If the principal lacks information about the agent and wants delegation to succeed (i.e. wants the agent to be accountable), then she must have the ability to learn from others. But learning from others is no trivial matter. Any attempt to learn from others leads to one of three possible outcomes.

- *Enlightenment.* When someone furnishes us with knowledge, we become enlightened. If we initially lack knowledge sufficient for reasoned choice and can obtain such knowledge only from others, then we can make reasoned decisions only if others enlighten us.
- *Deception.* If the testimony we hear reduces our ability to predict accurately the consequences of our actions, we are deceived. For deception to occur, the TP must lie to us *and* we must believe him.
- **The third outcome is that we learn nothing**. When we learn nothing, our beliefs go unchanged and we gain no knowledge.

Both enlightenment and deception, in turn, require persuasion, which is a successful attempt to change the beliefs of another. The key to understanding whether the principal can learn from the TP is to understand the conditions under which persuasion occurs.

Most scholars of communication and politics, dating back to Aristotle, focus on a TP's *internal character* (e.g. honesty, ideology, or reputation) as a necessary condition for persuasion. If a TP lacks the right character, then these scholars conclude that the TP will not be persuasive. Lupia and McCubbins (1998) argue that persuasion need not be contingent upon personal character; rather, *persuasion requires that a listener perceive a TP to be both knowledgeable and trustworthy*. While a perception of trust can arise from a positive evaluation of a TP's character, Lupia and McCubbins show that *external forces can substitute for character*, and can thus generate persuasion in contexts where it would not otherwise occur. Moreover, when these forces give the principal an accurate perception of the TP's interests, then these forces generate enlightenment as well. Institutions can create precisely the external forces needed in order to make a TP appear knowledgeable and trustworthy.

Three external forces affect what the principal and TP say and do, or that can make the TP "trustworthy" to the principal. The first force is *verification*, or whether or not the principal can verify the statement of the TP. We represent verification as follows: after the TP speaks, but before the principal chooses, nature reveals to the principal (with some probability) whether x is better or worse for her. In words, we examine the case where TP statements can be verified as true or false before the principal makes her choice. "Nature" here is obviously a reduced form model of a much more complicated process. Nonetheless, it is sufficient for us to establish this first external force.

The second force is *penalties for lying*, represented as a cost that the TP must pay when it sends a false signal. This penalty directly affects the TP's utility. Our motivation for focusing on penalties for lying are the explicit fines levied on people who lie (e.g. in cases of perjury) and the losses in valued reputations for honesty that result from being caught making false statements.[11]

The third external force is *observable, costly effort* that the TP must pay to send any signal. Intuitively, there is a cost for almost any cognitive task, and speaking is no exception. In addition, TPs can undertake more or less costly efforts to make their voices heard. In the international context, TPs can hire or sponsor high level commissions of prominent (and highly paid) experts, conduct publicity events, or even mobilize members of associations – all understood in other theoretical contexts as forms of mass participation designed to pressure political leaders but which can be understood here as costly and observable efforts to exercise voice (Keck and Sikkink 1998).

Verification, penalties for lying, and costly effort cover the range of effects that external forces can have on communication. Verification affects the manner in which the principal receives the TP's statement. It is independent of any costs associated with making statements. Both penalties for lying and costly effort affect the TP's costs and are independent of the manner in which the signal is received. Penalties for lying are a simple example of statement specific costs. Costly effort is an example of communication costs that are independent of what is said.

From the theory, we find that the following conditions are individually necessary and collectively sufficient for persuasion:

- The principal must perceive the TP to be trustworthy and the principal must perceive the TP to have the knowledge she desires.

---

[11] While we focus on the case where these costs are common knowledge, our results are robust to the assumption that the principal is uncertain about them. Note also that other statement specific costs, such as rewards or penalties for telling the truth, have similar dynamics.

Directions for future research

- Absent external forces, persuasion requires perceived common interests and perceived TP knowledge. In the presence of external forces, these requirements can be reduced. As the likelihood of verification, the magnitude of the penalty for lying, or the magnitude of costly effort increase, the extent to which perceived common interests are required decreases. In other words, with respect to persuasion, external forces can be substitutes for common interests (and for each other).

Conditions for successful delegation

There are two general conditions that determine the outcome of delegation, and a set of more precise conditions that determine when each of the two general conditions is satisfied. The first general condition for successful and thus accountable delegation is the *knowledge condition*. The knowledge condition is fulfilled if and only if the principal can correctly infer whether the agent's proposal is better or worse for her than the status quo. The second general condition is the *incentive condition*. To satisfy the incentive condition, the agent must have an incentive to make a proposal that is better for the principal than the status quo. This second requirement is satisfied if either the agent and principal have common interests or if external forces motivate the agent to propose an alternative that is better than the status quo for both he and the principal. The relationship between delegation and these two general conditions in our model is as follows:

Theorem 1: *If both the knowledge and the incentive conditions are satisfied, then delegation succeeds. If neither condition is satisfied, then delegation fails.*

If both conditions are satisfied, then the agent makes a proposal that enhances the principal's welfare and the principal knows enough to accept it. In this case, the outcome of delegation is better for the principal than the status quo – delegation succeeds. When neither condition is satisfied, the principal cannot hold the agent accountable for his actions and the agent has no incentive to increase the principal's welfare – delegation fails.

If *only one* of the two conditions is satisfied, then the worst that can happen, from the principal's perspective, is the retention of the status quo. To see this, consider two cases. First, if only the knowledge condition is satisfied, the principal knows enough about the agent's proposal to base its decision on whether the proposal is better or worse for it than the status quo. In this case, it can reject any welfare-reducing proposal and no delegation will occur. Therefore, the worst outcome it can obtain is the status quo. Alternatively, if only the incentive condition is satisfied, then the agent makes a proposal that improves the principal's welfare. In this case, if the principal rejects the proposal, it gets the status quo and no delegation occurs, otherwise it does better.

The knowledge condition requires that the principal distinguish whether the agent's proposal is better or worse for it than the status quo.

Theorem 2: *The knowledge condition is satisfied only if:*

- *the principal's prior knowledge is sufficient for her to distinguish proposals that are better for her than is the status quo from proposals that are worse for her; or*
- *she can learn enough to make the same distinctions. When the principal initially lacks knowledge, the conditions for persuasion and enlightenment are necessary for the satisfaction of the knowledge condition.*

Recall that delegation is accountable if both the knowledge and the incentive conditions are satisfied and fails if neither is satisfied. Therefore, Theorems 1 and 2 imply the following: if the incentive condition *and both* of Theorem 2's two conditions fail, then delegation is not accountable. By contrast, the consequence of delegation is no worse than the status quo for the principal if *either* of the two conditions in Theorem 2 *or* the incentive condition is satisfied. Moreover, if the incentive condition *and either* of the two conditions in Theorem 2 is satisfied, then delegation is accountable.

These two theorems also imply that *the principal need not know very much about what her agents are doing in order to ensure accountable delegation.* For example, if the incentive condition is satisfied and either the principal has sufficient prior knowledge about the consequences of the agent's proposal *or* gains enough knowledge by observing the agent's costly effort *or* is sufficiently enlightened by the TP's testimony, then delegation is accountable.

The incentive condition requires that the agent offer a proposal that makes the principal better off than does the status quo.

Theorem 3: *The incentive condition is satisfied only if:*

- *the principal's ideal point is closer to the agent's ideal point than it is to the status quo and the agent gains more than C if the principal chooses his proposal instead of the status quo, or*

- *the knowledge condition is satisfied and there exists a point that both the principal and the agent (after paying C) prefer to the status quo. (If the principal initially lacks knowledge, then the conditions for persuasion and the conditions for enlightenment are the keys to the satisfaction of the knowledge condition.)*

To see why Theorem 3 is true, consider the following. In our model, the agent must weigh the costless option of making no proposal against the costly option of making a proposal. Therefore, it is always better for him to propose nothing than to propose something that is worse for him than the status quo. Put another way, a necessary condition for the satisfaction of the incentive condition is that there be at least one alternative that is better for the principal than the status quo and that the agent prefers to the status quo so much that he is willing to pay C to achieve it. If no such alternative exists, then any proposal that is better than the status quo for the agent leaves the principal worse off than the status quo and vice versa.

If the agent's ideal point is better for the principal than the status quo and allows the agent to recover the costs of proposing it, then, in equilibrium, he proposes it when he makes a proposal. We call this the Interest Condition. If the agent's ideal point does not fit this description, then satisfaction of the incentive condition requires a knowledgeable principal. This can be achieved when the principal learns from a persuasive speaker or TP.

Stated intuitively, when the agent faces a principal who can distinguish better proposals from worse proposals, then he knows that proposing any point that is worse for the principal than the status quo, including his own ideal point, leads to the status quo as the outcome of delegation. In these conditions, the agent should only make a proposal that makes both himself and the principal better off relative to the status quo. By contrast, if the same agent faces a principal who is incapable of distinguishing worse from better proposals, then he has no incentive to make a proposal that benefits the principal. Therefore, when there exists a proposal that both the principal and agent (after paying C) prefer to the status quo, satisfaction of the knowledge condition is also sufficient for satisfaction of the incentive condition.

In figure 12.2, we diagram Lupia and McCubbins's conclusions about the relationship between persuasion, enlightenment, and delegation. The direction of causality is from left to right. For example, the relationship between penalties for lying and successful delegation is as

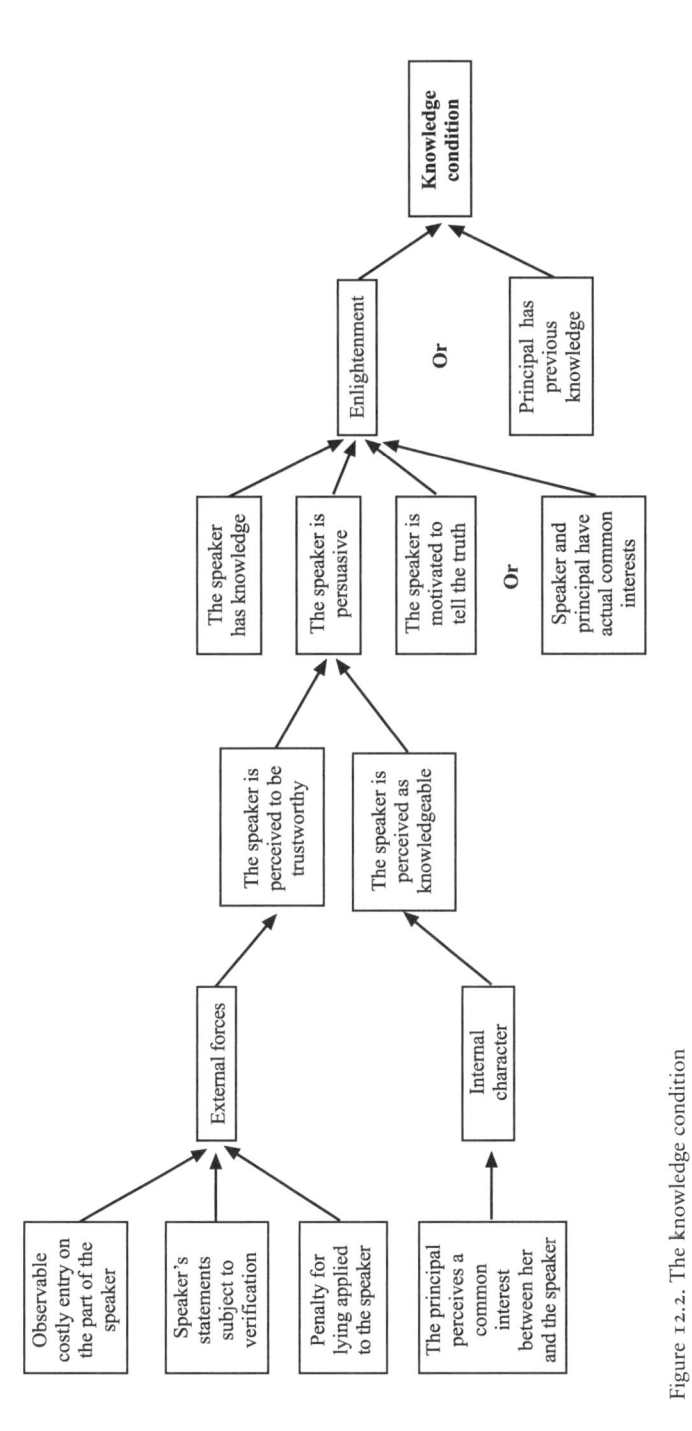

Figure 12.2. The knowledge condition

Directions for future research

follows: "Penalties for lying applied to the speaker" are left of, and have an arrow pointing to, "The speaker is perceived to be trustworthy"; "The speaker is perceived to be trustworthy" is a step to the right and has an arrow pointing to, "The speaker is persuasive"; "The speaker is persuasive" has an arrow pointing to "Enlightenment," which, in turn, has an arrow pointing to the "Knowledge Condition." The lesson of following this particular path is that penalties for lying can produce successful delegation.

A more general lesson is that we can compare the likelihood of successful delegation in two or more international organizations by comparing the extent to which the concepts at the terminal branches on the left hand side of figure 12.2 characterize each setting. That is, if we could enumerate the extent to which factors such as "observable costly effort" and "speaker has knowledge," are at work, then we could rank order these international organizations in terms of their conduciveness to successful delegation.

Together, Theorems 1 through 3 imply, and figure 12.2 shows, that there are many routes to successful delegation. Many of them provide the principal with ways to adapt to her limited information. For example, delegation fails only if all of Theorem 2's conditions and Theorem 3's conditions fail. By contrast, delegation succeeds if any of the conditions in Theorem 2 and any of the conditions in Theorem 3 are satisfied. Theorems 1, 2, and 3 reveal myriad ways to make delegation succeed, some of which require the principal to have very little information. Thus, it is the possibility of enlightenment by any number of means, and not necessarily principals who have expertise, that provides the sturdy ground upon which successful delegation can be constructed.

As diagrammed in figure 12.3, it follows that if the knowledge condition *and both* of Theorem 3's conditions fail, then delegation fails. By contrast, the consequence of delegation is no worse than the status quo if *at least one of the two* conditions in Theorem 3 *or* the knowledge condition is satisfied. Moreover, if the knowledge condition *and any* of the conditions in Theorem 3 are satisfied, then delegation is accountable.

DELEGATION AND INTERNATIONAL ORGANIZATIONS

Having identified the conditions necessary for success in a generic model of delegation, intended to apply to all arenas of social interaction, we now turn to three specific characteristics of delegation that may (or may not) be more common in international relations and form possible

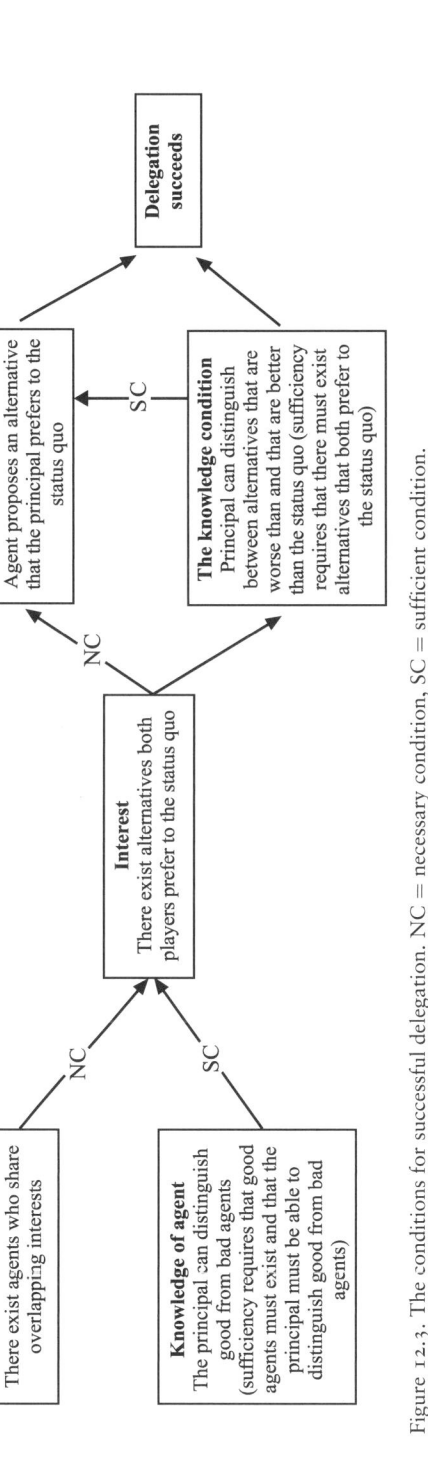

Figure 12.3. The conditions for successful delegation. NC = necessary condition, SC = sufficient condition.

objections to our model as applied to IOs. We find little reason to believe that delegation to IOs is different – or more difficult – than other delegation relationships. Although circumstances differ and the concerns manifested in these possible objections may sometimes hold, if the knowledge and incentive conditions are satisfied principals cannot be made worse off than the status quo even when delegating to IOs.

Possible Objection #1: There are fewer TPs qualified to "speak" about IO agents than about domestic agents.
The domestic political arena is rich with competing agencies and affected interest groups who can send costly signals to principals about an agent's proposal. It might be argued that fewer such TPs exist at the international level, potentially crippling the ability of principals to be enlightened about their agents. Although true that, in some issue areas, the international political arena may not be as institutionally and organizationally diverse as similar domestic arenas, there are nonetheless likely to be a sufficiently large number of potential TPs for three reasons.

Our theory requires that only one TP be able to signal a principal whether an agent's proposal is better or worse for her than the status quo. It does not require multiple parties. These single TPs, in turn, can take many forms, including national-level actors willing to pay the cost of observable effort to become informed about or make their voice heard about proposals by IO agents. TPs must, of course, themselves meet the knowledge and incentive conditions, and their compensation (if any) cannot be linked to that of the agent. These are non-trivial requirements that limit the number of TPs in any venue. But given that national-level TPs can be qualified to speak about proposals by IOs, there is no particular reason to expect that principals searching for information about international agents are necessarily handicapped relative to their purely domestic counterparts.

Moreover, with the growth of international civil society over the last decades (Keck and Sikkink 1998; Boli and Thomas 1999), and the explosion in the number of transnational NGOs, IOs, and other international actors, the pool of potential TPs has grown enormously. As a subject for future research, it may be that the expansion in the number of possible international TPs has facilitated the trend toward greater delegation in international relations (Goldstein et al. 2001). Indeed, it is likely that principals now find themselves not with a shortage of possible TPs but a cacophony of competing voices.

The logic of delegation to international organizations

In addition, states can always choose to create their own TPs – at some cost – to evaluate the proposals of IOs. This may be especially important in areas touching on national security issues, where information is more tightly held by both state principals and IO agents. In the case of weapons inspections regimes, for instance, the great powers retain extensive national agencies of their own to monitor the behavior of foreign states directly and as a check on the accuracy of reports by IOs. At one level, these national agencies may appear to be redundant capabilities that vitiate some or all of the gains from specialization that underlie delegation to IOs in the first place. As TPs, however, these national agencies gain new – indeed, essential – importance. With preferences closely aligned with their national principals, and distinct from those of IOs, these national TPs help resolve the paradox of why some of the most autonomous IO agents with some of the most significant delegated powers are found in the weapons inspection and arms control areas – issues over which we might expect states to be extremely reluctant to delegate authority (see Brown forthcoming).

In summary, since only one TP is, in principle, necessary for delegation to be successful, but the pool of TPs available at the international level is large (including many national level organizations) and growing, we find little reason to expect that delegation to IOs is likely to be less successful, on average, than delegation to domestic agents.

Possible Objection #2: Delegation to IOs is more often characterized by multiple principals, relative to delegation to domestic agents, and this creates the potential for greater agency slack.
Lyne, Nielson, and Tierney (this volume) develop the distinction between collective and multiple principals and examine the consequences of these different agency relationships for delegation. In collective principals, the members come to a joint decision (according to some rule) and then enter into a single contract with an agent, much as Congress, for instance, acts as a collective in deciding to delegate to an internal committee or the president. Similarly, states collectively set health policy and then delegate to the staff of the World Health Organization certain investigatory powers, including the ability to issue health and travel advisories (Cortell and Peterson). With multiple principals, each principal enters into a separate contract with the same agent, a relationship often thought to characterize federal agencies responsible to both Congress and the executive or, in an international context, the European Commission as a single agent reporting to both the Council of Ministers

Directions for future research

a. Delegation with multiple principals is possible

```
———+————+————+————+————+————
   Q    P₁    P*    A          P₂
```

b. Delegation with multiple principals is impossible

```
———+————+————+————+————+————
   P₁       Q         A         P₂
```

Figure 12.4. Delegation with multiple principals

and the European Parliament (Pollack, this volume). Clearly, both forms exist at both the domestic and international levels. In the absence of a systematic census of agency relationships, we are agnostic about which form is more common in either arena. Informally, although it is relatively easy for us to think of examples of collective principals delegating to IOs, it is harder to identify cases of true multiple principals.[12]

But even if multiple principals are more common relative to collective principals, the consequences for successful delegation are not necessarily more severe. In a case of multiple principals, the agent's incentives will be structured by the preferences of the principals, and the rules regarding their collective decisions and actions. Importantly, however, if the principals satisfy the knowledge condition – and both possess an ex post veto over the agent's policy choices, as in the model above – they can be made no worse off than the status quo under any conceivable preference ordering. This is best shown by example, as in figure 12.4.

Suppose there are two principals, and both must agree to the agent's action for the agent's choice to affect policy. If both principals are able to satisfy the knowledge condition, then the agent must satisfy both principals simultaneously. This may be possible, although difficult, if the status quo (Q) lies outside the ideal points of the principals, denoted P_1 and P_2, as in figure 4a. In figure 4a, where policies and ideal points are

---

[12] The closest analog to multiple principals is the practice of voluntary contributions to IOs, as opposed to assessed dues, that allow each member to make their payments contingent on certain activities or conditions.

assumed to line up on a single spatial dimension, A is the agent's ideal point, while P_1 and P_2 are the ideal points of the two principals. In this example, the agent would propose a policy, p*, that makes the first principal (P_1) only slightly better off than the status quo. P_1 would therefore accept p*. The second principal (P_2) would also accept p*, as it is closer to its ideal point than is the status quo, Q. More generally, whenever the status quo lies outside the range bounded by the ideal points of the principals, some proposal by the agent is possible, and if the principals satisfy the knowledge condition, the proposal will be accepted if made. Whether the agent chooses to make a proposal, however, depends on its preferences (and the costs of making the proposal). If A lies to the left of Q, no proposal will be made, leaving the principals with the status quo. If A lies to the right of Q, a proposal is possible.

On the other hand, if the status quo lies inside the range bounded by the ideal points of the principals, no proposal made by the agent would be preferred by both principals to the status quo. If both principals possess an ex post veto, the agent will always choose not to make a proposal. If preferences are aligned as in figure 4b, where Q is interior to [P_1, P_2], then the agent would find it impossible to make an acceptable choice and would therefore choose not to participate. Any proposal to the left of Q would be vetoed by P_2, and any proposal to the right of Q would be vetoed by P_1. This is the classic illustration of gridlock under divided government (McCubbins 1985, Epstein and O'Halloran 1999b). Whenever the status quo lies inside the range bounded by the ideal points of the principals, no proposal will be preferred by both principals and the agent, if it bears any cost at all in making a proposal, will choose not to do so.

The important conclusion here is that even when multiple principals exist, delegation can be successful as long as both principals satisfy the knowledge condition and possess an ex post veto. Moreover, even in delegation relationships with multiple principals when agency slack is normally expected to be a significant problem, if the several principals can satisfy the knowledge condition they can never be made worse off than the status quo by opportunistic agents. The status quo may not be a desired outcome for one or more principals, of course, but their unhappiness stems not from agency losses but from policy preferences that render cooperation impossible. This is, no doubt, a demanding set of conditions that may not always be met in the real world, but in principle the requirements for successful delegation can be met even when multiple principals exist. And, again, although the conditions may be severe, they are no more stringent in the case of delegation to IOs than in delegation to domestic agents.

Possible Objection #3: *The chain of delegation is longer in international than in domestic context and, therefore, more likely to fail.*
A "chain" of delegation involves multiple stages in which the same authority is granted conditionally from one actor to another (Nielson and Tierney 2003a). In the simplest case of two "links," the originating or "ultimate" principal (P_1) delegates to an agent (A_1), who in turn becomes a principal (P_2) and delegates to a second agent (A_2). In practice, delegation chains can be quite long. As individuals, for instance, we may hire an attorney to represent us in a lawsuit; our attorney, in turn, may hire a variety of associates to handle parts of the case; an associate may hire an investigator to acquire additional information. In this not uncommon relationship – albeit one in which we hope never to find ourselves – there are at least four links in the chain. The investigator is, in some sense, our agent, but only through the preceding links. Intuitively, it would seem that the potential for agency slack is very much greater the longer the delegation chain. Also intuitively, it might appear that delegation chains involving or ending with IOs must necessarily be longer than wholly domestic chains. On these grounds, states – and their ultimate principals, citizens – may be justifiably skeptical of delegation to IOs.

Our theory provides precise conditions for assessing the first intuition on increasing agency slack. Delegation can succeed in the serial fashion just described if and only if each principal at each stage satisfies the knowledge and incentives conditions for its immediate agent. In our relatively "short" chain with two links above, if the incentive and knowledge conditions are met, A_2 chooses to make proposal x, A_1/P_2 knows enough to whether to accept it (pass it on to P_1) or reject it (retain the status quo), and P_1 in turn knows enough whether to accept or reject it as well. If neither the incentive nor the knowledge condition is satisfied at any stage, delegation will fail. As above, if only one of the two conditions holds at any stage, the worst that can happen from P_1's perspective is that the status quo is retained. In our theory, therefore, as long as the knowledge and incentive conditions are met at every link, delegation can succeed regardless of the length of the chain.[13] We note, however,

---
[13] Note that in the model the principal always moves last or possesses an ex post veto over the agent's proposal. The theorems above – and extended here – hold only for

that satisfying the knowledge and incentive conditions at each link in a chain is an extremely demanding requirement, and one that becomes progressively less likely to be met as delegation chains become longer. Despite the difficulty of satisfying these demanding conditions for success, it is important to recognize that delegation is made through very long chains every day, which suggests that the problems are not insurmountable. Focusing on the knowledge and incentive conditions, however, sharpens the intuition behind claims that longer chains are more likely to fail. It is not the length of the chain per se that matters, but rather whether the knowledge and incentives conditions are met in the way described above.

If the knowledge and incentives conditions are less likely to be met in longer delegation chains, is this more of a problem for international or domestic delegations? Once again, we do not find obvious reasons to believe that the differences between international and domestic arenas are great – and certainly no general conclusion can be sustained without detailed empirical investigation. Principals, agents, and delegation itself are analytic concepts or analogies imposed by theorists to help classify and explain real world relationships. Principals and agents – and what constitutes an act of delegation – are defined by the analyst, not the parties themselves. This holds as well for the number of links in a delegation chain. It is possible to disaggregate many delegation acts into numerous parts, and thereby create longer chains. At one level, analysts write of Congress delegating United States foreign assistance policy to the Agency for International Development (USAID). At another level, however, it might be accurate to describe Congress as delegating to the political appointees who direct USAID, who then delegate to senior staff, who then delegate to regional or country experts, who then delegate to USAID employees stationed abroad who first propose projects for funding. The actual delegation is the same in both cases, but the second

---

the sequence of moves stated in Assumption 4 and depicted in figure 12.1. It seems intuitive that in longer chains of delegation, the ultimate principal (P_1 in our example) may not possess an ex post veto, in which case our theory is silent on the prospects for success. This may account for the common political principle that delegated authority cannot itself be delegated (Hamilton *Federalist 78*; Stewart 1975; Fisher 1985). For a recent exchange on the topic of international delegation, see Golove (2003), who argues that further delegation is not inconsistent with early constitutional thought, and Bradley (2003), who argues that such delegations can only entail non-self-executing treaty commitments (i.e. in our terms, only when the principal retains an ex post veto).

chain is described as being much longer. What chain length we describe depends on the analytic purpose for which the description is being used. As always, analysts must make "bets" on which links – and how many – are salient to the question they are asking (Lake and Powell 1999: 13–16).

As analytic constructs rather than "real" entities, it is impossible to conclude that delegation chains that include IOs are always longer than chains that end with domestic agents. We can again write that Congress has delegated authority over elements of development aid to the World Bank, which it does by passing authorizing and appropriating funds that are transferred to that agent – a simple one-link chain. But as above, we could greatly multiply the apparent number of links by including a host of intermediate steps between the passage of legislation in the United States and the ultimate dispersal of aid in developing countries. To argue that one chain is longer than another refers far more to our analytic purposes than to any fixed or absolute trait of an act of delegation.

One crucial difference between delegation to domestic and international agents, however, is that the latter often involves a "pooling" of sovereignty prior to the hiring of an agent. Although often confused with the length of the delegation chain, this is a distinct issue. In domestic acts of delegation, there is typically only one stage at which a collective principal aggregates "lower level" preferences and sets policy goals whose implementation may then be delegated to specialized agents. Voters, the ultimate principals in a democracy, elect representatives to the legislature, which then sums (through various rules and with more or less bias) the preferences of citizens into policy. The legislature may then choose to delegate implementation to an executive, directly to agencies, or even to municipalities and other lower levels of government. But importantly, there is only one "summation" point at which a collective decision is being made.

At the international level, however, there is in the case of collective principals a second summation point – often described as a pooling of sovereignty. Outside of the European Union and especially the European Parliament, which serves to sum preferences directly from voters, most delegations to IOs proceed through two summation points: first, from citizens through their government and, second, from governments through IOs. Collectively, the members of the IO may choose to delegate authority to that organization and its staff or to other IO agents to implement policy. The second summation point, however, is quite likely to produce a collective policy for the member states that is different from the ideal policy determined at the national level. This is not, directly, a problem of the length of the chain, but of the unique nature of the second summation point. To return to the aid example above, from the perspective of American voters and their elected representatives, the key difference between delegating to USAID and the World Bank is not the number of bureaus between the appropriation of funds and the delivery of aid, but rather that the Bank's collective decision-making structure takes into account the policy preferences of states other than their own – even despite the disproportionate influence of the United States within the latter organization. Indeed, as Milner and Thompson show in their chapters above, it is precisely the difference in ideal points between a state and the collective principal that allows delegation to the IO to create a credible commitment or screen other agents. This second summation problem need not preclude effective – and successful – delegation. But for clarity, it is important to recognize that the consequences of pooling sovereignty are distinct from the length of the delegation chain.

CONCLUSION

Delegation is a necessary component of modern international relations, and many people believe its success depends on the answer to the question, "When is delegation accountable?" We have shown that accountability in delegation depends on two conditions: the knowledge condition and the incentive condition. The satisfaction of both conditions turns on whether or not the principal can become enlightened, which itself depends on the conditions for persuasion and the conditions for enlightenment. Only when these latter conditions fail, does the principal's limited information and the strong tendency of principals and agents to have conflicting interests imply that delegation must fail to be accountable. Otherwise, accountability is possible, if not always likely.

Even though successful delegation is possible, it does not mean it is easy. The knowledge and incentive conditions can be satisfied, but not always. Nonetheless, from everyday interactions to national level policy-making, delegation is a common occurrence. Third-party testimony is an important part of successful delegation. The same is true for delegation to IOs. Indeed, we see no inherent reason why delegation to IOs should be more difficult than delegation to other types of agents. State principals must be mindful of the knowledge and incentive conditions, but this is true of all possible delegations.

Directions for future research

This chapter has emphasized the role of third parties in the success of delegation. As noted, this theme does not figure prominently in the chapters above. There has been an explosion of interest recently in NGOs and other transnational interest groups. They are often understood as purveyors of international norms who shape and alter the preferences of citizens and states (Keck and Sikkink 1998; Boli and Thomas 1999). Less frequently, NGOs are described as crucial fire alarms in monitoring compliance with international treaty obligations (Raustiala 1997). The study of delegation, and our model in particular, suggests that NGOs and other actors in "global civil society" may be equally or even more important in monitoring IOs in the exercise of delegated authority. By helping states satisfy the knowledge condition, NGOs increase the chances for successful delegation and, in turn, increase the prospects for international cooperation. They do so not by changing preferences, as sometimes supposed, but by enriching the information available to state principals. This volume focuses attention on PA theory and delegation, and emphasizes factors internal to the agency relationship. As PA theory has developed in other contexts, attention has turned to how principals can improve oversight and control by incorporating "outside" sources of information. The role of third parties in delegation is a promising avenue for future research in international relations as well.

References

Abbott, Kenneth W. and Duncan Snidal. 1998. Why States Act Through Formal International Organizations. *Journal of Conflict Resolution* 42 (1): 3–32.
  2000. Hard and Soft Law in International Governance. *International Organization* 54 (summer): 421–56.
Alchian, Armen and Harold Demsetz. 1972. Production, Information Costs, and Economic Organization. *American Economic Review* 62: 777–95.
Alesina, Alberto and David Dollar. 2000. Who Gives Foreign Aid to Whom and Why? *Journal of Economic Growth* 5: 33–63.
Alexandrova, Olga. 1991. Soviet Policy in the Gulf Conflict. *Aussenpolitik* 42 (3): 231–40.
Alter, Karen J. 2000. The European Legal System and Domestic Policy: Spillover or Backlash. *International Organization* 54 (3): 489–518.
  2001. *Establishing the Supremacy of European Law: The Making of an International Rule of Law in Europe.* Oxford: Oxford University Press.
  2003. Resolving or Exacerbating Disputes? The WTO's New Dispute Resolution System. *International Affairs* 79, 4 (summer): 783–800.
  2005. Agents or Trustees: International Courts in their Political Context. Unpublished manuscript.
  2006a. Exporting the European Court of Justice Model: The Experience of the Andean Common Market Court of Justice. Unpublished manuscript.
  2006b. Private Litigants and the New International Courts. *Comparative Political Studies* 39(1): 22–49.
Alter, Karen J. and Sophie Meunier-Aitsahalia. 1994. Judicial Politics in the European Community: European Integration and the Pathbreaking *Cassis de Dijon* decision. *Comparative Political Studies* 24 (4): 535–61.
Alvarez, Jose. 2003. The New Dispute Settlers: (Half) Truths and Consequences. *Texas International Law Journal* 38 (3): 405–41.
Ansolabehere, Stephen, John de Figueiredo, and James M. Snyder, Jr. 2003. Why is There so Little Money in US Politics? *Journal of Economic Perspectives* 17 (1) (winter): 105–30.
Arnold, R. Douglas. 1992. *The Logic of Congressional Action.* New Haven, Conn.: Yale University Press.

References

Arvin, B. Mak. 2002. *New Perspectives on Foreign Aid and Economic Development.* Westport, Conn.: Praeger.

Åslund, Anders. 2000. *Russia and the International Financial Institutions.* Washington, DC: Carnegie Endowment for International Peace.

Aufricht, Hans. 1964. *The International Monetary Fund: Legal Bases, Structure, Functions.* London: Steven and Sonds.

Azzam, Maha. 1991. The Gulf Crisis: Perceptions in the Muslim World. *International Affairs* 67 (3): 473–85.

Bacchus, James. 2001. The Role of Lawyers in the WTO. *Vanderbilt Journal of Transnational Law* 34 (4): 953–62.

——— 2002. Table Talk: Around the Table of the Appellate Body of the World Trade Organization. *Vanderbilt Journal of Transnational Law* 35 (4): 1021–39.

——— 2003. Leeky's Circle: Thoughts from the Frontier of International Law. Address to the Institute of Advanced Legal Studies, University of London, London, 10 April.

——— 2004. Open Doors for Open Trade: Shining Light on WTO Dispute Settlement. *Remarks to the National Foreign Trade Council*, Mayflower Hotel, Washington, DC, January 29.

Bailey, Michael. 2001. Quiet Influence: The Representation of Diffuse Interests on Trade Policy, 1983–1994. *Legislative Studies Quarterly* (February): 45–80.

Baker, James with Thomas DeFrank. 1995. *The Politics of Diplomacy.* New York: G. P. Putnam's Sons.

Baldwin, David A. 1985. *Economic Statecraft.* Princeton, NJ: Princeton University Press.

Baldwin, Robert E. and Christopher S. Magee. 2000. *Congressional Trade Votes: From NAFTA Approval to Fast-Track Defeat.* Washington, DC: Institute for International Economics.

Balogh, Thomas. 1967. Multilateral versus Bilateral Aid. *Oxford Economic Papers* 19 (3): 332–44.

Barnett, Michael N. 2002. *Eyewitness to a Genocide.* Ithaca, NY: Cornell University Press.

Barnett, Michael N. and Martha Finnemore. 1999. The Politics, Power, and Pathologies of International Organizations. *International Organization* 54 (4): 699–732.

——— 2004. *Rules for the World: International Organizations in Global Politics.* Ithaca, NY: Cornell University Press.

Barro, Robert. 1998. The IMF Doesn't Put Out Fires, It Starts Them. *Business Week* (December 7): 18.

Barro, Robert J. and Jong-Wha Lee. 2002. IMF Programs: Who is Chosen and What are the Effects? NBER Working Paper 8951. Cambridge, Mass.: National Bureau of Economic Research.

Bawn, Kathleen. 1995. Political Control Versus Expertise: Congressional Choices about Administrative Procedures. *American Political Science Review* 89: 62–73.

Bendor, Jonathan, A. Glazer, and Thomas Hammond. 2001. Theories of Delegation. *Annual Review of Political Science* 4: 235–69.

References

Bergman, Torbjorn, Wolfgang Müller, and Kaare Strøm. 2000. Parliamentary Democracy and the Chain of Delegation. *European Journal of Political Research* 37(3): 255–60. Special issue.

Berkov, Robert. 1957. *The World Health Organization: A Study in Decentralized International Administration.* Geneva: Librairie E. Droz.

Bernheim, B. Douglas and Michael D. Whinston. 1986. Common Agency. *Econometrica* 54, 4 (July): 923–42.

Beschloss, Michael and Strobe Talbott. 1993. *At the Highest Levels.* Boston: Little, Brown.

Bhagwati, Jagdish N. 2002. *The Wind of the Hundred Days: How Washington Mismanaged Globalization.* Cambridge, Mass.: MIT Press.

Bird, Graham. 1996. The International Monetary Fund and Developing Countries: A Review of the Evidence and Policy Options. *International Organization* 50 (summer): 477–511.

Bird, Graham and Dane Rowlands. 2001. IMF Lending: How is it Affected by Economic, Political, and Institutional Factors? *Journal of Policy Reform* 4 (3): 243–70.

Blackburn, Robert and Jörg Polakiewicz. 2001. *Fundamental Rights in Europe: The European Convention on Human Rights and its Member States, 1950–2000.* Oxford: Oxford University Press

Blix, Hans. 2004. *Disarming Iraq.* New York: Pantheon.

Boli, John and George M. Thomas. 1999. *Constructing World Culture: International Nongovernmental Organizations since 1875.* Stanford, Calif.: Stanford University Press.

Bordo, Michael D. and Harold James. 2000. The International Monetary Fund: Its Present Role in Historical Perspective. NBER Working Paper 7724 (June): 1–57.

Boughton, James M. 2001. *Silent Revolution: The International Monetary Fund, 1979–1989.* Washington, DC: International Monetary Fund.

Bradley, Curtis A. 2003. International Delegations, the Structural Constitution, and Non-Self-Execution. *Stanford Law Review* 55, 5 (May): 1557–96.

Bronars, Stephen G. and John R. Lott. 1997. Do Campaign Contributions Alter How a Politician Votes? Or, Do Donors Support Candidates Who Value the Same Things that They Do? *Journal of Law and Economics* 40, 1 (October): 317–50.

Brown, Chester. 2002. The Proliferation of International Courts and Tribunals: Finding Your Way Through the Maze. *Melbourne Journal of International Law* 3: 453–75.

Brown, Robert L. Forthcoming. Nonproliferation Through Delegation: International Agency and the Diminution of WMDs Threats. Ph.D. diss., University of California, San Diego

Buira, Ariel. 1983. IMF Financial Programs and Conditionality. *Journal of Development Economics* 12 (1): 111–36.

Burley, Anne-Marie and Walter Mattli. 1993. Europe Before the Court: A Political Theory of Legal Integration. *International Organization* 47 (1): 41–76.

Burnside, Craig and David Dollar. 2000. Aid, Policies, and Growth. *American Economic Review* 90 (4): 847–68.

References

Busch, Marc L. and Eric Reinhardt. 2000. Bargaining in the Shadow of the Law: Early Settlement in GATT/WTO Disputes. *Fordham International Law Journal* 24 (November–December): 148–72.

Bush, George and Brent Scowcroft. 1998. *A World Transformed*. New York: Alfred A. Knopf.

Calomiris, Charles W. 1998. The IMF's Imprudent Role as Lender of Last Resort. *Cato Journal* 17 (3) (winter): 275–94.

Calvert, Randall, Mathew McCubbins, and Barry Weingast. 1989. A Theory of Political Control and Agency Discretion. *American Journal of Political Science* 33 (3): 588–611.

Caprio, Gerard and Daniela Klingebiel. 2003. Episodes of Systemic and Borderline Financial Crises. World Bank Research Paper.

Carozza, Paolo G. 1998. Uses and Misuses of Comparative Law in International Human Rights: Some Reflections on the Jurisprudence of the European Court of Human Rights. *Notre Dame Law Review* 17 (5): 1217–37.

Carpenter, Daniel P. 2001. *The Forging of Bureaucratic Autonomy*. Princeton, NJ: Princeton University Press.

Caruson, Kiki and J. Michael Bitzer. 2004. At the Crossroads of Policymaking: Executive Politics, Administrative Action, and Judicial Deference by the DC Circuit Court of Appeals (1985–1996). *Law and Policy* 26 (3 and 4): 347–69.

Caves, Richard E. 1982. *Multinational Enterprise and Economic Growth*. New York: Cambridge University Press

Chalmers, Damian. 2004. The Satisfaction of Constitutional Rhetoric by the European Judiciary. Paper presented at the conference Alteneuland: The Constitution of Europe in an American Perspective, New York, April 28–30.

Chwieroth, Jeffrey M. 2003. Neoliberal Norms and Capital Account Liberalization in Emerging Markets: The Role of Domestic-Level Knowledge-Based Experts. Paper presented at the Annual Meeting of the American Political Science Association, Philadelphia, August 28–31.

Clark, Wesley K. 2001. *Waging Modern War: Bosnia, Kosovo, and the Future of Combat*. New York: Public Affairs.

Clines, Francis X. 1983. Administration Scores a Quiet Coup. *The New York Times*, December 28, B6, National Desk.

Cohen, Margot, Gautam Naik, and Matt Pottinger. 2003. Inside the WHO as it mobilized for War on SARS. *Wall Street Journal*, May 2, A1, A6.

Connaughton, Richard. 1992. *Military Intervention in the 1990s*. New York: Routledge.

Cooley, Alexander and James Ron. 2002. The NGO Scramble: Organizational Insecurity and the Political Economy of Transnational Action. *International Security* 27: 5–39.

Cooper, Scott. 2004. Third World Monetary Blocs: Small State Choice or Great Power Hegemony? *EUI Working Papers*, RSCAS no. 2004/30.

Cooter, Robert D. 2000. *The Strategic Constitution*. Princeton, NJ: Princeton University Press.

Cortell, Andrew and Susan Peterson. 2001. Limiting the Unintended Consequences of Institutional Change. *Comparative Political Studies* 34 (7): 768–99.

References

Council of Europe. Various years. *Yearbook of the European Convention on Human Rights*. The Hague: Martinus Nijhoff.

Cox, Gary and Mathew McCubbins. 1993. *Legislative Leviathan: Party Government in the House*. Los Angeles: University of California Press

Cox, Robert W. and Harold K. Jacobson, eds. 1973. *The Anatomy of Influence: Decision Making in International Organizations*. New Haven, Conn.: Yale University Press.

Crawford, Vincent and Joel Sobel. 1982. Strategic Information Transmission. *Econometrica* 50: 1431–51.

Dam, Kenneth W. 1982. *The Rules of the Game: Reform and Evolution in the International Monetary System*. Chicago: University of Chicago Press

Dell, Sidney. 1981. *On Being Grandmotherly: The Evolution of IMF Conditionality*. Essays in International Finance No. 144, October. Princeton, NJ: International Finance Section, Department of Economics, Princeton University.

Demirguc-Kunt, Asli and Harry Huizinga. 1993. Official Credits to Developing Countries: Implicit Transfers to the Banks. *Journal of Money, Credit, and Banking* 25 (3): 430–44.

Denzau, Arthur and Michael Munger. 1986. Legislators and Interest Groups: How Unorganized Interests Get Represented. *American Political Science Review* 80: 89–106.

DiMaggio, Paul J. and Walter Powell. 1991a. Introduction. In *The New Institutionalism in Organizational Analysis*, edited by Walter Powell and Paul DiMaggio. Chicago: University of Chicago Press, 1–38.

———. 1991b. The Iron Cage Revisited: Institutional Isomorphism and Collective Rationality in Organizational Fields. In *The New Institutionalism in Organizational Analysis*, edited by Walter Powell and Paul DiMaggio. Chicago: University of Chicago Press, 63–82.

Dixit, Avinash, Gene Grossman, and Ethan Helpman. 1997. Common Agency and Coordination: General Theory and Application to Government Policy Making. *Journal of Political Economy* 105 (4): 752–69.

Dogan, Rhys. 2000. A Cross-Sectoral View of Comitology: Incidence, Issues and Implications. In *Europe in Change: Committee Governance in the European Union*, edited by Thomas Christiansen and Emil Kirchner. Manchester: Manchester University Press.

Downs, George, David Rocke, and Peter Barsoom. 1996. Is the Good News About Compliance Good News About Cooperation? *International Organization* 50 (3): 379–406.

Dreher, Axel and Nathan Jensen. 2003. Independent Actor or Agent? An Empirical Analysis of the Impact of US Interests on IMF Conditions. Leitner Working Paper No. 2003–04. Yale University, New Haven, Conn.

Dreher, Axel and Roland Vaubel. 2001. *Does the IMF Cause Moral Hazard and Political Business Cycles? Evidence from Panel Data*. Institut für Volkswirtschaftslehre und Statistik No. 598–01, Universität Mannheim.

Dudley, Leonard and Claude Montmarquette. 1976. A Model of the Supply of Bilateral Foreign Aid. *American Economic Review* 64 (1): 132–42.

Eckaus, R. S. 1986. How the IMF Lives with its Conditionality. *Policy Sciences* 19: 237–52.

References

Ehlermann, Claus-Dieter. 2003. Experiences from the WTO Appellate Body. *Texas International Law Journal* 38: 469–88.
Eisner, Marc Allen and Kenneth Meier. 1990. Presidential Control Versus Bureaucratic Power: Explaining the Reagan Revolution in Antitrust. *American Journal of Political Science* 34 (February): 269–87.
Elster, Jon. 2000. *Ulysses Unbound: Studies in Rationality, Precommitment, and Constraints*. Cambridge and New York: Cambridge University Press.
Epstein, David and Sharyn O'Halloran. 1994. Administrative Procedures, Information, and Agency Discretion. *American Journal of Political Science* 38 (3): 697–722.
  1999a. *Delegating Powers: A Transaction Cost Politics Approach to Policy Making Under Separate Powers*. Cambridge: Cambridge University Press.
  1999b. Measuring the Electoral and Policy Impact of Majority-Minority Voting Districts. *American Journal of Political Science* 43 (2): 367–95.
Epstein, Lee and Jack Knight. 1998. *The Choices Justices Make*. Washington, DC: CQ Press.
Evans, Peter and Martha Finnemore. 2001. Organizational Reform and the Expansion of the South's Voice at the Fund. *G-24 Discussion Paper Series* (New York: United Nations).
Falk, Richard. 2004. The Iraq War and the Future of International Law. Paper presented at the Annual Meeting of the American Society of International Law, March 31–April 3. Available at <http://www.wagingpeace.org/articles/2004/04/19_falk_iraq-war-law.htm>.
Fama, Eugene. 1980. Agency Problems and the Theory of the Firm. *Journal of Political Economy* 88 (2): 288–307.
Farnsworth, Clyde H. 1987. US Proposals Hearten IMF and World Bank. *New York Times*, October 2, D1.
Felton, John. 1989. OAS Ministers Admit Failure in Effort to Oust Noriega. *Congressional Quarterly* 47 (34): 2223.
Fidler, David P. 2004. *SARS, Governance, and the Globalization of Disease*. New York: Palgrave Macmillan.
  2005. From International Sanitary Conventions to Global Health Security: The New International Health Regulations. *Chinese Journal of International Law* 4: 325–92.
Finch, C. David. 1988. Let the IMF be the IMF. *The International Economy* 1 (2) (January/February): 126–28.
  1994. *Governance of the International Monetary Fund by its Members*. Washington, DC: Bretton Woods Commission.
Fisher, Louis. 1985. *Constitutional Conflicts Between Congress and the President*. Princeton, NJ: Princeton University Press.
Fox, Jonathan and David Brown. 1998. *The Struggle for Accountability: The World Bank, NGOs, and Grassroots Movements*. Cambridge, Mass.: MIT Press.
Franchino, Fabio. 2000. Commission's Executive Discretion, Information, and Comitology. *Journal of Theoretical Politics* 12: 155–81.
  2001. Delegating Powers in the European Union. Paper presented at the Seventh Biennial International Conference of the European Community Studies Association, Madison, Wisconsin, May 31–June 2.

References

Freedman, Lawrence and Efraim Karsh. 1993. *The Gulf Conflict, 1990–1991*. Princeton, NJ: Princeton University Press.

Fuller, Graham. 1991. Moscow and the Gulf War. *Foreign Affairs* 70 (3): 55–76.

Furubotn, Eirik G. and Rudolf Richter. 2000. *Institutions and Economic Theory: The Contribution of the New Institutional Economics*. Ann Arbor: University of Michigan Press.

Gabel, Matthew J. and John D. Huber. 2000. Putting Parties in Their Place: Inferring Party Left–Right Ideological Positions from Party Manifestos Data. *American Journal of Political Science* 44 (1): 94–103.

Garrett, Geoffrey. 1995. The Politics of Legal Integration in the European Union. *International Organization* 49 (1): 171–81.

Garrett, Geoffrey, Daniel Kelemen, and Heiner Schulz. 1998. The European Court of Justice, National Governments and Legal Integration in the European Union. *International Organization* 52 (1): 149–76.

Garrett, Geoffrey and George Tsebelis. 1996. An Institutional Critique of Intergovernmentalism. *International Organization* 50 (2): 269–99.

Garrett, Geoffrey and Barry Weingast. 1993. Ideas, Interests, and Institutions: Constructing the EC's Internal Market. In *Ideas and Foreign Policy*, edited by J. Goldstein and R. Keohane. Ithaca, NY: Cornell University Press.

Garritsen De Vries, Margaret. 1976. *The International Monetary Fund, 1966–1971: The System Under Stress*. Washington, DC: IMF.

    1985. *The International Monetary Fund, 1972–1978*. Washington, DC: IMF.

    1986. *The IMF in a Changing World, 1945–85*. Washington, DC: IMF.

Gartzke, Erik and Dong-Joon Jo. 2002. The Affinity of Nations Index, 1946–1996. Version 3.0. Dataset. Available at http://www.columbia.edu/~eg589/datasets.html.

Gilligan, Thomas and Keith Krehbiel. 1989. Asymmetric Information and Legislative Rules with a Heterogeneous Committee. *American Journal of Political Science* 33: 459–90.

    1990. Organization of Informative Committees by Rational Legislatures. *American Journal of Political Science* 34: 531–64.

Gilpin, Robert. 2002. *The Challenge of Global Capitalism: The World Economy in the Twenty-First Century*. Princeton, NJ: Princeton University Press.

Glennon, Michael. 2003. Why the Security Council Failed. *Foreign Affairs* 82 (3): 16–35.

Global War. 2002. Interview with Gro Harlem Brundtland, Director-General of the World Health Organization. *Foreign Policy* 128: 24–36.

Godlee, F. 1994a. WHO in Crisis. *British Medical Journal* 309: 1424–28.

    1994b. WHO in Retreat: Is it Losing its Influence? *British Medical Journal* 309: 1491–95.

Gold, Joseph. 1979. *Conditionality*. Washington, DC: International Monetary Fund.

    1984. *Legal and Institutional Aspects of the International Monetary System: Selected Essays*. Vol. 2. Washington, DC: International Monetary Fund.

Goldstein, Judith, Miles Kahler, Robert O. Keohane, and Anne-Marie Slaughter. 2000. Introduction: Legalization and World Politics. *International Organization* 54 (3): 385–99.

References

Goldstein, Judith L., Miles Kahler, Robert O. Keohane, and Anne-Marie Slaughter, eds. 2001. *Legalization and World Politics.* Cambridge, Mass.: MIT Press.

Golove, David. 2003. The New Confederalism: Treaty Delegations of Legislative, Executive, and Judicial Authority. *Stanford Law Review* 55, 5 (May): 1697–1748.

Golsong, Heribert. 1958. Die Europäische Menschenrechtskonvention vor den nationalen Gerichten. *Deutsches Verwaltungsblatt* 73 (23): 809–12.

Gomien, Donna. 1995. *Judgments of the European Court of Human Rights.* Strasbourg, France: Council of Europe Press.

Gordon, Edward, Steven J. Burton, Richard Falk, Thomas M. Franck, and Constantine Nezis. 1989. The Independence and Impartiality of International Judges. *American Society of International Law Proceedings* 83: 508–29.

Gould, Erica R. 2003. Money Talks: Supplementary Financiers and International Monetary Fund Conditionality. *International Organization* 57 (3): 551–86.

2006. *Money Talks: The International Monetary Fund, Conditionality and Supplementary Financiers.* Stanford, Calif.: Stanford University Press.

Gourevitch, Phillip. 1998. *We Wish to Inform You that Tomorrow We Will Be Killed with Your Families.* New York: Picador.

Grant, Ruth W. and Robert O. Keohane. 2005. Accountability and Abuses of Power in World Politics. *American Political Science Review* 99 (1): 29–43.

Grieco, Joseph M. 1990. *Cooperation Among Nations: Europe, America, and Non-tariff Barriers to Trade.* Ithaca, NY: Cornell University Press.

Grossman, Gene M. and Elhanan Helpman. 1994. Protection for Sale. *American Economic Review* 84 (4) (September): 833–50.

2002. *Interest Groups and Trade Policy.* Princeton NJ: Princeton University Press.

Gruber, Lloyd. 2000. *Ruling the World: Power Politics and the Rise of Supranational Institutions.* Princeton, NJ: Princeton University Press.

Haftel, Yoram Z. and Alexander Thompson. 2006. The independence of international organizations: concept and applications. *Journal of Conflict Resolution* 50(2): 253–75.

Haggard, Stephen. 1988. The Institutional Foundations of Hegemony: Explaining the Reciprocal Trade Agreements Act of 1934. *International Organization* 42 (1): 56–94.

Hall, Richard L. and Frank W. Wayman. 1990. Buying Time: Moneyed Interests and the Mobilization of Bias in Congressional Committees. *American Political Science Review* 84: 797–820.

Hamilton, Alexander, John Jay, and James Madison. 1961. *The Federalist Papers (1787–88).* New York: The New American Library of World Literature.

Hammond, Thomas H. and Jack H. Knott. 1996. Who Controls the Bureaucracy? Presidential Power, Congressional Dominance, Legal Constraints, and Bureaucratic Autonomy in a Model of Multi-institutional Policy-Making. *Journal of Law, Economics, and Organization* 12 (1): 119–66.

Harris, D. J., M. O'Boyle, and C. Warbrick. 1999. *Law of the European Convention on Human Rights.* London: Butterworths.

Haskel, Jonathan E. and Matthew J. Slaughter. 2000. Have Falling Tariffs and Transportation Costs Raised US Wage Inequality? NBER Working Paper 7539. Cambridge, Mass.: National Bureau of Economic Research.

References

Heikal, Mohamed. 1992. *Illusions of Triumph: An Arab View of the Gulf War*. London: HarperCollins.
Helfer, Laurence and Anne-Marie Slaughter. 1997. Toward a Theory of Effective Supranational Adjudication. *Yale Law Journal* 107 (2): 273–391.
——— 2005. Why States Create International Tribunals: A Response to Professors Posner and Yoo. *California Law Review* 93 (May).
Helmke, Gretchen. 2002. The Logic of Strategic Defection: Court-Executive Relations in Argentina under Dictatorship and Democracy. *American Political Science Review* 96 (June): 291–303.
Hill, Jeffrey and Carol Weissert. 1995. Implementation and the Irony of Delegation: The Politics of Low-Level Radioactive Waste Disposal. *Journal of Politics* 57 (May): 344–69.
Hix, Simon. 2002. Parliamentary Behaviour with Two Principles: Preferences, Parties and Voting in the European Parliament. *American Journal of Political Science* 46 (3): 688–98.
Hoadley, J. Stephen. 1980. Small States as Aid Donors. *International Organization* 34 (1): 121–37.
Holland, Martin. 2002. *The European Union and the Third World*. New York: Palgrave.
Horsefield, J. Keith, ed. 1969. *The International Monetary Fund, 1945–65: Twenty Years of International Monetary Cooperation*. 3 vols. Volume 1: *Chronicle*, by J. Keith Horsefield. Volume 2: *Analysis*, by Margaret Garritsen de Vries and J. Keith Horsefield, with the collaboration of J. J. Gold and others. Volume 3: *Documents*, edited by J. Keith Horsefield. Washington, DC: International Monetary Fund.
Horsefield, J. Keith and Gertrud Lovasy. 1969. Evolution of the Fund's Policy on Drawings. In *The International Monetary Fund, 1945–1965: Twenty Years of International Monetary Cooperation*. Volume 1: *Chronicle*, by J. Keith Horsefield. Washington, DC: International Monetary Fund.
Huber, John D. 1998. How Does Cabinet Instability Affect Political Performance: Credible Commitment, Information, and Health Care Cost Containment in Parliamentary Politics? *American Political Science Review* 92: 577–92.
Huber, John. D. and Charles R. Shipan. 2000. The Costs of Control: Legislators, Agencies, and Transaction Costs, *Legislative Studies Quarterly* 25: 25–52.
——— 2002. *Deliberate Discretion? The Institutional Foundations of Bureaucratic Autonomy*. Cambridge: Cambridge University Press.
Huber, John. D., Charles R. Shipan, and Madelaine Pfahler. 2001. Legislatures and Statutory Control of Bureaucracy. *American Journal of Political Science* 45: 330–45.
Hug, Simon. 2003. Endogenous Preferences and Delegation in the European Union. *Comparative Political Studies* 36 (1–2): 41–74.
Hurd, Ian. 1999. Legitimacy and Authority in International Politics. *International Organization* 53 (2): 379–408.
——— 2002. Legitimacy, Power, and the Symbolic Life of the Security Council. *Global Governance* 8 (1): 35–51.
——— 2005. The Strategic Use of Liberal Internationalism: Libya and the UN Sanctions, 1993–2003. *International Oranization* 59 (spring): 495–526.

References

Imbeau, Louis M. 1988. Aid and Ideology. *European Journal of Political Research* 16: 3–28.

——— 1989. *Donor Aid: The Determinants of Development Allocations to Third World Countries: A Comparative Analysis.* New York: Peter Lang.

International Commission on Intervention and State Sovereignty. 2001. *The Responsibility to Protect.* Ottawa, Ontario: International Development Research Centre.

International Financial Institution Advisory Commission (IFIAC or Meltzer Commission). 2000. Final Report, March. Available at www.bicusa.org/usgovtoversight/meltzer.htm. Accessed on April 15, 2003.

International Monetary Fund. Exchange and Trade Relations and Legal Departments. 1978. *Conditionality in the Upper Credit Tranches: Issues for Further Consideration.* Washington, DC: IMF.

——— 1983. *Review of Upper Credit Tranche Arrangements Approved in 1981 and of Some Issues Related to Conditionality.* Washington, DC: IMF.

——— 1986. *Program Design and Performance Criteria.* Washington, DC: IMF.

——— Various years. *Annual Report of the Executive Board.* Washington, DC: IMF.

Jacobson, Harold K. 1973. WHO: Medicine, Regionalism, and Managed Politics. In *The Anatomy of Influence: Decision Making in International Organization*, edited by Robert W. Cox and Harold K. Jacobson. New Haven, Conn.: Yale University Press.

——— 1984. *Networks of Interdependence: International Organizations and the Global Political System.* 2nd edn. New York: Alfred Knopf.

James, Harold. 1996. *International Monetary Cooperation Since Bretton Woods.* Washington, DC: IMF.

Janis, Mark, Richard Kay, and Anthony Bradley. 1995. *European Human Rights Law.* New York: Oxford University Press.

Jeanne, Olivier and Jeromin Zettelmeyer. 2001. International Bailouts, Moral Hazard, and Conditionality. *Economic Policy* 33 (October): 409–32.

Jensen, Michael C. and William H. Meckling. 1976. Theory of the Firm: Managerial Behavior, Agency Costs, and Ownership Structure. *Journal of Financial Economics* 3: 305–60.

Jervis, Robert. 1983. Security Regimes. In *International Regimes*, edited by Stephen Krasner. Ithaca, NY: Cornell University Press.

Joergens, Konstantin J. 1999. True Appellate Procedure or Only a Two-Stage Process? A Comparative View of the Appellate Body Under the WTO Dispute Settlement Understanding. *Law and Policy in International Business* 30 (2): 193–230.

Johnston, Alastair Iain. 2001. Treating International Institutions as Social Environments. *International Studies Quarterly* 45 (4): 487–515.

Johnstone, Ian. 2003a. Security Council Deliberations: The Power of the Better Argument. *European Journal of International Law* 14 (3): 437–80.

——— 2003b. The Role of the UN Secretary-General: The Power of Persuasion Based on Law. *Global Governance* 9: 441–58.

Jordan, Robert S. 1967. *The NATO International Staff/Secretariat 1952–1957.* London: Oxford University Press.

References

Joskow, Paul and Roger G. Noll. 1981. Regulation in Theory and Practice: An Overview. In *Studies of Public Regulation*, edited by Gary Fromm. Cambridge, Mass.: MIT Press.

Joyce, Joseph P. 2002. Through a Glass Darkly: New Questions (and Answers) about IMF Programs. Wellesley College Working Paper 2002–04 (June). Wellesley, Mass.

Kahler, Miles. 1990. The United States and the International Monetary Fund: Declining Influence or Declining Interest? In *The United States and Multilateral Institutions: Patterns of Changing Instrumentality and Influence*, edited by Margaret P. Karns and Karen A. Mingst, 91–114. Boston: Unwin Hyman.

2001. *Leadership Selection in the Major Multilaterals*. Washington, DC: Institute for International Economics.

Kahn, Alfred. 1988. *The Economics of Regulation: Principles and Institutions*. 2nd edn. New York: John Wiley & Sons.

Kapur, Devesh, John P. Lewis, and Richard Webb, eds. 1997. *The World Bank: Its First Half Century*. Washington, DC: Brookings Institution Press.

Katzenstein, Peter. 1985. *Small States in World Markets: Industrial Policy in Europe*. Ithaca, NY: Cornell University Press.

Kay, Sean. 1998. *NATO and the Future of European Security*. Lanham, Md.: Rowman and Littlefield.

Keck, Margaret E., and Kathryn Sikkink. 1998. *Activists Beyond Borders: Advocacy Networks in International Politics*. Ithaca, NY: Cornell University Press.

Keener, E. Barlow. 1987. The Andean Common Market Court of Justice: Its Purpose, Structure, and Future. *Emory Journal of International Dispute Resolution* 2 (1): 37–72.

Kelley, Judith. 2005. Do States Care About Normative Consistency? The ICC and Bilateral Non-Surrender Agreements as a Quasi-Experiment. Paper presented to the Vanderbilt Law School International Law Roundtable on International Criminal Law and International Human Rights Law, January 27–29.

Keohane, Robert O. 1984. *After Hegemony: Cooperation and Discord in the World Political Economy*. Princeton, NJ: Princeton University Press.

Keohane, Robert O., Andrew Moravscik, and Anne-Marie Slaughter. 2000. Legalized Dispute Resolution: Interstate and Transnational. *International Organization* 54 (3): 457–88.

Keohane, Robert O. and Joseph Nye, Jr. 1977. *Power and Interdependence: World Politics in Transition*. Boston: Little, Brown.

Khalidi, Washid. 1991. Why Some Arabs Support Saddam. In *The Gulf War Reader*, edited by Micah Sifry and Christopher Cerf, 161–71. New York: Random House.

Kiewiet, D. Roderick and Mathew D. McCubbins. 1991. *The Logic of Delegation: Congressional Parties and the Appropriations Process*. Chicago: University of Chicago Press.

Killick, Tony. 1992. *Continuity and Change in IMF Programme Design, 1982–1992*. Washington, DC: Overseas Development Institute.

References

Kilroy, Bernadette. 1995. Member State Control or Judicial Independence: The Integrative Role of the Court of Justice. Paper presented at the Annual Meeting of the American Political Science Association, Chicago, August 31–September 3.

———. 1999. Integration through Law: ECJ and Governments in the EU. Unpublished manuscript, Department of Political Science, UCLA.

King, Gary, Michael Tomz, and Jason Wittenberg. 2000. Making the Most of Statistical Analyses: Improving Interpretation and Presentation. *American Journal of Political Science* 44 (2) (March): 341–55.

Kissinger, Henry A. 2001. The Pitfalls of Universal Jurisdiction. *Foreign Affairs* 80 (4): 86–96.

Klepak, Hal. 2003. Power Multiplied or Power Restrained? The United States and Multilateral Institutions in the Americas. In *US Hegemony and International Organizations*, edited by Rosemary Foot, S. Neil MacFarlane, and Michael Mastanduno, 239–64. New York: Oxford University Press.

Koremenos, Barbara, Charles Lipson, and Duncan Snidal. 2001. The Rational Design of International Institutions. *International Organization* 55 (4) (autumn): 761–99.

Krause, George. 1996. The Institutional Dynamics of Policy Administration: Bureaucratic Influence over Securities Regulation. *American Journal of Political Science* 40 (November): 1083–1121.

Krauthammer, Charles. 2001. The Failure of Multilateralism. *Washington Post*, reprinted in the *Guardian Weekly*, December 6, 20.

———. 2003. UN, RIP. *Washington Post*, January 21, A27.

Krehbiel, Keith. 1991. *Information and Legislative Organization*. Ann Arbor: University of Michigan Press.

Kroszner, Randall S. and Thomas Stratmann. 1998. Interest-Group Competition and the Organization of Congress: Theory and Evidence from Financial Services' Political Action Committees, *American Economic Review* 88 (5): 1163–87.

Krueger, Anne O. 1993. *Economic Policies at Cross-Purposes: The United States and Developing Countries*. Washington, DC: Brookings.

Kuemmel, Gerhard. 2003. Changing State Institutions: The German Military and the Integration of Women. Paper presented to the European Consortium for Political Research, Marburg, September 18–21.

Laffont, Jean-Jacques and David Martimort. 2002. *The Theory of Incentives: The Principal-Agent Model*. Princeton NJ: Princeton University Press.

Laffont, Jean-Jacques and Jean Tirole. 1993. Cartelization by Regulation. *Journal of Regulatory Economics* 5: 111–30.

Lake, David A. 1996. Anarchy, Hierarchy, and the Variety of International Relations. *International Organization* 50 (1) (winter): 1–33.

———. 1999. *Entangling Relations: American Foreign Policy in its Century*. Princeton, NJ: Princeton University Press.

Lake, David A. and Robert Powell. 1999. *Strategic Choice and International Relations*. Princeton, NJ: Princeton University Press.

Larkins, Christopher M. 1996. Judicial Independence and Democratization: A Theoretical and Conceptual Analysis. *American Journal of Comparative Law* 44 (4): 605–26.

References

1998. The Judiciary and Delegative Democracy in Argentina. *Comparative Politics* 30: 423–43.
Laver, Michael and Norman Schofield. 1990. *Multiparty Government: The Politics of Coalition in Europe*. New York: Oxford University Press.
Lazurus, David. 2003. Bush Tries to Weaken Tobacco Treaty. *San Francisco Chronicle*. April 30, A1.
LeoGrande, William. 1990. From Reagan to Bush: The Transition in US Policy Towards Central America. *Journal of Latin American Studies* 22 (3): 595–21.
Lesch, Ann Mosely. 1991. Contrasting Reactions to the Persian Gulf Crisis: Egypt, Syria, Jordan and the Palestinians. *Middle East Journal* 45 (1): 30–50.
Lewis, Paul. 1989. UN Health Agency Seeks Compromise on PLO. *New York Times,* May 7, A5.
Liebert, Ulrike. 2002. Europeanizing the Military: The ECJ and the Transformation of the Bundeswehr. Jean Monnet Center for European Studies Working Paper 2002/7. Florence, Italy.
Lijphart, Arend. 1977. *Democracy in Plural Societies: A Comparative Exploration*. New Haven, Conn.: Yale University Press.
Lippman, Thomas W. 1999. Budget Line Raises Flag; Helms Sees Red Over Increase for Inter-American Foundation. *Washington Post*, May 24, A25.
Lord Lester of Herne Hill. 1998. UK Acceptance of the Strasbourg Jurisdiction: What Really Went on in Whitehall in 1965. *Public Law* (summer): 237–53.
Lumsdaine, David H. 1993. *Moral Vision in International Politics: The Foreign Aid Regime, 1949–1989*. Princeton, NJ: Princeton University Press.
Lupia, Arthur. 1992. Busy Voters, Agenda Control, and the Power of Information. *American Political Science Review* 86: 390–403.
  1994. Shortcuts Versus Encyclopedias: Information and Voting Behavior in California Insurance Reform Elections. *American Political Science Review* 88 (1): 63–76.
Lupia, Arthur and Mathew McCubbins. 1994a. Learning from Oversight: Fire Alarms and Police Patrols Reconstructed. *Journal of Law, Economics, and Organization* 10 (1): 96–125.
  1994b. Who Controls? Information and the Structure of Legislative Decision Making. *Legislative Studies Quarterly* 29 (3): 361–84.
  1998. *The Democratic Dilemma: Can Citizens Learn What They Need to Know?* New York: Cambridge University Press.
Lutz, Ellen and Kathryn Sikkink. 2000. International Human Rights Law and Practice in Latin America. *International Organization* 54 (3): 633–59.
Maizels, Alfred and Machiko Nissanke. 1984. Motivations for Aid to Developing Countries. *World Development* 12 (9): 879–900.
Majone, Giandomenico. 2001. Two Logics of Delegation: Agency and Fiduciary Relations in EU Governance. *European Union Politics* 2 (1): 103–21.
Makinson, Larry. 2003. *Open Secrets: The Encyclopedia of Congressional Money and Politics*. Available at http://www.opensecrets.org/.
Malone, David. 2003. The UN, the United States, and Iraq. In *Rebuilding Societies in Crisis*, edited by Sally Armstrong et al., 69–98. Toronto: Canadian Institute of International Affairs.

References

Mansfield, Edward, Helen V. Milner, and B. Peter Rosendorff. 2002. Why Democracies Cooperate More: Electoral Control and International Trade Agreements. *International Organization* 56 (3): 477–514.

March, James G. and Johan P. Olsen. 1998. The Institutional Design of International Political Order. *International Organization* 52 (4): 943–69.

March, James G. and Herbert Simon, with Harold Guetzkow. 1958. *Organizations*. New York: Wiley.

Marks, Brian A. 1989. A Model of Judicial Influence on Congressional Policy Making: Grove City College v. Bell (1984). Unpublished manuscript, Department of Political Science, University of Washington.

Martens, Bertin, Uwe Mummert, Peter Murrell, and Paul Seabright. 2002. *The Institutional Economics of Foreign Aid*. New York: Cambridge University Press.

Martin, Lisa L. 1992a. *Coercive Cooperation: Explaining Multilateral Economic Sanctions*. Princeton, NJ: Princeton University Press.

   1992b. Interests, Power, and Multilateralism. *International Organization* 46: 765–92.

Matthews, Ken. 1993. *The Gulf Conflict and International Relations*. New York: Routledge.

McCarty, Nolan, Keith T. Poole, and Howard Rosenthal. 1997. *Income Redistribution and the Realignment of American Politics*. Washington, DC: AEI Press.

McCubbins, Mathew D. 1985. The Legislative Design of Regulatory Structure. *American Journal of Political Science* 29: 721–48.

McCubbins, Mathew D., Roger G. Noll, and Barry R. Weingast. 1989. Structure and Process, Politics and Policy: Administrative Arrangements and the Political Control of Agencies. *Virginia Law Review* 75 (March): 431–82.

McCubbins, Mathew D. and Talbot Page. 1987. A Theory of Congressional Delegation. In *Congress: Structure and Policy*, edited by Mathew D. McCubbins and Terry Sullivan, 409–25. New York: Cambridge University Press.

McCubbins, Mathew D. and Thomas Schwartz. 1984. Congressional Oversight Overlooked: Policy Patrols Versus Fire Alarms. *American Journal of Political Science* 2 (1): 165–79.

McDonnell, Ida, Henri-Bernard Solignac Lecomte, and Liam Wegimont, eds. 2003. *Public Opinion and the Fight Against Poverty*. Edited by D. C. Studies. Paris: OECD.

McKinlay, Robert. 1979. The Aid Relationship: A Foreign Policy Model and Interpretation of the Distributions of Official Bilateral Economic Aid of the US, UK, France, and Germany. *Comparative Political Studies* 11 (4): 411–64.

McKinlay, Robert and Richard Little. 1977. A Foreign Policy Model of US Bilateral Aid Allocations. *World Politics* 30 (1): 58–86.

   1978. A Foreign Policy Model of the Distribution of British Bilateral Aid, 1960–70. *British Journal of Political Science* 8 (3): 313–31.

McNamara, Kathleen. 2002. Rational Fictions: Central Bank Independence and the Social Logic of Delegation. *West European Politics* 25 (1): 47–76.

References

McNollgast. 1987. Administrative Procedures as Instruments of Political Control. *Journal of Law, Economics, and Organization* 3 (2): 243–79.

———. 1989. Structure and Process, Politics and Policy: Administrative Arrangements and the Political Control of Agencies. *Virginia Law Review* 75: 431–82.

Mearsheimer, John. 1994. The False Promise of International Institutions. *International Security* 19 (3): 5–49.

Meltzer, Allan H. 1998. Asian Problems and the IMF. *Cato Journal* 17 (3) (winter): 267–74.

Meltzer Commission Report. 1999. United States Congressional Advisory Commission on International Financial Institutions. Report to the US Congress on IFIs. Available at http://www.house.gov/jec/imf/ifiac.htm.

Merrills, J. G. 2001. *Human Rights in Europe: A Study of the European Convention on Human Rights*, 4th edn. Manchester: Manchester University Press.

Meyer, John and Brian Rowan. 1991. Institutionalized Organizations: Formal Structure as Myth and Ceremony. In *The New Institutionalism in Organizational Analysis*, edited by Walter Powell and Paul DiMaggio, 41–62. Chicago: University of Chicago Press.

Milgrom, Paul, Douglass North, and Barry Weingast. 1990. The Role of Institutions in the Revival of Trade: The Law Merchant, Private Judges, and the Champagne Fairs. *Economics and Politics* 2: 1–23.

Milgrom, Paul and John Roberts. 1990. Bargaining Costs, Influence Costs, and the Organization of Economic Activity. In *Perspectives on Positive Political Economy*, edited by James Alt and Kenneth Shepsle. Cambridge: Cambridge University Press.

———. 1992. *Economics, Organization, and Management*. Englewood Cliffs, NJ: Prentice-Hall.

Miller, Scott. 2005. Boeing, Airbus Fight to Go Before Quirky Trade Court. *Wall Street Journal*, June 3, 1, 14.

Milner, Helen V. 1997. *Interests, Institutions and Information: Domestic Politics and International Relations*. Princeton, NJ: Princeton University Press.

Milner, Helen V. and B. Peter Rosendorff. 1996. Trade Negotiations, Information and Domestic Politics. *Economics and Politics* 8: 145–89.

Mingst, Karen A. 1992. The United States and the World Health Organization. In *The United States and Multilateral Institutions: Patterns of Changing Instrumentality and Influence*, edited by Margaret P. Karns and Karen A. Mingst. London: Routledge.

Moe, Terry M. 1984. The New Economics of Organization. *American Journal of Political Science* 28: 739–77.

———. 1990. Political Institutions: The Neglected Side of the Story. *Journal of Law, Economics, and Organization* 6: 213–53.

Moravcsik, Andrew. 1991. Negotiating the Single European Act: National Interests and Conventional Statecraft in the European Community. *International Organization* 45 (1): 19–56.

———. 1998. *The Choice for Europe: Social Purpose and State Power from Messina to Maastricht*. Ithaca, NY: Cornell University Press.

———. 2000. The Origins of Human Rights Regimes: Democratic Delegation in Postwar Europe. *International Organization* 54 (2): 217–52.

References

Moseley, Paul. 1985. The Political Economy of Foreign Aid: A Model of the Market for a Public Good. *Economic Development and Cultural Change* 33 (2): 373–94.

Mueller, John. 1994. *Policy and Opinion in the Gulf War.* Chicago: University of Chicago Press.

Müller, Harald. 2004. Arguing, Bargaining and All That: Communicative Action, Rationalist Theory, and the Logic of Appropriateness in International Relations. *European Journal of International Relations* 10 (3): 395–435.

Murphy, Walter. 1964. *Elements of Judicial Strategy.* Chicago: Chicago University Press.

Murphy, Walter F., C. Herman Pritchett, and Lee Epstein. 2002. *Courts, Judges, and Politics: An Introduction to the Judicial Process.* 5th edn. Boston: McGraw-Hill.

Mutume, Gumisai. 2005. Criticism of IMF Gets Louder. Available on the Third World Network web site at www.twnside.org.sg/title/louder.htm.

National Public Radio. 2003. Disease Gatekeeper. *The Connection.* Available at www.theconnection.org/shows/2003/08/20030808_a_main.asap.

Nelson, Paul. 1995. *The World Bank and Non-Governmental Organizations: The Limits of Apolitical Development.* New York: St. Martin's Press.

Nielson, Daniel L. and Michael J. Tierney. 2003a. Delegation to International Organizations: Agency Theory and World Bank Environmental Reform. *International Organization* 57 (2): 241–76.

2003b. Principals and Interests: Common Agency and Multilateral Development Bank Lending. Draft manuscript (February).

2005. Theory, Data, and Hypothesis Testing: World Bank Environmental Reform Redux. *International Organization* 59 (3): 785–800.

Nielson, Daniel L., Michael J. Tierney, and Catherine A. Weaver. 2003. Bridging the Rationalist–Constructivist Divide: Re-engineering the Culture of the World Bank. Unpublished manuscript.

Niskanen, William A. 1971. *Bureaucracy and Representative Government.* Chicago: Rand McNally, 1971.

Noel, Alain and Jean Phillipe Therien. 1995. From Domestic to International Justice: The Welfare State and Foreign Aid. *International Organization* 49 (3): 523–53.

North Atlantic Treaty Organization. 2001. *NATO Handbook.* Brussels: NATO Office of Information and Press. Updated November 4, 2002. Available from http://www.nato.int/docu/handbook/2001/index.htm.

Nugent, Neill. 2000. *The European Commission.* New York: St Martin's Press.

2003. *The Government and Politics of the European Union.* 5th edn. Basingstoke: Palgrave Macmillan.

Oatley, Thomas and Jason Yackee. 2000. Political Determinants of IMF Balance of Payments Lending: The Curse of Carabosse? Unpublished manuscript, University of North Carolina at Chapel Hill.

2004. American Interests and IMF Lending. *International Politics* 41 (3): 415–29.

OECD. 1999. *A Comparison of Management Systems for Development Cooperation in OECD/DAC Members.* Paris: OECD.

References

2001. *International Development Statistics*. Paris: OECD.

Olson, Mancur. 1965. *The Logic of Collective Action: Public Goods and the Theory of Groups*. Cambridge, Mass.: Harvard University Press.

Omang, Joanne. 1985. Foundation Head Outmaneuvers Foes; Move to Oust IAF's Szekely Fails. *Washington Post*, July 1, A13.

Ovey, Clare and Robin White. 2002. *Jacobs and White, the European Convention on Human Rights*. 3rd edn. New York: Oxford University Press.

Papayoanou, Paul. 1997. Intra-Alliance Bargaining and US Bosnia Policy. *Journal of Conflict Resolution* 41 (1): 91–116.

Parks, Bradley and Michael J. Tierney. 2004. Outsourcing the Allocation and Delivery of Environmental Aid. Paper presented at the American Political Science Association Annual Meeting, Chicago, Illinois, September 1–4.

Parris, Henry. 1966. The Conseil d'État in the Fifth Republic. *Government and Opposition* 2 (1): 89–104.

Partsch, Karl Josef. 1956/1957. Die Europäische Menschenrechtskonvention vor den nationalen Parlamenten. *Zeitschrift für ausländisches und öffentliches Recht und Völkerrecht* 17: 93–132.

Pauwelyn, Joost. 2000. Enforcement and Countermeasures in the WTO: Rules Are Rules – Toward a More Collective Approach. *American Journal of International Law* 94: 335–47.

  2005. The Transformation of World Trade. *Michigan Law Review* 104 (1): 1–65.

Perle, Richard. 2003. Thank God for the Death of the UN. *The Guardian*, March 21.

Perrow, Charles. 1986. Economic Theories of Organization. *Theory and Society* 15: 11–45.

Pescatore, Pierre. 1981. Les Travaux du "Groupe Juridique" dans la négociation des Traités de Rome. *Studia Diplomatica (Chronique de Politique Etrangère)* 34 (1–4): 159–78.

Pierson, Paul. 1996. The Path to European Integration: A Historical Institutionalist Analysis. *Comparative Political Studies* 29 (2): 123–63.

  2004. *Politics in Time: History, Institutions and Social Analysis*. Princeton, NJ: Princeton University Press.

Polak, Jacques J. 1991. *The Changing Nature of IMF Conditionality*. Essays in International Finance, No. 184, September. International Finance Section, Department of Economics, Princeton University.

Pollack, Mark A. 1997. Delegation, Agency, and Agenda-setting in the European Community. *International Organization* 51 (1): 99–134.

  2002. Learning from the Americanists (Again): Theory and Method in the Study of Delegation. *West European Politics* 25 (1): 200–19.

  2003a. *The Engines of European Integration: Delegation, Agency, and Agenda Setting in the European Union*. Oxford: Oxford University Press.

  2003b. Control Mechanism or Deliberative Democracy? Two Images of Comitology. *Comparative Political Studies* 36 (1): 125–56.

Pollock, David. 1992. The "Arab Street?" Public Opinion in the Arab World. Washington Institute for Near East Policy Policy Paper No. 32. Washington, DC: The Washington Institute for Near East Policy.

References

Poole, Keith T. and Howard Rosenthal. 1997. *Congress: A Political-Economic History of Roll Call Voting*. New York: Oxford University Press.

Poole, Keith T., Howard Rosenthal, and Boris T. Shor. 2003. Voteview for Windows Version 3.0.3: Roll Call Displays of the US Congress, 1789–1988. Available at http://voteview.gsia.cmu.edu.

Popkin, Samuel. 1991. *The Reasoning Voter*. Chicago: University of Chicago Press.

Posner, Eric A. and Miguel De Figueiredo. 2004. Is the International Court of Justice Biased? Law and Economics Paper 234. University of Chicago Law School.

Posner, Eric A. and John C. Yoo. 2004. A Theory of International Adjudication. University of Chicago, Law and Economics, Olin Working Paper 206; UC Berkeley Public Law Research Paper 146. Available at SSRN: http://ssrn.com/abstract=507003.

Powell, Colin with Joseph Persico. 1995. *My American Journey*. New York: Random House.

Powell, Robert. 1999. *In the Shadow of Power: States and Strategies in International Politics*. Princeton, NJ: Princeton University Press.

Power, Samantha. 2002. *A Problem from Hell: America and the Age of Genocide*. New York: Perseus Publishing.

Przeworski, Adam and James R. Vreeland. 2000. The Effect of IMF Programs on Economic Growth. *Journal of Development Economics* 62: 385–421.

Purrington, Courtney and A. K. 1991. Tokyo's Policy Responses During the Gulf Crisis. *Asian Survey* 31 (4): 307–23.

Putnam, Robert. 1988. Diplomacy and Domestic Politics: The Logic of Two-Level Games. *International Organization* 42 (3): 427–60.

Randal, Jonathan C. 1989. PLO Defeated in Bid to Join World Health Organization. *Washington Post*, May 13, A1.

Raustiala, Kal. 1997. States, NGOs, and International Environmental Institutions. *International Studies Quarterly* 41 (4): 719–40.

  2000. Compliance and Effectiveness in International Regulatory Cooperation. *Case Western Reserve Journal of International Law* 32: 387–440.

Rich, Bruce. 1994. *Mortgaging the Earth: The World Bank, Environmental Impoverishment, and the Crisis of Development*. Boston: Beacon Press.

Risse, Thomas, Stephen Ropp, and Kathryn Sikkink, eds. 1999. *The Power of Human Rights: International Norms and Domestic Change*. Cambridge: Cambridge University Press.

Robertson, A. H. and J. G. Merrills. 1993. *Human Rights in Europe: A Study of the European Convention on Human Rights*. Manchester: Manchester University Press.

Robichek, Walter E. 1984. The IMF's Conditionality Re-Examined. In *Adjustment, Conditionality, and International Financing*, edited by J. Muns, 67–83. Washington, DC: IMF.

Rodrik, Dani. 1996. Why is there Multilateral Lending? In *Annual World Bank Conference on Development Economics, 1995*, edited by M. Bruno and B. Pleskovic. Washington, DC: IMF.

References

Rogoff, Kenneth. 1999. International Institutions for Reducing Global Financial Instability. NBER Working Paper 7265. Cambridge, Mass.: National Bureau of Economic Research.

Rogowski, Ronald. 1999. Institutions as Constraints on Strategic Choice. In *Strategic Choice and International Relations*, edited by David A. Lake and Robert Powell, 115–36. Princeton, NJ: Princeton University Press.

Romano, Cesare. 1999. The Proliferation of International Judicial Bodies: The Pieces of the Puzzle. *New York University Journal of International Law and Politics* 31 (summer): 709–51.

Rourke, Francis E. 1976. *Bureaucracy, Politics, and Public Policy*. 2nd edn. Boston: Little, Brown.

Ruggie, John Gerard, ed. 1993. *Multilateralism Matters: The Theory and Praxis of an Institutional Form*. New York: Columbia University Press.

Ryan, Missy. 2000. Small Agency, Big Target. *National Journal*, March 4.

Sanders, Bernard. 1997. Let the Asian Tigers Fend for Themselves. *Los Angeles Times*, December 10.

Sandholtz, Wayne and John Zysman. 1989. Recasting the European Bargain. *World Politics* 42 (1): 95–128.

Santaella, Julio. 1995. Four Decades of Fund Arrangements: Macroeconomic Stylized Facts Before the Adjustment Process. IMF Working Paper 74. Washington, DC: International Monetary Fund.

Schanzenbach, Max. 2004. Racial and Gender Disparities in Prison Sentences: The Effect of District-Level Judicial Demographics. Northwestern Law and Economics Research Paper No. 04–03. *Journal of Legal Studies* 34 (1): 57–92 (January 1995).

Scharpf, Fritz. 1988. The Joint-Decision Trap: Lessons from German Federalism and European Integration. *Public Administration* 66 (autumn): 239–78.

Scheffer, David J. 1997. The Future of International Criminal Justice (Transcript). *US Department of State Dispatch* 8 (8): 23–34.

Scheve, Kenneth F. and Matthew J. Slaughter. 2001. What Determines Individual Trade-Policy Preferences? *Journal of International Economics* 54 (August): 267–92.

Schimmelfennig, Frank. 2003. *The EU, NATO, and the Integration of Europe*. Cambridge: Cambridge University Press.

Schmidt, Susanne. 2000. Only an Agenda Setter? The European Commission's Power Over the Council of Ministers. *European Union Politics* 1 (1): 37–61.

Schneider, Andrea Kupfer. 2001. Institutional Concerns of an Expanded Trade Regime: Where Should Global Social and Regulatory Policy Be Made? Unfriendly Actions: The Amicus Brief Battle at the WTO. *Widener Law Symposium Journal* 7 (spring): 87–108.

Schraeder, Peter J., Stephen W. Hook, and Bruce Taylor. 1998. Clarifying the Foreign Aid Puzzle: A Comparison of American, Japanese, French, and Swedish Aid Flows. *World Politics* 50 (2): 294–323.

Schultz, Kenneth. 2001. *Democracy and Coercive Diplomacy*. Cambridge: Cambridge University Press.

Schwartz, Anna J. 1998. *Time to Terminate the ESF and IMF*. Cato Foreign Policy Briefing No. 48. August. Washington, DC: The Cato Institute.

References

Shaffer, Gregory. 2001. The World Trade Organization Under Challenge: Democracy and the Law and Politics of the WTO's Treatment of Trade and Environment Matters. *Harvard Environmental Law Review* 25 (1): 1–93.

Shanks, Cheryl, Harold K. Jacobson, and Jeffrey H. Kaplan. 1996. Inertia and Change in the Constellation of International Governmental Organizations. *International Organization* 50 (4): 593–627.

Shapiro, Martin. 1981. *Courts: A Comparative Political Analysis*. Chicago: University of Chicago Press.

Shapiro, Robert and Lawrence Jacobs. 2000. Who Leads and Who Follows? US Presidents, Public Opinion, and Foreign Policy. In *Decision Making in a Glass House*, edited by Brigitte Nacos, Robert Shapiro, and Pierangelo Isernia, 223–45. New York: Rowman and Littlefield.

Shelton, Dinah. 2003. The Boundaries of Human Rights Jurisdiction in Europe. *Duke Journal of Comparative and International Law* 13 (1): 95–154.

Sikkink, Kathryn. 1986. Codes of Conduct for Transnational Corporations: The Case of the WHO/UNICEF Code. *International Organization* 40 (4): 815–40.

Simmons, Beth and Lisa Martin. 2002. International Organizations and Institutions. In *Handbook of International Relations*, edited by W. Carlnaes. London: Sage.

Simon, Herbert A. 1955. A Behavioral Model of Rational Choice. *Quarterly Journal of Economics* 69: 99–118.

Slater, Jerome. 1969. The Limits of Legitimization in International Organizations. *International Organization* 23 (1): 48–72.

Smillie, Ian, Henny Helmich, Tony German, and Judith Randel, eds. 1998. *Public Attitudes and International Development Coordination*. Paris: OECD.

Smith, James McCall. 2000. The Politics of Dispute Settlement Design. *International Organization* 54 (1): 137–80.

Snidal, Duncan. 1985. The Limits of Hegemonic Stability Theory. *International Organization* 39 (4): 579–614.

Snyder, James. 1992. Long-term Investment in Politicians: Or, Give Early, Give Often. *Journal of Law and Economics* 35: 15–43.

Soros, George. 1998. *The Crisis of Global Capitalism: Open Society Endangered*. New York: Public Affairs.

Southard, Frank A. 1979. *The Evolution of the International Monetary Fund*. Princeton, NJ: Department of Economics, Princeton University.

Spence, A. Michael. 1974. *Market Signaling: Informational Transfer in Hiring and Related Screening Processes*. Cambridge, Mass.: Harvard University Press.

Spence, Michael. 1973. Job Market Signaling. *Quarterly Journal of Economics* 87 (3): 355–74.

Steger, Debra. 2002. The Rule of Law or the Rule of Lawyers? *Journal of World Investment* 3 (5): 769–92.

Stein, Arthur. 1990. *Why Nations Cooperate: Circumstance and Choice in International Relations*. Ithaca, NY: Cornell University Press.

Stein, Eric. 1981. Lawyers, Judges, and the Making of a Transnational Constitution. *American Journal of International Law* 75 (1): 1–27.

References

Steinberg, Richard H. 2004. Judicial Lawmaking at the WTO: Discursive, Constitutional, and Political Constraints. *American Journal of International Law* 98 (2): 247–75.

Stephan, Paul B. 2002. Courts, Tribunals and Legal Unification: The Agency Problem. *Chicago Journal of International Law* 2002 (3): 333–52.

Stewart, Richard. 1975. The Reformation of American Administrative Law. *Harvard Law Review* 88: 1667–1813.

Stiglitz, Joseph E. 2002. *Globalization and its Discontents*. New York: W. W. Norton.

Stiles, Ken and Deborah Wells. In press. On the Crossing of the Rubicons: Norm Dissemination and policy idiosyncracy in the United Kingdom. *Political Science Quarterly*.

Stokke, Olav. 1989. The Determinants of Norwegian Aid Policy. In *Western Middle Powers and Global Poverty: The Determinants of the Aid Policies of Canada, Denmark, The Netherlands, Norway and Sweden, Uppsala and Oslo*, edited by Olav Stokke. The Scandinavian Institute of African Studies in cooperation with The Norwegian Institute of International Affairs.

Stolper, Wolfgang, and Paul A. Samuelson. 1941. Protection and Real Wages. *Review of Economic Studies* 9: 58–73.

Stone, Randall W. 2002. *Lending Credibility: The International Monetary Fund and the Post-Communist Transition*. Princeton, NJ: Princeton University Press.

　2004. The Political Economy of IMF Lending in Africa. *American Political Science Review* 98 (4) (November): 577–91.

Stone Sweet, Alec. 2002. Constitutional Courts and Parliamentary Democracy. *West European Politics* 25 (1): 77–700.

Strand, Jonathan R. and David P. Rapkin. 2005. Regionalizing Multilateralism: Estimating the Power of Potential Regional Voting Blocs in the IMF. *International Interactions* 31: 15–54.

Strange, Susan. 1973. IMF: Monetary Managers. In *The Anatomy of Influence: Decision Making in International Organizations*, edited by R. W. Cox and H. K. Jacobson, 263–97. New Haven, Conn.: Yale University Press.

　1976. *International Monetary Relations*. New York: Oxford University Press.

Strøm, Kaare. 2000. Delegation and Accountability in Parliamentary Democracies. *European Journal of Political Research* 37: 261–89.

Swaine, Edward. 2005. Reserving. Available at SSRN: http://ssrn.com/abstract=700981.

Tallberg, Jonas. 2000. The Anatomy of Autonomy: An Institutional Account of Variation in Supranational Influence. *Journal of Common Market Studies* 38 (5): 843–64.

　2002a. Delegation to Supranational Institutions: Why, How and with What Consequence. *West European Politics* 25 (1): 23–46.

　2002b. Paths to Compliance: Enforcement, Management, and the European Union. *International Organization* 56 (3): 609–43.

Telhami, Shibley. 1993. Arab Public Opinion and the Gulf War. In *The Political Psychology of the Gulf War*, edited by Stanley Renshon, 183–97. Pittsburgh: University of Pittsburgh Press.

References

Terasawa, Katsuaki and William Gates. 1993. Burden-Sharing in the Persian Gulf: Lessons Learned and Implications for the Future. *Defense Analysis* 9 (2): 171–95.
Thacker, Strom C. 1999. The High Politics of IMF Lending. *World Politics* 52 (1) (October): 38–75.
Tharoor, Shashi. 2003. Why America Still Needs the United Nations. *Foreign Affairs* 82 (5): 67–81.
Thatcher, Margaret. 1993. *The Downing Street Years, 1979–1990*. New York: HarperCollins.
Thatcher, Mark and Alec Stone Sweet. 2002. Theory and Practice of Delegation to Non-Majoritarian Institutions. *West European Politics* 25: 1–22.
Thelen, Kathleen. 2004. *How Institutions Evolve: The Political Economy of Skills in Comparative-Historical Perspective*. New York: Cambridge University Press
Thompson, Alexander. 2006. Coercion through IOs: The Security Council and the Logic of Information Transmission. *International Organization* 60(1): 1–34.
Thompson, Alexander and Yoram Haftel. 2003. Theorizing and Operationalizing IO Independence. Paper presented at the Annual Convention of the International Studies Association, Portland, Oregon, February 25–March 1.
Tomz, Michael, Jason Wittenberg, and Gary King. 1998. CLARIFY: *Software for Interpreting and Presenting Statistical Results*, version 1.2. Cambridge, Mass.: Harvard University.
Tsebelis, George and Geoffrey Garrett. 2000. Legislative Politics in the European Union. *European Union Politics* 1 (1): 9–36.
　2001. The Institutional Foundations of Intergovernmentalism and Supranationalism in the European Union. *International Organization* 55 (2): 357–90.
Tsebelis, George and Amie Kreppel. 1998. The History of Conditional Agenda Setting in European Institutions. *European Journal of Political Research* 33: 41–71.
Ul Haque, Nadeem and Mohsin S. Khan. 1998. Do IMF-Supported Programs Work? A Survey of the Cross-Country Empirical Evidence. IMF Working Paper 98/169, December. Washington, DC: IMF.
Undén, Osten. 1963. About Law Courts in the United Nations and the Council of Europe. *Svensk Juristtidning* 165: 657–61.
US Chamber of Commerce. 1998. *How They Voted*. Washington, DC: Chamber of Commerce.
US Congress. House. 1964. National Advisory Council on International Monetary and Financial Problems. Secretary of the Treasury. Report of the National Advisory Council on International Monetary and Financial Problems: A Special Report on US Participation in an Increase in the Resources of the Fund for Special Operations of the Inter-American Development Bank. 88th Congress, 2nd sess. House Document No. 316. Washington, DC: GPO.
　1966. Conference Report on the Foreign Assistance Act of 1966 HR15750 to Amend Further the Foreign Assistance Act of 1961, as Amended and for Other Purposes. 89th Cong., 2nd sess. House Report No. 1927. Washington, DC: GPO.

References

1967a. Committee on Foreign Affairs. Report of the Special Study Mission to the Dominican Republic, Guyana, Brazil, and Paraguay. 90th Cong., 1st sess. House Report No. 219. Washington, DC: GPO.

1967b. House of Representatives. Committee on Foreign Affairs. Report on H.R. 12048 to Amend Further the Foreign Assistance Act of 1961, as Amended, and for Other Purposes. 90th Cong., 1st sess. House Report No. 551. Washington, DC: GPO.

US General Accounting Office. 1979. Report of the Financial Condition of the Inter-American Foundation September 30, 1978 and 1979. ID-79-29. Washington: GAO 18 May 1979. Washington, DC: GPO.

1982. Report to the President. Inter-American Foundation. GAO/ID-82-16. Washington: GAO July 1982. Washington, DC: GPO.

1999. Inter-American Foundation: Allegations of Improper Contracting and Personnel Actions at the Foundation. GAO/OSI-99-11R. Washington, DC: GPO.

2000. Report to the Chairman on Foreign Relations, US Senate Inter-American Foundation, Better Compliance With Some Key Procedures Needed. GAO/NSIAD-00-235. Washington, DC: GPO.

2001. International Monetary Fund: Efforts to Advance US Policies at the Fund. Report No. GAO-01-214, 1–78. Washington, DC: GPO.

Upton, Barbara. 2000. *The Multilateral Development Banks: Improving US Leadership*. Westport, Conn.: Praeger.

Van Houtven, Leo. 2002. Governance of the IMF: Decision Making, Institutional Oversight, Transparency, and Accountability. IMF Pamphlet Series No. 53. Washington, DC: IMF.

Vaubel, Roland. 1983. The Moral Hazard of IMF Lending. *The World Economy* 6 (2): 291–304.

1986. A Public Choice Approach to International Organization. *Public Choice* 51 (1): 39–57.

1991. The Political Economy of the International Monetary Fund: A Public Choice Analysis. In *The Political Economy of International Organizations. A Public Choice Approach*, edited by Roland Vaubel and Thomas D. Willett, 204–44. Boulder, Colo.: Westview Press.

Voeten, Erik. 2004. Judicial Behavior on International Courts: Ideology and Strategy on the European Court of Human Rights. Social Science Research Network Working Paper. April. Available at http://ssrn. com/abstract=705363.

2005. The Political Origins of the UN Security Council's Ability to Legitimize the Use of Force. *International Organization* 59 (3): 527–57.

Vreeland, James R. 1999. The IMF: Lender of Last Resort or Scapegoat? Paper presented at the Annual Meeting of International Studies Association, Washington, DC, February 16–21.

Wade, Robert. 2002. US Hegemony and the World Bank: The Fight Over People and Ideas. *Review of International Political Economy* 9 (2): 215–43.

Wallander, Celeste. 1999. *Mortal Friends, Best Enemies: German–Russian Cooperation after the Cold War*. Ithaca, NY: Cornell University Press.

Waltz, Kenneth N. 1979. *Theory of International Politics*. Reading, Mass.: Addison-Wesley.

References

Ward, Angela. 2000. *Judicial Review and the Rights of Private Parties in EC Law.* New York: Oxford University Press.

Weber, Steven. 1994. Origins of the European Bank for Reconstruction and Development. *International Organization* 48 (1): 1–38.

Weil, Gordon L. 1963a. The Evolution of the European Convention on Human Rights. *American Journal of International Law* 57 (4): 804–27.

1963b. *The European Convention on Human Rights: Background, Development and Prospects.* Leyden: A. W. Sythoff.

Weiler, Joseph. 1991. The Transformation of Europe. *Yale Law Journal* 100: 2403–83.

Weingast, Barry R. and Mark J. Moran. 1983. Bureaucratic Discretion or Congressional Control? Regulatory Policymaking by the Federal Trade Commission. *Journal of Political Economy* 91 (51): 765–800.

Wertman, Patricia A. 1998a. *The IMF and "Voice and Vote" Amendments: A Compilation.* Congressional Research Service Report No. 98-391 (April): 1–22. Washington, DC: Congressional Research Service.

1998b. *The International Monetary Fund's (IMF) Proposed Quota Increase: Issues for Congress.* Congressional Research Service Report No. 98-56 (January). Washington, DC: Congressional Research Service.

Williams, Douglas. 1987. *The Specialized Agencies and the United Nations.* New York: St. Martin's Press.

Williams, Frances. 2003. Tobacco Treaty "Could Be In Force Within a Year." *Financial Times,* May 22, 12.

Williamson, John. 1982. *The Lending Policies of the International Monetary Fund.* Washington, DC: Institute for International Economics.

Williamson, John, ed. 1983. *IMF Conditionality.* Washington, DC: Institute for International Economics.

Williamson, Oliver E. 1985. *The Economic Institutions of Capitalism: Firms, Markets, Relational Contracting.* New York: Free Press.

Wood, Adrian. 1994. *North–South Trade, Employment, and Inequality: Changing Fortunes in a Skill-Driven World.* Oxford: Clarendon Press.

Wood, B. Dan. 1988. Principals, Bureaucrats, and Responsiveness in Clean Air Enforcements. *American Political Science Review* 82 (March): 213–34.

Woodward, Bob. 1991. *The Commanders.* New York: Simon & Schuster.

2002. *Bush at War.* New York: Simon & Schuster.

World Bank. 2001a. *Annual Report 2001.* Washington, DC: World Bank.

2001b. *World Development Indicators.* Washington, DC: World Bank.

2004. Addressing the Challenges of Globalization: An Independent Evaluation of the World Bank's Approach to Global Programs. Operations Evaluation Department. Washington, DC: World Bank.

World Health Assembly. 1995. *Revision and Updating of the International Health Regulations.* WHA48.7, May 12.

2003. *Revision of the International Health Regulations.* WHA56.28, May 28. Available at http://whqlibdoc.who.int/wha/2003/WHA56_28.pdf.

World Health Organization. 1948. *Constitution of the World Health Organization.* Available at http://policy.who.int/cgi-bin/om_isapi.dll?hitsperheadin-

References

g=on&infobase=basicdoc&jump=Constitution & softpage=Document42#JUMPDEST_Constitution.

1983. *International Health Regulations 1969*, 3rd annotated edn. Available at http://policy.who.int/cgi-in/om_isapi.dll?infobase=Ihregandsoftpage=Browse_Frame_Pg42.

2002. *Global Crises – Global Solutions: Managing Public Health Emergencies of International Concern Through the Revised International Health Regulations* (Geneva). Available at http://www.who.int/csr/resources/publications/ihr/en/whocdsgar20024.pdf#Top.

World Trade Organization. 1994. *Results of the Uruguay Round of Multilateral Trade Negotiations: The Legal Texts*. Geneva: The GATT Secretariat.

1997. *European Communities: Regime for the Importation, Sale, and Distribution of Bananas*. WT/DS27/AB/R. September 9.

1998. *United States: Import Prohibition of Shrimp and Shrimp Products*. Report of the Appellate Body. WT/DS58/AB/R. October 12.

2000a. *United States: Imposition of Countervailing Duties on Certain Hot-Rolled Lead and Bismuth Carbon Steel Products Originating from the United Kingdom*. Report of the Appellate Body. WT/DS138/AB/R. May 10.

2000b. *European Communities: Measures Affecting Asbestos and Product Containing Asbestos. Communication from the Appellate Body*. WT/DS135/9. November 8.

2000c. *General Council – Minutes of Meeting – Held in the Centre William Rappard*. WT/GC/M/60. November 22.

2001. *European Communities: Measures Affecting Asbestos and Asbestos-Containing Products: Report of the Appellate Body*. WT/DS135/AB/R. March 12.

2003a. Working Procedures for Appellate Review. WT/AB/WP/7. May 1.

2003b. Report by the Chairman, Ambassador Peter Balas, to the Trade Negotiations Committee. TN/DS/9. June 6.

Wright, John R. 1996. *Interest Groups and Congress*. Boston: Allyn and Bacon.

Yackee, Jason. 2000. The Political Determinants of IMF Lending. Paper delivered at the Midwest Political Science Association. Chicago, April 27–30.

Ying, Leu Siew and Bill Savadore. 2003. WHO Says Mainland Officials Continue to Hinder Investigation. *South China Morning Post*, April 1.

Yourow, Howard Charles. 1996. *The Margin of Appreciation Doctrine in the Dynamics of the European Human Rights Jurisprudence*. The Hague: Kluwer Law International.

Index

Abbott, K.W. 16, 200, 205, 232, 256
accountability 42, 193, 235, 315, 337, 349, 355; of agents 50, 312, 347
adverse selection 116, 231, 238
Afghanistan 10, 250
Africa, IMF programs 160
agency 45, 140, 205; formal and informal 141, 144
agency losses 9, 24, 41, 169, 196, 226
agency slack 8, 24–26, 31, 255–78, 311, 343, 361, 364, 278; autonomy and 31, 33, 204; degree of 290, 304, 306; IMF 283–85, 291–303, 309; international organizations 255, 258–62, 261, 263, 279, 342; measurement of 285–87, 291–303; multiple principals and 35, 46; opportunities for 258, 262; variations in 282, 285, 307, 309
agenda-setting power 16; in the European Union 174, 177–78; in the IMF 147, 148, 149
agents 8, 31–33, 36–37, 145, 168–69, 199–228, 341–44; *see also* autonomy, control mechanisms, discretion, preferences of agents, permeability of agents; accountability 50, 346, 347; agenda-setting agents 16; arbitrating agents 17, 18; buffering 210–12, 213; characteristics of 25, 35–38, 200, 226, 227, 279, 345, 350; collaboration agents 16; competition between 30; conformity 43, 286, 290; coordinating agents 15; cost of establishing 14, 25, 26, 203; costs of monitoring 211, 345; and delegation of conditionality 285–91; domestic 41; dualism and ceremonialism 210–12, 222, 223, 224, 225; economic agents 204; enforcing agents 19; faithfulness of 46, 50, 75; human rights agents 212–25; incentives for 26, 362; influence of 32, 33; interpretation and reinterpretation of rules 206–7, 210, 212, 213, 224; opportunistic 24, 26; policy-biased 20, 27; political agents 204; sanctions 30–31, 169; scope conditions for 204; screening and selection procedures 28–29, 210, 227, 229, 231, 314, 317–21; self-reporting of activities 347, 348; shirking 8, 14, 28; size of pool of existing 205; slack: *see* agency slack; slippage 8, 28; specialization 25, 304; strategies 37, 199, 200, 201, 205–12, 226, 227; third-party testimony 348; and trustees 334, 335
Alchian, A. 9, 346
Alesina, A. 108, 109
Alexandrova, O. 243, 245
Alter, Karen J. 210, 274, 312
Ansolabehere, S. 94
Arnold, R.D. 86
Arvin, B.M. 124

Index

Asian Development Bank 59, 65
Åslund, A. 160
Atlee government, Britain 219
Aufricht, H. 292
autonomy 8, 31, 205, 212, 308, 341–44;
  and control mechanisms 221, 226;
  degree of 18, 21, 26, 32, 200, 221, 226;
  discretion and 18, 258, 279;
  formal and informal 141; of IO
  staff 143, 147; limiting 170; sources
  of 141–47, 142, 145, 161; of
  states 248
Azzam, M. 242, 244

Bacchus, James 274, 276, 278
Bailey, M. 86
Baker, James 239, 243, 245, 246, 302
Baldwin, D.A. 111
Baldwin, R.E. 84
Balogh, R. 114, 115
Barnett, M.; autonomy 141, 154, 207,
  254, 308; IMF 285, 304; international
  organizations 42, 194, 200, 205, 256,
  284, 347; UN 3
Barro, R. 77, 78, 81, 98
Barsoom, P. 332
Bawn, K. 170, 290, 291, 308
Bell, Peter D. 53
Bendor, J. 290, 291
Bergman, T. 199
Berkov, R. 264
Bernheim, B.D. 9, 58, 282
Beschloss, M. 238, 245
Bhagwati, J.N. 78
Bird, G. 77, 84
Bitzer, J.M. 328
Blackburn, R. 214
Blix, H. 235
Boli, J. 360, 368
Bordo, M.D. 87
Bosnia 235
Boughton, J. 85, 286, 287, 301, 302
Bradley, A. 214, 215, 221, 223
Bradley, C. 365
Bretton Woods Act 85, 150
Britain 219
Bronars, S.G. 94

Brown, C. 333
Brown, D. 209
Brown, R. 361
Broz, J. Lawrence 77–100
Brundtland, Gro 266–67, 270
Buira, A. 162
bureaucracies, political 204, 253
Burley, A.-M. 32
Burnside, G. 108
Busch, M.L. 336
Bush, Pres. George H. 239, 240, 241, 242,
  243, 247
Bush, Pres. George W. 229, 241,
  242, 250

Calomiris, C.W. 95
Calvert, R. 44, 46
Candau, Marcolino 268
Caprio, G. 97
Carozza, P.G. 225
Carpenter, D.P. 227
Caruson, K. 328
Cassis de Dijon case 314
Castanza, George 201
Caves, R.E. 348
chain of delegation 78, 79, 115, 116,
  347, 364
Chalmers, Damian 325
Cheney, Dick 240
Chicken game 15
China, SARS 270
Chwieroth, J.M. 288
civil society, international 360, 368
Clark, W.K. 258, 288
Clines, F.X. 53
coalitions 22, 46, 59, 61, 233, 253
coercion 235, 236, 238, 239, 247,
  248, 252
Cohen, M. 270
Cold War 123, 126, 132
collaboration dilemmas 15, 16
collective choice problem 16, 200, 227
Colombia 151
Comparative Manifesto Project 125
conflict of interest 142–45, 158, 347, 349
conformity 281–310
consensus 81, 148

395

Index

contract between principal and agent 7, 27, 196, 202, 286; discretion and 259; incomplete nature of 17, 18, 174; and international courts 334; rewriting 324–26
control mechanisms 26, 199, 212, 289, 303–6, 307; autonomy and 205, 221, 226; design of 170, 212; effectiveness of 34, 103; selection of 169, 170, 256; variation in 282
Cooley, A. 11
Cooper, S. 19
cooperation 10, 11, 13, 33
coordination 15, 20, 113
Cooter, R.D. 27
Cortell, Andrew P. 141, 255–78, 310, 361, 278
Council of Europe 16, 361
Cox, G. 17
Cox, R.W. 258
Crawford, V. 233
credibility 18–19, 30, 110, 174, 240, 342
credible commitment 18, 168, 170, 171, 189; European Union 171, 172, 178, 187, 191; measurement of 173
crisis situations 35, 77, 79, 97; Asia 83; Mexico 83, 87, 90; Russia 160, 284, 303

Dam, K.W. 150
decision-making 21–23, 43, 45, 56, 143, 345; collective 16–17, 20, 35, 59, 344; European Union 177, 188; IMF 78, 81, 86, 96, 98, 148; international courts 315, 318, 319, 334; multilateral development banks 56, 57; World Bank 367
delegation 8, 23–33; accountable 354–58, 367; chain of 78, 79, 115, 116, 347, 364; domestic 12, 107–33, 366; incentive condition for 354, 355–56, 358, 360, 364, 365, 367; interest condition for 356; knowledge condition for 354, 355, 357, 358, 360, 363, 364, 365, 367; model of 349–54; successful 344–58, 359, 367

delegation to international organizations 10–12, 23, 107, 140–64, 341–65; and autonomy 341–44; benefits of 6, 13–20, 22, 23, 289; causes and consequences of 4; comparative analysis of 195; costs of 26, 32, 304; definition of 7–12, 201; discretion-based 27; and expertise 172; failure of 66, 349; fiduciary logic of 172, 189, 312, 331; functional logic 166, 167, 187; incentives for 230; informational rationale for 170, 189; institutional design 21–23, 166, 167; motivation of 12–23, 30, 111, 195, 342; nature of 11–12, 283, 347–49; and re-contracting 12; third-party actors 345
Dell, S. 150, 156, 157, 285, 291
Demirguc-Kunt, A. 84
Demsetz, H. 9, 346
Denzau, A. 86
developing countries 156, 157, 158, 159, 162; and the IMF 156, 157, 158, 159, 162; and the WHO 266; and the WTO 325
development aid: *see* foreign aid
DiMaggio, P.J. 191, 202, 205, 210
discretion 8, 27–28, 173, 194, 226, 257, 258; autonomy and 18, 258, 279; degree of 15, 19, 169; uncertainty and 27
dispute resolution 17–18, 30, 255, 343
distributional conflict 142–45, 158
Dixit, A. 9, 282
Dogan, R. 180
Dollar, 108, 109
donor countries 108, 122–23, 127
Dornsife, Cinnamon 57
Downs, G. 332
Dreher, A. 77, 81, 83
Dudley, L. 108, 109

Eastwood, Clint 201
Eckaus, R.S. 162
Ehlermann, Claus-Dieter 272, 274, 275, 278
Eisner, M.A. 204
El Salvador 52–53

Index

Elster, Jon 328
Enron 211
Epstein, D. 169, 182, 185, 363; costs and benefits of delegation 189, 290, 291; US Congress 12, 168, 170, 171, 172, 173, 175
Epstein, L. 331
European Central Bank 195
European Commission 3, 166, 175–89, 227, 361; administrative law and judicial review 180–81; agenda-setting power 177–78, 180, 187, 188, 194; appointment and dismissal procedures 179–80, 190, 193; autonomy 33, 35, 213; comitology committees 180; common commercial policy 183, 184, 186, 188; competition policy 183, 184, 186, 188; control mechanisms 179–81, 182, 183, 185; decision-making rules of 177, 188; delegation of functions in secondary legislation 185–87, 189; delegation of functions in the Treaties 176–77, 182, 184, 185; discretion 172, 175, 178, 179, 181–85, 186, 194; Equal Treatment directive 323; functions delegated to 187, 193; implementation and regulation functions 178–79, 183, 187, 188, 194; influence of 337; informational role 174, 187; institutional checks 181; judicial review 183; *Lawless* decision 216; monitoring and enforcement functions 174, 178, 183, 187, 188, 194; oversight procedures 180; preferences 180; speed and efficiency 187, 189; tasks and composition 176–77; voting rules 177, 262
European Convention of Human Rights 212, 214, 215, 224, 225
European Court of Auditors 181, 191
European Court of Human Rights 20, 212, 214, 227, 317, 320, 323; access to 221, 222; appointment of judges 318; autonomy 213, 217–18, 220, 222, 224, 225, 324; *Barber* decision 325; delegation to 26, 329; *Golder vs. United Kingdom* decision 224; influence of 31, 32, 214; individual petition 215, 216, 221, 223; jurisdiction of 215, 221; *Lawless vs. Ireland* decision 222, 223; margin of appreciation 216, 225; membership of 216, 219; permeability 217–18, 225; recontracting 325; role of 329; *Tyrer vs. UK* decision 224; *Vagrancy* decision 223; *Wenhoff vs. FRG* decision 224
European Court of Justice 3, 178, 180, 195, 196; access to 28, 209; autonomy 313; *Cassis de Dijon* case 314
European Ombudsman 181, 191
European Parliament 190–93, 195, 361; supervisory role of 192, 194, 192
European Union 28, 32, 124, 165–88, 188; autonomy 342; competition policies 19; credible commitment 176, 178, 186, 187, 188, 189, 191; *see also* European Commission; development aid 108, 132; institutional structure 176, 193; member states 166; multiple principals 192–93; Treaties 176; voting rules 325
Evans, P. 288
expertise 170, 172, 173, 186, 189, 290, 304; *see also* specialization
externalities 15–16, 109

Fahd, King 242
Falk, Richard 229
Fama, E. 9
Farnsworth, C. H. 302
Federal Election Commission 89
Federal Financial Institutions Examination Council, Country Exposure Lending Survey 89, 97
Felton, J. 249
Fidler, D.P. 267, 268, 269, 270
Figueiredo, John de 94
Figueiredo, Miguel de 317
Finch, C. David 302
Finch, D. 153
Finnemore, M. 288; autonomy 141, 154, 207, 254, 308; IMF 285, 304; international organizations 43, 194, 200, 205, 256, 284, 347; UN 3

"fire alarms" 28, 202, 208
Fisher, L. 365
flexibility 145, 146, 159, 249, 250
foreign aid 41–75, 115, 120, 123, 75;
    benefits for donors 122; bilateral 109,
    114, 118; commitments to 122, 126,
    127, 128–29, 130–31, 133, 134–35,
    136–37; conditional 109, 138; costs of
    111–14; information about and
    evaluation of 116, 117–18, 119, 120,
    138; multilateral 114, 118, 119; policy
    57, 60, 62, 70–72, 73, 107–33
forum shopping 29, 247–53
Fox, J. 209
France 242, 245
Franchino 173, 180, 182, 183, 185–86
free rider problem 16, 228
Freedman, L. 237, 240, 241, 243, 245
Fulbright, Sen William 114
Fuller, G. 245
Furubotn, E.G. 24

G-7 65, 66, 112
Gabel, M.J. 125
Garrett, Geoffrey 59; European Court of
    Justice 313, 314, 324, 325
Garritsen de Vreis, Margaret 157, 158, 162,
    163; IMF board 143, 161, 162;
    IMF staff 153, 158, 161, 162, 163
Gates, W. 237, 239
GDP 65, 123
Germany 246
Gilligan, Thomas 233, 237
Gilpin, R. 42
Glazer, A. 290, 291
Glennon, Michael 229
Global Outbreak Alert and Response
    Network 269
Global Public Health Intelligence
    Network 269
globalization 79, 84, 89, 95, 102; protests
    against 3, 5, 277
Godlee, F. 268
Gold, J. 143, 148, 161, 291, 292, 296, 297
Golder vs. United Kingdom 224
Goldstein, J.L. 5, 17, 181, 324, 360
Golove, D. 365

Golsong, H. 219
Gorbachev, M. 238, 241, 245
Gordon, E. 319
Gould, E. 31, 78, 79, 141, 202,
    281–310
Gourevitch, P. 3
Grant, R.W. 18, 316, 328, 335, 337
Grieco, J.M. 56
Grossman, G. 9, 86, 120, 282
Gruber, L. 22, 203
Gulf War, 1990–91 237–47
Gump, Forrest 201
Gutt, Camille 150

Haggard, S. 51
Haftel, Y. 232
Haiti 305–6
Hall, R. 94
Hallstein, Walter 188
Hamilton, A. 365
Hammond, T.H. 44, 46, 112
Harris, D.J. 221, 224
Haskel, J.E. 84
Hawes, Michael Brewster 77–100
Hawkins, Darren 3–24, 54, 228
hegemony 62, 66, 73, 123, 195
Heikal, Mohamed 238, 244
Helfer, Lawrence 313, 331, 332
Helmes, Jesse 53
Helmke, G. 220
Helpman, E. 9, 282
Hess, Rudolph 216
Hill, J. 204
HIV/AIDS 268
Hix, S. 45
Hoadley, J.S. 117–18
Holland, M. 108
Horsefield, Keith 150, 151, 291, 292;
    IMF autonomy 152, 153, 154–55, 156;
    IMF conditionality 285, 291, 292
Huber, J.D. 125, 168, 170, 225, 226;
    discretion 173, 226; monitoring and
    enforcement 290, 291
Hug, Simon 192
Huizinga, H. 84
human rights policy 32
Hurd, Ian 254, 336, 337

Index

Imbeau, L.M. 57
IMF 3, 22, 26, 29, 32, 37, 44, 77–100, 291, 342; agency slack 303; Articles of Agreement 87, 147, 151, 161; automaticity 149, 150; autonomy 31, 342; Board of Governors 81, 143; as a collective principal 287–89; commercial bank exposure 98; *Conditionality Dataset* 289, 291, 295, 297; confidential information 161–63; decision-making 78, 81, 86, 96, 98, 148; delegation of conditionality 291–92; directors' preferences 81, 82; Early-Warning System 97; Executive Directors 86, 102, 103, 140, 152; Extended Fund Facilities programs 96; influence of lobbying on loan decisions 80; "lapse of time" procedure 153; lending decisions 77, 96–102, 296; negotiation and approval of programs 149, 154; policy and policy-makers 86–87; political interference 292, 302, 309; principal preferences 300–3; private actors and 78, 79, 82, 83–85, 96, 102, 103; quotas 80, 87, 88, 90, 91, 92, 148; size of loans 100; slack 283, 291–303; structure of 80–82, 147–49, 288; success of programs 305, 309; third-party actors 308, 309, 310; transparency 78, 79, 82, 141, 304; and the USA 34, 82, 85–86; voting rules 80, 262, 287
IMF conditionality 140–64, 281–310; agreements 284, 289; binding conditions 157, 292, 293, 294, 295, 297, 299, 303, 305; conformity 295–99, 303; consultation clauses 293, 297; guidelines 147–59, 160, 163, 287, 291, 299–300, 303, 307; phasing 293, 295, 296, 303, 304; preconditions 159–61
IMF Executive Board 81, 148, 158, 287, 292, 343; and conditionality 159, 160, 292, 302; relationship with staff 147, 152, 153, 155, 159
IMF staff 142, 148, 152, 155, 163, 288, 292; authority of 153, 155, 156, 164;
autonomy of 35, 141, 153, 154, 159, 161, 163; and conditionality 149, 152, 159; expertise 162, 305
IMF Stand-By programs 96, 148, 151, 292; binding conditions and 293, 294; mechanisms for implementing 155–59, 293, 294, 300
information 109, 138, 140–64, 229–54; asymmetric 194, 231, 347, 348, 349; borrowing countries and 146; confidential 159; demand for 172; hidden 25, 347, 348; imperfect 170; and international organizations 229–54; private 141–47; problems of 116; transmission of 233, 237, 252, 253
institutional checks and balances 29–30, 206
institutional design 167, 170, 255, 256, 263, 341
institutional rules 21–23, 42, 56, 208
Inter-American Court of Human Rights 320
Inter-American Development Bank 34, 42, 47, 59, 65, 342; delegation to 46, 54, 74; Social Progress Trust Fund 47, 50, 51, 52
Inter-American Foundation 42, 46, 48, 52, 53, 74; budget 53; coordination with other agencies 48, 49; monitoring and reporting requirements 49, 50; multiple principals 53
International Atomic Energy Agency 16
International Bank for Reconstruction and Development 64, 108
international community 231, 234, 238, 260
International Court of Justice, and the US 325, 330, 334
international courts 31, 37, 312, 315, 317, 319, 322–24, 332, 338; access to 315, 332, 333, 335; appointment of judges 320, 321, 330, 331–32, 337; autonomy 324, 343; control of 214, 321–22, 330; decision-making 315, 318, 319, 334; delegation to 327, 329, 337; design of 332, 333; independence of 331–34, 335, 336, 337

399

Index

international courts (*cont.*)
  interpretation of rules 337; jurisdiction of 315, 332, 333, 335; legitimacy 330, 336; non-compliance with rulings 329, 336; political influence 315, 316–31, 335; prosecutors in 321; re-contracting 317, 333; reservations 323; sanctions 324–26, 327; slippage 316, 322, 336; standard of review 322–24
International Criminal Court 14, 29, 319, 320; and the US 312, 317, 336
International Criminal Tribunals 320, 321
International Development Association 108
International Health Regulations 267, 268, 269
international organizations 3–24, 29, 44, 233, 284, 358–67; accountability 41, 42; as actors 5, 200; autonomy 140, 342; constraints on staff activity 144; constraints on states 234, 238, 241, 242, 248, 252; control of 4, 5, 66, 73, 261; culture of 42, 280; decision-making rules of 45, 56, 235, 239; and information 147, 229–54; membership of 232, 235, 250, 252, 253, 254; neutrality of 232, 234, 247, 248, 252; preferences 248, 257, 259, 261, 262, 280; public confidence in 120, 121; regional 252, 253, 319; responsibilities 5, 145, 235; screening function 231, 232–37, 238–43, 247, 248, 249, 253; and slack 255, 258–62, 263, 279, 342; and state preferences 282; variation among 247–53, 306–9; voting rules 257, 261, 262, 279
international organization staff 143, 256, 257, 259–60, 279; autonomy of 143, 144, 260; international staff 257, 260–61
International Sanitary Regulations 267
International Tribunal for the Law of the Sea 320
Iraq 8, 235, 237–47, 250; "Arab solution" 241, 243; public opinion and 243–47, 246; US war on 229, 230
isomorphic mimicry 327, 329, 330

Jacobs, L. 237
Jacobson, H.K. 258, 264, 265, 266
Jacobsson, Per 156
Jacoby, Wade 228
James, H. 87, 158, 284, 291
Janis, M. 214, 215, 221, 223
Japan 246
Jeanne, O. 83
Jensen, M.C. 346
Jensen, N. 81
Joergens, K.J. 275
Johnston, A.I. 261, 337
Johnstone, Ian 337
Jordan, R.S. 259
Joskow, P. 348
Joyce, J.P. 77
judicial independence 321, 326

Kahler, Miles 284, 285; IMF conditionality guidelines 301–2; IMF staff autonomy 153, 158, 159
Kahn, A. 350
Kaplan, J.H. 25
Kapur, D. 286, 288
Karsh, E. 237, 240, 241, 243, 245
Katzenstein, P. 56
Kay, R. 214, 215, 221, 223
Kay, S. 259
Keck, M.E. 208, 337, 353, 360, 368
Keener, E.B. 330
Keleman, Daniel 313, 324
Kelley, J. 336
Keohane, R.O. 10, 13, 16, 18, 203; international organizations 41, 56, 167, 168, 235, 260, 332
Keynes, John Maynard 149, 150
Khalidi, W. 242
Khan, M.S. 305
Kiewiet, D.R. 17, 287, 290, 346; agents 24, 25, 44, 256, 290, 291
Kilroy, Bernadette 314
King Fahd, Saudi Arabia 238
King, G. 93
Kissinger, H.A. 214, 241
Klepak, H. 56
Klingebiel, D. 97
Knight, J. 331

Index

Knott, J.H. 44, 46, 112, 290, 291
Koremenos, B. 5, 24, 167, 200
Kosovo 250, 252
Krause, G. 204
Krauthammer, C/ 3, 229
Krehbiel, Keith 172, 233, 237, 252
Kreppel, A. 188
Kroszner, R.S. 94
Krueger, Anne 302
Kuemmel, G. 324

Lacomte, S. 118, 119, 132
Laffont, J.-J. 116, 346
Lake, David A. 3–24, 56, 204, 234, 341–65, 366; Iraq war 237, 242, 244
Larkins, C.M. 220
Latin America 249
Laver, M. 59
Lawless vs. Ireland 216, 222, 223
Lawrence, J. Broz 77–100
Lazurus, D. 266
Lee, J. W. 77, 81, 98, 270
legislative committees 232, 233, 237, 250, 252
legitimacy, democratic 167, 191, 192
LeoGrande, W. 250
Lesch, A.M. 238, 244
Lester, Lord 220
Lewis, J.P. 286
Lewis, P. 267
Liebert, U. 324
Lijphart, A. 20
Lippman, T.W. 49, 53
Lipson, C. 5, 24, 167, 200
Little, R. 108, 109
lobbying 77
lock-in (creating policy bias) 19–20
Lott, J.R. 94
Lovasay, G. 291, 292
Lumsdaine, D.H. 109, 114, 118, 124–25
Lupia, A. 120; information 233, 236, 348; model of delegation 345, 346, 350–52, 356; non-government organizations 120
Lutz, Ellen 324
Lyne, Mona M. 75, 361

Magee, C.S. 84
Mahler, Halfdan 267
Maizels and Nissanke 108, 114
Majone, Giandomenico 328; delegation to courts 316, 328; European Union 174, 186, 278; logic of delegation 172, 187, 189, 312, 331
Makinson, L. 94
Malone, David 250
Mansfield, E. 119
March, J.G. 260, 350
Marks, Brian 327
Marshall Fund 150
Martens, B. 11, 51, 114, 116
Martin, Lisa L., 140–64; cooperation 13, 15, 56; credibility 18; international organizations 5, 234, 304
Martimort, D. 116
Matthews, K. 237
Mattli, W. 32
McCubbins, Mathew 28, 341–65; agents 24, 27, 256, 290, 291, 308; delegation 17, 327, 332, 345, 346, 350–52, 356; discretion 28, 258; "fire alarms" 28, 202, 208; information 25, 233, 236, 304, 348; multiple principals 44; non-government organizations 120
McDonnell, I. 118, 119, 132
McKinlay, R. 108, 109
McNamara, K. 327
McNollgast, 12, 20, 32
Mearsheimer, J. 344
Meckling, W.H. 346
Meier, K. 204
Meltzer, A.H. 95
Meltzer Commission 3, 83, 282
Merrills, J.G. 215, 216, 221, 222, 223
Meunier, Sophie 314
Mexico 83, 87, 90, 284
Meyer, J. 210
Milgrom, P. 7, 235, 327
Miller, S. 255, 273
Milner, Helen V. 15, 51, 107–33, 348, 367
Mingst, K.A. 266
Mitterand, F. 245
Moe, T.M. 19, 25, 181, 204

Index

money-center banks 77, 80, 83, 86, 89, 96, 98, 102; campaign contributions 79, 89, 93, 94, 96
monitoring and reporting requirements 28, 169, 174, 206, 347; costs of 290, 304, 348
Montmarquette, C. 108, 109
moral hazard 80, 83, 84, 86, 95, 116, 231
Moravcsik, A. 19, 64, 73, 191, 332; European Court of Human Rights 20, 215, 219; European Union 171, 187; international organizations 42, 56, 214; preferences 191, 260
Moseley, P. 115
Moubray, G. L. L. de 284
Mubarak, Pres. Hosni 244
Mueller, J. 241, 242
Müller, H. 337
Müller, W. 199
multilateral aid 111–14, 114–22
multilateral development banks 16, 41, 342; as collective principals 46, 54–59; decision-making rules of 56, 57; number of actors involved 56–57, 66, 74, 75; preferences of their principals 43, 57–58; social loans 34, 55, 74
multilateralism 107–33, 248
Munger, M. 86
Murphy, W.F. 331
mutual policy adjustment 10, 11
Mutume, G. 255

Naik, G. 270
Nakajima, Hiroshi 267
NATO 235, 252, 257, 258, 259
Nelson, P. 209
neo-functionalism 32
Nissanke, M. 108, 114
non-government organizations (NGOs) 120, 210, 269, 276, 341, 360, 368
Nicaragua 52–53, 325, 334
Nielson, Daniel 3–24, 27, 75, 141, 286, 347; delegation 347, 364; multilateral development banks 54, 75; multiple principals 46, 54, 64, 200, 205, 212, 361; preferences 21, 46, 256, 287
Niskanen, W.A. 288, 308

Noel, A. 57
Noll, R.G. 308, 327, 348
Noriega, Manual 249
North, D. 327
normative institutional isomorphism 192–93, 194, 196
Nugent, N. 174
Nye, J. 56

OAS 249, 252
Oatley, T. 56, 66, 77, 78, 83, 84, 255
O'Boyle, M. 221, 224
O'Halloran, S. 169, 182, 185, 363; costs and benefits of delegation 189, 290, 291; US Congress 12, 168, 170, 171, 172, 173, 175
Olsen, J.P. 260
Olson, M. 22, 235
Omang, J. 48
organization costs 235, 236, 239, 240, 241, 248, 249
Organization for Economic Cooperation and Development (OECD) 16, 120, 123; country-specific aid policy reviews 119–20; Creditor Reporting System 60; development aid 112, 113; Development Assistance Committee 110, 117–18, 119
Ovey, C. 215, 224

Page, T. 27, 28, 258
Panama 249–50
Papayoanou, P. 235
Parks, B. 22
Partsch, K.J. 219
Pauwelyn, J. 329, 336
peacekeeping 14
Perle, R. 229
permeability of agents 37, 202, 211; degree of 202, 208–10, 212, 213; European Court of Human Rights 223, 224, 225
Perrow, C. 205
persuasion, conditions of 352–54, 367
Pescatore, Pierre 188, 330
Peterson, Susan 141, 255–78, 310, 361
Pfahler, M. 173
Pierson, P. 32, 205, 261, 326

Index

pivotal-players model 59, 61, 62
Polak, Jacques 158, 285, 297
Polakiewicz, J. 214
"police patrols" 28
policy bias ("lock-in") 19–20
policy externalities 15–16, 109
political parties 124, 125, 132
Pollack, D. 28, 141, 244
Pollack, Mark 64, 205, 212, 221; European Court of Justice 313, 326; European Union 17, 45, 188; slack 261, 262, 286
Poole, K.T. 89
Popkin, S. 236
Posner, Eric 317, 318, 332, 336
Pottinger, M. 270
Powell, Colin 240, 249
Powell, R. 19, 366
Powell, W. 191, 202, 205, 210
Power, S. 3
power 13, 21–23, 37, 76, 124, 326
preferences; of agents 7, 29, 30, 36, 209, 256, 279, 308, 310; aggregation of 21, 22, 75, 287; among IMF EDs 140; of collective principals 300, 302; conformity with 290, 309; of donor governments 110, 118; heterogeneity of 6, 13, 20–21, 36, 142, 232, 254, 256; of IO staff 142, 144, 145, 147, 163, 164; measurement of 62, 287; of principals 7, 34, 42, 67–69, 70–72, 117, 212, 233, 287; revealed 79, 81, 327; short- and long-term 171; for social policy 54; of states 142, 143, 144, 145, 163, 248
principal-agent theory 3–24, 107–33, 142, 167–75, 368; control and conformity 281; goal of 225; and international courts 334–38; and legal scholarship 331–32; limitations of 282, 306–9, 310, 316; models 75; predictions of 289–91, 307; screening and selection procedures 256; slack 256; strengths of 41, 303–6, 309, 341
principals 7, 41–75, 289; agency losses 9; characteristics of 33–35, 279, 345, 350; complex 44–46, 74; IMF 285–91;

models of 66, 74, 75; need for information 35; single 42, 45; strategies 345; structure of 35, 41
principals, collective 44, 84, 114, 115, 207, 213, 231, 366; decision-making 35, 46, 287; delegation to multilateral development banks 43, 60, 61, 110, 139; European Parliament 167, 193; and hegemony 195; model of 58–59, 73, 74, 75; preferences 113, 283, 287, 300; slippage 112
principals, multiple 44, 45, 46, 54, 193, 345, 361, 362, 363; European Union 167, 192–93; models of 58, 61, 63, 64, 74; slack 46
Prisoner's Dilemma 16
Pritchett, C.H. 331
Program for Monitoring Emerging Diseases 269
proxy problem 173
Przeworski, A. 77
public goods 16
public opinion 110, 111, 115, 117, 118–19, 120, 125–26, 132–33, 139; Arab 238, 243; and coercion 236; in Europe 121, 146; and government policy 236; and international organizations 120–22, 236; measurement of 125–26; and military intervention 246, 251
Purrington, C. 246
Putnam, R. 237

Randal, J.C. 267
Rapkin, D.P. 22
rational choice theory 115, 166, 167, 170, 328
Raustiala, K. 332, 368
Reagan Administration 48, 50, 52, 301, 334
re-contracting 12, 307, 312, 314, 334, 335
regional development banks 30, 108
Reinhardt, E. 336
Rich, B. 3
Richter, R. 24
Risse, T. 208, 336
Roberts, J. 7, 235

403

Index

Robertson, A.H. 216, 221, 222, 223
Robichek, W.E. 150
Rocke, D. 332
Rodrik, D. 109–10
Rogoff, K. 84
Rogowski, R. 21
Romano, C. 333
Ron, J. 11
Ropp, S. 208, 336
Rooth, Ivar 151, 155
Rosendorff, B.P. 119, 120
Rosenthal, H. 89
Rourke, F.E. 204
Rowan, B. 210
Rowlands, D. 77
Ruggie, J.G. 107
rule of law 329
Russia 160, 243, 245, 284, 303
Ryan, M. 49

Samuelson, P.A. 84
sanctions 30–31, 169, 204, 314
Sanders, Bernie 95–96
Sandholtz, W. 43
Santaella, J. 294
Santer Commission 193
SARS 255, 263, 269
Savadore, B. 270
Scandinavian countries 112
Schanzenbach, Max 317, 318
Scharpf, F. 328
Scheffer, D.J. 14
Scheve, K.F. 84
Schimmelfennig, F. 337
Schmidt, Susannah 337
Schneider, A.K. 325
Schraeder, P.J. 109
Schulz, Heiner 236, 313, 324
Schwartz, A.J. 95
Schweitzer, Pierre-Paul 157, 158
Scowcroft, Brent 239, 240, 242, 243
Shaffer, Gregory 272
Shanks, C. 25
Shapiro, Martin 328
Shapiro, R. 237
Shelton, D. 214, 225
Shevardnadze, Eduard 240, 245

Shipan, C.R. 168, 170, 173, 225, 226, 290, 291
shirking 8, 14, 28, 47
Sikkink, K. 208, 266, 324, 336, 353, 360, 368
Simmons, B. 5
Simon, H. 350
slack: *see* agency slack
Slater, J. 252
Slaughter, Anne-Marie 260, 313, 331, 332
Slaughter, M.J. 84
slippage 8, 28, 231, 234, 316
Smillie, I. 119
Smith, James McCall 333
Snidal D. 16, 22, 24; institutional design 167, 200; international organizations 5, 191, 232, 256
Snyder, J.M. 94
Sobel, J. 233
social learning 196
Social Policy Index 60, 61, 62, 66, 67–69, 73
Soros, G. 78
Southard, Frank 148, 152, 154, 155, 156, 286
sovereignty 216, 219, 234, 239, 328; pooling of 366
Soviets 243, 245
Spaak, Paul-Henri 188
specialization 13–15, 25, 27, 145, 230, 342
Spence, A.M. 231, 346
states 3–24, 37, 56–57, 123, 334–38; cooperation 10, 13, 33, 124; interests of 313, 314, 327; voting power 56, 60
states, preferences of 23, 57–58, 75, 145, 163, 164, 200, 282; and multilateral development banks 57, 60; and the IMF 142, 144; and the European Court of Human Rights 216
Steger, D. 273
Stein, E. 15, 56, 329
Steinberg, Richard 319, 321, 331
Stephan, P.B. 313
Stewart, R. 365
Stiglitz, J.E. 3, 78, 86
Stiles, K. 219
Stokke, O. 57
Stolper, W. 84

404

Index

Stone, Randall 18, 81, 143, 160, 302, 305
Stone Sweet, A. 166, 316, 328
Strand, J.R. 22
Strange, Susan 148, 152, 153, 156
Stratman, T. 94
Strom, K. 199, 205
Sudden Acute Respiratory Syndrome (SARS) 255, 263, 269
supranational organizations 165
Swaine, E. 323
Sweden 219, 222

Tallberg, Jonas 28, 258, 313, 337
Tallbott, S. 238, 245
Taylor, B. 109
Telhami, S. 244
Terasawa, K. 237, 239
Thacker, Strom 56, 66, 73, 77, 81, 284
Thatcher, Mark 166
Thatcher, Margaret 239, 240
Thelen, K. 326
Thieren, J.P. 57
third-party actors 352, 360, 367, 368
Thomas, G.M. 360, 368
Thompson, Alexander 120, 229–54, 367
Tierney, Michael J 3–24, 27, 75, 141, 286, 347; delegation 347, 364; multilateral development banks 54, 75; multiple principals 46, 54, 64, 200, 205, 212, 361; preferences 21, 46, 256, 287
Tirole, J. 346
Tomz, M. 93
transactions costs 18, 168, 169, 187, 190, 191, 235; institutional 166, 167
transparency 119, 235, 277
trust 352, 353
trustees 18, 47, 316, 317, 334, 335, 343
Tsebelis, G. 188, 208
Tyrer vs. UK 224

Ul Haque, N. 305
uncertainty 19, 24, 172, 203, 230, 350; and discretion 27, 291; and information 173, 237; proxies for 173
Undén, Osten 223
UNICEF, NGO consultative committees 210
unilateralism 10, 33, 248, 249–50

United Nations 3–4, 108, 204; Secretary General 29, 337
United Nations Security Council 31, 32, 36, 44, 253, 262, 345; and the 2003 Iraq war 8, 26, 229, 230, 237–47, 250; membership of 20, 247, 250, 319
Upton, B. 54
USA 77–100, 103, 115, 319; Chamber of Commerce 95; Congressional voting on IMF policy 47, 82, 85–86, 87–96; delegation of foreign aid 42, 45–46, 367; export-oriented industries 92, 95; Federal Election Commission 89, 92; Federal Financial Institutions Examination Council, Country Exposure Lending Survey 89, 97; foreign aid policy 46–54, 112, 365; Foreign Assistance Act 47, 51; hegemony 123, 126, 132; House Committee on Foreign Affairs 47, 51; and the IMF 22, 77–100, 152, 284, 301; and IMF conditionality 150, 151; and international courts 312, 317, 330, 336; and Iraq 237, 238–43, 246; multiple principals 50–54; Senate Foreign Relations Committee 53; as a single principal 47, 74; skill levels of Congressmen's constituents 89, 90, 93, 95; Social Policy Index 62, 64, 66; Supreme Court, *Marbury vs. Madison* decision and the UN Security Council 235, 326; war on Afghanistan 10, and the World Bank 112

Vagrancy case 223
Van Houtven, L. 81
Vaubel, R. 77, 83, 288, 308
veto 35, 59, 112, 262
Voeten, Erik 254, 317, 318–19
voting rules 195, 255–78, 279, 327, 344, 345; European Commission 177, 325; IMF 80, 262, 287; NATO 257; UN Security Council 262; World Bank 56; WHO 261, 263, 265, 271; WTO 271, 275, 276
Vreeland, J.R. 77

Index

Wade, R. 28
Wallander, C. 235
Waltz, K.N. 344
Warbrick, C. 221, 224
Ward, A. 181
Wayman, F.W. 94
Weaver, 286
Weber, S. 203
Webb, R. 286
Wegimont, L. 118, 119, 132
Weil, G.L. 216, 222
Weiler, J. 329
Weingast, Barry 44, 286, 308, 313; European Court of Justice 313, 314; international courts 327, 328
Weissert, C. 204
Wenhoff vs. FRG 224
Wertman, P.A. 85
Whinston, M.D. 9, 58, 291
White, Harry Dexter 149
White, R. 215, 224
Williams, D. 266, 267
Williams, F. 266
Williamson, J. 151, 159, 285, 301
Williamson, O.E. 7, 9, 17, 24, 199, 348
Wittenberg, J. 93
Witteveen, Johannes 162
Wolfowitz, Paul 29
Wood, A. 84, 204
Wood, B.D. 204
Woodward, B. 240, 242, 249
World Bank 3, 27, 29, 30, 44, 108, 367; Articles of Agreement 112; collective nature of 112; conditionality 111; decision-making 367; members' preferences 64; membership of 112; social loans 54, 59
World Development Indicators 60, 123
World Health Assembly 265, 266

World Health Organization (WHO) 16, 33, 44, 255–78, 361; Committee on Communicable Diseases 268; communicable disease surveillance and response 267, 271; constitution 264, 268; Executive Board 265, 268; expert committees 264, 265; information from non-state sources 268, 269; mandate of 270, 271; politicization of 266; procedures 271; SARS 270; secretariat 264, 265; slack 263, 271; staff 260, 263, 266, 270; technical assistance 265; travel alerts 270; voting rules 261, 263, 265, 271; World Health Assembly 265, 266
WorldCom 211
Wright, J.R. 94
WTO 3, 255–78; access to 274; *amicus* briefs 276, 277, 278, 325; Appelate Body 255, 260, 271, 272, 275, 320; Appelate Body membership 273, 274; Asbestos case 277; consensus 261, 271, 275, 277, 278; dispute resolution process 255, 271, 272, 273, 278; General Council 275, 277; legitimacy of 278; NGOs (non-government organizations) 276, 277; non-state actors and 272, 276, 277; reform of the legal process 331; rules of 322; screening and selection procedures 273; secretariat 272; slack 275, 276, 278; transparency 277; voting rules 271, 275, 276

Yackee, J. 56, 66, 77, 78, 83, 84, 255
Ying, L.S. 270
Yoo, John 313, 332
Yourow, H.C. 216, 225

Zettelmeyer, J. 83
Zysman, J. 43

Other books in the series (continued from page ii)

Jean Ensminger, *Making a Market: The Institutional Transformation of an African Society*

David Epstein and Sharyn O'Halloran, *Delegating Powers: A Transaction Cost Politics Approach to Policy Making under Separate Powers*

Kathryn Firmin-Sellers, *The Transformation of Property Rights in the Gold Coast: An Empirical Study Applying Rational Choice Theory*

Clark C. Gibson, *Politicians and Poachers: The Political Economy of Wildlife Policy in Africa*

Avner Greif, *Institutions and the Path to the Modern Economy: Lessons from Medieval Trade*

Stephen Haber, Armando Razo and Noel Maurer, *The Politics of Property Rights, Political Instability, Credible Commitments, and Economic Growth in Mexico, 1876–1929*

Stephan Haggard and Matthew D. McCubbins, eds., *Presidents, Parliaments, and Policy*

Ron Harris, *Industrializing English Law: Entrepreneurship and Business Organization, 1720–1844*

Anna L. Harvey, *Votes without Leverage: Women in American Electoral Politics, 1920–1970*

Murray J. Horn, *The Political Economy of Public Administration: Institutional Choice in the Public Sector*

John D. Huber, *Rationalizing Parliament: Legislative Institutions and Party Politics in France*

John E. Jackson, Jacek Klich, Krystyna Poznanska, *The Political Economy of Poland's Transition: New Firms and Reform Governments*

Jack Knight, *Institutions and Social Conflict*

Michael Laver and Kenneth A. Shepsle, eds., *Making and Breaking Governments: Cabinets and Legislatures in Parliamentary Democracies*

Margaret Levi, *Consent, Dissent, and Patriotism*

Brian Levy, Pablo T. Spiller, eds., *Regulations, Institutions, and Commitment: Comparative Studies of Telecommunications*

Leif Lewin, eds., *Ideology and Strategy: A Century of Swedish Politics*

Gary D. Libecap, *Contracting for Property Rights*

John B. Londregan, *Legislative Institutions and Ideology in Chile*

Arthur Lupia and Mathew D. McCubbins, *The Democratic Dilemma: Can Citizens Learn What They Need to Know?*

C. Mantzavinos, *Individuals, Institutions, and Markets*

Gary J. Miller, *Managerial Dilemmas: The Political Economy of Hierarchy*

Douglass C. North, *Institutions, Institutional Change and Economic Performance*

Elinor Ostrom, *Governing the Commons: The Evolution of Institutions for Collective Action*
Daniel N. Posner, *Institutions and Ethnic Politics in Africa*
J. Mark Ramseyer, *Odd Markets in Japanese History: Law and Economic Growth*
J. Mark Ramseyer and Frances McCall Rosenbluth, *The Politics of Oligarchy: Institutional Choice in Imperial Japan*
Jean-Laurent Rosenthal, *The Fruits of Revolution: Property Rights, Litigation and French Agriculture, 1700–1860*
Michael L. Ross, *Timber Booms and Institutional Breakdown in Southeast Asia*
Shanker Satyanath, *Globalization, Politics, and Financial Turmoil: Asia's Banking Crisis*
Norman Schofield, *Architects of Political Change: Constitutional Quandaries and Social Choice Theory*
Norman Schofield and Itai Sened, *Multiparty Democracy: Parties, Elections and Legislative Politics*
Alastair Smith, *Election Timing*
David Stasavage, *Public Debt and the Birth of the Democratic State: France and Great Britain 1688–1789*
Charles Haynes Stewart, *Budget Reform Politics: The Design of the Appropriations Process in the House of Representatives, 1865–1921*
Robert Thomson, Frans Stokman, Christopher Achen and Thomas Koenig, eds., *The European Union Decides: Testing Theories of European Decision-Making*
George Tsebelis and Jeannette Money, *Bicameralism*
Nicolas Van de Walle, *African Economies and the Politics of Permanent Crisis, 1979–1999*
Georg Vanberg, *The Politics of Constitutional Review in Germany*
John Waterbury, *Exposed to Innumerable Delusions: Public Enterprise and State Power in Egypt, India, Mexico, and Turkey*
David L. Weimer, ed., *The Political Economy of Property Rights: Institutional Change and Credibility in the Reform of Centrally Planned Economies*